Territoriality and Conflict in an Era of Globalization

Predictions that globalization would undermine territorial attachments and weaken the sources of territorial conflict have not been realized in recent decades. Globalization may have produced changes in territoriality and the functions of borders, but it has not eliminated them. The contributors to this volume examine this relationship, arguing that much of the change can be attributed to sources other than economic globalization. Bringing the perspectives of law, political science, anthropology, and geography to bear on the complex causal relations among territoriality, conflict, and globalization, leading contributors examine how territorial attachments are constructed, why they have remained so powerful in the face of an increasingly globalized world, and what effect continuing strong attachments may have on conflict. They argue that territorial attachments and people's willingness to fight for territory appear to have much less to do with the material value of land than they have to do with the important symbolic role it plays in constituting people's identities, and producing a sense of security and belonging in an increasingly globalized world.

MILES KAHLER is Rohr Professor of Pacific International Relations at the Graduate School of International Relations and Pacific Studies, University of California, San Diego. Publications include *Governance in a Global Economy* (co-edited with David Lake, 2003), *Legalization and World Politics* (co-editor, 2001), *Leadership Selection in the Major Multilaterals* (2001), *Capital Flows and Financial Crises* (editor, 1998), and *International Institutions and the Political Economy of Integration* (1995).

BARBARA F. WALTER is an Associate Professor of Political Science at the Graduate School of International Relations and Pacific Studies, University of California, San Diego. She is the author of *Committing to Peace: The Successful Settlement of Civil Wars* (2002) and co-editor with Jack Snyder of *Civil Wars, Insecurity, and Intervention* (1999).

Territoriality and Conflict in an Era of Globalization

Edited By

Miles Kahler and Barbara F. Walter

CAMBRIDGE
UNIVERSITY PRESS

CAMBRIDGE UNIVERSITY PRESS
Cambridge, New York, Melbourne, Madrid, Cape Town, Singapore, São Paulo

Cambridge University Press
The Edinburgh Building, Cambridge CB2 2RU, UK

Published in the United States of America by Cambridge University Press,
New York

www.cambridge.org
Information on this title: www.cambridge.org/9780521675031

First published 2006

Printed in the United Kingdom at the University Press, Cambridge

A catalogue record for this book is available from the British Library

ISBN-13 978-0-521-85833-5 hardback
ISBN-10 0-521-85833-X hardback
ISBN-13 978-0-521-67503-1 paperback
ISBN-10 0-521-67503-0 paperback

Contents

v

Figures

Tables

Contributors

HALVARD BUHAUG is a Research Fellow in the Department of Sociology and Political Science, Norwegian University of Science and Technology, Trondheim, Norway.

ERIK GARTZKE is Associate Professor of Political Science in the Department of Political Science and the Saltzman Institute of War and Peace Studies, Columbia University, New York, New York.

NILS PETTER GLEDITSCH is a Researcher at the Centre for the Study of Civil War (CSCW), International Peace Research Institute (PRIO), Oslo, Norway.

HEIN E. GOEMANS is Assistant Professor of Political Science at the University of Rochester, Rochester, New York.

MILES KAHLER is Rohr Professor of Pacific International Relations at the Graduate School of International Relations and Pacific Studies, University of California, San Diego, La Jolla, California.

DAVID A. LAKE is Professor of Political Science at the University of California, San Diego, La Jolla, California.

TERRENCE LYONS is Assistant Professor at the Institute for Conflict Analysis and Resolution, George Mason University, Fairfax, Virginia.

DAVID NEWMAN is Professor of Political Geography at Ben Gurion University of the Negev, Beer Sheva, Israel.

ANGELA O'MAHONY is Assistant Professor of Political Science at the University of British Columbia, Vancouver, British Columbia.

KAL RAUSTIALA is Acting Professor of Law at the UCLA School of Law, Los Angeles, California.

JOEL ROBBINS is Associate Professor of Anthropology at the University of California, San Diego, La Jolla, California.

BETH A. SIMMONS is Professor of Government at Harvard University, Cambridge, Massachusetts.

BARBARA F. WALTER is Associate Professor of Political Science at the Graduate School of International Relations and Pacific Studies, University of California, San Diego, La Jolla, California.

Acknowledgments

This project began with a simple observation. Numerous scholarly studies have shown that territorial disputes are more likely to escalate, are more likely to produce a high number of fatalities, and are more conflictual than non-territorial confrontations (i.e., Luard 1986; Holsti 1991; and Hensel 1994). Yet globalization and technological innovation have also seemingly reduced the importance of territory, at least in terms of its economic and strategic value. Why has territory continued to be a key source of violent conflict even as goods, capital, and populations move increasingly seamlessly across borders?

To date, scholars have focused on the connection between territorial stakes and conflict, and between globalization and conflict, but not on the effects of globalization on territoriality and territorial conflict. Our goal was to fill in these missing links by exploring what effect, if any, globalization may have on territorial attachments, stakes, and institutions, and what effect these changes may then have on territorial conflict. In the course of the project, territoriality itself and changes in territoriality over time became a more prominent part of the enterprise.

The project began with a two-day workshop in La Jolla in March 2001. Our first aim was simply to identify and assemble those scholars in a variety of disciplines working on issues related to territoriality. Participants were drawn from political science, anthropology, geography, and law, and deployed a range of methodological and epistemological approaches. The workshop produced two surprises. The first was that many of the participants had never met before and most were unaware of each other's research programs. The second surprise was that the group generally agreed that the next big contribution would come from exploring the origins of territorial attachments; only by understanding the sources of territorial attachments could we begin to comprehend how globalization (and the various processes associated with it) might influence people's willingness to fight for land.

This initial workshop led to two additional conferences held in January 2003 and January 2004. During these conferences draft chapters were presented and discussed, and special efforts were made to solicit feedback from a variety of discussants both within and outside the scholarly community. In addition to the authors, John Agnew, Ibrahim Elbadawi, Håvard Hegre, Saskia Sassen, John Vasquez, and Marie Henehan were active members of the group and contributed to our thinking in important ways. Gershon Shafir, Jerry Cohen, Ronnie Lipschutz, David Laitin, William Wood, and Mark Zacher also gave generously of their time, reviewing drafts and offering guidance for the project. Two anonymous reviewers for Cambridge University Press offered a final set of helpful suggestions on the text. Much gratitude and thanks are due to Lynne Bush for her expeditious editorial work and to John Haslam at Cambridge University Press, whose support and guidance were essential to the publication of this book.

This project received financial support from several sources. The Institute on Global Conflict and Cooperation, the Division of the Social Sciences, the Graduate School of International Relations and Pacific Studies, and the Sociology Department at the University of California, San Diego provided the initial seed money that allowed us to organize our first conference in 2001. Our greatest thanks, however, go to the Carnegie Corporation of New York, whose two-year grant made this project possible. The statements made and views expressed in the volume, however, are solely the responsibility of the authors. Those who have worked with Stephen J. Del Rosso, Jr., Chair of International Peace and Security at the Carnegie Corporation, know that his contribution to any project is much more than financial. His intellectual guidance helped shape this project in many significant ways, and we are grateful to him for his insights and advice.

Finally, we wish to thank each of our authors for their hard work throughout the project. Their graciousness and goodwill in tolerating our subtle and not-so-subtle requests for revisions made our editorial roles a pleasure rather than a burden.

MILES KAHLER AND
BARBARA F. WALTER
San Diego

1 Territoriality and conflict in an era of globalization

Miles Kahler

The world of the early twenty-first century displays both persistent attachments to territory and violent conflict over those territorial stakes. Even as interstate conflict has declined, many costly internal conflicts have taken on a territorial dimension. The persistence of territoriality and the conflict that it inspires run counter to one popular view of the consequences of growing globalization: capital, goods, and populations display increased mobility, and their detachment from territory should reduce the importance of conventional territorial boundaries. Globalization has produced changes in territoriality and the functions of borders, but it has eliminated neither. We do not live in a "borderless world" or one that has seen the "end of geography" (Ohmae 1990; O'Brien 1992). Conflict over territory continues in an increasingly integrated world.

Spanning the social sciences, the authors in this volume present converging investigations into the complex causal relations among territoriality, conflict, and globalization. The study of globalization and the persistence of ethnic conflict have stimulated an interest in borders of all kinds, questioning their permanence and defining the consequences when social and cultural identities do not coincide with political boundaries and territorial claims.[1] The contributors display skepticism toward both an unreconstructed view of the sovereign territorial state and the competing claim that globalization has completely transformed the existing territorial regime. The modern territorial state is seen as one historically bounded exemplar of territoriality, rather than the defining expression of territorial rule. Scrutiny of the concept of territoriality leads to a more contingent and mutable formulation of unit variation rather than the conventional, static view of territoriality within international relations – a "Westphalian" system populated by precisely delimited, territorial states (Kahler 2002).

At the same time, changing territoriality is not equated with deterritorialization in an era of globalization. Early arguments claimed that globalization – particularly global economic integration – was eroding or "hollowing out" the role of the nation-state as governance moved to global and regional international institutions and devolved to sub-national units. In addition, private actors seemed to claim a role in governance that would substitute for, rather than complement, the role of national governments. Subsequent investigation has revealed a modern nation-state that is far from obsolete or absent from national governance. No universal shift in the location of governance has taken place. Rather, national governments, which have remained bounded territorial units, have adapted in order to retain the effectiveness and accountability demanded by their constituents. New forms of governance have emerged in the face of competing demands from the forces of integration and the claims of constituents (Kahler and Lake 2003).

Territoriality as the creation of actors over time, globalization as one of the determinants of territoriality rather than a force for its eradication – these broad viewpoints inform all of the chapters that follow. Disagreement over which actors are most important and how constrained their actions may be will become apparent. To question territoriality and the consequences of globalization would not set this study apart from many others. In three ways, however, it also advances the exploration of territoriality, globalization, and conflict:

1 Although states (and groups) continue to contest territory, often violently, the reasons for particular *territorial attachments* have remained obscure. Explanations are advanced, here and elsewhere, for a general increase in the importance of territorial stakes, but even in eras when territory appears of declining importance, specific territorial attachments can be mobilized into politics in ways that reinforce conflict. Globalization has in some cases strengthened those attachments and in others diluted them. In the first part of this volume, several models are advanced for the construction and persistence of such attachments. They provide alternative micro-foundations for changes in territoriality.

2 Although major interstate conflict has declined in recent decades, territorial conflicts remain prone to escalation and difficult to resolve. Conflicts within the borders of states often display a territorial dimension that has similar effects on their deadliness and persistence. Territoriality defined as *territorial stakes* clearly influences conflicts; globalization affects those stakes and may predictably increase or diminish the likelihood of conflict between and within states. Globalization may also have different effects on interstate conflicts and those erupting within the borders of existing states. Explaining the effects of globalization on territorial stakes and, through those stakes, on violent conflict is a central aim of authors in the second part.

3 Finally, the micropolitics of territorial attachments and territorial stakes contribute to the construction of *territorial regimes* – territoriality defined as domestic and international institutions. Boundaries are often seen as sources of dispute and symbols of conflict, barriers to movement and frontiers for military defense. As institutions that legitimate territorial claims, however, settled borders also play a central role in conflict reduction. Policy jurisdictions may match territorial borders, or they may bear only a rough relationship to a territorially defined space. Globalization and conflict influence the regime of borders and jurisdictions and its changes over time. An exploration of territorial regimes and their determinants lies at the center of part III.

Controversies surrounding the changing nature of globalization, territoriality, and violent conflict have centered on their definition and their consequences. Each has inspired a rich scholarly and policy literature over the past decade. Causal links among the three have been posited, but their investigation is far from complete. The volume at hand draws on interdisciplinary investigation of these features of the global system in order to better define them, to explore their change over time, and to propose causal relationships among them.[2] Changes in territoriality lie at the core of this research agenda, changes shaped by both globalization and past conflict that in turn increase the probability either of continuing conflict or of its resolution.

Territoriality and globalization defined

Territoriality

For anthropologists and geographers, who view territoriality over long historical spans and across cultural divides, territoriality has two dimensions: delimitation of boundaries and behavior within those boundaries. Robert Sack, for example, defines territoriality as "the attempt by an individual or group to affect, influence, or control people, phenomena, and relationships, by delimiting and asserting control over a geographic area" (1986, 19). Each of these dimensions has demonstrated wide variation over time and across societies.

In modern political science, sociology, and international relations, territoriality has been defined more narrowly in terms of spatially defined political rule. Recent explorations of territoriality have questioned the axiomatic hold that the modern state has had in defining territorial rule, however. This new look at unit variation has unearthed the territorial and non-territorial rivals of the modern territorial state and emphasizes the contingent nature of the eventual success and expansion of this particular territorial template.[3] Hendrik Spruyt and Charles Tilly, for example, emphasize the importance of city-leagues and city-states in late medieval Europe, rivals to the territorial state that enjoyed considerable success before falling to its greater military power and institutional advantages (Tilly 1990; Spruyt 1994). Andreas Osiander (2001) challenges the claim of a sharp Westphalian break that separates the modern state system from earlier conceptions of sovereignty and territoriality.

Even this narrower definition contains three dimensions of variation. First, individuals and groups can be distinguished by their *territorial attachment and detachment*: their identification with a particular territory and the precision and intensity of that identification. As Terrence Lyons describes, certain groups of migrants, particularly economic migrants, demonstrate little identification with their previous homeland. Diasporic communities, however, display a close affinity with a homeland that may often be more mythical than real, but one that has significant behavioral implications nonetheless (Lyons, this volume).

Territorial attachment is in turn a major determinant of the *stakes* that actors, particularly political elites, discern in territory. For those preoccupied with the role of territorial claims in violent conflict among or within units, this second dimension of territoriality is central: territory may be more or less important (as compared to other objectives) as a stake in bargaining among key actors. Over time, governments and groups have awarded greater or lesser value to land in their disputes.

Conflicting territorial claims may involve stakes of two types. Tangible territorial stakes include varying degrees of control over land and sea, as well as over the resources and populations that are part of those spatial claims. More puzzling and difficult to explain, however, are the symbolic stakes that are often invested in territorial conflicts. At the level of the polity, these stakes are often determined by the prior (and constructed) territorial attachments of groups. As a result, territories that are devoid of resources or substantial, ethnically related populations may still become the site of violent disputes. Unraveling the sources of territorial attachment will help to explain the symbolic stakes that lie at the heart of many territorial conflicts.

Finally, challenges to a timeless Westphalian order that are based on an awareness of the fluidity of territoriality require the introduction of *territorial regime* as a third dimension of changes in territoriality. Territorial regime narrows the concept of territoriality by reducing both the actors and the behaviors of interest. A territorial regime governs the spatial exercise of authority by political elites or governments. As defined earlier, such a regime is constituted by the norms, institutions, and practices associated with territorial governance. Its two principal constituents are *border delimitation* and *jurisdictional congruence*. Border delimitation captures the means by which political units separate themselves from other units, means that can be characterized by more or less precision and permanence. Jurisdictional congruence measures the degree to which exclusive political authority across policy domains coincides with those boundaries.

These dimensions of territorial regimes have displayed considerable variation over time. For example, Friedrich Kratochwil (1986) contrasts border delimitation practices and jurisdictional authority among pastoral or nomadic peoples with the institutions of ancient empires and the contemporary states system. The introduction of fixed property among the Mongols – a different and more permanent sort of control over territory – led to a decline in their mobility, which had been a major strategic asset deployed against the Chinese empire, and to the institution of new and more permanent hierarchical relations with their sedentary neighbors (Kratochwil 1986, 21). Michael Saltman (2002) has described a similar transition among the Kipsigi, a formerly pastoral people in Kenya. The dimensions of territoriality have also differed across regions as well as among different types of units. Amitav Acharya describes the pre-colonial interstate system in Southeast Asia as "loosely organised states existing side-by-side without clearly defined territorial limits" (Acharya 2000, 21).[4] In pre-colonial Africa, an abundance of land coupled with relatively low population meant that authority faded rapidly from the center to the ill-defined edges of the polity (Herbst 2000). The Westphalian image of precisely delimited borders and exclusive, congruent jurisdictions within those borders has been an exception rather than a norm even within western Europe, as Peter Sahlins (1989) demonstrates in the case of the Pyrenees border between France and Spain. Although this border was one of the first to be agreed in early modern Europe, it was initially defined in jurisdictional terms – the rule of the two sovereigns over particular subjects – rather than as strictly territorial rule. Those jurisdictions continued to overlap for some time.

Globalization

Globalization is a term laden with political freight and theoretical ambiguity. For some, globalization encompasses a host of changes in international politics that can be traced to radically reduced costs of international transportation and communications. Robert O. Keohane and Joseph Nye, for example, define globalization as an increase in globalism, which is described as "networks of interdependence at multi-continental distances" (Keohane and Nye 2000, 2). Defined in such a way, globalization becomes so all-encompassing that its usefulness for explanation is reduced. Given its scope, endogeneity seems to be defined into the concept, and tracing the direction of causality becomes very difficult.

For the purposes of exploring its consequences for territoriality and military conflict, globalization will be more narrowly defined as economic integration at the global level, a reduction in the barriers to economic exchange and factor mobility that creates one economic space from many.[5] Economic globalization, which is central to most contemporary debates about globalization's reach and its consequences, is driven by both the technological changes noted above and the political choices of governments. Although measured through economic indices, it is not a purely technological or economic process. Trade-based measures are often deployed to estimate levels of globalization, but a definition of economic globalization should include investment and migration as well. Contemporary economic integration is driven by capital market integration and foreign direct investment by multinational corporations as much as by the opening of markets to trade in goods and services. Cross-border migration may also have important political implications, as the diasporas described by Terrence Lyons demonstrate. Finally, globalization, even when defined as economic integration, may vary over time. The pre-1914 era of globalization, despite high levels of economic integration, differed from contemporary globalization in both economic constituents and territorial outcomes.[6] That variation is noted by several of the authors when assessing the significance of globalization for changes in territoriality.

Explaining territorial attachments

Territorial attachments are often identified as contributors to conflict within and between states. Systematic analysis of interstate territorial conflict points to the importance of symbolic attachments to territory: the intrinsic value of territory (in terms of its economic or demographic significance) cannot account for a substantial share of disputes and violent conflict over territory (Diehl 1999a, x–xi). Domestic political dynamics drive territorial conflict as much as the strategic value of the territory in dispute, and those political dynamics are often rooted in the symbolism of territory rather than its measurable value (Huth 1999, 68; Hensel 1999, 117–19).

The lack of coincidence between homeland attachments and countries of residence also lies at the heart of many ethnonational disputes *within* existing states, disputes that may also have a strong international dimension. Homelands may match perfectly the boundaries that delimit a particular state, but that outcome is relatively rare. The homeland may be external to the state of residence of an individual or group (as in the case of diasporas). It may also be only a portion of an existing state, as in the case of many secessionist movements. Or, as in irredentist movements, a homeland may span the territory of more than one state. In any of these cases, homeland selection may point toward conflict between states or between groups and their states of residence (Barrington et al. 2003, 292–94). In conflicts between governments and ethnonational groups, Monica Toft (2003) has discovered that populations concentrated territorially and lacking any other homeland are more likely to turn to violence to achieve their ends in the face of state resistance to greater autonomy.

Given the underlying importance of territorial attachments in many conflicts and growing evidence that the homeland "is a perception, susceptible to change over time" (Toft 2003, 313), a model that explains the creation, maintenance, and demise of territorial attachments would also contribute to an explanation for many territorial conflicts. Four such models are presented in the first part of this volume. Hein Goemans argues that the homeland originates in the classical setting of insecurity familiar to students of international politics. The need for collective defense offers powerful incentives for a clear principle that will allow identification of membership in the group. Territoriality has often provided that core principle, offering advantages of coordination both to followers – who can more easily monitor their leader(s) – and to the elite who can more reliably count on the support of the population in common defense (Goemans, this volume, 31).

As Goemans describes, these rationalist assumptions help to explain the emergence and survival of a group norm for defense of the homeland, but the choice of a *particular* homeland requires further explanation through a set of focal principles that are deployed to identify the contours of the homeland, focal principles that change over time. Peter Sahlins (1989), for example, describes how the focal principle of "natural" frontiers, defined by mountain ranges or rivers, became more accepted in the boundary delimitation of early modern Europe, often displacing historical (and mythical) claims. Although these focal principles often appeared to disguise simple strategic interests, they also took on a life of their own in the professional work of geographers, cartographers, and diplomats. In his account of colonial boundary surveys in British Guiana, D. Graham Burnett describes the ways in which different focal principles could conflict: finding a boundary that referred to historical occupation, followed natural features of the landscape, offered visibility, and allowed access to surveyors fixing its position was often impossible. The selection of one focal principle rather than another could produce persistent border disputes, such as those that Guyana inherited from its colonial ruler (Burnett 2000, 209–10).

Joel Robbins (chapter 3) presents a case of territorial detachment in his account of the Urapmin of Papua New Guinea, a group who, under the influence of cultural (religious) and economic globalization, reject their existing territorial domain in favor of alternative identities. The homeland in this case is not a reservoir of positive emotional attachment, but a persistent barrier to religious and economic aspirations. Robbins recreates at the local level a parallel to the territorial reconstitution traced by others at the national and international levels. Two competing versions of globalization's effects on such local territorial attachments emerge: on the one hand, globalization may provoke an identity backlash that deepens symbolic territorial attachments at the local level; on the other, globalization, in this case defined more broadly than economic globalization, may provide a menu of new identities, competitors that undermine or usurp older symbolic attachments to territory. The Urapmin were hardly participants in the global economy; as Robbins points out, globalization was more an aspiration than a reality. Territorial detachment owed more to an imported transnational religious identity, Pentecostal Christianity, which provided a symbolic alternative to deities rooted in their locale. Religion in this case eroded attachment to a local homeland, in striking contrast to the "geopiety" described by David Newman in Israel.

Newman (chapter 4) traces reterritorialization and the development of territorial attachments at the local level. Like other authors in this volume, he rejects a simple trajectory from globalization to a borderless world, particularly when invisible borders are constructed every day at the local level. For many ethnoterritorial conflicts, the creation of territorial facts on the (local) ground has been a central instrument in creating new landscapes and new territorial realities. As Newman argues, borders as dynamic institutions incorporate a " 'bottom up' process of change, . . . which emanates from the daily functional patterns of the ordinary people living in the borderland region, as much as the traditional 'top down' approach which focuses solely on the role of institutional actors, notably – but not only – governments" (Newman, this volume, 102–3).

Territorial expressions of conflict, through such processes as residential segregation and differential distribution of resources, are part of the micro-level means for reshaping territory that may later be reflected at the more familiar level of national borders and conflicts. As Peter Sahlins (1989) describes in the case of neighboring Catalan villages that faced each other across the French–Spanish border, local politics could embroil national governments and call on national claims to promote local ends, just as national governments could at times mobilize local populations in their own strategies on the frontier. At the Finnish–Soviet border, Anssi Paasi contrasts the attitudes of national elites toward the border – a stance of fear and "otherness" – with the younger generations who live near the border and have been "completely socialized" to its existence. For them, the border is "part of the routine of everyday activities and part of the security that springs from the routinization of action" (1996, 268–69). The potential conflict between local territorial compartmentalization or compromise and national strategies may also undermine efforts at conflict resolution.

A final set of actors may be strengthened by globalization and in turn reinforce the high symbolic stakes and politically significant attachments associated with territory: diasporas. Although diaspora is a contested concept, attachment to a homeland outside the state of residence is a key factor separating diasporic communities from other migrants: " 'the old country' – a notion often buried deep in language, religion, custom or folklore – always has some claim on their loyalty and emotions."[7] That homeland is defined territorially, often more precisely and emotionally by diasporas than by homeland residents themselves. Terrence Lyons (chapter 5) examines those attachments and their determinants in the case of conflict-generated diaspora groups. He also traces the attitudes of diasporas toward territorial politics in the homeland. Diasporas may provide an important external constituency with intense preferences regarding territorial conflict, one with resources to back up their political attitudes. Diasporas also share a particular relationship to globalization. Although the conflict-generated diasporas described by Lyons were not created by globalization, contemporary globalization has provided both avenues for retaining intensive communication with the former homeland and, occasionally, the economic incentives to maintain those links. Paradoxically, globalization allows diasporic communities to reinforce starkly territorial definitions of the homeland and to heighten the territorial stakes in both internal and interstate conflicts.

Territorial stakes, globalization, and conflict

Territory remains a potent source of conflict between states, one that has persisted into the current era of globalization. Even if proximity is controlled, territorial stakes remain important in many militarized disputes and wars. Territorial disputes are more likely to escalate: militarized disputes over territory are much more likely to involve a militarized response by the target state and are more likely to escalate to full-scale war. Territorial conflicts – both interstate and intrastate – are more likely to be protracted and difficult to settle. The tangible stakes associated with territorial disputes (strategic location, economic value, and shared ethnic groups) clearly explain some of the active territorial claims between states, but far from all.[8]

For conflicts internal to states as well as those between states, the ability to mobilize political support over a territorial conflict derives from the salience of such conflicts, which, in turn, is often based on symbolic attachments and appeals. Such mobilization often makes territory – an eminently divisible stake – an intractable issue by creating effective indivisibility.[9] Goemans, for example, argues that attachment to a particular focal principle in defining the homeland may produce bargaining failures. If territorial concession calls into question the underlying focal principle that defines the territory that should be defended, the intrinsic value of territory could fail to predict its perceived implications for group survival.

The direct effect of globalization on violent conflict has most often been investigated through dyadic measures of economic interdependence. Most research points to a positive relationship between interdependence and peace, although skeptical voices remain.[10] Here the principal concern is globalization's effects on territoriality – defined as the territorial regime or the salience of territorial stakes – and whether those changes in territoriality have discernable effects on territorial disputes and the militarized conflicts that may follow from them. If globalization, through either changes in territorial regimes or a reduction in intrinsic or symbolic territorial stakes, lowers the frequency of territorial disputes between states or groups, its contribution to a reduction in violent conflict could be substantial. Such effects could also be used to reshape strategies for the resolution of such disputes.

David Lake and Angela O'Mahony (chapter 6) connect changing territorial stakes and interstate conflict through the variable of changing state size. State size in the international system demonstrates a clear and significant pattern of increase in the nineteenth century and decrease in the twentieth century. For Lake and O'Mahony, increasing state size is accompanied by an increase in the importance of territorial stakes for state elites and a greater propensity for conflict over territorial issues. A simple increase in conflict over territory, however, need not lead directly to an increase in militarized disputes or wars fought over territory. Following the rationalist theory of war, Lake and O'Mahony point out that many such disputes could be resolved peacefully in the absence of failures of bargaining, such as information asymmetries, inability to commit credibly, or barriers to divisibility.

Lake and O'Mahony make a critical link between changing territorial stakes and the likelihood of war by demonstrating that an increase in the value of territory produces a result equivalent to a reduction in the *relative* cost of waging war under a familiar rationalist model. An increase in state size, which implies increasing territorial stakes, should therefore produce a greater probability of interstate conflict. This expectation seems to be confirmed by a cycle of rising and declining interstate territorial conflict that tracks the rise and decline of state size. Their findings are confirmed by others. As measured by Kalevi J. Holsti, territory declined as a percentage of issues in interstate war in the nineteenth century (1815–1914) as compared to the previous century (1715–1814), but only because other issues – ideological and national – emerged during the period. As Holsti notes, "territory continued to be the main indicator of a nation's power, as it had been since the days of Louis XIV" (1991, 151). Using a somewhat different periodization, Paul Hensel discovers that territory has remained a relatively constant source of militarized disputes, although the 1920–39 period (decades of low global economic integration) witnessed the highest percentage of territorial issues in such disputes (Hensel 2002, 40).

The influence of globalization on the dynamics of state size and interstate conflict is ambiguous, however. Lake and O'Mahony detect different effects over time, in particular during the pre-1914 and post-1945 eras of advancing global economic integration. One familiar model, that of Alberto Alesina and Enrico Spolaore (2003, chap. 6), predicts that increasing global economic integration should favor the creation of smaller states. In the late nineteenth century, however, state size increased: the predicted effects of globalization were either more than offset by technological changes that permitted states to project power over larger areas or average state size would have grown even larger in the absence of globalization. In the most recent period of globalization, on the other hand, trends toward economic openness and larger numbers of unitary democracies have reinforced one another and the century-long pattern of smaller states (Lake and O'Mahony, this volume). Kal Raustiala, in his investigation of the territorial characteristics of the US domestic legal regime (chapter 9), also questions whether the effects of globalization are consistent across historical periods. Foreign direct investment and intra-industry trade have been more characteristic of global economic integration in recent decades, creating incentives for assertions of extraterritorial regulatory jurisdiction. Globalization only had this effect, however, because of a prior expansion of the regulatory reach of the state domestically. Other international changes – in the security environment and in relative power – have had more influence on the evolution of US legal territoriality.

In teasing apart the distinct effects of economic development and globalization on violent interstate conflict, Erik Gartzke's results (chapter 7) also qualify the effects of globalization on territorial stakes and territorial conflict. Economic development has contradictory implications for conflict: on the one hand, enhancing capabilities and creating a larger pool of potential disputants and, on the other, reducing the significance of territorial stakes. Overall, the propensity of more economically developed states to engage in territorial disputes declines, but non-territorial conflict actually increases with development. Even this outcome reduces conflict over territorial stakes, a particularly dangerous form of interstate conflict.

To the degree that globalization spurs economic development, it will also contribute to this reduction in conflict over territorial stakes. If globalization spurs industrialization, the value of land as a factor of production (and incentives to conquest) will decline as well, reducing the incentives for territorial acquisition (Zacher 2001). Globalization also disperses industrial production and integrates it in far-flung networks. Territorial acquisition is therefore unlikely to produce control over significant economic sectors or technologies. Stephen Brooks (1999) argues that the central role of foreign direct investment in contemporary globalization may allow governments to substitute that instrument of external economic influence for the older instrument of conquest. Each of these economic changes is associated with contemporary globalization (but not to the same degree with pre-1914 globalization); each also reduces the incentives for territorial acquisition.

Gartzke, however, argues that the empirical evidence demonstrates little independent effect of globalization on territorial conflict. As demonstrated in other spheres, globalization does not appear to have a strong "deterritorializing" effect on warfare. Globalization does reduce interstate disputes overall, but it demonstrates, according to Gartzke, no differential effect on territorial conflicts. He suggests that the dyadic effects of globalization – the constraint that economic interdependence exercises on conflict and the enhancement of signaling abilities – are too weak to overcome the dynamics of territorial conflict, "conflicts of an intensity where integration is neither an effective deterrent, nor a particularly useful signal of resolve."[11]

Halvard Buhaug and Nils Petter Gleditsch (chapter 8) provide a third skeptical view of the influence that globalization exerts on territorial conflict. Rather than emphasizing territorial stakes, however, they concentrate on state capabilities and the effects that technological changes associated with globalization may have on patterns of conflict. In parallel with other authors in the volume, they criticize a simple association of globalization with the "death of distance." Predictions that conflict will become less associated with regional neighborhoods and with geographically proximate adversaries are challenged. The technological changes that have reduced the cost of many long-distance economic transactions have not spilled over completely into military technology, which remains more constrained by geography. Like Gartzke, they find only a weak relationship between globalization and the decline of territorial conflicts, lending further support to others in this volume who reject an overarching deterritorialization as a necessary consequence of globalization.[12]

Territorial conflicts between states remain a significant and dangerous part of interstate violence, but the incidence of such conflicts has declined since the nineteenth century. Globalization appears to have played a relatively minor role in that decline. As Lake and O'Mahony point out, the pre-1914 era of globalization witnessed both increasing state size and an increase in violent territorial conflict. Kal Raustiala's reading of the territorial logic of legal regimes at the time confirms this relationship: globalization and traditional Westphalian territoriality were at least able to cohabit during that era. Gartzke undermines the independent role of globalization by examining economic development and its effects on territorial conflict. Rich countries have greater capabilities, which result in involvement in more conflict, but those conflicts do appear to revolve around non-territorial stakes. Globalization, however, seems to have at best a weak effect on the incidence of conflict over territorial stakes.

The effects of globalization on interstate conflict do not demonstrate a radical undermining of territoriality. Its effects on conflict within states may be more pronounced and could exacerbate such conflicts. Internal conflicts represent the largest share of violent conflicts in recent decades, and a large number of internal conflicts have territorial stakes.[13] Wars within states have also proven resistant to settlement in recent decades, producing a cumulation of ongoing civil wars since 1945.[14]

Existing models of violent conflict within states suggest plausible causal connections between globalization and this pattern. The insurgency model of James Fearon and David Laitin provides one such link (2003, 77). The core of their model involves a contest between an ineffectual and arbitrary central government and a rural insurgency based in inhospitable terrain and drawing on a large population. Territoriality and globalization figure in their results through the effects of the territorial regime. First, the international territorial regime has sustained "quasi-states" with weak administrative capability, "badly financed, organizationally inept, corrupt, politically divided, and poorly informed about goings-on at the local level" (ibid., 80). Government weakness permits insurgencies to persist.

A second feature of the territorial regime, internal administrative boundaries, is rarely functional in the settlement of internal territorial conflict. For one important group of insurgencies, labeled "sons of the soil" by Fearon (2004), conflicts over land or natural resources are intensified by in-migration to the peripheral area by a more populous (and land-hungry) dominant group, often supported by the central government. These conflicts, particularly important in Asia, also tend to be among the most protracted. Although boundary regimes are increasingly clear at the international level and borders can serve as institutional supports for conflict resolution, few if any such territorial conventions exist within states. As Goemans describes, pre-existing administrative boundaries have often provided a relatively peaceful focal point for state disintegration (most notably in the former Soviet Union), but that convention is only triggered by prospective state failure.[15] Perversely, a clear-cut territorial regime *between* states and the absence of such a regime *within* states may offer strong incentives for armed resistance and secession. If globalization also provides economic incentives for smaller territorial scale, the case for a violent attempt at separation may appear even more attractive.

A second link between globalization and internal conflict lies in the resources that support such insurgencies. Both the insurgency model of Fearon and Laitin (2003) and the "greed and grievance" model of Paul Collier and Anke Hoeffler (2000) point to tradable resources – often high-value, low-volume contraband such as diamonds, opium, or cocaine – as crucial stimulants and supports for violent internal conflict. Since these resources are found in delimited areas of the national territory, globalization also reinforces the territorial character of the conflict. Without access to a world market and specifically the trading networks that permit such products to reach that market, the resource base for many internal conflicts would wither. The diasporas described by Lyons are another resource that globalization provides to insurgent movements. Overall, globalization may tilt local balances of power against weak central governments and in favor of peripheral insurgencies.

Territorial regimes in an era of globalization

Territorial regimes – territoriality defined as institutions – reflect the territorial attachments and stakes of key actors and also shape those definitions of territoriality. Two contributions, by Kal Raustiala (chapter 9) and Beth Simmons (chapter 10), provide a final reading of the complex relationships among territoriality, globalization, and conflict. Each concentrates on one of the dimensions of territorial regimes. Raustiala examines changes in jurisdictional congruence; Simmons re-evaluates border delimitation.

The pre-1914 era of globalization witnessed a normative consolidation of what is often labeled the Westphalian territorial regime – two centuries after the Peace of Westphalia – as well as its incorporation into state practice. Although the nineteenth century had produced experiments in federal and decentralized governance in Europe, in its final decades a diverse realm of "federative politics" had been replaced by the centralized nation-state (Binkley 1941). This transformation affected both dimensions of the territorial regime. On the one hand, boundaries came to be formally delimited in the contemporary sense. As Peter Sahlins describes in his history of the border region between France and Spain, the Treaty of the Pyrenees, which "inaugurated the first official boundary in the modern sense" in 1659, was only the starting point in a process of border delimitation.[16] The construction of a more precise boundary regime was only completed in the Treaties of Bayonne in 1866 and 1868. Over two centuries, both national elites and local communities contributed to the social and political demarcation of the boundary between the two societies (P. Sahlins 1989).

At the same time, throughout Europe and other parts of the world, jurisdictional congruence – exclusive political control across policy realms within the delimited boundaries – became the norm for the first time. This was perhaps most important in the realm of identity, which lay at the core of the emerging nation-state. As Charles Maier (2000) describes, identity space and decision space were now closer to coincidence. This coincidence was reflected in a growing national and international aversion to dual nationality – that each individual should have one nationality and only one – a norm that was consolidated in bilateral treaties, such as the Bancroft treaties signed by the United States and in a 1930 League of Nations convention (Koslowski 2001, 205–07).

Mercenaries, once commonplace parts of national military forces, also began to give way to citizen armies during the nineteenth century (Avant 2000).

In central economic policy domains, a similar process of delimitation and assertion of exclusive jurisdiction also took hold during the late nineteenth century. Territorial currencies grew in importance, after centuries in which several currencies – public and private – had typically circulated within national borders. The strengthening of exclusive territorial currencies was closely linked to the building of the national territorial state, through policing of national tender laws, extension of state control over currencies that were accepted by state offices, and the use of currencies as significant national symbols. The process was driven by technological capability, in particular the ability to produce standardized currencies, as well as the reduction in transaction costs that a common currency implied (Gilbert and Helleiner 1999). As in other dimensions of the new national jurisdictions, territorial currencies only triumphed in the mid-twentieth century. Before 1914, alternative models, such as currency unions and free banking, remained potent challengers (Helleiner 2003).

Somewhat paradoxically, given the claims that are often made regarding the territorial effects of globalization, these shifts toward the consolidated territorial nation-state took place during decades of growing international economic integration. That earlier era of globalization figures prominently in the contribution of Kal Raustiala to this volume. In his examination of extraterritoriality (jurisdictional claims beyond territorial boundaries), he discovers that the era of globalization in the nineteenth century marked a movement in American constitutional jurisprudence toward strict territoriality (as defined above). This territorial principle applied to American citizens and to the citizens of other "civilized" states. Toward weaker, non-European states during this era of imperialism, globalization encouraged extraterritoriality, extending the jurisdictions of powerful states beyond their borders in order to protect their citizens and favor their firms. In some cases, the extraterritorial regime was governed by a set of unequal treaties (as in the case of China); in others, the extension of jurisdiction implied rule in a more complete sense – imperialism (Binkley 1941, 165–68).

From a legal regime founded on jurisdictional congruence in the late nineteenth century, the United States has moved to a more heterogeneous territorial regime in the early twenty-first century. In certain respects, the mixed legal regime of the United States described by Raustiala tracked the evolving international territorial regime. The legal regime of delimited borders and jurisdictional congruence that emerged in Europe in the late nineteenth and early twentieth centuries spread around the world after 1945. The post-1945 territorial regime incorporated elements of the earlier period and at the same time modified those constituents under the influence of decolonization. Given the military and political weakness of many of the new states, an even more rigid attachment to territorial rules, norms, and practices that established clear borders and ensured national government control within those borders became a central aim of political elites. Technological advance and resource claims have also driven border delimitation, a trend that culminated in the United Nations Conference on the Law of the Sea (UNCLOS). UNCLOS established maritime Exclusive Economic Zones for the first time, a substantial extension of qualified territoriality into the oceans.

At the same time, contemporary territoriality also demonstrates change in several key dimensions that may be explained in part by globalization. Although precise border delimitation has been retained and even expanded, congruence of policy jurisdictions with the national territorial domain has eroded, in what John Ruggie terms "the unbundling of territoriality" (1993, 165). This process of reducing the congruence of policy domains with territorial limits has been driven by globalization. The revival of interest in regional currency unions (with Europe's EMU as the most prominent example) or the "borrowing" of another government's policy regime (in the form of dollarization) are only two examples from economic policy. Increased cross-border migration has put pressure on the demographic boundary regime, producing a reversal in international norms against dual citizenship (Koslowski 2001). Overall, in Maier's terms, identity space coincides less with decision space.

Raustiala notes a parallel development in American jurisprudence, which has extended the reach of both American regulatory law and, for citizens at least, the spatial scope of the Constitution. Extraterritoriality – claims by the state that its legal reach exceeds its territorial jurisdiction – has grown in American jurisprudence since 1945. Globalization provides incentives for governments presiding over increasingly integrated economies to expand their regulatory regimes. These extraterritorial claims have become less constrained as confidence has grown that peace among the advanced industrialized countries will persist. In this respect and others, however, Raustiala argues that conflict has been as important as globalization in shaping the territorial regime in US law. The constitutional rights of US citizens are now confirmed regardless of their physical location, the result of jurisprudence confronting the realities of Cold War military deployments. Territoriality has been maintained in the case of aliens, resident and non-resident, as security threats posed by more open borders have become more salient (Raustiala, this volume). The heterogeneous – some would say incoherent – legal regime that has emerged from this complex of international change suggests a patchwork in which the previous territorial regime of strict jurisdictional congruence has been overturned, but no new alternative has replaced it.

Territoriality may incorporate a different balance between globalization and conflict in the future, an alteration that will be reflected in changed domestic legal regimes. If globalization and international attachment to human rights increase, regimes of harmonization that reduce the disparity between national jurisdictions and international practice may take shape. On the other hand, in a future filled with higher perceptions of external threat, the line between citizen and non-citizen may be sharpened once again, although without a reinstatement of old-style jurisdictional congruence.

Although both contemporary globalization and international conflict may have contributed to regime change on the dimension of jurisdictional congruence, both eras of globalization have been marked by continued and perhaps growing attachment to a well-defined border regime. This observation seems to undermine claims that globalization has rendered borders *less* important, at least for economic exchange. Beth Simmons resolves this apparent paradox by treating international borders as institutions. As such, agreed borders provide valuable benefits to neighboring states in the form of increased certainty and reduced transaction costs. Simmons demonstrates the opportunity costs that countries bear when their borders are disputed, even when those disputes are not militarized. Those costs, measured in terms of bilateral trade forgone, are in many cases substantial. Good borders make good traders. Globalization, by increasing the prospective gains that may result from settled borders, offers incentives for a well-bordered world (Simmons, this volume).

The apparent effects of globalization on the territorial regime in the contemporary era differ significantly from its effects before 1914. Three possible explanations can be advanced for this puzzle. First, as Lake and O'Mahony argue, the effects of globalization before 1914 may have been swamped by other trends – technological and institutional – that created strong incentives for an increase in state size through territorial expansion. Certainly, the persistence of a strong regime of border delimitation in both eras (whatever the economic significance of those borders) is explained in large measure by technological advance. Second, globalization itself may have changed in character. An agent-centered view of globalization's effects emphasizes changes in the sectoral character of foreign investment. Foreign investors in the earlier era of globalization insisted on territorial control to guarantee their economic stakes; after 1945, new forms of investment changed the territorial program of economic agents (Kahler 1984). Finally, although more powerful states have a wider array of options for expanding their jurisdictional reach, the territorial regime influences their choices. The norm against territorial conquest, for example, has strengthened since 1945, despite persistent claims of extraterritorial jurisdiction (Zacher 2001).

Globalization, conflict, and changes in territoriality

Despite differing methodological approaches and concentration on different dimensions of territoriality, each contributor to this volume rejects a simple causal path from globalization to deterritorialization to reduced conflict. Globalization does not produce a world in which territorial attachments of individuals and groups, territorial stakes claimed by governments, or the territorial regimes constructed by states have been consistently devalued. Although changes in territoriality are apparent, much of that change can be attributed to sources other than economic globalization.

Territorial attachments remain profound in much of the globalized world – and not only, as Newman emphasizes, on its least globalized margins. Conflict may exercise a more significant influence on the attachment of populations and elites to territorial focal principles for defining themselves and their homelands, as Goemans argues. As Robbins claims, economic globalization may figure in territorial detachment only as a vague aspiration for the future, and religious globalization may offer a sounder basis for an uncomfortable divorce from a longstanding spatial identity. Globalization and even national policies may fail to penetrate the powerful local processes of border formation and territorial claims described by Newman. By increasing ease of communication and economic transfers, globalization may permit diasporic attachments to old and often unseen homelands to flourish, hardening territorial claims and propagating territorial conflict.

Changes in the frequency of violent territorial conflict among states may also owe less to globalization than has often been argued. Lake and O'Mahony note the influence of globalization on the decreasing size of states in the twentieth century (although not in the earlier, pre-1914 era of globalization). Even so, the rise of unitary democracies plays an equally important role in the relative decline of territorial stakes in interstate conflict. Gartzke assigns economic development a more significant and unambiguous role than globalization in the decline of territorial disputes and warfare. Buhaug and Gleditsch find little evidence that warfare demonstrates the same "death of distance" that some have found for economic transactions in a globalized world.

Territorial regimes have changed substantially over the past century, but once again, globalization is only one of the sources of change. Extraterritoriality, measured by Raustiala in the evolution of American constitutional jurisprudence, has both domestic and international sources. Globalized states with greater regulatory scope have been more tempted to expand their extraterritorial jurisdiction *if* the risk of military conflict is low. The pressures exerted by globalization for an erosion of jurisdictional congruence are therefore qualified by both domestic and international variables. At the same time a different globalization – the growing reach of the US military during the Cold War and new cross-border threats in the post-Cold War era – has also moved the spatial dimensions of the American legal regime. Paradoxically, globalization serves to confirm another dimension of the territorial regime that emerged in the nineteenth century: more precise border delimitation. Simmons offers persuasive evidence that settled borders provide substantial benefits in an era of growing cross-border economic exchange. However, other trends – technological and political – have also propelled governments in the same direction, as noted by Peter Sahlins and other historians.

Rather than endorsing a simple and popular notion that globalization has produced a borderless world, one in which territoriality has declined in significance and conflict over territorial stakes is rare, the authors in this volume offer a more complicated causal story, one in which globalization's effects on territoriality have differed over time and have been highly conditioned and sometimes outweighed by other variables. International and internal conflicts have both reflected changes in territoriality and induced change in territorial attachments, stakes, and regimes. Globalization has encountered obstacles since the late 1990s: the Asian financial crisis, the terrorist attacks of 11 September 2001, the end of the stock market bubble in the United States, and the SARS epidemic. There is little evidence, however, that the integration of the world economy has gone into reverse. Understanding the often uneasy cohabitation of globalization with an evolving territoriality will remain central both to our understanding of international politics and to the alleviation of violent conflict.

NOTES

The author thanks Kelly Wurtz for his research assistance. Jonathan Kirshner and members of the Olin Institute Economics and National Security Seminar at Harvard University offered helpful comments on an earlier version of this chapter.

1 For an example from the field of anthropology, see Donnan and Wilson 1999; in history, Burnett 2000 and P. Sahlins 1989.

2 This research project, co-directed by Barbara Walter (University of California, San Diego), is supported by a grant from the Carnegie Corporation of New York. The authors represented in this volume are drawn from the disciplines of anthropology, law, political science, and geography.

3 For a survey of research on unit variation, see Kahler 2002.

4 Acharya is describing the mandala system of O. W. Wolters, the galactic polity of Stanley Tambiah, and the theatre state of Clifford Geertz.

5 The logic underlying this definition of globalization follows closely Kahler and Lake 2003a.

6 For a comparison of pre-1914 globalization and contemporary globalization, see Kahler and Lake 2003a.

7 R. Cohen 1997, ix. Compare to Shain and Barth 2003, 452.

8 The preceding findings regarding territorial conflict are drawn from Huth 1996, Huth 2000, Hensel 2000, Hensel 2002, Vasquez 2004, Vasquez and Henehan 2004, and Walter 2003.

9 On the divisibility of stakes and war, see Fearon 1995.

10 Russett and Oneal 2001; Morrow 1999 for a skeptical view.

11 Gartzke, this volume, 177. On the value of economic integration in facilitating costly signaling, see Gartzke and Li 2003.

12 Although territorial MIDs (Militarized Interstate Disputes) have declined as a proportion of MIDs in recent decades, they find a slight increase in the proportion of territorial wars over the same period (Buhaug and Gleditsch, this volume, 209).

13 On the growing importance of internal conflicts relative to interstate conflicts, see Eriksson and Wallensteen 2004; Sarkees et al. 2003.

14 Fearon and Laitin (2003, 77) counter the conventional wisdom that the outbreak of civil wars has increased since the end of the Cold War. Instead, the apparent increase results from their failure to end.

15 The importance of existing administrative boundaries as focal principles for new state formation is confirmed in Goemans, this volume.

16 The quotation is from Kratochwil 1986, 33.

Part I

Territorial attachment and detachment

2 Bounded communities: territoriality, territorial attachment, and conflict

H. E. Goemans

Introduction

In the first half of the twentieth century the study of territory and its role in international politics was very much in fashion among political scientists. Since then, however, the study of territory has lost much of its appeal among political scientists and has largely (but not completely) been left to political geographers. In the last decade or so, however, territory and territoriality have received renewed attention among political scientists. It should not be surprising that scholars in international relations have been at the forefront of this renewed attention to territory and territoriality. The importance of territory has long been recognized in the origins and escalation of disputes between states. Nonetheless, only recently have scholars who put territory front and center in their study of international conflict revealed that disputes over territory are more likely to escalate to war than any other type of dispute (Huth 1996; Diehl 1999b). The importance of territoriality – exclusion by area (Sack 1986) – is less well understood among political scientists, but it seems that some scholars have begun to recognize that territoriality is a, if not the, fundamental ordering principle of the modern state system (see Spruyt 1994; Wagner 2004). The third main concept discussed in this volume, "globalization," has received much attention in recent years precisely because it seems to challenge this fundamental ordering principle of the modern state system. Globalization proposes that exclusion by area loses its importance in "a world of flows." (See Paasi 1999 and Newman, Gartzke, Raustiala, and Simmons, this volume.)

My goal in this chapter is to offer a rationalist theoretical framework to explain how and why people become attached to "their" territory. Specifically, I seek to answer the following central question: how and why do people become attached to some territory – often far away from where they live – but remain unattached to other territory nearby? (I should emphasize here that I seek to explain not the cognitive or emotive state of "attachment" but the behavior it induces since that is the only way to measure "attachment.") An explanation of such territorial attachments, I propose, will not only contribute to our understanding of the causes and consequences of territorial disputes, but also to our understanding of the causes and consequences of "globalization." It will, I hope, allow us to better assess in what ways and how much "globalization" will challenge and affect both domestic and international politics.

The recognition that territorial attachment plays an important role in international relations is not new. For example, differential evaluation of "homeland" versus "non-homeland" territory played an important role in the discussions on extended deterrence during the 1950s and 1960s. The United States' nuclear umbrella over Europe faced a credibility gap precisely because Americans could not be counted on to value Berlin and West Germany as much as they valued New York or California. Attachment to territory, specifically to a "homeland," is thus often argued to help explain why people are willing to sacrifice blood and treasure to gain, hold and protect, or invest in such territory (Schelling 1960 and 1966; D. Friedman 1977, 59; for a contrasting view on how people *devalue* their territory, see Robbins, this volume.)

While political geographers have produced fascinating work on territorial attachment and "homelands" (Paasi 1996 and 1999; Newman 1999; White 2000; Yiftachel 2001b), to date no one has offered a rationalist causal mechanism to explain attachment to territory. In this paper I offer such a rationalist causal mechanism to shed new light on the causes and consequences of territorial attachment, a mechanism that can explain why people are willing to sacrifice their blood and treasure for their territory's defense. The main themes in my argument can be summarized briefly. Following Schelling (1960 and 1966) I argue that boundaries form focal points. But arguing that boundaries form focal points only puts the essential question one step further back: what coordination game do these focal points solve? Schelling (1960, 67–68) argued that the underlying coordination game helps solve the problem of multiple equilibria in interstate bargaining over territory. Thus, Schelling proposes that borders are focal points and are *drawn following focal principles* as the result of interstate bargaining. While I recognize this dynamic is an important force helping to shape borders, I propose a second mechanism to explain why borders are focal points and drawn following focal principles. This mechanism focuses squarely on the strategic interaction *within* the state.

I argue that territorial specification of group membership – for example, "we" live "here" – has been and in many places still is a particularly powerful and attractive way to coordinate group members to provide a collective defense.[1] Just like any other way to specify group membership, a territorial specification of the group is most powerful when it is easily communicated and readily comes to mind for potential group members. The territory that specifies group membership will therefore, I argue, be defined by focal principles (Kreps 1990). Historically, the most important focal principles have been natural frontiers, less (as is often assumed) because they sometimes form defensive barriers than because they are common knowledge.[2] A second important focal principle is common culture; individuals can coordinate around a common language, religion, or even the geographical spread of sugar palm trees.[3] The common culture of "nationalism," I argue, is merely a special case; the general and fundamental mechanism of territorial attachment is one of coordination for the provision of the collective (technically, club) good of collective defense.[4] Two other powerful and oft-invoked focal principles to define the group's territory have been territorial precedent as in prior historical formation where a group lays claim to the territory of a predecessor state or polity and cartography, as in Africa where almost half of all borders were drawn along lines of longitude and latitude.[5] As I will argue below, territorial specification of group membership produces a "homeland," "fatherland," or "motherland." (My use of the term "homeland" is slightly unconventional because it does not claim any necessary link between nationalism or ethnicity and homeland.) The territory becomes a "homeland" precisely because it is to be commonly defended, because all group members share similar obligations for its protection and because it defines who "we" are. In the previous literature, scholars explore the meaning and power of "homeland" by posing a poorly defined "emotional attachment" to an undefined piece of territory, failing to explain why some territory is part of the homeland while other territory is not. In contrast, my argument proposes a causal mechanism: group members will sacrifice their blood and taxes for the defense of the homeland because the territorial definition of the group sharply and clearly distinguishes "us" from "them" and thereby facilitates monitoring of both leaders and followers in the provision of collective defense. In essence, therefore, I emphasize territorial identification over ethnic identification of group members. Thus, while "[e]thnic network theory argues that group affiliation serves as an enforcement mechanism to prevent cheating and sanction contracts" (Congleton 1995), I argue that group affiliation can be promoted as – if not more – easily by territoriality, which then activates the same enforcement mechanisms necessary to get collective defense off the ground. The theoretical scaffolding that forms the bulk of this paper, the explanation why boundaries are focal points and follow focal principles, solves several important out-standing puzzles in international relations. Because the territory that defines the group – from now on referred to as the homeland – is defined by focal principles, it will be *indivisible*. Failure to defend and fight for the homeland as specified by the focal principle will unravel the coordination necessary for collective defense. Similarly, cession of terri-tory that the focal principle defines as part of the homeland breaks the power of the coordinating principle. It is the indivisibility of the principle that therefore explains why (and which) territory is a potent source of conflict (Fearon 1995). When groups invoke clashing focal principles to define their homelands, and competing focal principles lay claim to the same territory, disputes will be much more likely to start and much more likely to escalate to war.[6] While some political scientists have argued that territorial disputes are more likely to escalate to war because homeland territory is indivisible, to the best of my knowledge, only Walter (2006) has specified a mechanism to explain the source of this indivisibility, a variation on the chain-store paradox. The focal principle logic offers a new and competing explanation for the indivisibility of territory and offers new insights into other impor-tant puzzles. The most important of these, I would suggest, is that my focal principle argument helps explain why states *repeatedly* and *protractedly* dispute and fight for one specific piece of territory while never disputing many other pieces of territory that are equally or more valuable for its power. The focal principle argument also offers a new perspective on globalization and suggests that "globalization" may be the result of coordination for the provision of public goods at a different *scale* as territoriality loses its advantages in facilitating coordination for common defense (Knight 1999b). In the remainder of this paper, I first present the main theoretical building blocks of the argument. Next, I sketch some theoretical and empirical im-plications. Finally, I offer abbreviated tests of two implications of the argument. I first examine the first case of specification of a homeland by focal principles on the European continent. I show that well before the age of "nationalism" King Philip the Fair of France (1285–1314) specified the boundaries of France with a focal principle and that this principle *consistently* guided his territorial policies. Next I focus on the so-called age of "nationalism." I examine the new international borders of countries that were divided as a result of secession or parti-tion in the twentieth century. I find that in the great majority of cases (70 percent), the new international borders overwhelmingly follow previous internal administrative boundaries, rather than the distribution of military force, nationality, or ethnicity.

Collective defense and territoriality

Any substantially sized group faces a free rider problem in defense. Individuals would like to enjoy the benefits of collective defense but would also prefer to shirk and shift the costs of contributing to a collective defense to others. The only way to successfully establish a collective group defense is through (sometimes decentralized) enforcement. To enforce, it is of course essential to be able to identify shirkers and deserters, and to identify deserters it is necessary to know who is expected to fight in the first place. It is impossible to anticipate all contingencies and sources of attack or threat and thus impossible to specify and sign a contract that specifies who should fight under which circumstances (Kreps 1990). Coordination around a focal principle to define group membership is a powerful mechanism to help overcome the free rider problem. To coordinate group members, each has to know who qualifies as a group member, thus, where the group begins and where it ends. Territorial specification of the group, through the definition of a homeland, establishes both who is a group member – an essential first step required for collective action (Ostrom 2000, 149) – and, as we shall see, a group norm to fight for the homeland.

Territory and territoriality is a particularly powerful way to define group membership, especially when potential groups are composed of heterogeneous individuals.[7] While political geographers have long argued that territoriality and territorial divisions actually promote group identification and cohesion and that territorial divisions often precede group formation and identification, they have not provided the required causal mechanisms (Newman 1999, 3–4; Paasi 1996; Orridge 1982, 46; see also P. Sahlins 1990; Horowitz 1985, 201). As defined by Sack (1986, 19), territoriality is "the attempt by an individual or group to affect, influence, or control people, phenomena, and relationships, by delimiting and asserting control over a geographic area." Territoriality, by definition, involves a form of "classification by area"(Sack 1986, 21).[8] Classification of group membership by area, I argue, has enormous advantages over other potential classifications such as language or ethnicity in the provision of a collective defense. It is often very difficult if not impossible to distinguish a member of one ethnic group from a member of a different ethnic group, and individuals can speak multiple languages. This not only makes it difficult to detect shirkers, but also makes it difficult to detect and credibly communicate that an attacker was not a group member (and therefore that a collective defense is warranted). Moreover, members of ethnic or linguistic groups often live widely dispersed, intermingled with members of other groups. Such dispersed groups face higher transaction costs for a common defense because they are more difficult to organize, and free riders will be more difficult to identify. Mobilization to defend far-flung members of a linguistic or religious community may require the projection of force over vast distances, which drastically lowers the probability of success. Successful defense of the group often requires a spatial concentration of force which requires control over lines of communication and supply. A territorial definition of the group automatically includes protection of these vital requirements of successful collective defense.[9] Another advantage of a territorial definition of the group, as James Anderson (2001, 27) points out, is that

the need to delimit the "relevant political constituency" each time – difficult, time-consuming, and perhaps impossible to achieve by purely democratic means – is obviated by having the standard "pre-given framework;" and *it gains legitimacy from being created before and independently of particular contemporary issues*. It is further distanced from particular issues through having a more abstract or general spatial basis in territory rather than in social attributes. It avoids a recurring "problem of origins" and the regress of "who decides the decision makers." (emphasis added)

Finally, territoriality is a powerful principle because historically threats focused on control over land as one of the main sources of wealth. In summary, it is the greater credibility of a territorial definition of the group for collective defense – because of military advantages and monitoring – that has historically promoted territoriality over language, ethnicity, religion, and other potential principles.

As Spruyt (1994, 155) pointed out, "[b]orders enabled sovereigns to specify limits to their authority . . . and also precisely specify who their subjects were." Both aspects – setting limits to the sovereign's authority and specifying subjects – play a crucial role in overcoming the free rider problem in the provision of a collective defense. A territorial specification of the group makes it possible for subjects to monitor the leader, for the leader to monitor his or her subjects, and thus to coordinate for collective defense. First, if the leader fails to fight to defend the territory that is used to specify the group and only that territory, his subjects learn he is unprincipled and pursuing private goals at their expense. Therefore, his subjects will be more likely to punish and remove him. Second, territorial specification of the group (either from above by the leader or "spontaneously" from below) allows the leader to monitor his subjects; subjects living within the territory who fail to fight for the homeland can be identified and punished, perhaps even excluded from future defense.[10]

Specification of a homeland enables group members to monitor the leader because it ties the hands of the leader; without a specified homeland the leader may underprotect or exploit his subjects. If the leader tells the group members to fight for territory outside of the previously specified homeland, he may as well ask them to fight anywhere and everywhere, at any time and every time. Any leader who tells his group members to fight for more (or less) than the homeland will thus make it clear to all group members that he or she is unprincipled and pursuing his or her own private goals, and not acting in the group's collective interest. Such a signal coordinates the expectations of the group members about the type of leader. Violation of the norm by the leader increases the likelihood that group members will shirk or attempt to remove the leader. A leader can credibly state: "fight for the homeland or suffer my wrath" because it is costly to make the statement and later be found dishonest.

The leader also benefits in the long run from specification of a homeland. First, it increases the probability his subjects will actually fight for each other when he calls for their sacrifices for the defense of the homeland. Second, it allows him to signal his type and thereby increases the probability of staying in power. Specification of a homeland also benefits the leader in his interactions with other leaders in the international system. Leaders of other states similarly have incentives to monitor the leader and by fighting or failing to fight for the homeland the leader signals his type to the international community. An aggressive leader who fights for territory beyond the homeland signals potentially unlimited ambition, and invites coordination against him by the leaders of other countries.[11]

At the same time, the specification of a homeland changes the cost/benefit calculus of group members in their decision to comply and fight or shirk in favor of compliance. Specification of a homeland makes it more likely that the leader will enforce his call to arms, and punish shirkers and deserters. (Failure to punish shirkers and deserters would signal he is not committed to the norm.) Thus, a group member who shirked in previous rounds will be punished or simply not be defended when he is attacked in future rounds. By increasing the probability of enforcement and/or punishment, group members will 1) become more likely to fight and 2) increase their estimate that others will become more likely to fight and help enforce the norm. Moreover, the group norm of defense of the homeland together with a territorial specification of the homeland increases the probability of successful deterrence because other groups and states know it is credible that group members will fight for the homeland *and only for the homeland*. A specification of the homeland, by this logic, not only informs group members about the territory to be commonly defended and their duties, it also informs other groups that non-homeland territory is unlikely to be attacked. It is thus the very conditionality of the specification of the homeland – fight for the homeland and only the homeland – that makes it less likely that group members will actually have to fight at all for the homeland. Specification of a homeland is therefore beneficial for the group members because it 1) allows the group to monitor the leader and thereby helps ensure the group will fight only for limited aims; 2) increases the probability that group members will come to each other's aid, thereby increasing the probability of successful defense; and 3) makes it less likely that the norm will have to be invoked because others will know that the people are more likely to fight.[12]

Focal principles for the homeland

I argued above that the territorial specification of the group – the creation of a homeland – facilitates collective defense. In this section I will argue that specification of a homeland is not and indeed cannot be done arbitrarily and relies on *focal principles*. I argue that specification of the homeland requires "some sort of principle or rule that has wide (preferably universal) applicability and that is simple enough to be interpreted by all concerned" (Kreps 1990, 93). Such a principle or rule provides what Schelling called a "focal point" or "focal principle." Reliance on focal principles thus significantly shrinks the set of likely territorial specifications. Among the focal principles that have historically been invoked to specify the homeland are natural frontiers, common culture, prior historical formation, and cartography.

Leaders must rely on principles and cannot arbitrarily specify territory as homeland for two main reasons. First, leaders cannot arbitrarily specify territory as homeland because a specification not based on clear, easily understood, and communicable principles will fail to co-ordinate group members. To overcome the collective action problem and monitor shirking, all group members must know who else is a group member. To make collective defense of the homeland possible, every group member must know not only who is a group member, but also that all other group members know who is a group member, and that all other group members know that he knows that they know who is a group member, *ad infinitum*. In other words, which territory qualifies as homeland must be common knowledge (Hardin 1995; Chwe 2001;

Lewis 1969). Moreover, any arbitrary specification may also seem to be arbitrarily changed, or designed solely for the selfish interest of the leader. Taken together, these arguments suggest that arbitrary and unprincipled specification is difficult to monitor and therefore does not effectively tie the hands of a leader. Arbitrary and unprincipled specification of territory as homeland therefore defeats its very purpose.

Before the era of instant mass communication, the need for a principle understood and known by all to coordinate group members meant that the leader could only specify a homeland by reference to commonly available, widely known, and relatively simple symbols or principles, because only such principles could qualify as common knowledge. Historically, natural frontiers have been a particularly salient and attractive principle for several reasons. First and foremost, natural frontiers offer a salient principle because their location will be common knowledge for everyone who lives in the area. Second, drawing boundaries along rivers was a principle already well established in antiquity (Lugge 1960, 15; Squatriti 2002, 32–33). Third, natural frontiers may sometimes – but by no means always – offer military advantages for defense (P. Sahlins 1991, 248). (I will return to natural frontiers as a focal principle below.)

Once a focal principle is chosen or has spontaneously emerged, both leaders and group members will have incentives to further instill the principle in the minds of other subjects. Once the specification of the homeland has a "taken-for-granted" status, enforcement of the norm to fight for the homeland becomes cheaper. Indoctrination in the focal principle occurs through education and by applying the principle outside of its original domain (Paasi 1996; Harp 1998; Escudé 1992; Lustick 1993; Kreps 1990, 127).

Moreover, once specified, leaders and group members will not deviate from the focal principle, even if it is not the best solution in a particular instance, for three main reasons (Kreps 1990, 127–28). First, the principle will be taken into other areas. From specification of the territory to be collectively defended, the focal principle can be applied to other coordination games. In one striking example, the focal principle was applied to define which cucumbers would be kosher.[13] If the principle is the solution to several different and seemingly unrelated coordination games, application in different areas will reinforce the general power of the principle. Over time, as the principle becomes a general solution to several coordination games, its broad applicability helps foster an even broader and more general "attachment to the homeland." Second, in a particular instance the principle might not be in the interests of leaders and followers, but still benefits *the group* because other groups and states will observe whether the principle is followed or not. In other words, in their relations with other states, the group and state benefit from a reputation for consistently applying the principle. Third, even if the principle is inefficient in particular instances, *the leader* benefits from a faithful application because it signals his long-run credibility.

Nevertheless, exogenous changes in the system may produce a switch in focal points. First, the costs of enforcement may change because of an exogenous shock, such as a change in military technology, or because of the rise of a new ideology which significantly affects the relative costs of enforcement of potential principles. Second, exogenous changes may affect the optimal size of the market or even the optimal size of the state (Alesina and Spolaore 2003). Such changes may bring the economic and military viability of a state into doubt, which in turn produces incentives to change the focal point (Schelling 1978). Lustick (1993), although arguing from a radically different perspective, offers tantalizing illustrations of competing elites who battle over focal principles and the conditions for the victory or defeat of one side or the other.

Leaders will obviously expose themselves and their subjects to danger if they pick a focal principle that will bring the state into enduring conflict with militarily vastly superior rivals. (For reasons of space, I must largely bracket the role of other states here. However, other states and groups and the threats they represent help determine the group size – and thus territorial extent – necessary for a successful defense.) Even though the subjects may willingly sacrifice for the homeland, enforcement of the principle would be prohibitively costly and extremely unlikely to succeed. If it becomes obvious that such sacrifices must be in vain, coordination on the principle is likely to break down. An exogenous shock to the balance of power may therefore tip coordination from one focal principle to another that is less costly to enforce.

Having shrunk the set of potential definitions of the homeland to those specified by focal principles, four main factors will help determine which focal principles are likely to be chosen. First, leaders have incentives to pick the principle that is the cheapest to enforce. Therefore, leaders prefer focal principles that have a dedicated core of supporters (for example, because the principle applies to other important coordination problems). Such groups of supporters will enforce compliance with the norm to sacrifice for the defense of the homeland out of material self-interest or for ideological motivations. The ideal supporters are so-called true believers who will enforce compliance with the norm not so much out of self-interest (for example, doing so protects group cohesion and self-interest), but because they genuinely do not care about the costs of enforcement (Hardin 1995; Petersen 2001). "Nationalists" are a prominent example of such "true believers." To promote the coordinating power of the principle (and the advantages they derive from it) "nationalists" will seek to extend the coordinating power of "nationalism" beyond its original domain. Under some conditions, especially when they constitute a k group (Schelling 1978), nationalist true believers can tip coordination from a previous territorial focal principle such as natural frontiers to the territorial principle of common culture. I should emphasize that I argue that nationalism does not produce territorial attachment by itself. Rather, I argue that nationalism – as would be the case for any ideology – suggests that people have already coordinated on some principles for some common purpose. Prior *cultural* coordination on "nationalism" thus can promote *territorial* coordination on "nationality."

Second, leaders obviously can have self-interested motives to prefer one focal principle over another. As in gerrymandering, specification of the homeland according to one focal principle may bring a political majority while another focal principle may shift the domestic balance of forces against the leader. More generally, different focal principles specify different territorial configurations which will have distributional consequences for the leader and the domestic political elite. In addition, leaders themselves can obviously be "true believers" and prefer one principle over another for ideological reasons.

Third, as Kreps (1990, 128) points out, the principle should align with the sort of contingencies that are likely to arise. Even though it is impossible for leaders and followers to think about all possible threats, it is sometimes possible to anticipate which principle is best suited to deal with the most dangerous threats. For example, the external environment can help determine whether a particular focal principle is useful to specify the homeland and distinguish group members from non-group members. Thus, on a continent such as Latin America where the great majority of individuals speak the same language, adhere to the same religion, and are of the same ethnic group (in Latin America, the descendants of European immigrants), the principle of common culture does little to distinguish Argentineans from Uruguayans or Chileans, and Argentina from Uruguay or Chile.[14]

Fourth, the knowledge that is *common* knowledge differs from group to group and distinguishes many potential groups from each other. Since the principle that coordinates individuals must be common knowledge, the particular history and knowledge base of potential groups often plays a decisive role in determining which principles are likely to emerge. Thus, to predict which focal principles a leader and group are likely to coordinate on from the large number of possibilities – a number already significantly smaller than the infinite number of arbitrarily drawn borders – a thorough knowledge of the history, symbols, customs, and practices of potential group members is required.

The arguments in the sections developed above suggest that we can significantly shrink the set of potential homeland definitions (from what at first would seem to be an infinite number of possibilities); it is unlikely, however, that we will be able to exactly predict which focal principle a group or leader will choose ex ante. It seems much more likely that we can predict a narrow range of potential principles. This lack of pinpoint precision does not make my argument unfalsifiable. As I shall elaborate below, the argument can easily be falsified by ex ante determining which focal principle is used to define the homeland and then test whether this predicts the specific territory for which the group will subsequently fight. In other words, if the focal principle specifies territory "A" to be part of the homeland but not territory "B" and both pieces of territory currently are under the control of a foreign state, my argument predicts that the group will claim and fight for "A" but not "B."

In the section above, I explained how focal principles facilitate collective defense, how they promote the norm to fight for common defense of the homeland, why the focal principle is likely to spread to other domains, the conditions that promote the emergence of a particular focal principle, and the conditions under which group members will become more likely to switch from one principle to another. In the next section I discuss four focal principles that have historically been invoked and present an historical example for each principle. While I compiled this list inductively, I discuss how each principle relates to the underlying theoretical argument discussed above.

Natural frontiers   The principle of natural frontiers specifies the territory of the homeland by reference to "nature" and topographical features, for example mountains, rivers, seas, and the like. (On the role and use of natural frontiers see P. Sahlins 1990; Schultz 1991.) Such topographical features seem to come to mind easily as focal principles, as illustrated by Kreps' psychological experiment where two groups of students were asked to divide a list of eleven American cities – Atlanta, Boston, Chicago, Dallas, Houston, Kansas City, Los Angeles, Miami, New York, Philadelphia, and San Francisco – into two lists with only one city in common. While the principle of alphabetical order would seem to offer as good a guide, Kreps found that about 75 percent of the students participating in the experiment divided these cities according to which side of the Mississippi River they were on (Kreps 1990, 121).[15]

Especially in the eighteenth and nineteenth centuries, the principle of natural frontiers seems to have been the dominant principle invoked to specify the territory of the state. This should not be surprising, as the European states had explicitly agreed in the treaties of Nijmegen (1678), Ryswyck (1697), and Utrecht (1713) that natural frontiers, first rivers, subsequently also mountains, should be used to delimit their boundaries. The principle and its use go back much further in time, however. For example, in the reign of Philip the Fair (1285–1314) and for some time later, the boundaries of France were explicitly defined by the "four rivers." The Saône, the Rhône, Meuse, and Escault (Schelt) separated the kingdom of France from the Holy Roman Empire (Kern 1911, No.274, 201–06; Zeller 1933).[16]

The power of the principle of natural frontiers to specify the boundaries of kingdoms was indeed so great that cartographers would invent nonexistent mountains and mountain ranges to trace political boundaries (P. Sahlins 1990, 1428). Political philosophers such as Hume, Montesquieu, and Rousseau explicitly referred to the principle of natural borders to divide the states on the European continent. Thus, Rousseau claimed "[t]he lie of the mountains, seas, and rivers [in Europe], which serve as boundaries of the various nations which people it, seems to have fixed forever their number and size. We may fairly say that the political order of the Continent is in some sense the work of nature" (P. Sahlins 1990, 1436, see also fn. 46).

In America as well, the principle of natural frontiers played an important role from early on. Thus, Benjamin Franklin, George Washington, and Thomas Jefferson already talk of America reaching the Mississippi or even the Pacific. In the Federalist Papers No.2, John Jay claimed that "It has often given me pleasure to observe that independent America was not composed of detached and distant territories, but that one connected, fertile, widespread country was the portion of our western sons of liberty . . . *A succession of navigable waters forms a kind of chain round its borders, as if to bind it together*" (emphasis added; note also the reference to the principle of territorial contiguity). Only subsequently does Jay invoke the principle of common culture, claiming that Americans are "a people descended from the same ancestors, speaking the same language, professing the same religion."

The principle is alive and well in the twentieth century. During the "Continuation War" in the 1940s, Finnish newspapers and magazines, and even the government's Information Office, claimed territory from Russia on the basis of a natural border (Kosonen 1999, 97). Both the Congress and Muslim League pushed for the use of river beds as boundaries in the partition of India of 1948, arguing that rivers provided defensible natural barriers (Chester 2002). There are many examples where pairs of states have specified their borders by explicit reference to natural frontiers. Thus, the Treaty of Peking of 1860 delineated the boundary between Russia and Imperial China as "following the mountains, great rivers, and the present lines of Chinese permanent pickets" (Kratochwil 1986, 31).

I argued above that one consideration in the choice of principle is how it aligns with the sort of contingencies that are likely to arise. One important contingency used to be invasion by a hostile force. Since natural frontiers sometimes provide good defensive positions and strategically defensible borders, the principle of natural frontiers would seem attractive when the main threat is seen as an invasion by an outside force and the particular natural frontier provides a defensive advantage (and is therefore particularly likely to be promoted by the military). In addition, natural frontiers often differentiate ways of life, and affect cultural and economic exchange. Thus, Kratochwil points out that mountain crests or watersheds are usually sparsely populated, and exchanges across mountains are relatively minimized (Kratochwil 1986, 32). Natural frontiers therefore can also affect the cost of enforcement. Not only will it be more difficult and costly to transport enforcement officers in large numbers across natural frontiers, it may also be more costly to enforce the homeland norm in drastically different cultural settings.

Cartography and maps   The cartographic principle specifies the territory of the homeland by reference to cartographical conventions and maps. Sometimes cartography and maps are invoked to back up other principles such as natural frontiers and cultural homogeneity; however, cartography and maps can also serve as principles on their own (D. Wood 1992; Harley 1989 and 1990; Monmonier 1995; Weissberg 1963). Straight lines of longitude and latitude have long been used to delineate borders. One advantage of such straight lines, it could be argued, is that they "reduce the zone of contact between two sovereign territories to the absolute minimum, making it relatively easy and cheap to police them" (van Schendel 2003, 243). Not surprisingly, reference to cartographic principles was especially pronounced in cases where rival countries attempted to delineate unexplored territory. Thus, fully 42 percent of borders in Africa are drawn along lines of longitude and latitude (Herbst 2000). The US–Canadian border is similarly drawn by reference to cartographic conventions, and the slogan "Fifty-four forty or fight" rallied Americans in their dispute with Canada over the western provinces.

Maps are particularly powerful icons, sanctioned by their supposedly objective scientific status (Harley 1989 and 1990; D. Wood 1992). Maps standardize our images of the world and shape our mental structures (Harley 1989, 13). By offering such supposedly scientific images of the world and mental structures, the visual images of and from maps have been invoked to define a homeland. Maps have been drawn in the shape of a woman, a man, or a beast since the sixteenth century. But, as Kosonen (1999, 96) notes, "few of these earlier map-figures have survived as an often used symbol – unlike Finland." Especially during the "Continuation War" of 1941, Finland was often depicted on maps as the "Finnish maiden." "[T]he maiden first appeared in the form of a map in 1907 (Velikulta April 18, 1907), and was regularly drawn in the following decades, too. The shape of Finnish territory must have given the idea to combine the maiden and the map, but as imagery, it proved to be a very effective way to enhance the national message" (Kosonen 1999, 97). Similarly, in the nineteenth century France was often pictured on maps as "a face, with Paris as the eye, Brittany as the nose and the Loire estuary as the mouth" (M. Anderson 1996, 3, fn.17). In the second half of the twentieth century, France was often identified as a hexagon, "l'Hexagone" (Weber 1984–86). Another well-known example where the image represented on the map powerfully captures the imagination and has become a symbol for the country is the "boot" that is Italy.

But even when maps do not refer to such well-known images, the shape of a country on a map can become an icon and a symbol on its own. (Such icons then often spread and can be found on a variety of goods, such as labels in clothing and postage stamps.) Benedict Anderson provides a good example of how the visual image of the map affected conceptions of the homeland for Indonesians and West Papuans alike.

Dutch colonial logo-maps [of West New Guinea] sped across in the colony, showing a West New Guinea with nothing to its East, unconsciously reinforced the developing imagined ties . . . *[W]hat brought the often quarrelling young West Papuan nationalists together, especially after 1963, was the map.* Though the Indonesian state changed the region's name from West Nieuw Guinea, first to Irian Barat (West Irian) and then to Irian Jaya, it read its local reality from the colonial-era bird's-eye atlas . . . [T]he state itself, and through it the Indonesian population as a whole, saw only a phantom "Irianese" (orang Irian) named after the map. (B. Anderson 1991, 176–78, emphasis added)

Kosonen (1999, 91) shows similarly how newspaper maps "had a strong impact on defining Finland, its territory and borders in the minds of the general public, especially since 1899." In a fascinating study, Cutts Dougherty, Eisenhart, and Webley (1992) found that schoolchildren in Argentina were systematically better at completing a deliberately incomplete map of Argentina than were British school-children at completing a deliberately incomplete map of Great Britain. This should probably not be surprising given that geography received a lot of attention in the Argentine curriculum and was explicitly designed to be an essential tool in nation building (Escudé 1988 and 1992).

Common culture   The principles of natural frontiers and car-tography represent the purest cases of coordination on a territorial specification of the group for collective defense. In the sections below, we shall see that even when individuals have (already) coordinated on a cultural principle to define group membership, territorial principles have nevertheless consistently been subsequently invoked to coordinate for a collective defense.[17] As I noted above, three main reasons help explain why a territorial coordination for collective defense trumps a cultural one. First, a territorial specification of the homeland to be commonly defended allows for better monitoring, not only of potential shirkers but also whether the attack on group members comes from outside the group. Ethnic and linguistic differences can be and often have been hard to detect and very often do not lead to a clear-cut categorization of individuals into one group or the other.[18] Second, territory has historically been a – if not the – major source of wealth, and conquest is a fate that the territory's inhabitants face in common. The threat of territorial conquest is therefore best countered by a col-lective territorial defense. Third, because the use and projection of force requires a spatial concentration of force, territoriality has a distinct advantage over groups that live intermingled with other groups over a wide area.

The principle of cultural homogeneity specifies the territory of the homeland by reference to a pre-existing group. The principle proclaims that "our" land is where "we" live (England is where English people live). The pre-existing group is defined by some cultural attribute, most often language, religion, or ethnicity, and "nationality" (Yiftachel 2001b). The principle of common culture proclaims not just that group members should live in the same state, but also that this state should extend to and control the territory where these people live. In other words, the territorial specification of the state should corres-pond with the distribution of cultural similarities and dissimilarities.

In the literature on nationalism, for example, we find countless assertions that state and nation should be congruent (A. Smith 1992, 47;
Hechter 2000, 65; D. Friedman 1977, 72) and myriad examples in
the literature where this principle is assumed to be the basis for territorial
claims. Thus, Fearon argues that "the claims that give rise to ethnic
conflict will typically extend only as far as there are 'brethren' to bring
into Greater Ruritania, or brethren for Ruritania to intervene to protect"
(Fearon 1998, 110).

The principle of cultural homogeneity became especially prominent
after World War I. In his original draft for Article 10 of the Covenant
of the League of Nations, Woodrow Wilson even endorsed changing
territorial boundaries if the demographics and distribution of "races"
changed.

The Contracting Parties unite in guaranteeing to each other political independence and territorial integrity; but it is understood between them that *such territorial adjustments, if any, as may in the future become necessary by reason of changes in
present racial conditions and aspirations or present social and political relationships,*
pursuant to the principle of self-determination, and also such territorial readjust-
ments as may in the judgments of three-fourths of the Delegates be demanded by
the welfare and manifest interest of the people concerned, may be effected, if
agreeable to those peoples. (Baldwin 1992, 223; emphasis added)

I argued above that leaders have strong incentives to instill a focal
principle for collective defense in the minds of their (potential) group
members. One particularly powerful tool has been the education system.
Greek school geography in the late nineteenth century is but one of a
great many attempts to instill the principle of cultural homogeneity
as the basis of claims to territory currently not under the control of
the state. The prominent Greek geographer Spyridon Moraitidis
declared in 1880 in his school geography:

In the fourth grade we show our students the totality of Greek lands . . . We teach
them that these lands are Greek, that is to say that they are in the possession of
and inhabited by people who are close to us, who are of the same origin, have the
same religion, and speak the same language as us. But a part of them (we point
to the land delimited by the boundary) is free, because the king of the Greeks,
George, reigns there, that we Greeks have chosen as a king; and a part (we show
the rest of the Greek lands in Europe and Asia) are subject of the King of the
Turks, the Sultan. (Peckham 2000, 87)

In modern times, the principle of common culture seemed so powerful
that it has often been turned on its head. Thus, states have often
attempted to culturally homogenize their population, for example by
insisting on one official language within territories under their control

(White 2000; Weber 1976).[19] Cultural homogenization, however, has gone far beyond language to include architectural styles and landscapes (White 2000; Herb 1999, 21; Newman 1999, 13). Attempts to promote coordination on common culture thus often include homogenization of the cultural landscape, sometimes by force (Armstrong 1997).

A major problem for the principle of cultural homogeneity is that it can be very difficult to apply in practice, since populations often intermingle, and clear lines separating populations with different religions, languages, and ethnic characteristics can be very difficult to draw. The intermingling of culturally heterogeneous populations probably makes enforcement of the principle of cultural homogeneity more difficult and costly, since members of other groups may try to enforce their own principle of cultural homogeneity. The attempts to draw borders along lines of "nationality" after World War I show the enormous difficulty of drawing boundaries along lines of common culture. When asked whether they considered themselves Austrian or Italian, respondents often answered: "What do you mean? We are the people from 'here'" (see Burghardt 1988).[20] More fundamentally yet, the question to be answered before any plebiscite is who – and what *area* – is to be included in the plebiscite in the first place.

However, the principle of cultural homogeneity may have some particular advantages as well. It may be cheap to enforce if it can rely on "true believers" in the cause of cultural homogeneity. Hardcore nationalists and fundamentalists can significantly lower the costs of enforcement, since they are willing to enforce it for free. Hardcore nationalists will work hard to make the "national" identity more salient, and social psychology has shown that if group identity becomes more salient group members are more likely to comply with group norms (Spears et al. 1997).

Prior historical formation   The principle of prior historical formation specifies the territory of the homeland by reference to an antecedent territorial formation, in particular by claiming a relation with a prior cultural group and its – supposed or alleged – territory. The principle posits that the homeland is where the group's ancestors (once) lived. It is a form of claim by historical descent: since "our forefathers" once lived there, and we are entitled to their heritage, the land is rightfully ours. Kings and Lords who claimed a certain territory rightfully belonged to them, because it rightfully belonged to their ancestors, historically have made great use of the principle of prior historical formation.[21]

The political geographer George White presents a particularly striking example of the importance of the principle of prior historical formation to territorially define a group. In the struggle for independence from the Ottomans, a "nationalist Romanian" elite had formed, spread out roughly over three territories each with their own political organization: Walachia, Moldavia, and Transylvania. To found their nation-state, however, the elite needed to specify a principle to identify who qualified as "Romanian." As White argues, no straightforward ethnic, linguistic, or religious differentiation could be invoked to distinguish would-be Romanians from non-Romanians. However, neither was there a well-defined territory with a long common tradition that was commonly understood as "Romanian," as was the case, for example, for Hungary. I quote from White at length.

Even though unification could certainly be argued for, a single state had to be identified sometime in history that gave birth to the Romanian nation, a state with which Walachians, Moldavians, and Transylvanians could all identify. The identification of an early state was required not only to prove the legitimacy of the Romanian nation but also to delimit spatially the Romanian nation-state, *which in turn provided a means for identifying who should and should not be a Romanian.* Indeed, boundaries determined identity as much as identity determines boundaries. The search for a single state that included within it Walachia, Moldavia, and Transylvania finds only one example in the last thousand years: that of Michael the Brave, who unified the three principalities in 1600 . . . Michael the Brave's state, however, lasted less than a year. It would be impossible to argue that such a short-lived state was able to set up a field of spatial interaction intense enough to mold its inhabitants into a single people. Even if the state was able to do so, it had a major weakness which it could not overcome. Namely, it postdated Transylvania's incorporation into the Hungarian Kingdom . . . In the study of their territory, Romanian nationalists noted that their territory had been the Roman province of Dacia, named after the state and people that the Romans had conquered. Therefore, their strain of Latinness must have come from the mixing of Romans and their indigenous Dacians. The pre-Roman Dacian state was also attractive, and indeed meaningful, because its territory roughly coincided with that of the modern principalities of Walachia, Moldavia, and Transylvania. It was a territory with which Walachians, Moldavians, and Transylvanians could identify collectively. (White 2000, 125–26, emphasis added)

This example shows the deliberate attempt by the elite to find and instill a focal principle to coordinate the inhabitants of three previously separate provinces in a common struggle against a powerful opponent. It shows, moreover, the first-mover advantage of the elites from the three provinces of Walachia, Moldavia, and Transylvania.

History is replete with examples where claims to territory were based on an appeal to the principle of a prior historical formation. For example, in the seventeenth century French claims to territory were often based on the prior historical formation of "Gaul," in particular as articulated in Julius Caesar's *De Bello Gallico*. Thus, in the 1659 Treaty of the Pyrenees between Spain and France, the French–Spanish border was drawn along the Pyrenees, "which anciently divided the Gauls from the Spains" (P. Sahlins 1991, 44). In the nineteenth century, Greeks laid claim to extensive territories on the basis of their descent from the prior historical formation of the Byzantine Empire (Peckham 2000). More recently, of course, many Zionists have claimed Israel and "Judea and Samaria" on the basis of a prior historical formation, specified in the Bible.[22] Many disputes over territory in Latin America have stemmed from competing claims to be the rightful inheritor of the Vice Royalty of de la Plata (Escudé 1988 and 1992). As Murphy argues, "the justifications now offered in support of territorial claims are almost invariably couched in terms of recovery of territory that historically belonged to the claiming state" (Murphy 1990, 532; see also Newman 1999, 4).

Perhaps even more than the principle of cultural homogeneity, the principle of prior historical formation relies on education to indoctrinate the population (Escudé 1988 and 1992; Harp 1998). The people have to be told not only who constitutes the current group, but also why they are descended from a previous group and where that previous group lived. Cartography and historical atlases have played a particularly important role in this indoctrination (see above).

Observable implications

The theoretical framework developed above first explained how territorial specification of the group enables collective defense and how such territorial specifications will rely on and be further strengthened as focal principles. I next described the four focal principles that have historically been invoked most often to define the territory – and group – that is to be commonly defended. The value of this theoretical framework of course depends on whether it helps us understand and predict empirical patterns better than the competing theories. The theoretical framework makes (at least) three macro-predictions that can be used to assess its power.

First, the argument predicts that when the homeland is defined by focal principles it will be indivisible. Abrogation of the principle and a failure to claim and fight for the homeland defined by the principle will unravel the coordinating power necessary for a collective defense. It is the resulting indivisibility of the homeland, in turn, that helps explain why disputes over territory are more likely to escalate to war (Fearon 1995). The quantitative literature on war has indeed found that disputes over territory are more likely to escalate to war than disputes over other issues, but causal mechanisms have been sorely lacking to explain this striking finding (Vasquez 2000). While "indivisibility" has often been invoked, with the exception of Walter (2006) no mechanism has been provided to explain when and why territory – which at first would seem eminently divisible – becomes indivisible.

Second, the argument predicts that states will claim and fight for territory that fits the focal principle but not for territory that does not fit the focal principle. A brief case study (below) of the reign of Philip the Fair (1285–1314) shows that this French king specified the boundaries of France with a focal principle – the "four rivers," the Saône, the Rhône, Meuse, and Escault (Schelt) – and that this principle *consistently* guided his claims for territory (Kern 1911, No. 274; Strayer 1980, 15, 28–29, 352; Lugge 1960, 175–76).[23] This is not some arbitrarily chosen case, but the first documented instance I could find of the specification of the territory to be commonly defended on the European continent by reference to a focal principle, centuries before the rise of nationalism.

Third, the argument predicts that when territories are exchanged or new countries come into being, the new boundaries will follow focal principles. Against the baseline realist argument, thus, I argue that the new boundaries will *not* be drawn following the military penetration and occupation of territory, nor fit a grab of all the valuable resources within military reach. Rather, when one country secedes from the mother country, or when the mother country is partitioned into two or more new states, the new international boundaries will be drawn following focal principles and focal points. In the next sections I will offer a brief test of the second and third of these predictions.

Philip the Fair (1285–1314)

The late thirteenth and fourteenth centuries were a time of remarkable change in Europe. This was not only a time when the concept (if not the word) of sovereignty appeared but also the time when basic loyalties shifted from the Church, community, and family to the emerging state (Strayer 1970, 9, 36, 47; see also Strayer's "The Laicization of French and English Society in the Thirteenth Century," chap. 16 in Strayer 1971). As Strayer (1970, 47) notes, "The highest duty of every subject was now supposed to be the preservation and well-being of the state." An essential element in this shift was the definition of the state as a territorial unit: the understanding, knowledge, and establishment of definite boundaries to the state (Strayer 1971, 259).[24] The most influential models of this gradual change were England and France. But of these two France was the more important model; "the fact that the French were the first to solve the nearly universal problem of creating a state out of virtually independent provinces made the French model preeminent in Europe" (Strayer 1970, 49).

The evidence suggests that whereas French nobles and subjects previously coordinated on a common defense of Christendom, around the fourteenth century they tipped to coordinate around a French homeland specified by the Four Rivers. In the common defense of Christendom, nobles from all over Europe stopped the Arab advance at Poitiers in 732 and later participated in large numbers in the Crusades. Christianity even provided the focal principles for thinking about space in these times. Following Orosius, scholars conceptually organized space, regions, and peoples by distinguishing Christianity from Heathens (Reimitz 2000, 114).[25] The shift to loyalty to the state or kingdom as a territorial unit is of obvious importance, since my theory aims – in part – to explain how such loyalty is established. Fortunately, we can more or less pinpoint in time when this happened, since Strayer claims that "the transfer of loyalty to the king and the definition of the kingdom as a territorial unit took place almost simultaneously, culminating in the reign of Philip the Fair" (Strayer 1971, 302). In the rest of this paper, I will show that Philip the Fair was able to construct a homeland norm and persuade his subjects to sacrifice for the "defense of the realm." Moreover, I will show that Philip's construction of a homeland norm and his subsequent foreign policy behavior fit my theory of the homeland.

Philip the Fair is the first French king to systematically claim and exercise the right to levy taxes (and manpower) for "defense of the realm." This phrase is (exceedingly) rare in royal documents in the twelfth century and when, found, it invoked the aid of the patron saints rather than the king's subjects to help provide defense (Strayer 1971, 292). In Philip's reign, however, the claim imposed a territorial obligation on all the king's subjects (ibid.). Such a claim of course implied "that subjects had been convinced that they were members of a kingdom and that this kingdom was worthy of being defended" (ibid.).[26]

Two things are particularly remarkable about Philip the Fair's actual attempts to levy taxes and manpower for "defense of the realm." First, the king's levies of money and manpower for "defense of the realm" were the first general taxes in France (Strayer 1980, 394; Brown 1973, 19–20) and were generally accepted, even by the barons and the clergy.[27]

Subjects were notably less willing to pay taxes for other purposes. Second, when in 1313 and 1314 the threat that led to the tax abated quickly, the king revoked the tax and paid restitution (under the doctrine of *cessanta causa*) (Brown 1973, 19; see also Strayer 1980, 85). Invocation of emergency power in the name of "defense of the realm" thus on the one hand enabled the king to far extend his powers beyond their old limits (Strayer 1971, 297). On the other hand, the king was clearly severely constrained in his ability to invoke "defense of the realm."

It is obviously puzzling for political scientists that the king's subjects (including even the clergy who were normally exempt) accepted the king's right to levy taxes and manpower for "defense of the realm." My framework, however, offers an explanation. Philip's ancestors had demanded enormous sacrifices from their subjects, their barons, and the clergy, and had been able to do so because these sacrifices were for a series of Crusades and were supported by the Church. French subjects and barons had initially willingly fought in the Crusades for the Holy Land. Later, however, Crusades were launched for less noble purposes, against the Aragonese and for Sicily. More and more it became apparent that the Church was using the later Crusades as one more tool to further its own secular goals and its own secular foreign policy. These Crusades brought little or no benefit to the great majority who fought in them, and the French nobility in particular suffered, as compared to the German nobility (Michaud 1973, 347). Indeed, at the time learned opinion was definitely wary of more Crusades. For example, "Humbert de Romanis repeats the objections that were made in his time against undertaking crusades. Some said that wars, of whatever kind they might be, only served to promote the shedding of blood, and that there were quite enough of those that could not be avoided, and of those that people were obliged to make in self-defense" (Michaud 1973, 60–61). When the Council of Lyon (1274) decreed that a new Crusade should be undertaken, the enthusiasm of the faithful was no longer anything "but the smoking remains of a burnt cloth" (Michaud 1973, 60).

Under these circumstances, a king who could credibly claim to fight for self-defense and self-defense only would be a welcome relief for all the king's subjects. As I argued in the theoretical section above, specification of the homeland allows the subjects to monitor the king, while at the same time making it more likely that when the king calls for defense of the homeland, his subjects will contribute. In short, specification of a homeland facilitates collective defense. I argue that Philip the Fair specified a (French) homeland which allowed his subjects to monitor whether he was acting in their collective interest, while, at the same time, they were willing to sacrifice for that homeland. My claims are bolstered by several facts. First, Philip the Fair, unlike his ancestors, never went on a Crusade.[28] Second, as we shall see below, with one minor exception Philip fought for and claimed *only* territory that fit the specification of the homeland.

I argued not just that specification of a homeland is beneficial; I argued that a homeland will be uniquely specified, and specified by a focal principle or a focal point. It is therefore important to note that

Philip did have a stronger desire than any of his predecessors to establish fixed and definite boundaries with the Empire, and perhaps a clearer idea of what a boundary was. If he was to be supreme and final judge of all people who were "in regno et de regno" then it was important to know what the *regnum* was . . . During the reign there was a deliberate attempt to work out a theory of the proper boundaries of France.

(Strayer 1980, 15, 351; see also Lugge 1960, 165, fn.507 and 169, fn.526)

Philip specified the French homeland with a clear focal point, the Four Rivers – the Rhône, Saône, Meuse, and Scheldt – a focal point clearly nested in the principle of natural frontiers (Kern 1911, No. 271, 200; Kern 1910, 15–17). As the French government wrote the Pope before August 1297 regarding French rights to Lyon: "A King of France had two sons, of whom one became King of France and the other Emperor. As they came into conflict about the boundaries of the Kingdom and the Empire and found themselves battle ready in opposing camps, mutual friends helped them determine that the Scheldt, Meuse, Rhône and Saône would be the boundaries of the Kingdom and the Empire" (Kern 1911, No. 274, 205).[29] France's southern boundary was formed by the Pyrenees, while the Four Rivers formed the eastern and northern boundaries.

The French argued – and some of the princes of the Empire agreed – that the eastern boundary of France was formed by four rivers: the Rhône, the Saône, the Meuse, and the Scheldt. There were gaps in this argument, first, the actual physical gaps between the rivers, and, second, the obvious fact that in some places – the Vivarais, for example – lands that had long been recognized as imperial were on the west side of a boundary river. Nevertheless, the four-river line seemed logical (it was hard to find any other simple description of the boundary) and roughly in accord with the facts. *Philip used the formula successfully throughout his reign.*

(Strayer 1980, 352, emphasis added; see also Lugge 1960, 175–76)

Although the Treaty of Verdun (843), which divided Charlemagne's empire among his three sons, established boundaries which very roughly approximate the Four Rivers, it deserves emphasis that the boundaries of the Treaty of Verdun and those established by the Four Rivers principle do not match (Kern 1910, 16, 315; Longnon 1922, 176).[30] The Four

Rivers clearly present a *principle*, easy to understand and apply; claims to the prior historical formation produced by the Treaty of Verdun would require a great number of exceptions to the principle.

Since I argued that specification of the homeland relies on a focal principle or a focal point, it is essential to examine whether this principle and these focal points were indeed common knowledge for Philip's subjects. The historians leave no doubt that the principle of river boundaries and the focal point of the Four Rivers were very well known among the king's subjects (see in particular Kern 1911, No. 278a, 210–19; No. 271, 200; C. Wood 1967; Lugge 1960, 165, 173–74, 205, 209; Strayer 1970, 56, especially 381–83; Dion 1947, 40, 80–82). Pounds (1951, 148, emphasis added), for example, notes

> The boundary established at Verdun between the kingdom of Charles (*Francia*) and that of Lothaire (*Lotharingia*) followed, if only very approximately, the valleys of the Scheldt, Meuse, Saône and Rhône, lying now to one side, now to the other of these rivers ([A. Longnon, *Atlas historique de la France*] (Paris: 1884–1907), Plates XI–XV). Its course changed during the middle ages in response to influences. One was the gradual clearing and settlement of the waste land in which lay the frontier zone. Disputes arose between the communities on each side of the frontier for possession of resources of timber and game, and the growing number of disputes led to a greater precision in demarcating the frontier. Secondly, *the popular mind refused to consider a frontier, approximating so closely to the line of the rivers, as being anything other than the rivers themselves*. Already in the ninth century Regino of Prüm described Lotharingia as bounded by the Meuse and the Rhine. This opinion came eventually to be widely held. The short distances which separated the Scheldt from the Meuse and the Meuse from the Saône presented few difficulties and occasioned no serious disputes. The boatmen on the lower Rhône still in the nineteenth century took passengers from "*le royaume*," or France, to "*l'empire*" and back. Leopold of Bebenburg, writing in the fourteenth century described the Treaty of Verdun as giving to the French king all to the west of the Meuse. In the Debate of the Heralds (c. 1450) the French herald boasts of the beauty of the French rivers, of which, he remarks, the Saône separates Germany from France. They were marked, he wrote, by the Rhône and the Saône up as far as the borders of Lorraine. Near here rises the Meuse, which serves as a frontier until it reaches the province of Hainault. A day's journey hence is the source of the Scheldt, which forms the frontier as far as its union with the sea.

Strayer suggests that the court system of the later Capetians contributed significantly to facilitating this common knowledge and building the recognition of the king as the final authority in the realm (Strayer 1970, 19, 53).

Throughout his reign, Philip the Fair levied taxes for the "defense of the realm" only for territory within the Four Rivers. Territory beyond the Four Rivers, even if a longtime fief of his family (Provence)[31] or recently acquired by him personally (county of Burgundy), he never claimed as part of the realm (with one small exception). However, he consistently claimed suzerainty for territories within the Four Rivers, whether the disputed territory was large or small. Thus, he claimed "suzerainty over the Ostrevant, the part of the county lying west of the Scheldt, from the count of Hainaut," which the count was finally forced to acknowledge (Strayer 1980, 349, 352; see also Dion 1947, 44). When he defeated the Count of Bar, the count was similarly forced only to concede the part of the county west of the Meuse as a fief of the king (Kern 1911, No. 144, 93; Havet 1881, 387). Philip also forced the bishop of Viviers to acknowledge that the Vivarais – although long considered a part of the Empire – was part of the kingdom, because it lay on the west bank of the Rhône (Longnon 1922, 176). As Strayer (1980, 353) notes, "This was all the king wanted; the bishop was left with extensive rights of government in his district." This remarkable pattern also holds in his conflicts with more powerful nobles, the King of England over Aquitaine, the Count of Foix, and the Count of Flanders (Strayer 1980, 15). In his conflict with James of Aragon over the Val d'Aran, Philip and his lawyers made some remarkable arguments. The bases for the French claim were straightforward: the Val d'Aran was French because it lay on the French side of the Pyrenees and had been subject to French lords. What is remarkable is that Philip claimed his realm to be indivisible, with each part worth as much as every other. The French king "could not surrender a part of his realm; de facto possession by others could not extinguish royal rights." The French even told the Aragonese that Philip would defend the Val in the same way as he would defend Paris (Strayer 1980, 28–29, see also 352).[32]

What is far more surprising, perhaps, is that after Philip bought the county of Burgundy from Count Otto for 100,000 *livres tournois* and a life-rent of 10,000 l. t, he never tried to incorporate it into the kingdom (Strayer 1980, 354–55).[33] The county of Burgundy lay east of the Saône and was thus clearly outside of the kingdom. Consistent with the Four Rivers focal point, Philip admitted it was a fief of the Empire (Strayer 1980, 354). Strayer (1980, 356) notes that the county was listed in Mignon's inventory as *"terra foreana."* If the county was *foreign* territory, the king could clearly not levy taxes from the realm's nobles for its defense, nor would the nobles be under the obligation to pay taxes for the "defense of the realm" to defend territory outside of the realm.[34]

The only instance I found where Philip claimed territory beyond the line of the Four Rivers was the city of Lyon.[35] All of the county and most of Lyon lay on the east bank of the Saône, but Philip claimed and won

Lyon as part of the kingdom nevertheless. While this is an exception to Philip's policy to claim suzerainty only over land that lay within the Four Rivers, Philip and his lawyers nevertheless explicitly referred in the negotiations to the Four Rivers as the boundaries of the kingdom (Kern 1911, No. 74, 205; see also No. 285, 229). Two points may help mitigate this exception. First, while Lyon lay in the Empire, it was not subject to the Empire (Strayer 1980, 359). Second, Lugge (1960, 174) notes that Lyon already counted in the early thirteenth century as politically part of "Francia."

I close this examination of the reign of Philip the Fair with two observations. First, it is clear that in the absence of any French nation or nationalism, it is impossible that the homeland was shaped by nationalism. To quote again from Strayer at length:

On the other hand, while the idea of France as a nation could hardly have existed, and while the idea of France as a complex of concordant cultures was just beginning to take shape, the idea of France as a political unit had some validity. There was a *regnum Francie* with definite borders (at least in theory); one was either in this *regnum* or out if it. If one was "in regno et de regno," then one had to recognize the "superiority" and the competence of the king as the final judge. These principles were generally accepted, though there could be disputes about their exact meaning. Very few people who were in the *regnum* wanted to be out of it; they simply wanted it to bother them as little as possible. In fact, since the kingdom of France was the strongest political unit in western Europe, and since its leaders were held in high esteem, there were some advantages, both material and psychic, in being part of that kingdom. The idea that there was an obligation to defend the *regnum* could be accepted, even by people who would never have said that they were "French." (Strayer 1980, 388–89)

(Note that the homeland norm brought material benefits, which in turn helps explain its persistence and survival.)

New international boundaries

To test the third prediction – that when territories are exchanged or new countries come into being, the new boundaries will follow focal principles – I examine all secessions and partitions of the twentieth century.[36] Cases of decolonization are excluded but would all follow the principle of prior historical formation. Initial research strongly suggested that new international boundaries were not drawn based on military conquest but overwhelmingly on the principle of prior historical formation, specifically previous internal boundaries. Further research only served to strengthen this conclusion. Table 2.1 lists the partitions and

Table 2.1. *Partitions and secessions of the twentieth century*

Country	Mother Country	Date	Match	Source
Panama	Colombia	3 November 1903	Yes	EIB
Norway	Sweden	1905	Yes	EIB
Albania	Ottoman Empire	28 November 1912	No	EIB
Finland	Russia	6 December 1917	Yes	EIB
Estonia	Russia	May 1918	No	EIB
Latvia	Russia	November 1918	No	EIB
Austria	Austria-Hungary	16 November 1918	No	EIB
Hungary	Austria-Hungary	16 November 1918	No[1]	EIB
Czechoslovakia	Austria-Hungary	1919	Yes[2]	EIB
Lithuania	Russia	1919	No	EIB
Mongolia	China	July 1921	Yes	EIB
Burma	India	April 1937	Yes	Sukhwal
Iceland	Denmark	17 June 1944	Yes	EIB
Pakistan	India	15 August 1947	Yes	Chester
South Korea	Korea	15 August 1948	No[3]	EIB
Ireland	United Kingdom	18 April 1949	Yes[4]	EIB
North Korea	Korea	1 May 1949	No	EIB
Taiwan	China	December 1949	Yes[5]	Copper
East Germany	Germany	1949	No	Alexander
West Germany	Germany	1949	No	Alexander
North Vietnam	Vietnam	15 September 1954	No	IBS
South Vietnam	Vietnam	15 September 1954[6]	No[7]	IBS
Senegal	Mali Federation	20 August 1960	Yes	EIB
Cameroon	Nigeria	1 October 1961	Yes[8]	Anene
Burundi	Rwanda-Burundi	1964	Yes	EIB
Rwanda	Rwanda-Burundi	1964	Yes	EIB, IBS
Singapore	Federation of Malaya	9 August 1965	Yes	EIB
Bangladesh	Pakistan	26 March 1971	Yes	EIB
Turkish Republic of Northern Cyprus	Cyprus	15 November 1983	No	KM[9]
Namibia	South Africa	21 March 1990	Yes[10]	EIB
Georgia	Russia	6 April 1991	Yes	Polat
Croatia	Yugoslavia	25 June 1991	Yes	EIB
Slovenia	Yugoslavia	25 June 1991	Yes	EIB
Moldova	Russia	23 August 1991	Yes	Polat
Belarus	Russia	25 August 1991	Yes	Polat
Azerbaijan	Russia	30 August 1991	Yes	Polat
Kyrgyz Republic	Russia	31 August 1991	Yes[11]	Polat
Uzbekistan	Russia	31 August 1991	Yes	Polat
Tajikistan	Russia	September 1991	Yes	Polat
Estonia	Russia	6 September 1991	No[12]	Polat
Latvia	Russia	6 September 1991	No	Polat
Lithuania	Russia	6 September 1991	No	Polat
Macedonia	Yugoslavia	8 September 1991	Yes	EIB[13]
Armenia	Russia	23 September 1991	Yes[14]	Polat
Turkmenistan	Russia	27 October 1991	Yes	Polat

Ukraine	Russia	1 December 1991	Yes	Polat
Kazakhstan	Russia	16 December 1991	Yes	Polat
Bosnia-Herzogovina	Yugoslavia	3 March 1992	Yes	EIB
Czech Republic	Czechoslovakia	1 January 1993	Yes	Ratner
Slovakia	Czechoslovakia	1 January 1993	Yes	Ratner
Eritrea	Ethiopia	3 May 1993	Yes	EIB
East Timor	Indonesia	20 May 2002	Yes	CIA

Source: Polat refers to Polat (2002, 45–66). EIB refers to Biger 1995. Ratner refers to Ratner (1996, 598). CIA refers to Central Intelligence Agency 2004. IBS refers to US State Department 2004. KM refers to Kliot and Mansfield 1997. The Taiwan source is Copper 1996. The Burma case is verified using Sukhwal (1971, 222–24). The Alexander source refers to Alexander (1963, 241). The partition of India and Pakistan is analyzed in detail in Chester 2002. Anene refers to Anene 1970.

Notes: [1] The Burgenland region was granted to Austria post-World War I.

[2] Formed of Moravia, Ruthenia, Slovakia, and Bohemia.

[3] The thirty-eighth parallel is the marker of the boundary between North and South Korea.

[4] County and parish boundaries were elevated to the status of international boundaries.

[5] Taiwan was a Chinese province from 1886 to 1895, when the Japanese took control of the island.

[6] This is the date the boundary was delimited.

[7] The seventeenth parallel of north latitude is roughly what was chosen to determine the boundary.

[8] The international boundary follows a combination of Anglo-German and Anglo-French colonial boundaries. The boundary follows Anglo-German colonial era borders in the south and Anglo-French colonial borders in the north (Anene 1970, 52–55, 90–96, 138–40). This border roughly followed the line of mountains.

[9] Interestingly, the "Turkish advance halted along a line almost exactly identical with that proposed by Turkey as the demarcation of partition in 1965, and which had been rejected by the UN mediator Galo Plaza." Quoted from Kliot and Mansfield (1997).

[10] Agreements between European colonial powers account for almost all of Namibia's current boundaries.

[11] Although there are several interstate disputes concerning this border, it still largely conforms to previous internal boundaries.

[12] Even though the boundary was drawn along former administrative lines, none of the Baltic countries officially accepted these boundaries (Polat 2002, 45–66).

[13] The boundary with Serbia is disputed and relatively new.

[14] The Armenia–Azerbaijan boundary is disputed and problematic; however, the recognized international boundary conforms to existing administrative boundaries.

secessions of the twentieth century, the date of the partition/secession, and whether the new international boundaries matched the previous internal boundaries.

In case after case the principle of prior historical formation is invoked to specify new international boundaries. For example, "the Eritrean government explained that it only claims the 'colonial boundary,' meaning the line drawn between the Ethiopian imperial regime and Italian colony of Eritrea. This line was established through several international agreements at the beginning of this century, following the defeat of Italian troops at Adua in 1896. Three treaties are relevant to the present dispute: those of 1900, 1902 and 1908" (Peninou, 1998, 46). Similarly, "[t]he present-day international borders of Bosnia-Herzogovina are inherited from the Ottoman period. When Bosnia-Herzogovina was established in 1945 as one of republics [sic] of the Yugoslav federation, these historical boundaries served as a basis for its delimitation" (Klemencic 2000, 65).

When borders deviated from the principle of prior historical formation, almost without fail one of the other principles was invoked to specify the new international border. However, and surprisingly in the supposed "age of nationalism," the principle of common culture carried little weight. To be sure minor corrections along borders were occasionally made to include "ethnic brethren," but these corrections were minor indeed. Take the example of the "Former Yugoslavian Republic of Macedonia."

Except for the northern border, the present borders of the Republic of Macedonia were established in 1913. A change was made to the western border, through protocol signed in Florence in 1926. By this agreement the disputed Monastery of Naum was transferred to Yugoslavia which in turn gave up the area of Golo Brdo, which encompassed 27 villages with a predominantly Macedonian population. A change was also made on the eastern border in the Strumica Plain, which had belonged to Bulgaria. By the Neian Agreement in 1919 this area was transferred to Yugoslavia and the border was moved further east. The northern border of the Republic of Macedonia was drawn at the end of the Second World War. This border mostly followed ethnic divisions but did not coincide with the previous border of Serbia. (Milenkoski and Talevski 2001, 83)

Milenkoski and Talevski also note that "[t]he border with the Republic of Greece is mostly a latitudinal [one]. It goes over mountains, plains and water" (2001, 80).

Englefield (1992, 10) takes us one step further by noting that "[t]he boundary between the two republics [Serbia and Macedonia, HG] has no historical basis prior to 1945, and was delimited in 1945 and 1946. The boundary was drawn along the line of the Sar and Dukat mountains."

The example of the "Former Republic of Macedonia" makes a very important point. While the 1992 partition followed the post-1945/46 internal administrative boundaries, these previous internal boundaries were overwhelmingly *not* drawn along lines of ethnicity or "nationality."

Instead these previous internal boundaries overwhelmingly followed the principles of natural frontiers, cartography, and prior historical formation (for a similar example, see Sukhwal 1971, 224).

Conclusion

In this chapter I have sketched the outlines of a theory to explain territorial attachment and why people and states fight for some specific territory while never claiming other, just as valuable or more valuable, territory. I argued that specification of the homeland by a (focal) principle or point allows the people to monitor the leader and thereby facilitates collective action for a common defense. The theory offered a new explanation for why disputes over territory are more likely to escalate to war than disputes over other issues, and offered some novel predictions as well. I provided some very preliminary evidence that once specified, a focal principle that defines the homeland will constrain the territorial policies of the leader. I also offered some preliminary evidence that in cases of secessions and partitions, the new boundaries will follow focal principles and not, as seems to be commonly assumed, military conquest.

This framework can be extended and could throw new light on other important issues such as regional patterns of war and peace and system formation. While I paid little attention to international coordination on focal principles to specify the homeland, this could significantly affect international relations. For example, if the subjects in countries in a region all coordinate on one particular focal principle to specify their respective homelands, the homelands in such a region are significantly less likely to overlap, and those countries will then be less likely to promote conflicting territorial claims. Indeed, the desire to avoid war may actually even promote common coordination on a particular focal principle in a particular region. There is evidence that such international coordination occurred at different times in history. During Philip the Fair's reign, it seems that Philip and the Holy Roman Emperor Albert of Austria did indeed get together on one occasion to specify their mutual boundaries by reference to a focal principle: river boundaries (Dion 1947, 84). Centuries later, many of the major European states seem to have coordinated on a similar principle (first rivers, later also mountains) to establish their boundaries in the Treaties of Nijmegen, Ryswyck, and Utrecht. In the Treaty of Versailles and in Wilson's Fourteen Points, finally, we can catch glimmers of an attempt to internationally coordinate on the principle of common culture.

Territory and territoriality will most likely play an enduring role in politics. This paper offers a rationalist framework to explain this role, but it is only a beginning. I can only hope that the arguments I have developed promote renewed attention to the study of territory and territoriality in international politics.

NOTES

For their comments on earlier versions and drafts of this project, I am very grateful to the participants in the workshops on "Globalization, Territoriality, and Conflict," held at The Institute for International, Comparative, and Area Studies (IICAS) at the University of California San Diego, January 2003 and January 2004, and in particular to the organizers, Miles Kahler and Barbara Walter. In addition I would like to thank Brett Benson, Debra Boucoyannis, David Carter, Giacomo Chiozza, Rom Coles, Scott de Marchi, Tanisha Fazal, Erik Gartzke, George Gavrilis, Ron Hassner, Yuko Kawato, Keith Labedz, Jeffrey Legro, Erika Seeler, Taylor Siedell, David Soskice, Oren Yiftachel, Robert Walker, T. Camber Warren, and especially Craig Koerner. Mistakes, omissions, and other assorted infelicities remain my responsibility.

1 Political geographers have recognized for a long time the role territoriality can play in defining group membership. John Agnew (1994, 54), for example, notes that "[s]ystems of rule or political organization need not be either territorial, where geographical boundaries define the scope of membership in a polity a priori (for example, in kinship or clan systems space is occupied as an extension of group membership rather than residence within a territory defining group membership as in territorial states), or fixed territoriality (as with nomads)." The *locus classicus* is Sack (1986); see also Newman (1999, 3–4), Paasi (1996), Orridge (1982, 46), P. Sahlins (1990), and Horowitz (1985, 201).

2 Archeologists have found that the use of natural frontiers goes back to the earliest civilizations. Seeking to explain the conditions under which war gave rise to the state, Carneiro (1970, 734–35) proposes "to look for those factors common to areas of the world in which states arose indigenously – areas such as the Nile, Tigris–Euphrates, and Indus valleys in the Old World, and the Valley of Mexico and the mountain and coastal valleys of Peru in the New. These areas differ from one another in many ways – in altitude, temperature, rainfall, soil type, drainage pattern, and many other features. They do, however, have one thing in common: they are all areas of circumscribed agricultural land. Each of them is set off by mountains, seas, or deserts, and these environmental features sharply delimit the area that simple farming peoples could occupy and cultivate."

3 Almost any Cambodian will still respond to the question about their home-land with the saying, "Wherever sugar palm trees grow is Cambodian soil." This stems from a few episodes in relatively recent history, most prominently one that took place in the wake of independence from the French. In the mid-1950s, Cambodia succeeded in reclaiming a piece of the southern

reaches of the Mekong from Vietnam, partly (or at least so the government trumpeted) because of its obviously Cambodian nature – evidenced by the presence of said trees. So groups of villagers much farther north along the Cambodian–Vietnamese border internalized this lesson and decided that a great way to assert their claim to the disputed northern part of the border was to plant more of these trees as far eastward as they could. This went on for roughly a decade and was vaguely successful – or, at least, no one challenged the practice while Phnom Penh, Saigon, and Hanoi had bigger problems on their minds – until the US bombings began. The Cambodian villagers realized that they had effectively created more ground cover for the Viet Cong and so promptly cut down all the trees, relinquishing the territory in the hopes of peace. I would like to thank Sophie Richardson for this anecdote, based on her conversation with the 2001 Cambodian co-Minister of Defense, Prince Sisowath Sirirath.

4 Peter Sahlins (1991) shows how the adoption of "French" and "Spanish" national identities by inhabitants of the Cerdanya valley actually was the indirect *result* of the establishment of an international border in the Treaty of the Pyrenees of 1659. Thus, the border created identities, and not the other way around.

5 Note that this principle may have been focal for the European powers that carved up Africa in the nineteenth century, especially at the Congress of Berlin (1884), but is highly unlikely to have been focal for Africans themselves, who had not been exposed to the focal powers of maps and geographic education.

6 As suggested by Schelling (1960, 67–68), however, just like individuals, countries can also coordinate on principles to specify international boundaries and thereby attempt to limit international conflict.

7 Many countries bestow nationality and citizenship based on whether or not the individual was born within the territory of the state (*ius soli*). The competing but less prevalent principle *ius sanguinis* bestows citizenship and nationality on the basis of blood ties with someone who was or is a citizen. Very often, however, the question whether the ancestor was a citizen in the end depends on whether or not the ancestor was born in the territory.

8 Accordingly, James Anderson (2001, 19) argues that territoriality is "a 'spatial strategy' which actively uses territory and borders to classify and communicate . . . Its valuable strengths are that it can greatly simplify issues of control and provide easily understood symbolic markers 'on the ground', giving relationships of power a greater tangibility and appearance of permanence."

9 This is why non-contiguous states are few and far between and have declined in number over time. It can be argued that the big breakthrough of the treaties of Augsburg (1555) and Westphalia (1648) was that religion was defined territorially: *cuius regio, eius religio* (whose the region is, his the religion).

10 It is not difficult to specify a formal model in the manner of Weingast (1997) that generates these results. Assume the leader can announce a principle to determine which Dukes and Duchies are included in the homeland.

Assume furthermore an iterated game where Dukes are always uncertain which Duke and Duchy will be attacked next. When one of the Dukes and Duchies included under the principle is attacked from abroad, the leader can decide to support the Duke and Duchy or concede. If the leader supports the Duke, the other Dukes included under the principle individually decide whether or not to come to the Duke's defense or shirk. If the leader concedes, the other Dukes individually decide to punish or not punish the leader. In equilibrium, the leader will support a Duke if this Duke is in good standing at time t. The other Dukes will join in defense of the Duke under attack if the leader supports, punish the leader if he concedes and the Duke was in good standing, and otherwise not punish. A Duke will be in good standing at time t if he is in good standing at $t - 1$ and supports the leader if the leader defends at $t - 1$, and punishes the leader if the leader conceded at $t - 1$ and a Duke attacked in a previous round was in good standing. Otherwise, the Duke is not in good standing at time t. This logic can be straightforwardly extended to a game between the Duke and his subjects in his Duchy. I thank David Soskice for his invaluable help in articulating this game.

11 Mancur Olson (2000, 207–08) suggests that specification of a homeland may also benefit leaders because it allows them to reap the greater rewards of stationary banditry compared to roving banditry. Thus, he argues, "complete uncertainty about what territory an autocrat will control implies roving banditry. The advantages of stationary over roving banditry are obviously greatest when there are natural and militarily defensible frontiers."

12 Following Hardin (1995, 82, 132), we can also construct a functionalist explanation for power and persistence of the norm. He argues that "*An institution or a behavioral pattern X is explained by its function F for group G if and only if*

1 F is an *effect* of X;

2 F is *beneficial* for G;

3 F maintains X by a causal *feedback* loop passing through G."

Following Hardin's notation, if **F** is the greater likelihood of successful defense of the group **G** that follows from the homeland norm **X**, for example, fight for the homeland, then the homeland norm contributes to the power of the group, the increased likelihood of successful common defense, and a decreased likelihood of attacks on the homeland. This greater power is beneficial for virtually all members of the group, which therefore becomes even more likely to enforce and capable of enforcing the homeland norm against the occasional defector. See Hardin 1995, 132; see also Levi 1997.

13 "In Israel, Suddenly Cucumbers are Not Kosher." *New York Times*, 10 September 2000.

14 Note that the example of Latin America already spells trouble for the conventional wisdom that "nationalism" or common language determines the homeland. If common culture, common language, or common descent sufficed to determine states, Latin America would have only two or three states. Latin American countries have largely appealed to earlier (Spanish) administrative boundaries (Escudé 1992, 5–6).

15 Notably, foreign students seem to have known that they were at a disadvantage in the game. And they were, because they lacked the common knowledge available to Americans.

16 Using the same principle but a different focal *point*, Danton asserted in 1793 that France's territorial limits "are traced by nature. We reach them in the four corners of the horizon, on the Rhine and the Atlantic, in the Pyrenees and the Alps. These are France's boundaries" (Vigarello 1997, 475). This example shows that a principle may still allow for different specifications of the homeland, and that second level focal points may be necessary to definitively specify the homeland.

17 Before I examine prior group identification by reference to common culture, however, I should record my considerable skepticism about its historical prevalence before the late nineteenth century. Against the notion of primordial nations and primordial cultural groups, medieval historians have shown that group identifications often changed, that kinship or language were neither necessary nor sufficient criteria for group membership, and in particular that group membership was more often based on territoriality rather than the other way around (Geary 2002; Reynolds 1997, chap. 8; Strayer 1980, 388; see also Lugge 1960).

18 Historically we rarely see group members collectively come to the defense of co-nationals or co-religionists living beyond the boundaries of the state. Note that expatriates typically do not have the same right to be defended by the group as do people who live within the territory of the group.

19 Note that such homogenization can also be used to increase the economic benefits of combining different groups into one common country (Gellner 1983).

20 Karl Deutsch used this anecdote to telling effect in his classes at Harvard. I thank R. Harrison Wagner for relaying it to me.

21 It may be noted as an aside that the principle relates to notions of the territory of the state as property, and seems related to a Lockean vision of the appropriate territory of a state (Locke 1988, chap. 16: "On Conquest"). See also Gilbert (1998, 101–03).

22 As Ron Hassner never fails to point out, however, the Bible offers many different and conflicting definitions of that territory. If the principle of prior historical formation is based on some divine bequest, it may be relatively cheap to enforce because the clergy and committed religionists will help to enforce it for free.

23 A more powerful test – which I must postpone, but for which I am currently gathering data – would be to *ex ante* code the focal principle in force at any particular time for each of a group of countries, say Latin America, and then examine whether these focal principles predict the territorial claims and wars between states. Sources to code the focal principle in force include officially sanctioned maps and geography textbooks, as well as citizenship laws and speeches of important political actors.

24 It is striking to note that temporally this roughly coincides with a shift in the title of the king from "King of the Franks" to the "King of France" (Lugge 1960, 174, 203; C. Wood 1967).

25 By the early Middle Ages, the word *patria* no longer referred to an earthly fatherland but under the influence of the Church now referred to the Kingdom of Heaven (Kantorowicz 1997, 235–35).

26 To be sure, the idea of a territorial kingdom was not invented by Philip the Fair and its growth can already be seen during the reign of Philip Augustus. But as Strayer (1971, 293–94) points out, there is an important qualitative and quantitative shift in summonses of taxes and support for "defense of the realm" under Philip Augustus and Philip the Fair.

27 As Strayer (1971, 304–05) notes

> Philip the Fair was in a very different position [than Philip the Bold]. For the first time in almost a century the king of France had to wage a long, dangerous, and expensive war. For the first time in two centuries a French king found himself involved in a bitter controversy with the pope. The test could no longer be avoided. Philip had to demand men and money from all parts of his kingdom. He had to assert that all people living within certain boundaries were "in regno et de regno" (in the kingdom and part of the kingdom), and hence were required to aid in the defense of the kingdom. He had to insist that loyalty to king and kingdom took precedence over all other loyalties, including loyalty to the pope and to the church.
>
> Philip did not, of course, succeed completely in making these claims effective. He had to compromise in many cases. He received less money than he wanted, and he had to leave more power in the hands of some bishops and barons than he would have liked. The amazing thing is that he succeeded as well as he did and that his success did not require, to any significant degree, the use of force. Every part of what he considered to be the kingdom of France contributed men and money to his campaigns. Every part of the kingdom supported him in his controversy with Boniface VIII. There was, naturally, opposition to his policies, but the opposition usually took the form of legal protests and could be handled by political manipulation or decisions of the royal courts. Only at the very end of the reign, when both king and people were weary after years of crisis, were there serious rebellions . . . The relative moderation of the demands of the rebels shows how successful Philip had been in gaining acceptance for his basic doctrines. The baronial leaders admitted that defense of the kingdom took primacy over all other loyalties and privileges.
>
> Even Boniface VIII was forced to "[admit] that the clergy, like all other subjects, were bound to pay taxes for the defense of the kingdom in which they lived" (Strayer 1971, 339).

28 Nor did he fight for his Angevin cousins in Naples as his father had done before him (Strayer 1980, 11). At the Council of Vienna, Philip promised to take the cross and combat the infidels, but even at the time this promise was not taken seriously, and he never fulfilled his vow, which, according to Michaud, was "taken with perfect indifference" (Michaud 1973, 100). Runciman also claims that Philip's vow was just a temporary smoke-screen (Runciman 1954, 432–34; see also Brown 1973, 23).

29 My own rough translation of

> Item invenitur in scripturis et litteris antiquis fidem facientibus, quod olim
> quidam rex Francie habuit duos filios, quorum unus fuit rex Francie et alter
> imperator, et quod magna briga fuit inter eos orta super finibus regni et
> imperii, et ipsis in campis congregatis cum armis paratisque ad occidendum
> hincinde fuit inter eos per amicos communes concordatum, quod quatuor
> flumina, Scalcus, Moza, Rodanus et Sagona, essent pro finibus de cetero
> regni et imperii.

However, see also Kern (1911, No. 285, 229).

30 "Par suite de ces divers événements, la frontière orientale du royaume
atteignit la Meuse au sud de Verdun, cette Meuse qu'on s'habituait alors à
considérer, à l'est de la Champagne, non seulement comme la limite natur-
elle du royaume, mais aussi comme la limite légale, en prenant trop au pied
de la lettre ce que les chroniqueurs rapportaient du partage de l'empire
carolingien en 843" (Longnon 1922, 176).

31 "The county of Provence was held by his kinsmen, the kings of Naples, and
Philip scrupulously observed the Rhône boundary and that of both banks of
the Saône" (Strayer 1980, 351).

32 The king and his advisors are basically arguing that the realm is indivisible, a
straightforward implication of the focal point theory developed above. In the
end, Philip conceded *possession* of the Val d'Aran to the Aragonese, but
reserved the question of *property* (Strayer 1980, 28–30).

33 In terms of the theory offered above, the example shows that even if the
principle may have been suboptimal in this particular instance in the short
term – because Philip could not in the county levy taxes for the defense of the
realm, nor could he levy taxes in the realm for the defense of the county –
Philip stuck to it nevertheless.

34 While international relations scholars have argued that nobles fought for their
king because of *personal* bonds of loyalty between lord and vassal, this
example suggests that not just personal bonds, but also an obligation to the
"realm" could motivate the nobles to fight and sacrifice. See Strayer (1971,
305) where he argues that "The baronial leaders admitted that defense of the
kingdom took primacy over all other loyalties and privileges."

35 Dion (1947, 83) mentions that at two other places – Luxeuil (in Haute-
Saône) and Châtenois (Vosges) – the limits of the kingdom extended beyond
the line of the Four Rivers in the time of Philip the Fair.

36 I would like to thank David Carter for his excellent research assistance in
gathering these data.

3   On giving ground: globalization, religion, and territorial detachment in a Papua New Guinea society

Joel Robbins

One of the founding images of the recent wave of globalization discourse has been that of the deterritorialized migrant. Adrift without roots in an economically integrated world, the migrant has stood as a figure for the future of us all in an era in which territory was supposed to lose its role in structuring economic and political life. In the wake of the enthusiasm this image generated, whole bodies of social theory grew up that took the experience of the migrant as the norm and used it as a basis from which to critique older theories of culture and society based on notions of territorial identification and stability (for a review, see Papastergiadis 2000). Yet as the period of early enthusiasm has passed, many social scientists have come to realize that the majority of people in the world are not on the move, and that many of those who do move do not in the course of doing so necessarily lose their feelings of attachment to their home territories (see Lyons, this volume). The shift from one position to the other has not, however, been merely an idle pendulum swing, for what the discussions surrounding issues of movement and deterritorialization have demonstrated is that the links between people and territories are complex and require examination in their own right if we are to understand how they might change in response to social forces such as globalization.

One of the important themes of this volume is that, to borrow the terms of Newman's chapter, people's attachment to territory has both "tangible" dimensions, relating to issues of resources and defense, and "symbolic" ones, and that the importance of the symbolic ones has become more and more evident as globalization has threatened to attenuate the importance of the tangible ones. Thus several of the chapters in this volume demonstrate that the symbolic importance territory holds for people – its role in constituting their identities, providing them with a felt sense of security and belonging – has not been quick to fade in the face of economic globalization (Goemans, Lyons, and Newman, this volume). Similarly, studies of cultural globalization have often emphasized that the spread of Western cultures tends to sharpen people's commitments to the uniqueness of their local, often territorially defined, cultures rather than dull them (Robertson 1992; M. Sahlins 1992 and 2001). Such findings indicate the importance of moving beyond considerations of the tangible value of territory to study the nature and dynamics of symbolic attachment to it.

This chapter aims to explore some of the symbolic dimensions of territorial attachment by making use of the anthropological method of examining a single case in detailed and locally meaningful terms. The case in question is a distinctive one because it involves the members of a small society in Papua New Guinea (PNG), the Urapmin, who have collectively decided that they are willing to give up their territory to a mining company if that company will move them to a modern town somewhere else in the country, and this despite the fact that their territory has always been crucial in defining their collective and personal identities. The Urapmin, who have very little contact with the global market, have been led to this decision both by their imaginative representations of what participation in economic globalization would be like and by their conversion to a Pentecostal style of Christianity that devalues territorial attachment and provides people with ritual means for overcoming it. By looking at how the interplay of economic imaginings and religious beliefs and practices have loosened territorial attachment in the Urapmin case, I will argue, we can shed light on the construction of territorial attachments more generally: by seeing how territorial attachments unravel, that is, we can gain a better sense of how they are made. Furthermore, we can enrich the study of the processes of territorial detachment that have been so central to work on globalization by examining the forms they take in a situation in which migration is not a factor. As many contributions to this volume attest, continuing commitments to territory and to the distinctive cultural identities people routinely see it as underwriting are often sources of conflict. Thus a case such as that of the Urapmin, one in which people are ready to give up territory for other goods, takes on comparative importance. Uncovering the conditions in which territory has lost its hold on people in this one case suggests lines of future research on how it might come to do so in others, lines I consider briefly in the conclusion.

Territorial detachment among the Urapmin

The Urapmin are a group of 390 people whose territory falls within the West Sepik Province of PNG. They were first significantly contacted by

Westerners in the late 1940s when their region was brought under Australian control. In the early 1990s, when I carried out fieldwork among them, almost all Urapmin adults continued to work, as their ancestors had, as subsistence gardeners and hunters, procuring their livelihood on the basis of their extensive knowledge of the land they inhabit. With names for every stretch of ground, and with sacred and secular stories connected to all of their territory's major and many of its minor features, Urapmin saturate their everyday conversation with references to their land and its importance to their lives. Their attachment to their territory thus appears at first glance to be secure, as it usually does among communities in PNG and elsewhere in the world where everyone owns their own ground and makes their living from it.

As prevalent as the signs of territorial attachment were in the daily life and talk of the Urapmin during the early 1990s, however, the quality of their tie to their land was changing in significant ways. During the mid-1980s, a consortium of multinational companies and the PNG government opened the Ok Tedi mine four days' walk to the south of Urapmin on the other side of the imposing mountain range that forms the central spine of PNG. Though built in an area as remote as Urapmin, Ok Tedi was briefly the world's largest producing gold mine, and it has continued to be a major source of copper into the present. The town that services the mine, Tabubil, is the centerpiece of what is reported to have been one of the most expensive infrastructural construction projects in mining history, costing a billion US dollars to complete. It has 24-hour power, an airport, paved roads, several grocery stores, banks, and countless houses made of sawn timber in the style of the developed world. For most Urapmin, who live without electricity in houses made of bush materials (in the early 1990s even the government offices for their District had power only sporadically when there was fuel to run one of their generators), Tabubil presents them with the one close look they have been able to have at a kind of Western lifestyle they have heard much about and have come to imagine themselves wanting to live.

Since Ok Tedi was built, its owners and other companies have devoted resources to looking for other gold and copper deposits in the area around it in the hopes of developing other mines that could make use of its extensive infrastructure. In the late 1980s, as part of one of these efforts, prospecting groups from the Kennecott company began coming sporadically to Urapmin to collect soil samples. While there is some gold in Urapmin, the prospect has always been marginal in the company's eyes because of its great distance from Tabubil and even from other local "centers" with airstrips. Yet despite Kennecott's sense that the Urapmin prospect was most likely quite marginal, for the Urapmin the prospecting group's visits spurred a sense of expectation that profound changes were on the horizon. Chief among these imagined developments was that the Urapmin would be able to turn their land over to Kennecott and would in exchange be moved to a city somewhere else in Papua New Guinea, there to live what they saw as the developed lives of city-dwellers.

The extent to which the Urapmin took seriously their dreams of leaving their land behind came out quite chillingly in 1991 when a representative of the PNG mining commission and several Kennecott employees helicoptered in to Urapmin to hold a meeting that would decide whether the government would renew Kennecott's prospecting license for another term. Figuring this meeting would be the most important political event in their history (and certainly the first in which a representative of the national government, no matter how lowly, would be present), the Urapmin prepared an elaborate and highly symbolic pageant that they planned to present upon the helicopter's arrival. It would begin as they carried the visiting dignitaries from the helicopter on litters, not to honor them, but to drive home the point that there are no roads or cars in Urapmin. Then, as the performance developed, a man and a woman would jump out of the bushes wearing, respectively, the traditional penis-gourd and grass skirt. The Urapmin Councilor – their elected representative to the modern political system – would then say:

we surprised you with our penis gourds and grass skirts. But this is still what we are. If you have a mother and a father [i.e. sufficient resources] tear off our grass skirts and penis gourds and replace them with trousers. We must become just like you.[1]

After several more displays designed to drive home similar messages of need and entreaty, the Council would finish by saying "if you have the power, take our land and destroy it and move us to a town somewhere else."

The pageant that ended with this stark request to be removed from their own territory, a territory Kennecott was invited to "destroy," was the product of many weeks of discussion and planning involving most of the important adults in the community. As they came together to script their presentation, they publicly formulated the course they hoped their future would take. Their request that the company destroy their land and move them, then, was not a mere rhetorical turn of phrase. It accurately represented a collective consensus on a desirable course of action. How did this course of action come to seem to the Urapmin to be both desirable and viable?

The Urapmin have come to want to give up their territory in the course of a complex history of globalization in which economic changes have been minimal but fantasies of economic change have been vivid and highly motivating (Appadurai 1996). At the same time, religious globalization in the form of conversion to Protestant, Pentecostal-style Christianity has been more successful at introducing significant cultural change that is both symbolic and institutional – changing not only the ways people imagine their prospects but how they live their lives together day to day. I will argue that economic globalization in Urapmin, despite its paltry material effects, has been crucial in motivating the Urapmin's desire to leave their territory: without the image of an economic life they cannot live at home before them, the Urapmin would have no desire to leave their territory behind. Yet it is their Christian conversion that has made their detachment from their territory viable. Their Christianity has provided them with the conceptual and ritual means to dissociate themselves from their land and in so doing has been crucial in bringing them to the point at which they can imagine themselves able to barter their territory for the promise of a different kind of life.

Although my argument will unfold through an examination of the different contributions economic and religious change have made to the transformation of the Urapmin territorial regime, the claim that their experience illuminates the dynamics that underlie symbolic territorial detachment more generally depends upon a prior argument that before these changes took place the Urapmin were in fact symbolically tied to their territory in ways comparable to the way other, more well-known groups have been and continue to be tied to theirs. This is the argument I make in the next section.

Territory and identity in pre-contact Urapmin

There are two distinct levels on which the Urapmin are attached to their territory. The most immediately apparent to the observer is what we might call the personal level. All Urapmin adults have extensive knowledge of the major features of the Urapmin territory as a whole and even more detailed knowledge of those parts of the territory on which they garden and hunt. Some of this knowledge draws on mythical and historical narratives (about which more below), but much of it comes from personal experiences or stories handed down in families. As one walks with people on the footpaths that criss-cross Urapmin, they routinely point to particular trees, rocks, and other distinctive features of the landscape and recall what members of their families did in their vicinity in the past, or they pick out a place in the forest where a successful wild pig hunt had allowed them to give meat to the people of several villages, or they note the tree where initiators took sap to rub them with when they initiated them, or places where they gardened with their fathers and mothers when they were young, producing food they gave to all their relatives. Such running comments on the meanings the landscape holds for people indicate that it is sedimented with highly charged personal memories like these, such that few parts of it are insignificant to people's personal lives. As it does elsewhere in PNG, the land thus serves the Urapmin as an emotionally charged store of information about their personal histories and the shape of the social lives (Feld 1996; Kahn 1996; Schieffelin 1976; Weiner 1991).

The extent to which the Urapmin tether their memories and hence in important respects their conception of their society to their landscape is worth underscoring, for it enriches the sense in which we can talk about the symbolic nature of people's connection to the land, and gives added depth and scope to Newman's point in this volume that territorial attachment plays itself out on the micro as well as the macro level.

Yet as important as this extensive personal attachment to the landscape is for the Urapmin, for the current argument it is overshadowed by what I will call their collective sense of attachment to their territory. The Urapmin have traditionally had and continue in important respects to have an almost Westphalian conception of the connection between linguistic/ethnic groups and discrete, clearly bounded territories. They see themselves and their neighbors as defined by a set of characteristics that includes political autonomy, cultural and linguistic distinctiveness, and the grounding of these features in the possession of rigidly demarcated territories. Hence people's connections to their land are meaningful not only for their personal sense of themselves, but also for their sense of belonging to the collectivity they call Urapmin.

Far less common in PNG than the kind of personal connection to place described above, this territorially defined, collective one is rooted in the details of traditional Urapmin religion and mythology. Sketched briefly, the Urapmin and their neighbors all understand themselves to have been created by Afek (lit. "the Old Woman"), a creator spirit who lived in mythical times. She came from the East and traveled throughout the highland areas of what are now the West Sepik and western provinces, creating different ethnic groups at the various places she stopped along the way. She gave each group its own territory and language. She also determined traditional relations of alliance and enmity between groups, such that some groups fought each other from the time of creation until the enforced colonial peace of the mid-twentieth century, while other groups where dedicated to assisting one another in battle. She also gave each group its own special ritual competencies within a region-wide division of religious labor aimed at ensuring the agricultural and reproductive success of all groups of the region. This ritual system counterbalanced the centrifugal tendencies of the system of traditional warfare and ensured that all of the groups would see themselves as part of a single humanity. At the same time, the division of ritual labor upon which it was based foregrounded the fact that each group had its own identity and autonomy, an autonomy linked to their territories and the ritual sites they housed.

The Urapmin continue to view their region and the world beyond in territorial terms they have inherited from this mythical and religious tradition. They have, for example, learned to use the modern governmental apparatus to defend their territorial claims, bringing cases to the government court when members of neighboring groups have tried to annex land at the periphery of their holdings. Moreover, they have come to recognize that the rest of the world is organized in territorial terms similar to their own. Hence, they have had little trouble grasping the idea that they are now citizens of a territorially defined nation-state, and they imagine that all other people in the world must be as well (Robbins 1998). Modern notions of territoriality are thus one aspect of global culture they have taken up with ease.

The personal, intimate connections all Urapmin adults sustain with the land upon which they live establish a profound symbolic attachment to their territory. Their tradition of collective territorial understanding demonstrates that this attachment is central to the definition of group identities in a way that is similar to what we find in cases more familiar to those interested in the significance of territorial attachments to contemporary global politics. It is against the background of these strands of symbolic attachment to their territory that the recent Urapmin willingness to sever their territorial ties takes on comparative importance.

Development and the drive for territorial detachment

In the Urapmin case, economic globalization has been much more a matter of aspiration than of actual changes in economic process. But even as the Urapmin have yet to realize their hopes for economic change, the goals they have set for themselves continue to significantly influence their social lives and in particular the way they think about their bond to their territory. An important part of the impetus for them to give up their territory follows from the desires for change that economic globalization has stimulated.

The Urapmin would very much like what they call "development." The meaning this term has for them is complex, but at the minimum it refers to the attainment of a lifestyle in which people work for cash, buy food from stores, and live in houses made of permanent materials. Although it is easy for those of us who live this lifestyle to imagine that the Urapmin desire for it is quite natural, I would suggest that we would be better off seeing it as a puzzle. In fact, no one has tried to sell the Urapmin on the virtues of the developed life. From the beginning of the colonial era patrol officers suspected there would be little chance of development in the region the Urapmin inhabit, and to avoid future disappointment they did not work to convince the people of the area of the benefits of large-scale economic change. As a patrol officer in 1965, during the colonial era, noted in his report when the Urapmin asked about the possibility of development coming to them, "one can only emphasise to them their great distance from anywhere" (Robbins 2004a, 102). Furthermore, most Urapmin have little experience of the market economy in any but its most bare bones, back-blocks form: the forms it takes at the government center of Telefomin, a six-hour walk away, where people can occasionally get casual work clearing dirt roads of weeds in return for slight wages they use to buy soap, salt, and other foodstuffs and household commodities from extremely pricey, sparsely stocked stores that fly their goods in from the mining town of Tabubil. True, a few Urapmin had experiences in the 1970s working on copra and tea plantations – environments where workers' economic activities were carefully controlled and consumption possibilities limited – and people now have the image of Tabubil before them to provide an ideal of what developed life might look like. But the colonial-era patrol reports indicate that the Urapmin desire for development pre-dates Tabubil's construction by a good fifteen years and started before more than a couple of men had had plantation experience. So the question remains why people with relatively little experience of the developed world would want so desperately to join it.

In examining the appeal economic development holds for the Urapmin, it is crucial to understand how they see their traditional economic lives. With the exception of a division of labor based on gender, most Urapmin do not carry out specialized productive tasks. All men clear gardens and hunt, while all women tend gardens, collect water and firewood, and weave net bags out of string they make from tree bark. Every family consisting of an adult married couple can thus perform most of the tasks of Urapmin subsistence for themselves, and in this respect families are largely economically autonomous. In fact, although most Urapmin live at least part of the time in villages, families routinely demonstrate their autonomy by spending a good deal of time living alone in houses they build near their gardens, and at any given time there are also a few families living wholly on their own in single-family homesteads far from any villages. Yet despite the fact that most households are autonomous in the realm of production, all Urapmin exchange foodstuffs and items such as net bags with other families every day. The items they exchange are not ones any family would expect to be lacking in their own gardens or be unable to make for themselves. Instead, it is a matter of A giving B a sweet potato today and B giving A one several days later. Despite the fact that this exchange produces no "profit," as some Urapmin now put it, it is extremely common and accompanies the bulk of everyday socializing between families. Because of it, people almost never spend a day without eating some common food someone else has given them, nor do they pass a day without giving food to someone else.

Summarizing very briefly a good deal of important work in economic anthropology, we can begin to explain this pattern by noting that the traditional Urapmin economy is a gift rather than a commodity economy (the *locus classicus* of this type of analysis is Mauss 1990 [1925]; Gregory 1982 provides an influential contemporary account). Gift economies are founded on the norm of reciprocity: that one must receive what is given and make an appropriate return at a later time, ideally so that the initial giver can then give again. In a gift economy people give not to acquire specific goods they do not already have, but rather to establish and maintain relationships. As the Urapmin say, to eat food you have grown or hunted yourself is "to eat without purpose," whereas to give your own food away and eat the food of others is to use food to do important social work. It is the same with one's net bags or other goods – one gives them away in order to enter reciprocal exchange relationships that will render one rich not in things but in personal connections.

Gift economies can be complex, and the literature on them is vast. My purpose here is not to describe the Urapmin economy in detail (see Robbins 1999), but rather to point out that in it people produce things not in the first instance in order to use them or exchange them to get other things, but rather in order to have something to give to others so that they can establish and maintain social relationships with them. What is crucial is to have things to give so that others are willing to receive and reciprocate. It is in giving that one demonstrates the success and creative power of one's labor and, by extension, one's moral qualities as a person (Burridge 1969; Strathern 1988). These in turn allow one to participate as a full member of Urapmin society.

Because it is fundamental to producing the goods one exchanges, one's territory in places like Urapmin is intimately linked to the gift economy (Hirsch 2004). By Urapmin reckoning, their territory was valuable precisely because it provided them with a reliable basis on which to produce the goods they needed to successfully participate in the gift economy both within Urapmin and in the wider region articulated by the traditional religious system. Their territory, they reckon, is more fertile than that of many of their neighbors and reasonably well stocked with game. Moreover, due to the very steep grade of their holdings, they, unlike most others, have pandanus trees (which are very sensitive to microclimate) coming into fruit all year long, providing them with a constant supply of what people consider one of the most desirable and socially potent non-meat food gifts. Finally, all of the people of their region have traditionally understood Urapmin land to produce the best tobacco, and visitors still come from days away to trade prestige goods for it. This gave Urapmin people as firm a foothold in the regional luxury economy as they had in the more mundane, but also more fundamental, economy of everyday goods exchange. Since the region represented to all intents and purposes the limit of the known world for the Urapmin, their full participation in it amounted to the achievement of full moral status in the whole of the human world. Their ability to assume this status leads the Urapmin, who in general are not inclined to boast, to proclaim quite directly that they possess "good land," land that in traditional terms well supported their efforts to construct themselves as a "good people" by producing goods they could deploy in gift exchanges with all of the kinds of people whom they encountered.

The satisfactory tie joining Urapmin territory and their gift economy began to come unraveled during the colonial and postcolonial era as the scope of their social world widened. The primary problem was that, as the Urapmin came to see it, their land no longer allowed them to produce goods that they were able to exchange with all of the various people with whom they wanted to have relationships. They could still produce the foodstuffs and material goods that were central to local exchanges. To a large extent, they were also able to maintain their regional exchange relations, especially as people continued to value their tobacco (Robbins 1999). Yet even as they were able keep most of their regional relationships active, by the mid-1960s, the point when they began to ask patrol officers about development, they recognized that without an airstrip or the regular government and mission presence their neighbors enjoyed (see below), they were clearly falling behind in terms of their ability to lay hands on Western goods to exchange. This raised the specter of their falling out of the regional system altogether. More alarming even than this threat, however, was their complete lack of enduring relations with Westerners. Westerners clearly wanted nothing the Urapmin had to give. During early patrols, Westerners had exchanged salt and bush knives with the Urapmin for food and sometimes employed their labor as carriers, but they did so on the commodity economy basis of entering into brief relationships in order to exchange goods (including labor) rather than exchanging goods to build long-term relations. Hence, specific individuals seldom came around a second time, and during the independence era that began in 1975 few Westerners ever appeared at all. Since independence, the Urapmin tend only to encounter Westerners in places like Tabubil or the government offices for their district in Telefomin, and those they do encounter continue to prove uninterested in sustaining reciprocal relations. The educated Papua New Guinean elite who have come to run the country during the postcolonial era are similarly indifferent to Urapmin efforts to build relationships.

In a gift economy, the greatest failure is not having nothing to consume but rather having nothing to give (Robbins 2003). In regard to Westerners and the postcolonial elite, the Urapmin have since contact found themselves in precisely this position. And because a person's moral worth is tied up in their exchange relations, to discover a whole social world in which one cannot participate on the basis of reciprocal exchange is to see oneself as at least in some respects a failure as a person.

An incident that occurred at the meeting to renew Kennecott's prospecting license discussed above indicates how frustrating the Urapmin have found their inability to develop reciprocal exchange relations with Westerners. It also demonstrates the extent to which they hope to bring Westerners into relationship with themselves on gift rather than commodity economy terms. The incident turned on the fact that the PNG government requires that companies compensate landowners for any trees they cut down or land they disturb during the course of their prospecting activities. Once the main part of the licensing meeting had ended, and Kennecott's license had been renewed, the leader of the prospecting group approached the Urapmin Councilor to give him the compensation payments owed for the work done under the previous license. By Urapmin standards this payment, likely to have been worth a thousand or more US dollars, would have been a major windfall. The Councilor, however, refused to take it. "Bring us the money another time," he told the Kennecott representative. "It's more important that you should come back and that you should build a mine." Although the Kennecott representative explained that it would be best if he gave the payments now, the Councilor was insistent and the helicopter left without the payments being made.

The rationale for the Councilor's refusal of the payment is not hard to construe if one looks at the situation from the point of view of someone evaluating the situation in gift economy terms. In those terms, the goal is to collect relationships and the way to do that is to keep a constant flow of exchanges going. Things are given in order to create debts that require future gifts to resolve them. The Urapmin have given part of their land to Kennecott and, as creditors, have the right to expect a future return: a return that they hope will be a mine. At the same time, many Urapmin realize that the market economy works differently in that people operating on its terms extinguish debts immediately through purchase and then are not bound to each other in ongoing relationships. It is this kind of relationship-ending exchange the Councilor, one of the more sophisticated Urapmin when it came to the ways of the market, was hoping to avoid by refusing the payment. Having found in their land the one thing they could give to Westerners that Westerners appeared to be willing to receive, he and other Urapmin did not want to erase the debt until they could attain the kind of return that, like a mine, would allow them to produce goods they could give back to Westerners to keep their relationships with them alive. As an anthropological student of gift economies once put it, "debt is social structure." Having finally managed to find a debt that put them into a structural (that is, enduring, or at least so they hoped) relationship with Westerners, the Urapmin did not want to see it repaid in a way that would bring it to a definitive end.

As it happened, Kennecott eventually sold the Urapmin prospect and never returned, and as far as I know the payments the Councilor refused that day were never made (though they may have been after I left in early 1993). In this respect, Kennecott's behavior confirmed the pattern whereby Westerners routinely fail to enter into the kind of reciprocal relations with the Urapmin by which the Urapmin come to see themselves as full members of the human community.[2] The challenge this failure presents to the Urapmin sense of themselves fuels their continuing hopes for a mine and, more to the point here, their growing disappointment with their territory. They are inclined now to refer to their land as "deep jungle," indicating by this phrase their difficulty in wresting from it the products that seem so easily produced in more "developed" cities elsewhere in PNG and in the rest of the world and that the people who live in those places demand if they are to enter into relations of exchange. It is the Urapmin feeling that they can no longer use their territory to produce goods that will help them foster all of the kinds of human relations they want to foster that makes that territory something they are willing to give up.

But wanting to give up one's territory in exchange for something else is not the same as being able to imagine oneself able to do so. Given their complex, symbolic attachments to their land, how can the Urapmin conceive of leaving it behind? My argument is that it has been their encounter with the globalization of Christianity that has given them the means for imagining what such detachment would be like and the ritual tools with which to begin effecting it even before a mine has been built.

Christianity and symbolic detachment from territory

Shortly after the Australians formally colonized the area around Urapmin and opened a government district office about a six-hour walk to their west, the Australian Baptist Missionary Society set up shop on the government station. Because the Urapmin were remote from the station (their territory was far more than a six-hour walk for those not used to mountainous bush walking), had a small population, and did not have ground suitable for the construction of an airstrip, they were never directly "missionized." Instead, starting in the early 1960s, elders in the community sent young people out to study with missionaries living among their neighbors. These young people, and local people from groups that had been directly missionized, brought news of Christianity to those Urapmin who remained at home.

The effects of the Urapmin discovery of Christianity were not immediate, and by the mid-1970s few had converted who had not left Urapmin to study Christianity elsewhere in the region. But in 1977 a charismatic Christian revival movement spread throughout the highlands of PNG. When it reached Urapmin, people began to be possessed by the Holy Spirit and to have various ecstatic experiences that convinced them that the Christian conception of the world was true. Over the course of a year, all of the Urapmin converted to the Pentecostal-style Christianity the revival introduced, and since 1978 the Urapmin have seen themselves as a completely Christian community that has abandoned its traditional religion.

This is not the place to explain why the Urapmin converted or to describe the nature of their Christian beliefs and rituals in detail (see Robbins 2004a). It is important to note, however, that the Urapmin grasp of Christian doctrines is more sophisticated than one might imagine would be the case among an unmissionized, recently converted, remote population. Most Urapmin men under forty and women under thirty are literate in the Tok Pisin lingua franca of PNG and read the New Testament in that language. They devote a good deal of time to studying their Bibles and are concerned not to compromise what they define as the orthodoxy of their practice by developing what they understand to be syncretic forms of worship. It is legitimate, then, to speak of them for analytic purposes as Christians and to use their case to shed light on how Christianity, or at least Pentecostal forms of Christianity, influences people's territorial attachments.

Christianity in general is centered on a message it takes to have universal rather than territorially or ethnically bound significance, and it has from the outset emphasized social and geographic expansion. It also defines salvation as an ultimately otherworldly state. Finally, its focus is on the person of Christ, not on a particular place it takes to be holy (Davies 1994, 375). For these reasons, it is not by nature a territorially focused religion (Davies 1994; Sack 1986; J. Smith 1978, 1987). In general it supports, as Sack (1986, 102) notes that its early forms did, "a non-physical, non-territorial . . . sense of community." This is a sense of community in which "physical entities as such – land, Jerusalem, Temple – cease to be significant, except as types of realities which are not in essence physical" (Davies 1994, 366). To be sure, some churches historically and in the present have modulated this fundamental emphasis on territorial detachment, and some, such as the Catholic Church, have developed elaborate forms of territorial or-ganization (Sack 1986). But the bulk of Christian churches fall toward the deterritorialized end of any continuum one might make of the extent to which various religions promote attachment to territory among their followers.

Were one to make such a continuum, one would find that the Pente-costal types of churches of which the Urapmin church is an example would fall toward the far end even of the Christian portion of it. Such churches are defined by their emphasis on the importance of the ecstatic gifts of Holy Spirit, and this generally gives them an otherworldly and often (as in the Urapmin case) intensely millennial cast. With their eyes directed heavenward, there is little attachment to what the Urapmin call "things of this ground." Furthermore, Pentecostal churches are often independent in the sense of being locally run by those empowered by the Spirit to lead and only loosely, if at all, tied to central offices that might establish territorially based hierarchies. There is thus no tendency in Pentecostal-style Christianity to sacralize particular geographies or otherwise promote people's symbolic attachment to territory.

Yet Pentecostalism does more than simply counsel an indifference toward territorial concerns. In places like Urapmin, places where people's pre-conversion attachment to their land has been strong, it often requires believers to actively work to break the spiritual ties that bind them to their territory. This is so because Pentecostalism does not question the validity of traditional beliefs in territorial spirits (Robbins 2004b). Instead, it confirms the reality of traditional spirits by emphasizing the need for converts to come to recognize them as demonic and to work to put an end to their influence on people's lives. Because such spirits are territorially based and serve to give the land its meaning in important respects, to demonize them and attempt to break their hold on the land is to desacralize one's territory. It is this desacralization that makes symbolic detachment possible. We can illustrate the dynamics of this process by looking more closely at the Urapmin case.

Traditional Urapmin religion was in large part focused on helping the Urapmin to use their territory productively. Many of its rituals, including its large-scale public ones, were designed to entreat ancestors to make the land prosper and help with hunting. Cult houses were spread throughout the Urapmin villages and contained bones of ancestors to which offerings were given for help in the hunt and with gardening. People also kept bones of close relatives in their houses for further help with hunting and with pig rearing. Most elaborately, a central cult house contained the bones of major ancestors. The rituals carried out in this cult house were crucial to the agricultural success of all Urapmin and to that of their neighbors. The ancestors, in the form of their bones, were thus spread out throughout Urapmin territory and when properly worshiped made that territory productive.

With the coming of the revival in 1977, the Urapmin deliberately set about dismantling this traditional ritual system. Leaders of the revival removed the bones from all of the cult houses and private homes. They destroyed those of minor ancestors and put those of major ones in caves in the forest. At first people waited to make sure that the Christian God would be powerful enough to make their gardens grow and to prevent the ancestors from punishing the Urapmin for their sacrilege. When God proved able to do so – as gardens grew and people remained free of major illnesses sent by the ancestors as punishment – the Urapmin determined to sever all relations with their ancestors, leaving the bones of the major ones in the caves to which they had been brought. From that time forward, the history of Urapmin occupation of their territory, a history that formerly took tangible form in the bones of their ancestors, has ceased to be relevant to their ability to work the land. God now helps them in this, just as he would help them as

Christians to prosper on any other territory or perform any other work they might be able to secure elsewhere. That they now lack special, ritual competencies that allow them to work a particular territory is an important sense in which the Urapmin are no longer tied to their land.

The Urapmin break with their ancestors has been very clean. All important productive rituals are now Christian in nature, and people rarely mention their ancestors except when defending land-ownership claims. The same cannot be said of the Urapmin attempt to break with the other kinds of spirits that inhabit their territory. These spirits, which we can call "nature spirits" because they own particular features of the landscape (lands, rocks, streams) and particular animal species, have proven much more difficult for the Urapmin to turn away from.

Urapmin believe that all significant parts of the landscape are owned by nature spirits. These spirits existed before the Urapmin were created. The creator woman Afek had to promise these spirits possession of almost all of the earth in order to negotiate space to make villages for the human beings she wanted to create. Thus the Urapmin are late-comers to their land, and their ownership claims to resources vis-à-vis one another are always secondary to the claims of the spirits (Robbins 2003). For the most part, spirits allow the Urapmin to use the land and other resources they own as long as the Urapmin follow a stringent set of taboos regulating their use. All adult illnesses that end short of death, however, and all infant illnesses and deaths, are attributed to spirits who are angry because a taboo has been broken.[3] With every illness and every childhood death in the community, then, the Urapmin are reminded of the existence of the spirits and of the force of their proprietary claims.

One of the central tenets of Urapmin Christianity is the idea that God created all of the things of the world for people to use. For this reason, from a Christian point of view the spirits' claims on the land and its resources are illegitimate. The Urapmin should not have to follow any taboos regarding the use of their territory. Now, the Urapmin say, is "free time" – a time where no taboos are in effect. To a great extent the Urapmin have realized their vision of free time by discarding the bulk of the taboos they once practiced. They have done so because they enjoy the freedom taboo abrogation has brought, but more importantly because, as they now understand it, to follow taboos is to display a lack of faith, since it suggests that one does not believe God is strong enough to prevent the nature spirits from taking revenge for their breach.

But as much as the Urapmin are committed to the doctrine of free time, they remain wary of the nature spirits. It can hardly be otherwise, since they continue to get sick and infants continue to die, and they have no other explanation for these occurrences. Furthermore, by demonizing these spirits, Urapmin Christianity acknowledges that they exist and are powerful. The continued presence of these spirits on the Urapmin landscape produces what is one of the primary tensions in Urapmin life. On the one hand, Urapmin believe that if they are to act as good Christians they should disregard the spirits and their taboos completely. On the other, they must deal with problems of sickness and infant death that they are sure the spirits cause in retaliation for this Christian behavior. A class of possession mediums, women who are possessed by the Holy Spirit, has developed in response to this tension. There was no tradition of possession in Urapmin, but since the revival began there have been women, known as "Spirit women," who are able to become possessed by the Holy Spirit at will. People come to them when they or their children are sick. When they come, the Spirit women go into a trance and the Holy Spirit shows them which nature spirits are responsible for the sickness. They then pray with the afflicted, asking God to pry off the spirits (who are understood to be clutching their victims) and remove them from Urapmin territory, binding them in hell.

When sicknesses linger, particularly in children, Spirit women go further and order parents to carry out traditional pig sacrifices in which the spirits are given the "smell" of the cooking pig and asked to take that in exchange for the victim. The Urapmin have taken steps to Christianize these sacrifices by involving the Spirit women in them and by surrounding them with prayers. But they also recognize that these sacrifices are the one traditional type of ritual they still practice. They worry over this, and the continued resort to sacrifice is very controversial. One should not have any positive, exchange-type relations with the spirits, they say, and they remind each other that normatively Jesus was to have been the last sacrifice. But no one wants to see a child die if the death might have been prevented, so in the end people tend to resort to sacrifice if children's illnesses linger or begin to appear severe.

The problems spirits cause, both in terms of the illnesses they inflict and the traditional, "heathen" rituals required to deal with them, lead the Urapmin to desire a life in which their territory is entirely free of them. Addressing this hope, Spirit women sometimes hold rituals designed to rid whole areas of Urapmin territory of spirits. Often several will come together in a village or other area where people have been sick. They all become possessed at the same time, moving around the area praying and banishing the spirits to the forest. Then they plant small wooden crosses in the ground to form a fence meant to prevent the spirits from returning. People do not discuss the effectiveness of these rituals to any great extent after they have taken place, and one suspects that the first illness to come to a community after such a ritual has been completed indicates that it has not been a perfect success. But it remains true that people hold out the image of a land free of spirits as something they would like one day to achieve.

The tension that marks Urapmin spirit beliefs and the rituals those beliefs underwrite – a tension that stems from their desire to be fully rid of the spirits and their inability, even with the help of the Christian God, to realize this desire – is, I would argue, a symbolic reflection of the reality of their current situation. They are aware of and hope to participate in a world in which they will not be dependent upon their territory – hence the intimations they have of a land free of the territorial entanglements the spirits represent. Yet at the same time they are still dependent on that territory. They live and work on it in largely traditional ways, hence their inability to discard completely the spirit beliefs that represent that dependence. In terms of the focus of this chapter, what is symbolized by these contradictory beliefs in God's overwhelming power and the spirits' tenacity in the face of it is precisely the struggle for territorial detachment in Urapmin life.

Given this, it is interesting to note several developments in Urapmin spirit belief and ritual that have attended Kennecott's prospecting effort. Just as the Urapmin think of spirits as originally owning all of the natural resources upon which they draw, having learned about gold they now assume that the spirits own that as well. The Urapmin conceive of spiritual ownership in markedly physical terms: the spirits clutch tightly that which belongs to them. Kennecott's failure to find enough gold to begin mining operations is therefore caused by the spirits refusing to release the gold to the prospectors. In response to this, the Urapmin hold pig sacrifices and special Spirit women rituals when Kennecott's teams come to do their work. The pigs are presented to the Kennecott workers (who inevitably pay for them, just as they buy other local foods during their visits), but as in sacrifices to heal sickness their smell is delivered to the spirits, who are asked to release the gold and to forgo causing the Urapmin to become sick in retaliation for the disturbances the prospecting will cause. Along with this sacrificial carrot offered to the spirits, the Spirit women also wield the stick of the Holy Spirit and deploy it in ritual efforts to render areas to be explored free from the control of the nature spirits.

While these ritual efforts are clearly rooted in traditional sacrificial patterns, they also differ significantly from them. Traditional Urapmin sacrifices and even what we might call "traditional" Urapmin Christian healing rituals involving Spirit women aim to redress problems with the nature spirits that have followed upon specific instances of Urapmin disregard for the spirits' taboos. The sacrifices and spirit-removal rituals the Urapmin practice in the prospecting context, by contrast, focus on buying off the spirits' claims to resources before the Urapmin have violated any taboos (Robbins 1995). They are prophylactic and assume the possibility that the spirits might completely relinquish their hold on the land in return for sacrifices or under the sway of the power of the Christian God. These rituals thus constitute a new way in which the Urapmin are negotiating the possibility of freeing themselves from the spiritual demands that tie them to their territory. If they could buy off the spirits, they reckon, the prospecting would go well and then they could give their land to Kennecott without having to fear any spiritual reprisal.

In the previous section, I indicated that the Urapmin drive for deterritorialization was a product of their desire for development. I have presented their Christianity here primarily as a means for realizing the deterritorialized state their desire for development pushes them to seek. Yet there are also respects in which Urapmin Christianity, like their desire for development, encourages the Urapmin to define themselves in non-territorial terms. They have, for example, come to see themselves as members of a worldwide Christian community that they identify with as more powerful than either their regional or national communities (Robbins 1998). Convinced of the imminence of the second coming, they are also inclined to disregard "the things of this ground," and this too has led them away from identifying themselves in territorial terms. The "destruction" of their territory they hope for at the hands of Kennecott will be only a prelude to the complete earthly destruction of the last days. From this perspective, people's most salient identity is their Christian one. Territorial ties are at best transient. Yet as influential as all of these ideas have been in Urapmin thinking, they alone could not have effected their territorial detachment – just as their desire for development was not on its own capable of accomplishing this.[4] It is their Pentecostal belief that territorial attachments understood through ties to ancestors and nature spirits can be undone by Christian ritual that has allowed them to effect an attenuation of their bond to their territory. Ritual has provided the tool by which detachment has become in some respects real, helping to give their global imaginings a practical purchase on their still distinctly local lives.

Conclusion

The chapters in this volume primarily focus on the resiliency of territorial attachments in the face of economic globalization. Many of them demonstrate not only that globalization has failed to render territorial attachments a thing of the past, but also that such attachments continue to be a major source of conflict in the contemporary world. In relation to these themes, the case discussed here is doubly awkward. First, the Urapmin have by any usually accepted, hard-edged definition of economic globalization largely failed to globalize. Second, despite this failure they have, under the influence of those parts of globalization understood more broadly that they have experienced, reached a point where they are quite willing to give up their territory in order to realize the goals of economic change they have set for themselves. This chapter has explained how they have come to the point where they both want to and feel able to give up their territory. By way of concluding, it is worth considering how this case, despite its appearance of awkwardness, might raise points of comparative interest in relation to the volume's main themes.

A first point that it confirms is that, as Newman discusses, in studying territoriality it is important to pay attention to everyday forms of territorial attachment and, we might add, detachment. What are the practices through which attachment and detachment are made real in people's lives? Because religion is so important in the Urapmin case, I have focused on ritual means of relating people to territory. Given ritual's powerful ability to fix symbolic representations and stabilize social practices, this approach would likely prove fruitful in other cases as well.

The emphasis I have laid on detachment as a negotiation or process also raises issues of comparative relevance. Focusing on particular territorial decisions – decisions of the kind "should we fight to retain this territory" or "should we give up this territory to bring a conflict to an end" – does not tell us as much as we might hope about people's attachment to their territory. It does indicate the decision they will render to a particular question at a particular time, but it does not tell us whether their territorial bonds are in general weakening, becoming stronger, shifting their bases, etc. Anthropological research, with its commitments to detail and to the appreciation of the complexity of cultural phenomena, has the beneficial effect of reminding us that such questions about territorial process are important as well, and that answers to them can play a role in helping us predict the directions future deliberations might take.

There is, finally, the comparative question of how different religions might be shaping territorial processes throughout the world during the current era of globalization. There is no space here for a detailed examination of this issue. It is, however, important to a consideration of the comparative value of the Urapmin case to situate the kind of deterritorializing Christianity they practice in global terms. Pentecostal-style Christianity is currently the fastest growing branch of Protestantism and many predict that it will soon surpass Catholicism "to become the predominant form of Christianity of the 21st century" (Casanova 2001, 435; see also Jenkins 2002).[5] Its growth has been particularly explosive in areas outside of the West, where two-thirds of its 523 million adherents live and where the bulk of its 9 million yearly converts are made (Barrett and Johnson 2002, 284).[6] It has thus been one of the great success stories of the recent period of cultural globalization (Robbins 2004b).

The speed and extent of the spread of this style of Christianity has important implications for changing regimes of territoriality. I noted earlier that Christianity should be seen as falling on the weak end of a continuum of religious emphasis on territoriality and that Pentecostal Christianity represents the weakest end of the Christian part of this continuum. This means that in the many places Pentecostalism is spreading, it is promoting rituals of detachment similar to those practiced in Urapmin. As evidence of this, one can note that one of the most influential trends in contemporary Pentecostalism has been the growth of what is called "spiritual warfare." Spiritual warfare is in large measure aimed at eradicating the influence of "territorial spirits" in a fashion roughly familiar from this account of Urapmin practices. A large body of theological writing has been devoted to this topic, and it has led to the development of ritual techniques such as "spiritual mapping" to identify the spirits who control particular areas and "power encounter" rites that can be used to defeat the spirits so identified (DeBernardi 1999; Kraft 2002). The spiritual warfare movement has become a force throughout the global South and in North America and has likely had a deterritorializing effect on popular thinking similar to the one that related Pentecostal ideas and practices have had in Urapmin.

The deterritorializing thrust of this kind of popular religion may come as a surprise to many readers. Those whose interest is not primarily in religion are most likely to think about contemporary religious expressions of territoriality as they have developed in various kinds of fundamentalism. It is certainly true that media discussion of issues related to this topic routinely focus on Jewish, Christian, Hindu, Islamic, and other types of fundamentalism. In closing, then, it is worth underscoring how profoundly Pentecostal-style Christianity, which in the Christian world is growing at a pace that far outstrips that of its fundamentalist cousin, differs from fundamentalist religion on issues of territory. As Stump (2000) has demonstrated, fundamentalisms of all sorts tend to find their way into territorial conflicts of various kinds. This is so, he asserts, because of fundamentalists' commitment to this-worldly activism to defend themselves against perceived threats and their devotion to the cause of remaking the secular world in their own image. Fighting for these causes is crucial to the development of fundamentalist identities and success in them constitutes a key sign of religious success. Pentecostals, by contrast, find their identities and assurance of salvation in their receipt of the gifts of the Holy Spirit – gifts they can receive anywhere and while living in any kind of community. Combined with their practices of territorial detachment, the largely deterritorialized nature of Pentecostal identities and ritual practices is perhaps why, to this point, Pentecostals have not been involved in any high-profile territorial disputes. Looking at globalization from the vantage point of this type of religion, then, provides material for new ways of thinking about the potential role religion might play in the transformation of territorial regimes in the current global era.

NOTES

1 To avoid cluttering the text, I have not included terms in the Urap language or in the PNG lingua franca Tok Pisin in this chapter. All terms, phrases, or quotations that appear in single quotation marks are translated from one of these two languages.
2 The notion that humanity is what is at stake in the transactions the Urapmin undertake is not an overstatement or merely Western rhetoric. Though I cannot develop the point here in the detail that I have elsewhere (Robbins 2003), the Urapmin in part define spirits and the animals the spirits control as different from humans on the basis of their failure to participate fully in the gift economy.
3 Urapmin believe all adult deaths are the result of sorcery. One is only vulnerable to sorcery practiced by someone to whom one owes something (although often dead people's debts to the sorcerers who allegedly killed them are very small). Perhaps because children do not have debts in the way adults have them, they never die of sorcery but are instead killed by nature spirits punishing their own or their parents' breaches of taboo. In the early 1990s, the infant death rate in Urapmin was very high, approaching 50 percent, and thus this belief in the spiritual murder of children was often put to work to explain the way of the world.
4 Along with their hopes for development and the deterritorializing thrust of their Christian beliefs, one might, in light of Goemans' chapter in this volume, note a third possible factor influencing the growing Urapmin willingness to

detach themselves from their territory. This factor would be the current irrelevance of their territory to issues of collective defense. In the era of colonial and postcolonial peace, the Urapmin no longer organize for self-defense – a task they see as legitimately undertaken only by the state. Following Goemans' argument that the primary function of territorial attachment is to allow people to rationally organize for self-defense, the loss of this function would make territory less important among the Urapmin. I have not developed this argument here because it was not a focus of my research, and because matters of development and Christianity so dominate how Urapmin now talk about their own lives that they demand the kind of weight they are given here. I mention the possibility of making this argument, however, because I think it is important to note that the Urapmin case provides a further indication of the plausibility of Goemans' account of the factors leading to territorial attachment.

5 Pentecostal-style Christianity, as I am using the term here, refers to forms of Christianity in which people believe that the gifts of the Holy Spirit are widely available today. It includes those known as classical Pentecostals, as well as those often referred to as charismatics and members of third-wave churches (for more on terminology, see Robbins 2004b).

6 Statistics on the number of adherents to Pentecostal-style Christianity worldwide are difficult to validate. The 523-million figure represents the high end of commonly accepted reckonings. Conservative estimates put the figure at 250 million (Martin 2002, xvii). Regardless of which figures one accepts, there is no dispute over the claim that the spread of this form of Christianity has been very rapid and has introduced profound cultural changes in many areas.

4   The resilience of territorial conflict in an era of globalization

David Newman

Introduction

The analysis of territory as a changing focus for political power has moved beyond the exclusive confines of the geographic discipline during the past decade. The study of territory and borders now constitutes a multidisciplinary research focus, drawing in political scientists, sociologists, anthropologists, and legal experts, as they seek to understand the role of territory in the contemporary globalized world (Coakley 1993; Diehl 1999b; Dijkink and Knippenberg 2001). The globalist position argues that we are moving into a deterritorialized and borderless world. At the same time, the existence of ethnoterritorial conflicts reminds us that many groups continue to lay claim to specific pieces of territory in what could be described as a primordial, pre-modern, fashion. This raises questions concerning the functions and role of territory as part of the changing world political map. This chapter seeks to examine this resilience of territory as a factor of major political and functional significance, focusing on such contemporary cases as Israel–Palestine and the Balkans.

The territorial discourse within political geography has experienced a renaissance during the past two decades (Agnew 2000; Paasi 2002). An important framework for understanding the role of territory as a key factor in the political organization of space, and as a basis for the re-emergence of political geography as a bona fide discipline after three decades of shunning due to its "guilt by association" with the German school of Geopolitik (Newman 2002a),was provided by Edward Soja in what proved to be a seminal paper published by the Association of American Geographers in 1971 (Soja 1971). Soja identified three main functional realms of territorial organization – control over the distribution of resources, maintenance of order and authority, and the legitimization of order through societal integration (Soja 1971, 7). Problematically, Soja then goes on to re-evaluate the discussion of the political organization of space through studies of human group territoriality, explaining territorial confinement and exclusiveness through the comparison of human and animal territoriality that was in vogue at that time (Ardrey 1966; Lorenz 1966). Gottman's (1973) analysis of the "significance of territory" and Sack's (1986) discussion of the theory and history of human territoriality broadened the conceptual framework for understanding territorial behavior beyond the deterministic dimensions of territorial size and shape to the symbolic level through which the role of territory in the formation, rooting, and consolidation of group and national identities, as part of socially constructed "homeland" spaces, is developed. The explicit linking between states, national identity, and territory was further elaborated by the newly formed Commission on the World Political Map during the 1980s and 1990s (Knight 1994a; Hooson 1994; Herb and Kaplan 1999). This contrasts with the recent interest in territory from political scientists who have refocused their work around the tangible dimensions of territorial size, shape, and proximity to neighboring territories within an interstate framework (Diehl and Goertz 1988; Goertz and Diehl 1992; Kocs 1995; Huth 1996; Vasquez and Henehan 2001). Political geographers have also analyzed the intrastate role of state territorial ordering and spatial compartmentalization as constituting the political compartments within which control mechanisms are implemented and political hegemony is maintained (Murphy 1989; Taylor 1994). More recently, the traditional compartmentalization and fixed role of territory has been questioned by geographers seeking to restate the role of territory in a world experiencing rapid global change (Agnew 1994; Taylor 1995 and 1996). Recent work by geographers has presented a counternarrative to the deterritorialization discourse (Paasi 1996 and 2002; Pringle 1997). But while territory is shown to retain its relevance, it is accepted that we require a much deeper understanding of the complexities underlying territorial behavior than that offered by the traditional geographical discourse, and to some extent by the contemporary political science discourse, of fixed and rigidly bordered spaces.

This chapter seeks to discuss these wider implications of territorial behavior in the context of contemporary territorial conflict. The first section of the chapter deals, briefly, with the globalization–territory debate, summarizing the counter-deterritorialization discourse that has emerged in recent years. As part of the theoretical framework, we will also address the notion of territory as a dynamic factor in its own right, as contrasted with the traditional view of territory as constituting the static outcome of the political decision-making process. The main section of the chapter will address three dimensions of territorial behavior. The first concerns territorial scale. The political organization of space is not limited to notions of the state but is equally, perhaps even more importantly, impacted at the local and micro levels of daily behavior and practices. Second, the chapter will move away from the exclusive concern with the tangible and concrete dimensions of territory, such as size, shape, and proximity to neighboring states, in an attempt to broaden the discussion on territorial conflict through an analysis of the intangible and symbolic dimensions of territory, reflected through feelings of territorial attachment and belonging to particular places and spaces. Territory constitutes an important component of our individual, group, and national identities, not simply because our state territories are delimited by fixed boundaries but because territory has a symbolic dimension which determines our attachment and affiliation to particular spaces and places, attachments which are taught – consciously and subconsciously – through processes of political and territorial socialization. Third, any discussion of territory must, by association, be concerned with the role of borders and boundaries as the essential demarcators of territorial compartmentalization. Since we reject the absolute notion of deterritorialization (in favor of a continuing process of reterritorialization and changing territorial configurations of power) we must, by definition, reject the notion of a borderless world. At the same time, globalization has impacted the functions and relative permeability of boundaries, and this is reflected in the way that conflicts are played out in a hierarchy of territories – some of them more visible and tangible than others.

Theoretical framework: territoriality in a globalized world

The territorial structures and compartments which have, for the past few hundred years, formed a basic component of the state system are experiencing structural change (Agnew 1994; Murphy 1996). The impact of globalization and the changing nature of the world political order have raised major questions concerning the role of the nation-state and the way in which territory continues to define the spatial extent of sovereignty (Johnston 1995; Taylor 1994 and 1995). Notions of a "borderless world" and political "deterritorialization" are seen as signaling a new world order in which the territorial component in world affairs is of much reduced significance. From the outset it should be stated that this chapter rejects the notion of deterritorialization, in the sense that there cannot be any form of political power or social control that is totally divorced from some form of territorial compartmentalization. We do accept the notion that territorial configurations of power are constantly changing, and the impact of globalization has affected these changes more substantially than simply changing the spatial configurations or boundary demarcations of states. The globalization discourse has resulted in a more subtle understanding of the multidimensional, and dynamic, components of territory as a mechanism through which society is bordered, ordered, and controlled (Albert et al. 1999). Territorial ordering remains an essential component of human behavior. We seek to control the spaces within which we live, to make them as exclusive as possible, and this is as true of the state spaces within which "our" groups practice sovereignty and political control as it is of the municipal and neighborhood spaces within which we attempt to influence quality of life characteristics, and as it is of our desire to control and defend our private and personal spaces.

Reterritorialization, as contrasted with deterritorialization, is the process through which territorial configurations of power are continually ordered and reordered. It is not something new. It has been taking place continuously as new states are created and others are vanquished. At certain times, such as the periods following the two world wars or the break-up of the Soviet Union, the tangible territorial reconfiguration and restructuring of the world political map has provided us with "new world orders," contingent on specific political events. Where contemporary globalization has impacted this process over and beyond the normal patterns of territorial change has been at the structural-technological level, with the global flow of capital and cyberspace changing the traditional functions of territorial fixation and border permeability. Here too, globalization is geographically differentiated – it affects some regions and not others. Thus, while borders are becoming more permeable in Western Europe, they are being constructed in other places, not least in those places where ethnoterritorial conflict remains the order of the day. Equally, while territories and virtual spaces impact the ordering process for much of the Western industrialized world, territorial rigidity remains the order of the day in those regions where levels of technology are relatively low and where states jealously stand guard over the fixed barriers separating their physical space from that of the neighboring regime.

The territorial compartments within which we live and carry out our daily life practices, some of them with fixed state or administrative boundaries, some of them with invisible and perceived borders (see below), constitute the essential spatial compartments of the hierarchical ordering process. The "territorial trap" (Agnew 1994) is the trap of fixed territories, while the end of "territorial absolutism" (Taylor 1996) is the transition from a static notion of territory to one that has its own internal dynamics of change. Neither of these concepts signals an "end to territory" or a deterritorialized world. Recognizing the territorial imperative as a dynamic factor in its own right means that a deeper understanding of the territorial factor in its diverse forms is more, rather than less, complex, if we are to come to grips with its role in contemporary ethnoterritorial conflict.[1]

Territory, in its classic geographical sense, is generally perceived as being the static outcome of the political process. Borders are demarcated, territory is allocated between groups or nations, and cartographers create fixed images of the territorial configuration of the state at a given point in time. Territory is perceived as an unchanging element or, at the most, an element that undergoes modifications in shape or size as a result of wars, accretions, cessions, or even earthquakes. In its most traditional sense, the physical attributes of territory have formed a deterministic frame for decision-making, with such notions as "natural" borders or "strategic topography" being viewed as the key territorial criteria impacting political and military decision-making.

It is this static, and largely outdated, notion of territory that has been challenged by the globalization discourse. Territory is dynamic in the sense that territorial change creates new spatial realities, which are, in turn, fed back into the political and decision-making processes. The construction of settlements, the superimposition of borders of separation, or – on a totally different scale – the allocation of development resources to one region at the expense of another, creates new socio-spatial landscapes, which become rooted in reality. Equally, the naming of landscapes according to the semantics of a particular ethnic group (such as the Hebraization of the Palestine landscape, the Polandization of the Silesian landscape, or the Albanization of the Kosovan landscape) creates territorial realities, which, after the passing of no more than one generation, become transformed into the territorial and cartographic "facts." These are the realities, which are then fed into the next round of decision-making on the part of political elites. Whether or not they can be justified from an ethical or historical perspective often becomes irrelevant in the face of power relations, as new attachments and affiliations to a new socially constructed homeland landscape become the contemporary reality. The resolution of ethnoterritorial conflicts is, more often than not, resolved around these contemporary realities, a continuation of the *uti possidetis* principle which came into being with the Westphalian state system and which, despite all globalization impacts, has not disappeared along with the nation-state (Castellino and Allen 2003).

Historical claims to sovereignty, especially those based on priority considerations, are used as part of the political polemic and the need to self-justify the territorial claim in the face of a counter-claim. But it is generally the contemporary political and territorial realities that serve as the basis for bargaining and compromise between states seeking conflict resolution.

Ethnoterritorial conflict in a globalized world

Ethnoterritorial conflicts exist in our globalized world. Moreover, some of them exist at the geographic margins of those regions from where emanates much of the globalization/deterritorialization argument. Some contemporary conflict regions, such as Cyprus, the Balkans, and Israel–Palestine, are all part of the expanding European ecumene. One of them, Cyprus, became part of the enlarged European Union in 2004, while the Balkan countries see themselves as candidates for inclusion in the EU within the next decade. Israel–Palestine borders the expanded EU (it now shares a maritime boundary with Cyprus) and enjoys special cultural and trading relations with the Community. It would therefore be too simple to attribute the existence of "primordial" ethnoterritorial conflict only to those regions that have not yet been affected by globalization or which are located at great distances from the core of the globalization/deterritorialization heartland. Territory remains contested where ethnic and national groups compete for power, where they seek the implementation of self-government, where they display high levels of spatial segregation, regional concentration, and territorial homogeneity, and where they continue to feel threatened by the "other" national group, such that participatory forms of power sharing are not perceived as guaranteeing them the political rights or physical safety they desire (Yiftachel 2001a).

Territorial scale, power relations, and control mechanisms

While public discourse tends to focus on the national scale of territorial conflict, such as the demarcation of state borders or the relationships between neighboring states, the vast majority of people are affected at the local and micro scales of territorial behavior. This is as true of the local territorial behavior with respect to daily life practices, such as municipal, health, and education districting and competition for scarce resources, as it is of the way in which national and ethnic conflicts are played out at this level through processes of spatial segregation, separation, and mutual exclusion.

We do not normally think about the impact of ethnonational conflicts at the local and micro levels of territorial analysis. Notions such as municipal government and the provision of public services are not normally associated with the national conflicts that take place between states and national groups. We have assumed an almost artificial distinction between the various levels of scale analysis, which are also reflected in the specific types of conflict that are perceived as belonging to each scale. National conflicts are about political power, self-determination, and sovereignty, while local conflicts are about municipal government, public services, and resource distribution, as though the latter have little to do with the former.

This form of binary separation between territorial scale and political functions is challenged in this chapter. It is precisely at the local levels of territorial behavior that some of the ethnic and national conflicts have their strongest impact, as rivalries are played out through the daily life practices of segregated groups residing within their own distinct urban neighborhoods, or in mono-ethnic villages and towns. Notions of homeland are translated into neighborhood turfs, where ethnic groups create their own distinct and homogeneous cultural spaces, send their own representatives to the local municipalities, and compete for resources along distinct ethnic and sectoral interests. Equally, urban neighborhoods have their own borders which are not normally crossed unless absolutely essential. These borders do not necessarily reflect the formal administrative division of the urban area into municipal subregions, not least because populations are much more dynamic and mobile than are municipal governments. Such borders may be perceived; they do not necessarily have clear demarcators. They may be based around highways or other transportation arteries within the city. But for those who reside within the segregated neighborhoods, they exist as lines beyond which people do not purchase a house, undertake economic transactions, or undertake other routine activities for fear of being in an unfamiliar and threatening space. The borders of ethnoterritorial ghettos do not have to be fixed, nor do they require physical delimitation elements such as walls or fences, but they are resilient in that they facilitate the processes of inclusion and exclusion through which territories and spaces retain their spatial homogeneity. In places of extreme ethnoterritorial conflict, forced segregation results from "ethnic cleansing," creating patterns of spatial homogeneity that become irreversible, regardless of the ethical issues involved.

Ethnoterritorial conflicts express themselves through processes of residential segregation. Conflicting groups reside within separate housing blocks, separate neighborhoods, and separate villages and townships, and each, respectively, constitutes majorities or minorities within separate regions and locales. Retaining territorial demographic homogeneity is a major factor in the perpetuation of ethnoterritorial conflict, if only because separation enables the maintenance of a system of control to be practiced by ethnic leaders, facilitated through processes of bordering, ordering, and managerialism. The role of managers acting as social gatekeepers to the housing market has been well documented in the planning literature.[2] Attributed to both the public and private sectors, the managerialist thesis attributed patterns of ethnoterritorial homogeneity to the influence of political and economic groups who have the power to mold spaces and territories according to their own interests. Within the private sector, housing realtors and real-estate agents can determine the type of residents who will be able to purchase housing in particular neighborhoods – either enforcing existing patterns of segregation through selling to the "right type of person" only, or facilitating the mass change of the ethnic and social composition of an entire neighborhood by enabling the gradual infiltration of "undesirable" people (defined in a variety of ethnic, social, and class terms) into what was considered a more exclusive neighborhood. The economic benefits for the realtors of maintaining segregation and/or facilitating wholesale territorial change are considerable. In homogeneous neighborhoods, incoming residents may be prepared to pay significantly higher prices to live among people of "their own kind," while the wholesale change of the ethnic or social composition of a neighborhood within a relatively short time period also ensures substantial economic gains for the private real estate managers.

While this may be understandable behavior within the private sector, the same tendencies are to be found within the public housing sector. The managerialist ideology of public housing agents, determining the criteria of who is eligible for subsidized housing, where such neighborhoods are to be constructed in the first place, and the level of social services and infrastructure to be provided, is an important factor determining the social and ethnic composition of densely populated microspaces. Even within these lower socio-economic and poverty neighborhoods, ethnic differentiation is often maintained between local and immigrant populations, as each attempts to maintain its own territorial homogeneity. Nowhere is this more evident today than in the public housing neighborhoods of Western Europe, as Muslim and Christian populations maintain their own residential segregation, shunning each other's neighborhoods and housing blocks and, as a result, creating an even greater sense of mutual misunderstanding and mistrust, spurred on by the interests of sectoral political leaders.

Even in those places where the more blatant elements of extreme conflict are absent, people who do not "belong" are made to feel uncomfortable and, sooner or later, choose to leave the neighborhood. Managerial practices are effective in changing or perpetuating the conditions of ethnoterritorial residential homogeneity through the creation of demand and supply criteria based on the desire for residential proximity and playing on the fear of difference. The perceived neighborhood and settlement borders have as powerful an impact on spatial practices as do the physical delimiters of fences and walls in determining the patterns of territorial exclusion.[3]

Micro levels of territorial contestation are visible in almost all situations of ethnoterritorial and national conflict. In the Balkans, Kosovans, Macedonians, Serbians, and Albanians live in distinctly separate mono-ethnic communities. Within towns that were once partially mixed, minority populations have either been driven out, or they reside within their own urban neighborhoods. The importance of the microterritorial dimension of the Israel–Palestine conflict is reflected in the residential segregation of Jews and Arabs in their own communities and villages, and in segregated neighborhoods inside "mixed" Jewish–Arab towns. It is expressed within the planning and legislative apparatus, which favors the zoning and development plans of the dominant national group over the subordinate (Coon 1992). It is also expressed through the unequal distribution of resources to ethnic communities and municipal authorities, which explains the highly differentiated levels of urban and rural development experienced in neighboring Jewish and Arab settlements respectively. Israelis and Palestinians reside in separate regions, separate villages and towns, while in the so-called "mixed" towns they reside in separate neighborhoods (Gonen 1995). The competition for resources between the neighborhoods takes on a clear ethnic pattern, as majority groups (in terms of power relations and not necessarily demographic majorities) determine patterns of development and zoning to the benefit of their own affiliates as part of the broader territorial conflict (Falah 1996a; Yiftachel and Yacobi 2003). The statutory planning authorities provide a powerful mechanism of territorial control, usually representing the interests of the state and its policies relating to majority–minority power relations and systems of control.

Under conditions of territorial residential homogeneity and segregation spurred on by conflict and contestation, groups operate within parallel and dual spaces of interactivity. Territory enforces and strengthens intergroup separation, as members of competing groups attend their own cultural institutions and places of worship, shop in their own commercial centers, and generally avoid meeting members of the "other" group, unless there is no other choice. The "no choice" option normally occurs under conditions of dominant–subordinate relations, where the subordinate group has no choice but to engage in economic transactions (such as Palestinians finding employment within the Israeli marketplace) or where there is a clear benefit to be derived (such as Israelis seeking a cheaper option for the purchase of services or goods within the Palestinian sector). But even this latter option is conditional on the extent to which any individual experiences the sense of threat or fear when crossing into the territory of the "other" group, in which case the potential economic benefit is outweighed by the potential safety cost. The geography of fear within the smallest of territories can be experienced in the existence of separate transportation systems (in Jerusalem for instance, the East Palestinian and West Jewish parts of the city have their own separate bus systems, while taxi drivers mostly operate within one part of the city exclusively).[4] Similar geographies of fear are experienced in Belfast through the complete separation of social activities, clubs, and, that most important of places of interaction, the pub. Catholics and Protestants maintain almost exclusive territorial separation in their daily lives, strengthening the mutual sense of mistrust and perceptions of fear and threat.

Attempts to resolve territorial conflicts also require a deeper understanding of the local dimensions of territorial behavior and segregation. Patterns of inter-ethnic interaction at the micro level are directly affected by the outcome of peace negotiations, though they do not normally appear on the negotiation agenda. In virtually all such conflicts, existing patterns of ethnonational segregation encourage even greater separation in homogeneous and exclusive national territories, contrasting strongly with the political polemics and public statements of leaders with utopian notions of future cooperation, integration, and normalization of relations. This is often based around the notion of "good fences creating good neighbors," especially in situations where the securitization discourse (the desire to feel safe and secure from the threat posed by the "other") determines the nature of the conflict-resolution agreements.

Thus territorial compartmentalization and the segregation of ethnic groups results from, and contributes to, conflict and mutual antagonism. Segregation and physical separation may promote the immediate territorial objectives of conflict resolution but it does not contribute to longer-term normalization. The segregation "mentality" itself promotes the continued separation and compartmentalization of ethnic groups into separate national entities (Waterman 2002). The desire to retain separate spaces in peace agreements hinders the achievement of cooperation and normalization of relations. In other cases, economic integration has proved to be the first step toward increased levels of inter-ethnic interaction, although this often takes place as part of a system of dominant–subordinate economic relations (Blacks in the white towns in South Africa, or Palestinians in the Israeli workplace) or as the construction of artificial "joint" workplaces (Protestant–Catholic factories along the Shankill Divide in Belfast where Protestants and Catholics enter from different sides, or the "peace parks" planned for the border areas between Israel and a Palestinian state (Kliot 2002)). While such localized solutions may promote inter-ethnic interaction, they only affect a small minority of the people. They also constitute obstacles to greater interaction, excluding members of the "other" group from working anywhere other than these special areas where they feel secure from the perceived threat posed by the former belligerent. The geography of exclusion continues to be a major factor determining patterns and intensity of contact or separation between protagonists (Sibley 1995). Specially constructed "joint" facilities send out a message that entry is limited to a new micro border landscape. Entry beyond the border into the homogeneous and segregated territories of ethnic exclusion is not considered part of the process through which normalization of inter-ethnic relations can occur.

The symbolic and non-tangible dimensions of territorial behavior

As noted in the introduction to this chapter, much of the recent discussion on territorial conflict has focused on the concrete and tangible dimensions of state territories (size, shape, topography, and so on) and their proximity to neighboring states as explanatory factors for the existence of conflict under certain conditions. This is a deterministic approach which has largely ignored the essential symbolic dimensions of territorial attachment experienced by residents of specific territories, for whom issues of border location or resource exploitation vis-à-vis neighboring states are only secondary to their feelings of "belonging" and rootedness within specific places and spaces. It is their readiness to defend their "homeland" territories to which they lay claim through historical priority (which group can trace its roots back to an earlier date) or duration (which of the groups can demonstrate continuous residence over a longer and uninterrupted period of time) that explains much territorial conflict (Burghardt 1973; Murphy 1990 and 2002). Processes of political and territorial socialization have helped create national identities within which territory forms a major component of identity construction. Homeland territories are special places, the location of historical and mythical events in the nation's history, imbued with exclusive significance, constituting the core of the self-determination experience. Ethnoterritorial conflicts demonstrate that it is much more difficult to share territory than it is to share power (although the two are often parallel processes). If a particular place is part of my historical narrative, then it cannot be, at one and the same time, part of your historical or national experience. At the symbolic level, political territories are mutually exclusive. This primordial attachment to territory lies at the root of much contemporary ethnoterritorial conflict, even for people who operate within a global and transboundary world, but for whom the "homeland" territory remains central to their own ethnic and national identities.

Diaspora attachment to homeland territory is, paradoxically, often the strongest. Whereas a group (and its descendants) who reside outside the homeland territory might be expected to have a weaker link to it, diaspora groups often express strong attachment to the core territory. In times of conflict, diaspora groups frequently take on even more extreme stances than the home population itself. As Lyons shows (Lyons, this volume), conflicts in the homeland often rely on support from diaspora groups in the form of political lobbying and/or the raising of finance. Diaspora groups are not prepared to relinquish territory or make compromises over the homeland spaces. Territory, for them, is an essential part of the way in which a distant national belonging is maintained, expressed in many cases through the myth of territorial history rather than the realities of the contemporary period. Some of the most radical supporters of the irredentist "Greater Land of Israel" idea and supporters of the West Bank settlement movement are the orthodox Jewish groups in North America – especially in Brooklyn and Toronto – who even demonstrate against Israeli political leaders on their visits to North America because these leaders are prepared to cede territory for the sake of peace and constitute, in the eyes of the diaspora superpatriots, traitors to the national cause.

But globalization has affected the attachment of diaspora groups to territory in two contrasting ways. In the first place, diaspora groups are now able to visit their ancestral territories more easily than in the past owing to improved mobility and transportation. They also possess much more information on the "state of the nation" because of the free availability of information. For some, this strengthens the bond with a territory that was, until recently, an abstract and distant concept, while for others the mythical uniqueness of the homeland territory takes on a more concrete image – a place to travel to, to visit family, and perhaps to do business. This is part of the general way in which globalization has impacted the significance of diaspora communities and the way in which these communities are currently undergoing a process of re-evaluation and internal restructuring.

In this respect, Zionism as a political movement constituted a unique form of territorial behavior. Although it cannot be divorced from the era of nationalism in which it emerged at the end of the nineteenth and beginning of the twentieth centuries, Zionism, unlike the other national movements of the time, focused on a place from which its adherents had been territorially detached for almost two thousand years. There was no clear place for the realization of Jewish nationalism (as contrasted with Jewish emancipation and equality) within the main Jewish residential concentrations of Central and Eastern Europe. These were all territories laid claim to by local populations claiming their own territorial sovereignty and independence. The term "Zionism" was itself an abstract form of territorial affiliation, referring to the ancient Jewish homeland in Palestine, a mythical land that could be located within a geographic reality. Early Zionist leaders rejected the idea of Uganda as an alternative territory on which an independent state could be established because this was not part of the homeland. To this day, notions of ancestral homeland, as derived from Biblical, Jewish, and Israelite history, are part of the contemporary political discourse used by some groups to explain why they refuse to relinquish territory as part of a peace agreement, why this territory constitutes, for them, the very core of contemporary Israeli national identity.

Attachment to territory is based around the identification of symbols and signs in the landscape, as well as the creation of territorial histories and myths that reflect the singular importance of one piece of territory over any other. Simply being present is often not sufficient when making competing claims for territory. Within the frame of national consciousness, we are subject to strong processes of territorial socialization, the aim of which is to emphasize the importance of "our" territory as a key element in personal and group identity, "the acquisition of identity with a political area" (Duchacek 1970; Paasi 1995 and 1996). A particularly acute form of symbolic attachment to territory concerns the use of "sacred" or "holy" spaces. The religious attachment to the land is much more than the construction of political homelands. The inherent belief that the land was given to a specific people by divine promise makes it the most intangible of all features. Notions of geopiety express an almost reverential and devotional attachment to the land, as history, myth, and religion become interwoven in a complex relationship between the residents of a particular piece of territory, which they believe has been given to them by divine right.[5] As expressed by the territorial irredentists and settlers within the Israel–Palestine context, most of whom draw their territorial maximalist ideology from their religious beliefs that this land was promised to them by a divine being, the cession of territory is akin to tearing a limb from a living body or organism. This territorial metaphor is even stronger given the fact that the contested territory – the West Bank (or in the Biblical terminology of the territorial irredentists, Judea and Samaria) – is, in their eyes, more central to the historical experience of the Jewish people than are those territories which constitute the spatial core of the modern state and which are not contested by the Palestinian–Arab population, such as the metropolitan core of the Tel Aviv–Gush Dan region along the Mediterranean coast. This is the land "promised" to the Jewish people by God and, as such, it simply does not feature as part of the normative discussion of tangible goods over which compromises can be made. At the same time, in an attempt to attract greater support for the cause of territorial maximalism, the religious settlers promote the tangible argument of securitization, rather than the intangible argument of religion and belief, as this speaks to a wider stratum of Israeli society. Security is an argument with which many identify, even if they have no religious beliefs.

Territorial semantics and narratives are important components in this debate. Within Israel–Palestine, the concept of the "whole" of the West Bank has different meanings for each national group. The Palestinians' claim to the "whole" of the West Bank effectively means relinquishing any historical claims to the rest of Palestine, the Israel that makes up over two-thirds of Mandate Palestine. This is a minimalist demand for them and explains their opposition to the continued existence of even one Israeli settlement established in this region after 1967. For most Israelis, the notion of the "whole" of the West Bank is perceived as a maximal demand. Thus, for Israelis, the symbolic and tangible territorial debates focus on the West Bank and Gaza Strip alone, whereas for Palestinians the tangible debate focuses on the West Bank, while the symbolic debate still focuses on all of pre-1948 Palestine. For Israelis, claiming the "whole" of this territory is seen as maximalist and indicative of further territorial claims in the future, while for the Palestinians it is inconceivable that having "given up" on two-thirds of the territory, they should be asked to make further concessions on the West Bank.

The exclusive attachment to territory reflects in the naming and renaming of places and locations in accordance with the historic and religious sites associated with the dominant political group. Not only did the outflow of Palestinian refugees bring about a change in the

Jewish–Arab demographic ratios, but it also brought about the replacement of an Arab–Palestinian landscape with a Jewish–Israeli landscape (Falah 1996b; Benveniste 2000). The names of abandoned villages disappeared from the map and these were replaced with alternative Hebrew names, while new Israeli settlements were called after incidents and people from ancient Jewish or modern Israeli history (Cohen and Kliot 1981 and 1992). Israeli settlements throughout the West Bank have taken on Biblical names associated with the specific sites as a means of expressing the Jewish "priority" in these places and the exclusive nature of the territorial attachment. The means by which new landscapes are created which replace or obliterate former landscapes are, in turn, transformed into the new concrete political realities on the ground.

While the concrete manifestation of territory, either as an economic resource or as a strategic asset, can be quantified by each side to the conflict, this is not the case with the symbolic dimension. For participants in ethnoterritorial conflicts, their respective territorial claims are rooted in their perceptions of exclusive ancestral homelands, filled with sites, locations, and myths that form an integral part of their national identity. As territory becomes the focus of competing claims, the conflict participants imbue specific sites with historic and religious importance, often through the use of historical and archaeological narratives, as a means of proving priority or duration and exclusive belonging to the territory in question (Burghardt 1973). Scholarly research within certain disciplines, such as history, geography, archaeology, and anthropology, is used as a means of "proving" the prior or exclusive attachment of one people to a specific piece of territory. The social construction of knowledge reflects power hegemonies within the state, between majority and minority populations, and in the way in which certain territory-related research topics are given preference by public sector funding agencies.[6]

Symbolic and metaphysical attachment to territory, defined as intangible or relational values by others, can often be the most critical forms of attachment in determining actual policy decisions with respect to territorial claims. It has been argued that territorial changes with high relational importance are the most likely to involve violence (Goertz and Diehl 1992), as indeed is the case with respect to the West Bank ("the historic and religious heartland of the ancient Land of Israel") or Jerusalem ("the eternal capital of the Jewish people, never again to be divided"). This is consistent with the logic that indicates that conflict resolution is less likely when issues are less tangible or divisible, when territories are perceived as exclusively "belonging" to one group of people and that all others are usurpers (Vasquez 1983; Fearon 1994).

Given the strong notion of homeland attachment, it is difficult to analyze the nature of territorial conflict and, by association, conflict resolution through concepts relating to economic value (Simmons, this volume) or through a statistical analysis of border length, territorial proximity, or shape and size of states.[7] For conflict resolution to be attainable, it is necessary to deal with the symbolic and emotional dimensions of the territorial attachment, the zero-sum characteristics (it "all" belongs to me), before bartering can take place at the level of the tangible and the concrete dimensions of the negotiations process. It is necessary to gradually transform the public discourse surrounding the conflict from the level of the symbolic to the tangible, to make the language of conflict resolution more familiar and less threatening to the public at large so that they can accept the compromises which are made on their behalf by political leaders.

The inability of Israelis and Palestinians to reach an acceptable territorial compromise is due in no small part to the cognitive dissonance between the leaders' willingness to compromise over the tangible dimensions of territory and boundaries, and the unwillingness of their respective domestic constituencies to relinquish what they perceive to be the symbolic heartlands of the national identity, particularly Jerusalem. Thus, it is not surprising that the Camp David summit in 2000, intended to bring about a final agreement between both sides, collapsed when two of the most symbolic issues, Jerusalem and right of return for Palestinian refugees, were put on the negotiating table.

Focusing on the symbolic and attachment characteristics of territorial behavior does not mean that we should ignore, altogether, the tangible – often deterministic – dimensions of territory. The securitization and economic discourses are the main components around which conflict resolution is achieved. But if the symbolic factors remain a central part of the public discourse, this can prevent political leaders from negotiating over the tangible issues. The public discourse has to be transformed, as much as possible, from the symbolic to the tangible – as has been the case with respect to sensitive issues such as Jerusalem (from an "eternal city" discourse to one which focuses on a metropolitan area which has Israeli and Palestinian neighborhoods and which can be divided along municipal lines) or Palestinian refugees (from an "inalienable right of return" discourse to one which focuses on compensation and alternative housing solutions). In addition, the cases referred to in this chapter (Cyprus, Balkans, Israel–Palestine) are all states whose territorial size is small. The contestation for territorial control and hegemony is more acute, the scarcer the territorial resource. Territorial conflict can take place over a few square meters of land, such as the Temple Mount/Western Wall in the Old City of Jerusalem, the steps leading up to the Coptic Church, or the tomb of Rachel in Bethlehem. In such cases, the symbolic dimensions of the conflict are highlighted, often as part of social construction on the part of the political elites, as a means of socializing the population into rallying around the national cause, and also as a means of "justifying" the exclusive claim to control to the international community.

Territorial compartmentalization, conflict, and borders

By definition, any form of territorial ordering requires the existence of a border or a boundary. Boundaries may have become more permeable than in the past, but they remain the hard lines that determine the territorial extent of the state and, by definition, the citizenship of those residing therein. Notwithstanding the "borderless world" discourse, the hard boundaries separating states in the international system remain important delimiters of power and partial sovereignty in the contemporary world (Newman and Paasi 1998; Kolossov and O'Loughlin 1998; Newman 2003). But borders, like territory, have to be seen from their role as "impactor," rather than simply "impacted," as a dynamic factor in their own right. As such, it is the process of bordering, rather than the course of the line per se, which is important to our understanding of how boundaries affect the nature of interaction, cooperation, and/or conflict between peoples (Van Houtum 2002).

Border studies have come a long way during the past decade. From the study of the hard territorial line separating states within the international system, much of the contemporary study of borders now focuses on the process of bordering, through which territories and peoples are respectively included or excluded within a hierarchical network of groups, affiliations, and identities. The lines that are borders are as flexible as they were once thought to be rigid, reflecting new territorial and aspatial patterns of human behavior. While modern technologies, particularly cyberspace, have made the barrier role of borders redundant in some areas, they have also served to create new sets of borders and boundaries, enclosing groups with common identities and interests who are dispersed throughout the globe, lacking any form of territorial compactness or contiguity.

Part of the transformation in border studies has been the recognition that borders are institutions, as contrasted to simply lines in the sand or on the map (Paasi 1998). This takes the study of borders/boundaries beyond the notion of "settled boundaries" (Simmons, this volume), leading us almost automatically to assume that the fact that most of the world's territorial boundaries have long been demarcated and are only infrequently the cause of major political instability, tensions, or conflict is sufficient proof that territory is of no great significance in a globalized world. Institutions are the frameworks through which political power is expressed and through which control is practiced. As such, borders remain an important part of that control mechanism – notably through their functions rather than their physical location per se. Like all institutions, borders have their own set of internal rules that govern their behavior, much of which becomes self-perpetuating and resistant to change. Border institutions govern the extent of inclusion and exclusion, the degree of permeability, the laws governing transboundary movement – exit from one side of the border and entry into the other side.

Institutions change in one of two ways. Either the rules and regulations governing their behavior are changed by those groups who make policy decisions, through built-in adaptive mechanisms such as internal auditing; or there is grass-roots change from below which challenges the continued existence of the functional norms of the institution. Since institutions are self-perpetuating and resistant to change, it often requires an increase in levels of transboundary interaction on the ground for the norms and regulations to undergo any formal process of change. Most border studies have focused on the government-imposed status of the border and its associated management mechanisms. This is partly because of the control function which is attributed to state territoriality, a function that can only be implemented through government practices when there are clearly defined borders that determine the parameters within which policies of control are shaped (Taylor 1994). The "end of territorial absolutism" means an end to the absolute control exercised by the State through practices of fixed territoriality. Thus governments are reluctant to relinquish control of the borders unless there is pressure from outside (globalization) or from below (localization). To study borders as dynamic institutions, it is therefore important to study the "bottom-up" process of change, emanating from the daily functional patterns of the ordinary people living in the borderland region, as much as the traditional "top-down" approach which focuses solely on the role of institutional actors, notably – but not only – governments (Kaplan and Häkli 2002).

The essence of a border is to separate the "self" from the "other." As such, one of the major functions of a border is to act as a barrier, "protecting" "us insiders" from "them outsiders" (Oommen 1995; Sibley 1995). They prevent the entry of undesired elements – be they people, goods, arms, drugs, or – albeit to a much lesser extent than in the past – information. The determination of just what can and cannot move beyond the border is a function of how the power elites of a given society or country view the border as an institution which protects those who are on the "inside" or are "here" from the (perceived) negative impact of those who have been excluded and are on the "outside" or are "there." The protection function takes on many forms – at the primordial level protecting the citizens of a country from invasion by foreign armies or from the inflow of illegal weapons across the border. The barrier function of borders also protects those inside from other "harmful" elements, such as drugs, migrant labor, competition in the marketplace, and so on. Cultural borders offer protection against infiltration of values which are not compatible with the hegemonic practices of the majority, be they social and economic status, religious affiliation, and/or residential homogeneity.

The existence of borders enables us to maintain some sort of order, both within the spaces and groups which are thus encompassed, as well as between "our" compartment and that of the "other" groups and spaces which are part of a broader system of global ordering (Albert et al. 2001; Van Houtum and Naerssen 2002). Territorial borders performed precisely this function under the Westphalian state system, where the principle of *uti possidetis* ensured the maintenance of interstate order through the mutual recognition and acceptance of territorial integrity and, hence, the notion of territorial sovereignty (Castellino and Allen 2003). The process of territorial ordering was imposed upon the political landscape by the power elites of the time, just as it was implemented during the era of decolonization, and just as it is today by those groups who determine the values and codes which enable some to be members, while others have to remain outside. Thus the bordering process creates order through the construction of difference, whereby "others" are expected to respect the rights of the self, if only because they desire their own rights to be respected in the same way, or because the nature of power relations is such that they have no alternative.

But borders are equally there to be crossed. From the moment they are established, there are always groups who have an interest in finding ways to move beyond the barrier. There is always an aspiration to cross borders into the forbidden, and often invisible, spaces on the other side of the wall, although at one and the same time we do not want the "others" to cross the boundaries into our own recognizable and familiar world. Difference is okay if we determine the rules of belonging. It is unacceptable if it is determined by someone else. Thus borders are sometimes imposed from the outside and sometimes from the inside.

Minorities are often as keen to prevent the majority from "coming in" as majorities are to prevent the minority from "breaking out." This is as true of the state as it is of ethnic and ghetto neighborhoods, and as it is of the personal spaces and borders that are perceived and created around the individual.

International boundaries are the legacy of contemporary state formation. Despite the opening of boundaries in Western Europe, the territorial legacy of partition, division, and boundary superimposition remains a prominent component in the world political map. All resulted from, or gave rise to, conflict at one stage. Many have been resolved peacefully over time, while others remain the source of ongoing conflict and ethnoterritorial tensions, claims, and counter-claims. The legacy of boundary superimposition is still evident in much contemporary territorial conflict, in Africa (Peninou 1998; Daniel 2000; Griggs 2000; Lemon 2002), Iraq–Turkey–Iran and the Kurdish homeland (Cizre 2001), and the Balkans (Englefield 1992; Klemencic 2000 and 2001). Problems of partition and division remain critical in Israel–Palestine, Northern Ireland, India–Pakistan, and North–South Korea (Fraser 1984; Waterman 1987 and 1996; Samaddar et al. 2004). The re-emergence of states in Central and Eastern Europe since the early 1990s has focused around existing boundaries, some of which were state boundaries in the past and were subsumed as internal administrative boundaries during the periods of Soviet or Yugoslavian rule, respectively (Forsberg 1995; Kolossov 1998; Motyl 2001). These boundaries have maintained their function as the prior demarcators of ethnic and national groups within the pre-existing territorial compartments. In short, the legacy of international boundary formation remains a central component in contemporary ethnoterritorial conflict.

Increasingly, issues of identity lie at the root of boundary conflicts as much as, if not more than, the extent to which the demarcation of the line enables one state to control valuable and scarce natural resources – such as water, oil, and minerals (Newman 2004). Where territorial lines cross both the resource and identity interface at one and the same time, the potential for boundary conflict is greatest, since minority groups do not necessarily benefit from the potential economic benefits of the natural resources. The demarcation, delimitation, and ultimate location of boundaries are a function of power relations. They will reflect the patterns of ethnic distribution where they serve the interests of the state(s). Otherwise, they will cut across ethnic areas, as in the Balkans or in the Kurdish areas of Iran, Iraq, and Turkey, creating ethnoterritorial minorities and subordinate populations. Rarely do the territorial borders of the state coincide with the identity borders of the national group and, as mobility of peoples increases, their function in determining national territories will become less significant.

The Israel–Palestine conflict is a good example of where the ethno-national conflict is expressed through the demarcation and imposition of boundaries – real and perceived – at the local level (Newman 1998b and 2002c; Falah 1997; Falah and Newman 1995). The "Green Line" boundary was superimposed upon the Israel–Palestine landscape as a result of Israel's War of Independence and the ensuing armistice talks between Israel and Jordan in 1948–49 (Brawer 1990 and 2002). The single functional landscape was divided into two politico-territorial entities, the one becoming the State of Israel, the other becoming known as the West Bank and remaining under Jordanian administration until Israel conquered this area in the Six-Day War of 1967. Since 1967, the West Bank has remained an occupied territory, while the Green Line boundary has remained an administrative line of separation. The recent unilateral establishment of the separation fence/wall by the Israeli government has refocused the conflict around the issues of territorial demarcation and the functional impact that the construction of a border will have on Israeli–Palestinian relations even after the implementation of a peace agreement.

The Green Line functioned as a sealed and armed boundary of confrontation for only nineteen years. While its barrier effects were removed in 1967, it has remained in place as an effective administrative boundary until the present, largely because Israel did not annex the occupied territories, retaining a clear distinction between the sovereign Israel and the administrative status of the West Bank, and between their respective populations. The "facts" that are the Green Line and settlements have had a major impact on the thinking of negotiators. The default cartographic image carried around by most Israelis and Palestinians is of a region separated into an Israel and a West Bank, with the line of separation at the Green Line. That this line did not reflect the spatial distribution of the Arab population in 1949, that it cut off a coastal plain from its hinterland, that it bisected some villages, and that it was a sealed line of separation for only nineteen years, does not play a major role in the negotiations aimed at finding an acceptable territorial solution to the conflict. Even where territorial change and exchange is suggested, the Green Line continues to serve as the default line from which modifications must be determined.

The border discourse gained prominence during 2003 as a result of the construction of the "separation fence/wall" between Israel and the West Bank. The wall has been justified by Israeli governments as constituting a barrier against terror and suicide bomb attacks, but it has been interpreted by most as an attempt to unilaterally impose a physical border of separation between the two peoples and their respective territories. However, the wall has been constructed in such a way that many Israeli settlements have remained in situ on the Israeli side of the wall. This has resulted from the unilateral rerouting of the wall/fence away from the Green Line and effectively annexing parts of the West Bank territory to Israel, an action which is unacceptable to the Palestinians and has met with a great deal of international criticism, not least from the International Court of Justice in the Hague. The existing power relations are such that the more powerful side, Israel, is able to determine where it desires the line of territorial separation, a line which, with an alternative political or demographic logic, could have been delimited in a different location.

The borders throughout the Balkans have not changed since pre-Soviet times. Following the recent civil wars, ethnic cleansing, and attempted genocides of the 1990s, the existing territories have become more homogeneous in terms of their ethnic populations (Klemencic 2000; Milenkoski and Talevski 2001), but minorities still remain in almost every country (Serbs in Kosovo, Albanians in Macedonia, Croats in Bosnia, and so on). Notwithstanding, the international peacekeeping forces (the UN, NATO, and the KFOR troops) have refused to consider even the most minor of border changes, as this would result in a domino effect throughout the region, while it is not even clear it would bring about a better system of ethnoterritorial partition of the region. A mutual geography of fear and/or threat maintains a clear separation between peoples, including those who have been driven from their homes on the "other" side of the boundary. It does not necessarily require the building of a physical fence or wall for strong ethnoterritorial boundaries to take effect at the local level. Nowhere is the micro-ethnic boundary more prominent than in the town of Mitrovica in Northern Kosovo. The river separates the Albanian majority in the south of the town from the Serbian northern neighborhoods. Serbians used to reside south of the river but were mostly driven out by the Albanian majority, an action that was perceived by the Albanians as being no more than revenge for the violence inflicted upon them by the Serbs. The bridge across the river is a vacant no-man's land, patrolled by United Nations and other peacekeeping forces, and over which Serbs or Albanians cross with the knowledge that this may endanger their physical safety.

A similar non-wall "existed" until recently in the city of Jerusalem, separating East Jerusalem Palestinian from West Jerusalem Jewish neighborhoods. Prior to the onset of the first intifada in 1987, Israelis and Palestinians crossed to the other side of the city with relative ease,

Palestinians finding employment in West Jerusalem, Israelis finding cheaper goods and services in East Jerusalem (Romann and Weingrod 1991; Dumper 1996; Wasserstein 2001). The markets of the old city were also frequented by members of both national groups. This is no longer the case. Where there was once a minimal level of economic interaction, these spaces are now almost totally ethnically homogeneous, as each fears crossing the boundary, despite the fact that there was no physical barrier preventing the crossing from taking place. The establishment of settlement suburbs in the east of the city now makes it almost impossible to demarcate a "clean" line of ethnoterritorial separation as part of conflict resolution.

A recent Belgian film, *The Wall*, demonstrates, somewhat absurdly, the bordering process and the way in which barriers can be created to reflect existing differences and socially constructed territorial identities, creating walls, barriers, division, and conflict where a single functional space existed. The hero of the film is a French-speaking owner of a fried-potato wagon in Brussels. The non-existent line dividing the French- and Flemish-speaking areas of the city goes directly through the middle of his wagon. His clients are both French and Flemish speakers. He himself resides in the French-speaking section of the city but remains for a Millennium eve party on the Flemish side. When he wakes up in the morning of the "new" era, it is to find that a concrete barrier of Berlin-wall proportions has been constructed through the heart of the city and has divided his wagon into two parts. He is unable to return to his home on the other side of the wall because he does not have a visa or the necessary documents. French speakers without documents are sought out by a neo-Nazi style police force. They attempt to arrest him, but he manages to escape and, with his Flemish-speaking girlfriend, to cross back to his own side of the city. But his sigh of relief lasts for no more than few moments when his girlfriend now finds herself subject to the same dangers and problems on the French side of the wall that he was subject to on the Flemish side. Creating a physical border in the heart of "borderless" Europe, in the city of the EU institutions, *The Wall* is a cynical look at the way in which such lines can be manipulated to perpetuate difference, and hence enmity and ethnic tensions, as powerful social constructions on the part of power elites.

Borders compartmentalize. They exclude and include. And they are generally characterized by their functions as barriers – preventing movement. But borders, and in particular border zones, can also be conceived as places of contact and interaction, as bridges rather than barriers. This is particularly important when discussing notions of conflict resolution. Walls and fences are normally constructed as a means of ethnoterritorial separation between peoples. They may provide a limited amount of physical security in terms of safety, but they also constitute artificial constructions that make the "other" side invisible. Invisibility breeds ignorance, which in turn creates a new dimension of fear – fear of the unknown emanating from the other side of the border. In a world where many borders are becoming increasingly permeable, borders should be seen as places of potential interaction, points of contact and transition between two neighboring territorial or social entities. The "borderlands" (Rumley and Minghi 1991) or "political frontier zones"[8] should be places where localized interaction takes place in those areas that affect the civilian quality of life of both peoples, such as joint management of the environment, cooperation between municipal entities in the creation of higher size thresholds for the efficient provision of public services, economic complementarity in the construction of commercial centers and industrial parks, as well as the standardization of transboundary physical infrastructure such as roads, electricity grids, and sewage networks. Borders would remain as the territorial demarcations of state control (or whatever is left of sovereignty), citizenship, and, in some cases, national identity, but would become increasingly permeable in terms of the daily practices of the borderland residents, enabling interaction and cooperation rather than barriers and separation. This is where the two discourses – the global opening of borders, and the "primordial" closing and separation of territories, meet. It is the point where the territorial dialectic of the globalization argument is most strongly felt.

Conclusion

To fully understand the resilience of territorial conflict in a so-called era of deterritorialization, it is necessary to understand the multidimensionality of territory – the symbolic along with the tangible, the local along with the national, and the role of territory as a dynamic factor impacting the decision-making process in its own right. The territorial factor cannot be dismissed as simply "primordial," as not relating to the modern world.

The process through which territorial conflicts are resolved reflects all three of the characteristics discussed in this chapter: territorial scale, territorial symbolism, and the bordering process. Studies in conflict resolution have shown that it is the intangible and symbolic factors which are the most difficult to resolve between belligerents. This is as true of territorial factors as it is of other political conflict characteristics. When territory is presented as a discourse about tangible goods, it can be resolved through a process of quantification, bartering, and exchange, resulting in the contraction or expansion of state territory (Lustick 1993; Knight 1999a; Newman 1999). Settlements can be dismantled, compensation can be offered to refugees, borders can be relocated, and territorial parcels can be offered in exchange for territory annexed by the other side. But territory does not stand alone, nor is it the argument of this chapter that the territorial factor should be preeminent in our understanding of contemporary ethnoterritorial conflict. Territorial contestation cannot be understood without recourse to two parallel and related processes – demographic balances and hegemonies, and the changing nature of power relations. Changing territorial configurations reflect the demographic balances between majority and minority populations while, even in our globalized world, it is not unknown for the territory–demography balancing act to be resolved through ethnic expulsions or even genocides. The territorial dynamics of the Balkans are such that existing spatial configurations of control have been left in situ (no border changes) while populations have been forcefully removed or destroyed in an attempt to create territorial homogeneity. In both Cyprus and Lebanon, population movements of the past twenty years have created ethnic homogeneous spaces which are unlikely ever to return to their former "mixed" dimensions and which lend themselves to federal solutions of power sharing. In Israel–Palestine, even the outflow of Palestinian refugees and the inflow of Jewish migrants has not created a level of ethnoterritorial separation which allows for the demarcation of a "clean" or "good" border given the existence of a substantial Arab–Palestinian minority inside Israel, the existence of a growing Jewish settler population in the West Bank, and the demand for Palestinian refugee repatriation (Falah and Newman 1995).

This multidimensional analysis of the territorial factor allows us to achieve a deeper understanding of why territory continues to play a role in some contemporary conflicts. We need to move beyond the traditional discourse of demarcation, proximity, size and shape of territories, and, by association, the borders within which territories are enclosed, to a more functional definition of the territorial phenomenon. Paradoxically, it is the discourse of globalization, the supposition that both territory and borders have become meaningless, that has opened up the debate concerning the alternative and complementary ways in which territory needs to be understood if we are to find ways of resolving those conflicts, which remain a source of regional and even global instability.

NOTES

1 The phrase "the territorial imperative" is taken from the title of a book by Ardrey (1966), which was required reading for most social science undergraduates in the late 1960s and 1970s.

2 The managerialist thesis was initially discussed by urban sociologist Ray Pahl in the late 1960s. See Pahl 1969. For an overview of and a pointer to further references, see Knox 1995.

3 Notions of difference, exclusion/inclusion, and perceived boundaries are cutting-edge themes in the contemporary border discourse. See Paasi 1996; Newman and Paasi 1998; Albert 1998; Dittgen 2000; Newman 2002b; Shapiro and Alker 1996; Van Houtum 2002; Van Houtum and Van Naerssen 2002. See also David Newman (forthcoming 2006), "The Lines that Continue to Separate Us: Borders in a Borderless World," *Progress in Human Geography* 30.

4 For a good analysis of interaction and transactions between East and West Jerusalem, see Romann and Weingrod 1991.

5 On geopiety, see Wright 1947; Yi Fu Tuan 1976; Newman 1998a.

6 For an interesting discussion of the social construction of territorial knowledge in the Israel–Palestine context, see Kliot and Waterman 1990; Falah 1994; Kellerman 1995; Newman 1996b.

7 For recent political-science writings on territory, see Diehl and Goertz 1988; Goertz and Diehl 1992; Kocs 1995; Huth 1996; Vasquez and Henehan 2001.

8 This is the traditional term used to define those areas in close proximity to, and impacted by, the existence of a state boundary. See House 1980. For models of borderland interaction, see Martinez 1994.

5 Diasporas and homeland conflict

Terrence Lyons

Diaspora groups link processes of globalization to conflicts over identity and territory. Globalization has increased cross-border migration and decreased communication and travel costs, thereby making it easier for migrants to form diaspora networks that build links between the original homeland and current place of residence. Those forced across borders by war commonly have a specific set of traumatic memories and hence create specific types of "conflict-generated diasporas" that sustain and sometimes amplify their strong sense of symbolic attachment to the homeland. "Homeland" is often understood in specific territorial terms where a space from which a group has been forcefully detached assumes a high symbolic value. Globalization has increased rather than decreased this particular type of territorial attachment and thereby shaped the dynamics of certain homeland conflicts.

Conflict-generated diasporas – with their origins in conflict and their identity linked to symbolically important territory – often play critical roles with regard to homeland conflicts. As other scholars have noted, diaspora remittances are key resources to a conflict and often sustain parties engaged in civil war. In addition, and the focus of this research, such diasporas frequently have a particularly important role in framing conflict issues. Diaspora groups created by conflict and sustained by memories of the trauma tend to be less willing to compromise and therefore reinforce and exacerbate the protractedness of conflicts.

This chapter proposes a conceptual framework to explore the links between diaspora groups and conflicts in the homeland and why diaspora identities often focus on a territorially defined sense of homeland. How do diaspora groups relate to conflicts in their homeland? Is there a particular type of "conflict-generated diaspora" whose members retain specific types of links to the homeland as a consequence of their traumatic separation? Does a link to a territorially defined homeland where territory takes on symbolic rather than instrumental value promote uncompromising positions with regard to conflict? Do diaspora groups tend to frame homeland conflicts in ways that inhibit compromise and constructive conflict resolution? If so, are there opportunities for third parties to work with conflict-generated diaspora groups to encourage them to support conflict resolution? After presenting a framework for analyzing conflict-generated diasporas, this chapter sketches how the Ethiopian diaspora has both the territorial attachment and tendency to make homeland conflict more protracted. The chapter concludes with a section that briefly examines several processes suggesting how diasporas may play roles that promote rather than inhibit constructive conflict resolution.

Migration and conflict-generated diasporas

The involvement of migrants and exiles in the political affairs of their homelands is not new and has taken many forms over the centuries (Foner 2000; Iwańska 1981). As the pace and scale of globalization has increased in recent years the location where key political, economic, and social developments take place is often outside the sovereign territory of a given state. Transnational politics in recent years has led, for example, to Mexican politicians campaigning for votes and financial support in southern California. Croatians in the diaspora reportedly provided $4 million toward Franjo Tudjman's electoral campaign and were rewarded with 12 of 120 seats in recognition of their crucial electoral role.[1]

Migration is a complex process, with those who flee conflict and form diasporas actively engaged in the political affairs of their homeland only a small segment of a much larger and more diverse population. According to the 2000 US census, the countries sending the largest number of immigrants to the United States were Mexico, China/Hong Kong/ Taiwan, the Philippines, India, Vietnam, the former USSR, Cuba, Korea, Canada, and El Salvador (Camarota and McArdle 2003). Most of these migrants are not refugees fleeing persecution or ongoing violent conflicts but rather workers, students, and their dependents, or individuals immigrating to reunify families. They therefore play less direct roles in any homeland conflicts.

Many of these economic migrants organize on the basis of small-scale kinship groups with a focus on sending remittances from the wage earner in the host state to relatives in the homeland. Workers' remittances, estimated to total $100 billion annually, are critical to the economies of many states. According to the report of the Inter-American Dialogue Task Force on Remittances (2004, 4), remittances accounted for nearly 30 percent of Nicaragua's GDP, 25 percent of Haiti's, 17 percent of Guyana's, 15 percent of El Salvador's, and 12 percent each for

Honduras and Jamaica. During the Christmas season, thousands of migrants with suitcases bulging with gifts travel from North America to El Salvador, part of a \$2 billion remittance economy.[2] The implications and impacts of these relationships are profound but, by design and impact, more economic than political (Faist 2000).

Diaspora populations are a particular subset of migrants and are characterized by the social networks that link groups in host countries to their brethren in the homeland. Joining a diaspora is largely a matter of choice, although the choice might be constrained by the membership requirement for access to jobs, housing, cultural and religious services, or other resources distributed by the diaspora group. An individual migrant may or may not be a member of a diaspora. The 2000 US census recorded 19,282,096 citizens who registered "Irish" as their ancestry and 337,554 who answered "Armenian" (2000 US census, table PCT 16). Only the small fraction of these who are involved regularly in the organizations and networks that seek to link the community in the United States back to the homeland are members of the diaspora. Similarly, not all of the estimated 300,000 Tamils in the United Kingdom play any role in that diaspora. Furthermore, some active members of diaspora groups and networks may have been born in the host country, may be of mixed ancestry, or may be several generations removed from the homeland. What defines a diaspora is participation in activities designed to sustain linkages to the homeland.

This chapter focuses on a specific subset of migrants and a specific set of "conflict-generated diasporas."[3] This focus is narrower than the larger topic of globalization and migration (that includes consideration of economic migration, transborder communities, and remittances). Conflict-generated diasporas are characterized by the source of their displacement (violent, forced separation rather than relatively voluntary pursuit of economic incentives) and by the consequent nature of their ties to the homeland (identities that emphasize links to symbolically valuable territory).[4] Like all diasporas, conflict-generated diasporas are characterized in part by the organizations and networks they develop to build, sustain, and reinforce links between those in the homeland and those in the host country.

Conflict-generated diasporas are driven across borders as a result of violent conflict. This trauma is vivid in the minds of the first generation and is often kept alive in subsequent generations through commemorations and symbols (Volkan 1997). In fact, one of the functions of diaspora networks and institutions is to ensure that the original cause of displacement is remembered and the grievance passed on to the next generation. In many cases the initial migration was large, rapid, and included entire extended families and villages. The central importance of conflict therefore continues to shape identities among certain diaspora groups in their new host country and serves as a focal point for community mobilization (Portes 1999).

This definition is much narrower than the definitions proposed by such recent works on diasporas as Gabriel Sheffer's *Diaspora Politics*. Sheffer defines "ethno-national diaspora" as a "social-political formation, created as a result of either voluntary or forced migration, whose members regard themselves as of the same ethno-national origin and who permanently reside as minorities in one or several host countries" (Sheffer 2003, 9). While Sheffer argues that whether migration was voluntary or forced does not matter for diaspora formations, others argue that cases where trauma is associated with the original dispersal often generate "a vision and memory of a lost or an imagined homeland still to be established" (Faist 2000, 197). Diasporas that are "born from a forced dispersion," according to Chaliland, often "conscientiously strive to keep a memory of the past alive" (Chaliland 1989, xiv). One way to keep the past relevant is to keep alive the hope of returning, once conditions allow, even if this aspiration is remote. What distinguishes conflict-generated diaspora groups from other types of migrant groups and diasporas is that this specific type of migrant has conflict in the past and an aspiration of return to the homeland in the future.

Clear cases of conflict-generated diasporas include the Oromo and Eritreans from Ethiopia; the Kurds from Turkey, Iran, and Iraq; Tamils from Sri Lanka; Armenians; Irish; and Palestinians. Each has a large number of members forcefully displaced by war and currently has a critical mass participating in organizations that seek to build and reinforce links from the host countries back to the homeland in conflict. These migrants are highly mobilized into strong diaspora networks in part because their identities are linked to stateless and marginalized groups (Sheffer 2003). If one's identity group is secure back home, then the need to organize political activities abroad is less compelling. Without a state to champion their rights, stateless migrants often compensate with strong diaspora networks. Such conflict-generated diasporas follow different patterns of behavior with regard to homeland conflict than those who may have fled conflict or political repression, as in Central America, Iran, or Vietnam. They also differ from the much larger population of migrants who cross borders more or less voluntarily in pursuit of opportunities.

Conflict-generated diasporas and "homeland"

The identity and social mobilization of conflict-generated diaspora groups relate to a very specific, symbolically important, and territorially defined "homeland." Some have suggested that globalization and the development of diasporic identities will make territory and boundaries less salient as "supranational" identities develop and political, social, and economic life becomes deterritorialized (Wahlbeck 1999, 27). Appadurai, for example, writes that "ethnicity, once a genie contained in the bottle of some sort of locality (however large) has now become a global force, forever slipping in and through the cracks between states and borders" (Appadurai 1996). David Newman and others, however, argue that there cannot be political power or social control totally divorced from some form of territorial compartmentalization. Globalization has not decreased the significance of territory but has led to a "new, more complex, understanding of the multidimensional, and dynamic, components of territory as a mechanism through which society is bordered, ordered, and controlled" (Newman, this volume).

Conflict-generated diaspora groups define their identity in large part by their strong attachment to a homeland that is defined in territorial terms. Rather than seeking to build a transnational virtual community, many diaspora groups retain and amplify attachment to the territorial aspect of their identity, even if they are physically distant from and even unlikely ever to travel to that territory. An Eritrean wrote that the Eritrean community in the United States was "an integral part of its colonized people at home. Therefore its mental state is constantly in conflict caused by feelings of guilt, nostalgia, and its unequivocal desire to bring about the liberation of its people" (Aradom 1990, 3). Conflict-generated diasporas are driven by a desire for transformation and liberation as much as by nostalgia and tradition (Adamson 2002, 155). A sense of solidarity and attachment to a particular locality can generate a common identity without propinquity, where territorially defined community and spatial proximity are decoupled without diminishing the salience of territoriality.

The concept of territorially defined homeland often is inherent in the conflict-generated diaspora's identity and therefore serves as a focal point of diaspora political action and debate. Povrzanovic-Frykman notes, "The homeland they do not live in any more is very likely to remain a crucial place of emotional attachment and decisively defines their strategies of identification" (Povrzanovic-Frykman 2001, 23). As the intrinsic value of territory diminishes, as day-to-day activities focus on the new place of residence, the homeland's symbolic importance may grow. Diaspora websites and publications emphasize the symbols of the nation-state – maps, flags, symbolic geographic features, or local plants (Bakker 2001). Often the language of exile emphasizes the links to homeland as very much an earthly place by speaking of the "original soil" and the need to maintain "roots" in times of dispersal and uprooting (Naficy 1991). Geographical detachment removes the territorial concept from the "concrete to the metaphysical realm and from one that has relatively clear boundaries to one that is unbounded and abstract" (Newman 1999, 13). As Yossi Shain notes:

For many homeland citizens, territory serves multiple functions: it provides sustenance, living space, security, as well as a geographical focus for national identity. If giving up a certain territory, even one of significant symbolic value, would increase security and living conditions, a homeland citizen might find the tradeoff worthwhile. By contrast, for the diaspora, while the security of the homeland is of course important as well, the territory's identity function is often paramount. (Shain 2002, 134)

For the diaspora, therefore, homeland is a special category of territory, laden with symbolic meaning for those who identify with it from afar (Toft 2001, 7; Morley and Robins 1993). As a consequence, diaspora groups are less likely to support compromise or a bargain that trades off some portion of the sacred homeland for some other instrumental end.

Diaspora networks: setting the terms of debate around homeland conflict

Conflict-generated diaspora groups form a link between conflict, territoriality, and identity. Diaspora social organizations often mobilize around providing support for actors engaged in the conflict back home. These networks frequently engage in political activism in support of the struggle back home, including lobbying the host country or international organizations for support, engaging in public education and consciousness raising, supporting projects on behalf of the victims of the strife, or more active fundraising for arms and other war materiel. In this way, these networks often become a factor that complicates processes of conflict resolution and may protract homeland conflicts.

In many cases, diaspora groups engage in lobbying and in public information campaigns to inform and to shape the foreign policy of officials in their new state of residence as well as in the larger international community. The Dutch organization Yesu Kitenga, which represents Lisanga from Congo, for example, states its mandate as "to provide reliable information from the homeland, to raise awareness among the concerned organizations and government decision makers

about certain politically motivated persecutions and human rights viola-
tions of which often little is known outside a country, but also guide the
policymakers towards adopting the right policy approach towards our
homeland" (cited in Mohamoud 2005).

The conflict back home is often the key to social mobilization in the
host country, and, if the conflict ended, another issue around which to
mobilize would be necessary or else the organization would decline.
O'Grady wrote about Irish American organizations that maintaining
their cohesion requires "an agenda that is driven by events in Northern
Ireland and capable of molding and solidifying that voting bloc." If the
Good Friday Agreement results in lasting peace, then "Irish-Americans
will have no reason to forge an agenda that will hold their reinvigorated
pressure group together" (O'Grady 1996, 7).

Most conflict-generated diasporas develop social networks both to
retain a sense of identity and to promote community self-help programs
for finding jobs and housing, and managing immigration issues in their
new host countries. They often form church groups, schools to maintain
native languages and cultural practices among their children, and social
clubs to celebrate religious holidays or to mark other symbolically important dates and ceremonies. These social networks often are used to
mobilize the diaspora in support of a party engaged in homeland conflict. Heroes' Day, for example, is an important day for community
mobilization among the Tamil diaspora. The TamilNet website reported
that Anton Balasingham, the Liberation Tigers of Tamil Eelam theoret-
ician, spoke at Heroes' Day events in London in 2002 while other
leaders of the insurgency spoke in Italy, Switzerland, Germany, Norway,
and France.[5] Annual events such as the Ethiopian soccer tournament in
North America bring thousands together not only to compete and so-
cialize but also to talk politics. Celebration of national holidays is a
particularly important way to maintain links with the homeland and
reaffirm borders between the diaspora community and the surrounding
host country population. Iranians in the diaspora scrupulously celebrate
Nowruz, the Iranian New Year held at the spring equinox. Furthermore,
these cultural events are instrumental in socializing the generation born
outside of the homeland to the issues that define their membership in a
diaspora group.

Globalization and the rise of the internet have shaped how diaspora
groups mobilize and communicate with likeminded members. There are
hundreds of sites devoted to different homeland conflicts as members of
dispersed groups seek to build community. Many of these diasporic
websites are quite complete, including nearly all aspects of life from
history and politics to culture and homeland recipes. "The aim of these

websites is to (re)construct a true nation and to create counter-knowledge about a specific region" (Bakker 2001). Symbols, flags, and maps are omnipresent.

A number of recent studies have focused on the question of diaspora funding of homeland insurgencies. Collier and Hoeffler conclude that "by far the strongest effect of war on the risk of subsequent war works through diasporas. After five years of post-conflict peace, the risk of renewed conflict is around six times higher in the societies with the largest diasporas in America than in those without American diasporas. Presumably this effect works through the financial contributions of diasporas to rebel organizations" (Collier and Hoeffler 2000, 26). While Collier and Hoeffler use data on American diasporas, the same pattern is evident with regard to groups resident in Europe. The Tamil diaspora provides critical funding to the Liberation Tigers of Tamil Eelam, and the links between diaspora fundraising and conflict have been noted with regard to the Kurdish Workers Party, the Provisional Irish Republican Army, and Croatian political and military movements.[6] Diasporas sometimes lobby host governments for increased support for states engaged in conflict, as demonstrated by the Eritrean, Armenian, and Croatian diasporas' efforts (Mooradian 2004).

Beyond and in many cases more important than the provision of financial resources, diasporas play critical roles in setting the terms of debate around issues of conflict and identity. The "old country" is often romanticized and past glories and grievances kept alive in an "allegiance to the land of memories" as a way of asserting continued belonging and of making sense of their current location in exile (R. Cohen 1997, 185). Benedict Anderson argues that such diaspora groups, which he labels "long-distance nationalists," are inevitably unaccountable:

> While technically a citizen in the state in which he comfortably lives, but to which he may feel little attachment, he finds it tempting to play identity politics by participating (via propaganda, money, weapons, any way but voting) in the conflicts of his imagined Heimat [homeland] – now only fax time away. But this citizenless participation is inevitably non-responsible – our hero will not have to answer for, or pay the price of, the long-distance politics he undertakes.
> (B. Anderson 1992, 13; see also B. Anderson 1994)

Pnina Werbner echoes this concern and notes that diasporas often "feel free to endorse and actively support ethnicist, nationalistic, and exclusionary movements" (Werbner 2002, 120). Finally, David Fitzgerald suggests that some members of diasporas advance a "model of citizenship that emphasizes rights over obligations, passive entitlements, and the assertion of an interest in the public space without a daily presence" (Fitzgerald 2000, 106). Political leaders back home are often ambiguous about the political influence of those who have left and now emphasize emotional issues, and who may have lost touch with everyday struggles in the homeland.

The emotional attachment to highly symbolic land often leads to a framing of conflict in the homeland in categorical, uncompromising terms. This point of view and the way it sets the terms of debate and strategy is quite powerful, because exiles tend to have greater access to the media and the time, resources, and freedom to articulate and circulate a political agenda than do actors in the conflicted homeland. The cost of refusing to accept a compromise is often low (if the diaspora members are well-established in Europe, North America, or Australia) and the rewards from demonstrating steadfast commitment to the cause are high (in personal/psychological terms, but also as a mechanism of social mobilization).

In some cases, leading intellectuals have sought exile in order to continue to engage in political debate and campaigning. Major cultural figures including authors, filmmakers, and musicians are frequently based abroad, and their framing of issues relating to identity, memory, and conflict resonates powerfully back home. Diaspora groups often control major media outlets both in host states and in the homeland. Armenians in the United States, for example, support one daily and eleven weekly newspapers in Armenia, along with countless newsletters, internet sites, and e-mail distribution lists (Tölölyan 2000). Major Congolese and other African musicians are based in Paris or Brussels. Videotapes or cassettes of exile political speeches or demonstrations may circulate in a homeland where participation in such activities is more dangerous. During the 1990s the Ethiopian government charged that the Voice of America's Amharic service encouraged demonstrations so that the opposition's point of view could be broadcast back to Ethiopia in newscasts (Sheckler 1998).

Uncompromising diaspora positions therefore often constrain the ability of actors in the homeland to propose different ways to understand the struggle or to engage in constructive conflict resolution. As suggested by Maney in his study of transnational movements and civil rights in Northern Ireland, external supporters "not only can exacerbate problems encountered by domestic coalitions but can also introduce additional obstacles to the effective pursuit of social change" (Maney 2000, 153). The devotion to the cause of the diaspora may make it more difficult for political actors back home to accept compromise solutions that may be condemned as appeasement or treason among the émigrés. In Armenia, for example, the first post-Soviet president Ter-Petrossian sought to base Armenia's foreign policy on state interests and make conciliatory gestures toward Turkey. The Armenian diaspora in the United States and France, however, regarded this as selling out their core issue of recognition of the Armenian genocide. Ter-Petrossian eventually fell to Robert Kocharian, who followed the diaspora's traditional anti-Turkish attitudes (Shain 2002, 126–27).[7] Conflict-generated diasporas therefore can complicate the processes of conflict resolution in the homeland.

The Ethiopian diaspora: attachment to territory and protracted conflict

A quick sketch of the Ethiopian diaspora in North America suggests some of the ways in which diaspora groups are linked to and shape the dynamics of conflicts and some of the puzzles with regard to diasporas and homeland conflicts. The purpose of this sketch is to illustrate that territory sometimes retains a high salience to diaspora groups and that the categorical framing of homeland conflicts by certain diaspora groups complicates efforts toward conflict resolution and tends to reinforce the protracted nature of homeland conflicts.

The overall Ethiopian community in the United States is estimated at 250,000, with a large concentration in the Washington, D.C., metropolitan area. The migrants have come in waves, with the first wave of royalists who fled the Marxist military government known as the Derg in the early 1970s followed by leftist opponents who fled the period of "Red Terror" in the mid- to late 1970s (Ford 2003). The rule of the Derg saw protracted conflict against the Eritrean People's Liberation Front as well as a series of nationally based insurgencies, including the Oromo Liberation Front (OLF) and most notably the Tigray People's Liberation Front (TPLF) that eventually created the Ethiopian People's Revolutionary Democratic Party (EPRDF) and seized power from the Derg in 1991. Since this transition, many in the diaspora have supported political organizations that are intensely hostile to the EPRDF regime.

The Ethiopian diaspora remains deeply linked to political, social, and economic developments back home. The community has a wide range of organizations and newspapers, maintains dozens of websites and e-mail lists, broadcasts a number of weekly radio and cable television shows, and has a strong influence on the strategies and tactics of political actors back in Ethiopia. The Ethiopian Sports Federation in North America has a soccer league with twenty-five teams and an annual tournament that draws tens of thousands: it is an opportunity to renew old friendships, build solidarity, listen to major diaspora musicians, and engage in political affairs as well as sports. The diaspora is by no means unified. Some favor the incumbent EPRDF government, others a range of opposition movements, and still others are supportive of movements such as the OLF, which seeks self-determination for the Oromo people (an estimated 40 percent of the Ethiopian population).

The diaspora community in Washington is a critical arena where Ethiopian politics is contested and the boundaries of debates established and affirmed. Ethiopian political leaders, including those in the government and in the leading opposition organizations and liberation movements, regularly send delegations to brief their respective communities in Washington and to solicit their support. The Ethiopian Ministry of Foreign Affairs has a General Directorate in charge of Ethiopian Expatriate Affairs and funds a radio station in Washington to channel its message to the diaspora.[8] The diaspora is powerful and has lobbied the US government and international financial institutions to reduce aid because of human rights conditions in Ethiopia, and has also raised funds for humanitarian and development projects. Pressure from Ethiopian American groups led several members of the US Congress to introduce the Free and Fair Elections in Ethiopia Act in 2004.

A series of incidents suggest that diaspora groups are critical to Ethiopian political players back home:

- When splits within the core EPRDF group known as the Tigray People's Liberation Front erupted in March 2001, both factions immediately sent high-level delegations to the United States to influence how the diaspora understood the intraparty conflict and to build support for their respective factions.[9]
- Leaders of the political opposition within Ethiopia, such as Beyene Petros (Southern Coalition), regularly travel to North America to solicit support and receive advice. When the Southern Coalition entertained the idea of engaging with the EPRDF regime and competing in the 1995 elections, the diaspora was sharply critical and threatened to label Beyene as a traitor. This pressure, along with continued harassment at home, ultimately led the Southern Coalition to boycott.[10]
- Many of the most vigorous and dedicated supporters of Oromo self-determination and the OLF are in the diaspora. These leaders insist on uncompromising and unqualified demands – liberation of all Oromia by military means. They support OLF military leaders who pursue this agenda rather than other Oromo leaders, such as those in the Oromo National Congress prepared to engage in political competition with the incumbent regime.

Ethiopians in the diaspora tend to have a territorially defined concept of an Ethiopian homeland that is central to their identity. For many, this "Ethiopia" continues to include Eritrea (independent since 1991) and stresses a romanticized set of royal attributes and symbols (despite the overthrow of the monarchy in 1974).[11] The Ethiopian diaspora is generally extremely hostile to the incumbent regime in Addis Ababa, but many rallied to the regime when the territorial integrity of the Ethiopian state seemed to be under threat from the Eritreans during the bloody 1998 border conflict. In many cases, defending the homeland trumped profound political differences.

In sharp contrast, most Oromos in the diaspora reject this concept of an "Ethiopian homeland" and regard the Ethiopian state as an empire in which northern groups (Amharas and Tigreans, referred to as "Abyssinians" by many Oromos) dominate the South. As a consequence, they argue that the Oromo people have the right to self-determination and an independent "Oromia" state. The Oromo diaspora therefore defines itself through its rejection of the territorially defined nation-state of Ethiopia and through its loyalty to and support for an independent Oromia. As with those whose identity relates to an Ethiopian homeland, the Oromo diaspora has a clearly territorially defined sense of identity. Maps, nationalist colors, and images of the Oromo national symbol, the odaa tree, cover the walls of Oromo restaurants, are displayed on bumper stickers, and fill Oromo websites and publications (Bulcha 2002; Gow 2002).

According to Mekuria Bulcha, approximately 200,000 Oromo refugees scattered across the globe, with 100,000 settling in North America, Europe, and Australia (Bulcha 2002). While economic considerations clearly also drove many Oromos out of Ethiopia, war and violence are core traumatic events that launched their displacement. Many Oromo refugees have settled in Germany and in Minnesota, where connections through Lutheran missionary societies helped some receive education and other services. These concentrations make them powerful constituents in certain areas. For example, approximately 12,000 Oromos live in Minneapolis, leading the mayor to proclaim 30 July, 2001 "Oromo Day."[12] The Oromo diaspora has established a wide range of organizations distinct from the Ethiopian diaspora organizations. There are Oromo Lutheran and Muslim organizations in North America, a regular Oromo Studies Association with a full range of academic conferences and a journal, and a well-attended annual soccer tournament.

This sketch suggests that the Ethiopian and Oromo diasporas are mobilized in part around a territorially defined homeland that is symbolically important. The conflicts in the homeland that drove many of the members of the diaspora abroad are core focal points of their identities. These conflict-generated diasporas are key players in the homeland conflicts, in part because they provide a great deal of financial support but also because they frame the conflicts through their control over media outlets and other institutions and venues where political strategies are debated and leadership legitimized. Because of the nature of their attachment to the homeland, many frame the conflict in an uncompromising manner and are committed to the support of the most militant leaders back home. The Ethiopian diaspora therefore has the capacity to make conflict resolution more difficult and the conflict more protracted.

Conflict resolution and diasporas: engagement and transformation

Understanding how conflict-generated diasporas reinforce dynamics that make conflicts more protracted is important for policymakers interested in promoting conflict resolution. How can external parties work to reduce, if not end, the roles diasporas play in making conflicts less inclined to settlement? As argued above, conflict-generated diasporas tend to have definite, categorical perceptions of homeland conflicts. If these perceptions can be reframed and made more complex and multifaceted through a process of dialogue, then the diaspora's role in the conflict may be changed. In addition, if a diaspora group shifts its support from the most militant leaders and organizations engaged in the homeland conflict toward a position that supports the leaders and movements seeking peace, then an important factor that makes conflicts more difficult to resolve can be reduced. Diasporas have the potential to be sources of ideas and support for peacemaking as well as forces making conflicts more protracted (Zunzer 2004).[13]

This chapter concludes by pointing to several examples of processes to encourage conflict-generated diasporas to shift their attitudes toward homeland conflict. These cases are presented to illustrate the potential of diasporas to promote peace back home and hence opportunities to promote conflict resolution by working with diaspora groups. More comparative case studies are necessary to draw clear conclusions and investigate which policy initiatives offer the most promise. A number of initiatives to promote dialogues among members of conflict-generated diasporas have taken place, and this section will outline several to suggest the potential of such interventions. Finally, the case of how Irish

American attitudes toward the conflict in Northern Ireland and the Good Friday peace agreement changed will be outlined to suggest how diasporas may promote dynamics that reinforce conflict-resolution processes under the right circumstances.

Engaging diasporas through dialogue

A number of conflict-resolution organizations have sought to engage members of conflict-generated diasporas into dialogue processes in order to counter the diaspora-driven dynamics that often lead to more protracted conflicts. Many of these projects are based on the supposition that there is something about how diaspora groups tend to perceive and frame homeland conflicts that makes resolution of such conflicts more difficult. Dialogue processes are therefore designed to contribute to changing these perceptions.

From 2000 through 2003 a group of graduate students and faculty at George Mason University's Institute for Conflict Analysis and Resolution (ICAR) conducted an "Extended Dialogue" with members of the Ethiopian diaspora (Lyons et al. 2004). Building on the work done by Harold Saunders, this Ethiopian Extended Dialogue (EED) demonstrated how engaging a conflict-generated diaspora in a process of conflict resolution has the potential to alter the perceptions of leaders within the diaspora community of the homeland conflict (Saunders 1999).

Much of the dialogue revolved around how members of the diaspora understood issues of identity, both in terms of their personal identities as members of a community divided as a result of conflicts and in terms of how identity drives many of the conflicts back in Ethiopia. To speak in very broad terms, the discussions tended to be three sided. One group of participants emphasized the overarching unity of Ethiopians and interdependence among the Ethiopian people. To them Ethiopia represented a glorious historical and territorial entity to which unity and loyalty was owed. For some, this conception of Ethiopia included the entire territory of the currently recognized state as well as the neighboring state of Eritrea.

Another group suggested that the starting point for understanding Ethiopia was to recognize the structural, colonial system of domination and oppression, and emphasized that certain groups, most notably the Oromo, had been incorporated into the Ethiopian "empire" state without their consent. The territorial space occupied by "Ethiopia" in this point of view included "Oromia," the territory occupied by the Oromo people who awaited their legitimate self-determination. To them, Ethiopia merely represented a geographic concept rather than a source of positive identity based on voluntary association. Thus, for the Oromo, Oromia rather than Ethiopia was their homeland, with clear territorial boundaries.

A third group also underscored the use of force and domination by successive despotic regimes from Northern Ethiopia against the people of Southern Ethiopia but worried about potential Oromo domination of smaller groups. This group shared the territorial definition of the homeland of the first but also the perception of oppression expressed by the second. These different perspectives on the conflict therefore had territorial dimensions in that each point of view had a different conception of what the space labeled "Ethiopia" should be. Competing visions of homeland that overlap and occupy the same finite territorial space make the Ethiopian conflict particularly difficult for members of the diaspora to discuss together and hence inhibit conflict-resolution processes.

Over the course of some twenty meetings with a core group, sufficient trust developed so that the quality of discussions changed. In the early meetings, many participants made statements of principle and expressed their positions with regard to the injustices that they perceived as causing the conflicts in Ethiopia. Over time, however, the discussions became more complicated as participants increasingly recognized how other groups also had legitimate grievances, how principles sometimes were in tension, and how, as common members of a diaspora, all had interests in promoting a just and sustainable peace. These more complex and complicated perceptions opened up new possibilities for recognizing new options with regard to conflicts in the homeland.

Other dialogue processes have sought to tap into the potential peace-making roles of diaspora groups. Search for Common Ground, an international nongovernmental organization based in Washington, D.C., had an initiative to use dialogue processes within the Macedonian and Albanian diasporas in North America. The goal of these discussions was to promote "inter-ethnic tolerance" between the two diasporas, which include "some of the most fervent advocates of nationalist views," and thereby to promote stability in Macedonia.[14] Another-conflict resolution organization, the Conflict Management Group, organized Diaspora Dialogues between Palestinian/Arab and Jewish Americans.[15] Finally, members of the Sinhala diaspora in Melbourne organized themselves into a group called "Shanthi" to establish dialogues with members of the Tamil diaspora in Australia.[16]

Northern Ireland: from promoting violence to promoting peace

The shift of support of leading Irish Americans from organizations such as NORAID, dedicated to supporting hard-line military leaders, to those such as Americans for a New Irish Agenda (ANIA), focused on providing support for political forces seeking a peace agreement, is an important part of the Good Friday Agreement story. The peace process in Northern Ireland is extraordinarily complicated and will not be summarized here. The role of President Bill Clinton and his Special Envoy to Northern Ireland George Mitchell were in part the product of a campaign by key Irish American leaders to shift the Irish American diaspora from supporting the most militant tendencies within the Irish Republican Army to supporting a political process that resulted in the Good Friday Agreement.

For many years, the Irish Northern Aid Committee (NORAID) was the most prominent Irish American group that provided support to parties engaged in the conflict in Northern Ireland. Michael Flannery, an ex-member of the North Tipperary brigade of the IRA, founded NORAID in 1970. The organization mobilized Irish Americans and dedicated itself to raising funds in support of the IRA. NORAID formally channeled funds to An Cumann Cabrach, a charity in the IRA orbit that supported families of prisoners, but the organization also reportedly served as a key conduit for gun smuggling. Flannery, in fact, was charged (but not convicted) with gun running in 1982 (Guelke 1996).

In the early 1990s, however, leadership among Irish American organizations interested in Northern Irish issues shifted. Senator Ted Kennedy, Speaker of the House Tip O'Neal, Senator Daniel Patrick Moynihan, and Governor Hugh Carey (nicknamed the "Four Horsemen") began to speak out publicly against violence and in support of nonviolent political movements such as John Hume's Social Democratic and Labour Party (SDLP). In 1991, Americans for a New Irish Agenda (ANIA) was founded, with *Irish Voice* editor Niall O'Dowd taking the lead. Representatives of the ANIA traveled to Ireland to encourage Sinn Féin leader Gerry Adams to engage in discussions with Hume. The goal was to reinforce and strengthen the political wing of the republican movement and thereby promote the peace process.

ANIA and others pressured Bill Clinton to speak out on the Northern Ireland issue during the 1992 campaign, and Clinton promised to appoint a special envoy and to grant Adams a visa. Those pressing for a visa for Adams argued that providing him the legitimacy and prestige of a trip to the United States would strengthen his position with regard to the hard-line militants and promote the movement of Sinn Féin into peace talks. ANIA set up the National Committee on American Foreign Policy and invited Adams to New York to address their conference in February 1994. Clinton granted the visa, over the objections of the British, unionists in Northern Ireland, the State Department, and the US embassy in London (O'Grady 1996). The IRA did not proclaim a ceasefire as Clinton had hoped during Adams' trip to the United States. Following a visit to Ireland by O'Dowd and Congressman Bruce Morrison, however, the IRA proclaimed a unilateral and unconditional ceasefire on 31 August 1994 (Cox 1999). The Irish American diaspora had clear influence on the dynamics of the peace process in the homeland.

The transition among leading Irish American organizations from NORAID to ANIA played an important role in supporting the Good Friday Agreement. NORAID represented and helped fund the most militant and uncompromising elements within the Irish republican movement. ANIA, in contrast, represented a different strain of the diaspora, with less categorical perceptions, that was willing to adopt a different set of tactics. In particular, ANIA recognized that the violence of the Provisional IRA could not win and that the best strategy was to strengthen the moderates in the SDLP and Sinn Féin and support peace talks. ANIA successfully lobbied Clinton and used the issue of granting a visa to Adams as a mechanism to provide a wider audience for the new thinking that Adams represented. In this way, a shift in the Irish American diaspora helped facilitate a shift from the uncompromising militants to the more politically minded moderates.

Conclusions

Conflict-generated diasporas are the product of and link together territoriality and conflict. Globalization has increased transborder migration, but in many cases this movement has not decreased attachment to homeland. Diaspora groups with their origins in conflict often cultivate a specific type of linkage where homeland territory takes on a high symbolic value and is a focal point for mobilization. As a result, diasporas often provide financial support to militants engaged in homeland conflicts. In addition, conflict-generated diasporas tend to frame conflicts in ways that are uncompromising and categorical, and this framing has significance for the political strategies of the parties back home. Parties directly engaged in the conflict in the homeland are frequently dependent on supporters in the diaspora for resources and for access to international media, international organizations, and powerful host governments, thereby giving diaspora groups influential roles in the framing of debates and the adoption of strategies relating to conflict. Because of the particular importance of symbolic territory and a conception of homeland to diaspora identities and a consequent framing of homeland conflict in categorical, uncompromising terms, diaspora groups often contribute to prolonging and protracting conflicts.

Despite this general pattern, there are cases where the attitudes and behavior of diaspora groups have changed. Various dialogue processes have sought to generate more complex views of the conflict in the homeland among at least some in the diaspora. The shift of Irish American support from some of the most militant elements within the Irish Republican Army to more politically minded leaders intent on engaging in negotiations provides another case. Conflict-generated diasporas have a tendency to reinforce those dynamics of homeland conflicts that lead toward protractedness, but this tendency is not inevitable.

NOTES

The author thanks Maneesha S. Wanasinghe-Pasqual and Roba Sharamo for their research assistance and Miles Kahler, Barbara Walter, John Agnew, Saskia Sassen, Bidisha Biswas, Christian Davenport, and Agnieszka Paczynska for comments on earlier versions.

1 See "Special Report: Diasporas: A World of Exiles," *The Economist,* 4 January 2003, 25–27.
2 Mary Jordan, "In El Salvador, a Christmas Avalanche," *Washington Post,* 21 December 2003.
3 On defining diasporas, see Safran 1991; Sheffer 2003; R. Cohen 1997.
4 Of course motives are inevitably mixed and distinguishing economic from political motives is difficult, as thousands of asylum cases every year demonstrate. But the distinction is important to understanding how diasporas are linked to homeland conflict.
5 TamilNet, "Tamil Diaspora Celebrates Heroes' Day November 26, 2003," available at http://www.tamilnet.com/art.html?catid=13&artid=10539.
6 On the LTTE, see Byman et al. 2001. On the PIRA see Horgan and Taylor 1999; and Arthur 1991.
7 Shain cites an observer as saying that hardliners in the Armenian diaspora "are said to care less about the homeland's present and future than about the past's dead" (Shain 2002, 121).
8 "Ethiopia: Finances a Radio Station in Washington," *Indian Ocean Newsletter* No. 1043, 24 May 2003.
9 When Beyene appeared at a meeting of the diaspora in Los Angeles, for example, pamphlets were distributed that accused him of accepting $3 million in exchange for agreeing to participate in the elections. These meetings were often contentious and sometimes escalated to require police intervention. See "Ethiopia: Diaspora Unconvinced and Angry," *Indian Ocean Newsletter* No. 953, 9 June 2001.

10 "Ethiopia: Negotiations in Washington," *Indian Ocean Newsletter* No. 658, 11 February 1995. See also Lyons 1996.
11 Many Ethiopian restaurants on Eighteenth Street in Washington fly the old imperial flag and have maps that include Eritrea as part of Ethiopia, despite Eritrea's existence as an independent state since 1991. Needless to say Eritrean and Oromo restaurants display other symbols and emphasize different maps.
12 See www.oromiaonline.com/News/MPLS_OromoDay.htm.
13 For an example of a conflict-generated diaspora working to promote peace-building, see the work by the Kacoke Madit group that has mobilized the Acholi diaspora to promote peace in northern Uganda at http://www.c-r.org/accord/uganda/accord11/kacoke.shtml.
14 See Search for Common Ground's website at www.sfcg.org for more details.
15 See "Diaspora Dialogues: Mission Statement," and Naseem Khuri, "Diaspora Dialogues," *Peace by Piece* (Winter 2003), both found at www.cmgroup.org.
16 See *Shanthi: An Online Journal Promoting Peace in Sri Lanka*, found at http://members.fortunecity.com/shanthi/reconciliation_between_the_sinha.htm.

Part II

Territorial stakes and violent conflict

6   Territory and war: state size and patterns of interstate conflict

David A. Lake and Angela O'Mahony

The average size of states within the international system expanded steadily during the nineteenth century, nearly doubling between 1816 and 1876, and then contracted over the twentieth century. In previous work, we found that two key characteristics of globalization, increasing economies of scale and economic openness, as well as regime type, were important explanations for this trend in average state size (Lake and O'Mahony 2004). The rise in territorial size during the nineteenth century was, in part, the product of a growing number of large, federal democracies made possible by increasing economies of scale, while economic liberalism allowed small, unitary democracies to prosper in the twentieth century.

In this chapter, we analyze how this trend in average state size affects interstate conflict. We predict that as average state size increased in the nineteenth century, larger national territories will become more valuable, leading to more interstate territorial disputes. Conversely, as average state size declined in the twentieth century, we expect interstate conflict to decline. Testing this hypothesis at both the systemic and the regional level, we find relatively strong support for this expectation in the pattern of interstate wars and in the issues underlying those conflicts.

We first summarize our earlier investigation into the patterns and causes of average state size since 1815. The second section section develops our theory of average state size and conflict, and the third section reviews the empirical evidence. In the fourth section, we examine changes in the issues that led to interstate war. In the Conclusion, we reflect on how our findings support a recurrent theme in this volume, specifically, that states and individuals have only an instrumental attachment to territory.

State size

As Figure 6.1 demonstrates, the average size of states increased dramatically over the nineteenth century, reached a plateau between 1876 and

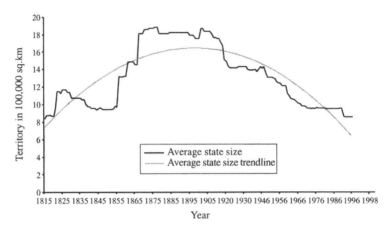

Figure 6.1. Average state size, 1815–1998.

1901, and then began an equally dramatic decline over the twentieth century. Over the course of two centuries, the average state grew from 832,000 square kilometers to 1.9 million sq. kilometers, and then shrank back to 854,000 sq. kilometers. Moreover, state size has retained the same log-normal distribution around this evolving mean over time. The trend toward greater size in the nineteenth century and then smaller size in the twentieth century was broadly based. Elsewhere, we document that this trend is not just an artifact of data availability or states entering the system as new members (Lake and O'Mahony 2004). We are confident that the rise and then decline in average state size over the last two centuries is a real, if heretofore unappreciated, "fact."

There is no simple explanation for this trend. State size is, most likely, a product of many factors, subject to contingency and chance, and path dependent. Our focus in this chapter is on the consequences of this trend in average state size for interstate conflict. Nonetheless, our previous research suggests that economies of scale in governance, economic openness, and regime type combine in subtle ways to explain, at least in part, this trend. We briefly summarize our earlier results here.

Expansion

Over the nineteenth century, technology evolved rapidly in ways that greatly expanded the ability of governments to project coercive force and to provide services to citizens over distance. Steam power allowed both military and commercial shipping to travel faster over greater expanses without regard for wind and enabled railroads to open up continental interiors, encouraging new areas of settlement while bringing goods to market at lower cost. The telegraph dramatically cut the time and expense of long-distance communication. These innovations, and many other less-celebrated improvements, not only led to the rise of nationally and, to a lesser extent, globally integrated markets and unprecedented levels of migration (O'Rourke and Williamson 2000), but they also allowed governments to exert power, enforce laws, and provide services at greater distances from their national capitals than ever before.

Governments responded to these new opportunities, especially in the latter half of the nineteenth century, in several ways. In one pattern, for which the United States and Russia are exemplars, states pursued continental expansion. Using the new technologies combined with the efficiencies of modern centralized administrative structures, they subjugated indigenous peoples and built massive but relatively integrated political units. On a smaller scale, perhaps because they faced other modern states on their peripheries rather than less developed and organized societies, Germany, Italy, and other powers unified their regions into national-states during this same period.

In a second pattern, states that faced very high costs of continental expansion, most notably Great Britain, built vast overseas empires. Our data on state size does not include colonial territories, but the history of Europe's overseas empires suggests a similar trend in territorial size, perhaps peaking a decade or two later. The mode of imperial expansion differed considerably by European state and peripheral region, but by the end of the nineteenth century nearly three-quarters of the globe was governed directly or indirectly by European countries – including several latecomers, famously Germany, that began to expand overseas only after they had consolidated their newly enlarged continental states. Both continental and imperial expansion appear to have a common root in the technological innovations that allowed states to reach further, faster, and deeper into more distant societies than at any time in the past.

Complementing but analytically distinct from the consequences of technological innovation was the spread of democratic and federal forms of government and the larger states they permitted. As we shall explain more fully in the theoretical section below, democracies are normally predicted to be and are, *ceteris paribus*, smaller than autocracies (Alesina and Spolaore 1997 and 2004). At the same time, democracies are also more likely to form federations than autocracies. Because they can allocate the provision of public services more efficiently across multiple levels of government, federal states will tend to be larger than unitary states. Where unitary democracies are small, federal democracies are *ceteris paribus* among the very largest states in the system (Hiscox and Lake 2000).

In a third pattern of territorial enlargement common to the late nineteenth century, otherwise independent and smaller democracies voluntarily pursued federation (Rector 2003). This pattern is distinct from the technological changes noted above, as suggested by the early creation of the United States from thirteen independent colonies. At the same time, however, technological innovation appears to have been required for the larger pattern to take hold. Several early nineteenth-century attempts in Central or South America to emulate the federal model of the United States failed (Gran Colombia, 1819–30, and United Provinces of Central America, 1823–38). Only after the middle of the nineteenth century, once the costs of transport and communication began to fall more rapidly, did federations survive in significant numbers. Indeed, nearly all of the democratic federal states that endure today were formed in this period, including Switzerland (adopting its modern federal constitution in 1848), Canada (1867), Australia (de facto independent since the 1850s, federated only in 1901), and others. Although there is some variance in the size of federal democracies, as the case of Switzerland suggests, they are all larger than their constituent units (by definition) and, on average, large relative to other types of states in the international system.

Interestingly, trade does not appear to have played a major role in influencing state size in the nineteenth century. Theory suggests that economic openness and international exchange should lead to smaller states. As the importance of protected national markets declines, and that of open international markets expands, smaller political units can more readily prosper and, thus, are expected to secede and form new sovereign states comprised of more homogeneous populations (Alesina and Spolaore 1997 and 2004). This effect, however, is not manifested in the trend in average state size. When the first period of globalization "took off" after 1870, state size was near its zenith and no contraction occurred for three decades. Although globalization was, in part, a consequence of the same technological innovations that permitted continental and imperial expansion, it is possible that the effects of economic openness were simply overwhelmed by the larger and perhaps more direct impact of technology on the costs to states of projecting power. It is also possible that economic openness restrained further growth in average state size after 1870, but this is a counterfactual that is difficult to evaluate given the unique and complex causal relationships found in the late nineteenth century.

Contraction

In the twentieth century, technological innovation continued, further lowering the costs of projecting state power over distance. The costs of transoceanic shipping continued to decline with the advent of containerization in the 1960s and 1970s. Similarly, air transport of both people and goods dramatically increased in quantity and decreased in price, especially after World War II. Telephony and, later, the internet, combined to produce virtually instantaneous communications at close to zero cost (Hufbauer 1991). Yet, where technological innovations led to larger states in the nineteenth century, they do not appear to have had a similar effect in the twentieth. Just as trade's effects were apparently muted in the previous century, technology's impact on state size appears muffled today, with perhaps the exception of the growth of the European Union, similar to the rise of the large, democratic, and federal states of the late nineteenth century (Rector 2003). Rather, the decline in average state size over the last 100 years seems best explained as a function of idiosyncratic factors in the immediate aftermath of World War I, increasing international economic exchange, and an increasing number of (unitary) democracies.

V. I. Lenin (1939) famously described World War I as a competition between the most advanced – and capitalist – states for territory in the periphery of the world economy. Although capitalism, a relative constant, was undoubtedly not the cause of this conflagration, there is an element of truth to Lenin's characterization of the war as the culmination of a process of territorial competition – a competition that was reprised twenty years later. The net effect of the war, for our topic here, was to reallocate the territory of the decaying imperial states of the ancient regime, most notably the Austro-Hungarian and Ottoman Empires. Out of these imperial ashes rose a set of new and smaller states in the Balkans and Eastern Europe. Just as the war itself was one of the two last great gasps of the old system of continental and imperial expansion, the new states created after the war may have been the progenitors of the new system of smaller states. These new states may have been premised on expectations of renewed economic openness following the war – expectations that were, of course, quickly dashed by increased protectionism in all the major powers. They may also have been a product of President Woodrow Wilson's call for national self-determination, or a sign of the presence of many smaller and sometimes antagonistic ethnic groups in the region. The early cases in this turn in average state size are hard to explain. Yet, this new trend was not limited to Europe. States everywhere had already started to become smaller on average after 1900; the trend merely accelerated after the war.

Over the twentieth century, two motors appear to have driven the move to smaller states. First, the world economy began a steady movement toward greater international economic openness after World War II. By the 1960s, levels of trade and overall economic interdependence, migration excepted, had returned to their pre-1913 highs and soon surpassed those levels in a new era of globalization. Theory predicts, and the evidence from the postwar period appears to support the hypothesis, that a world of increasing openness is more hospitable to smaller states. No longer dependent on their national markets, groups and regions are more willing to strike out "on their own" and assert their independence. This may be especially true for subnational regions in Europe that have been politically invigorated since the creation of the "single market" of the European Union.

Second, where the nineteenth century experienced growth in the number of federal democracies, which tend to be large, the twentieth century has seen several waves of progressive democratization in which the resulting unitary states tend to be relatively small. Indeed, the switch from federal to unitary democracies in the system is the only variable with sound theoretical foundations that actually correlates closely with actual state size over both the nineteenth and twentieth centuries. Technology explains the increase in state size in the nineteenth century, but not the decline in the twentieth; economic openness explains the contraction in state size in the twentieth century, but not the increase in the nineteenth. Regime type appears to be the best "proximate" explanation of state size. But just as federation may have emerged as a solution to increasing economies of scale in the first period, economic openness may interact with and, indeed, help sustain unitary democracies in a hostile international environment. Democracy helps promote the general interest in free trade over the particularistic interest in protection, and the prosperity engendered by economic openness may help bolster democracy. Regime type may be the best proximate cause, but it is itself a product of deeper causal forces.

In summary, our best estimate of the forces driving the amazing rise and decline in average state size over the last two centuries looks to be a combination of technological change and federation to explain the increase in territorial size in the nineteenth century, and a combination of economic openness and democratization in unitary states to explain the decrease in the twentieth century. We now turn to the question of the relationship between average state size and conflict.

State size and conflict

The theoretical literature on state size is small, but growing. The "state-of-the-art" model has been developed by Alberto Alesina and Enrico Spolaore (2004). We rely on this model above in our interpretation of territorial change. Here, we extend the model to conflict. Alesina and Spolaore posit a central tradeoff between economies of scale in governance, for which marginal cost is assumed to decrease monotonically with size, and preference heterogeneity, a cost that increases with size. Economies of scale derive both from producing public goods, such as national defense, at a fixed cost for a larger population, and from the division of labor within a larger domestic market. By themselves, economies of scale suggest there should be a single country that encompasses the globe. Preference heterogeneity is a cost borne by citizens for whom the policy preferred by the median voter is ever more distant from their preferred policy. As long as preferences and geography are correlated, and the policy enacted lies near the mid-point of any population, larger states mean that more and more citizens are increasingly dissatisfied with their government's policy. On this dimension, the optimal state has a mean of 1, with each person forming their own state reflecting exactly their own preferences. Actual state size, Alesina and Spolaore posit, is determined by the tradeoff between these two factors. Among their primary implications are:

- Reductions in the cost of or increases in the demand for public goods should lead, *ceteris paribus*, to larger states.
- Increased openness to trade, which reduces the relative benefits of national markets, should lead to smaller states.

Democracies will tend to form too many, overly small states. Since those near the periphery of the state receive the same public goods benefits as others, but suffer the costs of policies more distant from their ideal points, citizens will elect to secede and create more states than is optimal. By contrast, in autocracies, rulers earn rents from larger states and can more easily ignore the preferences of citizens at the periphery; as a result, they tend to form too few, overly large states. As discussed above, these expectations are generally borne out by the trend in average state size over the nineteenth and twentieth centuries, but not in a direct fashion.

Alesina and Spolaore offer only comparative static predictions of an equilibrium outcome. They do not posit a process of territorial change, and especially not a theory of war. To explain when territorial expansion or contraction will be peaceful, and when it will be violent, we augment their theory of state size with insights from the rationalist theory of war.

We posit, on the basis of Alesina and Spolaore's model and our earlier work (Lake and O'Mahony 2004) that as economies of scale increase, defined broadly to include the gains from specialization within a larger domestic market, countries on average increase in size (albeit with some lag and considerable diversity). We focus on average territorial size here as the end product of this link between the benefits of greater size and size itself. This implies, in turn, that as states increase in size, territory is becoming more valuable to the state and its citizens. Since this is a system-wide trend, we assume that all countries are affected in similar ways, regardless of whether or not they actually succeed in acquiring more territory. Thus, as average state size expands and, we infer, territory becomes more valuable, we expect states to compete more intensely for and bargain harder over territory that is 1) under the control of their neighbors; 2) in some third party that they and their neighbors might agree to dismember; or 3) "unclaimed" by a sovereign state.

As states struggle over the division of territory, bargaining may fail and war may ensue for one or more reasons (Fearon 1995; Powell 1999). States may possess private information with incentives to misrepresent that information to others. They may not be able to commit credibly to a particular division of the territory. Or territory itself may be indivisible (or lumpy), making settlements that reflect the precise distribution of capabilities impossible. These are the by now well-established tenets of the rationalist theory of war.

Most rationalist models assume that the issue in dispute, in our case territory, is "normalized" along an interval between 0 and 1, representing the good as a fixed value. As illustrated in Figure 6.2, the "dissatisfied" state (D), located at 0, covets all of the territory (summed to 1) and the "satisfied" state (S), located at 1, similarly desires all of the territory (summed at 0). D has an incentive to challenge S when the status quo division of territory (q) is less than its expected probability of victory (p). Powell (1999) describes this as a case where the existing distribution of benefits in the system does not reflect the distribution of capabilities. Since war is always costly to both sides, there always exists a bargaining range centered around p defined by the costs of fighting to the two states (represented here as d and s, respectively). Within this bargaining range, the two states would prefer any division of territory rather than fight. S will offer D a distribution of territory at p − d, and D, if it has the opportunity to make the first offer, will offer S a division of the territory at p + s, but in full information either offer will generally be accepted.[1] In turn, states are typically modeled as being uncertain of each other's

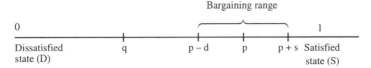

Figure 6.2. The costs of war and efficient bargaining.
Source: Adapted from Powell (1999, 92, Fig. 3.3).

costs of fighting (states have a prior belief about the distribution of their opponent's costs of fighting, but do not know their precise costs). As Powell explains most clearly, since concessions are also costly, each state makes an offer to the other likely to satisfy the "expected" type of opponent, but not necessarily every opponent. When the offer is "too small," bargaining breaks down. This generates a risk–return calculus that produces war when one or the other state believes its opponent has a high cost of fighting when, in fact, it has a low cost.

To incorporate changes in the value of territory simply, we retain the assumption that the issue lies along a fixed zero–one interval but redefine the costs of fighting (s, d) relative to the value of territory (v), or $s' = s/v$ and $d' = d/v$.[2] Thus, in this amendment, an increase in the value of territory is the same as a reduction in the relative cost of fighting. Given this shorthand, the standard predictions of rationalist theories of war carry through. Most important, Powell demonstrates that decreases in the costs of fighting shrink the bargaining range and increase the probability of war for all distributions of capability (except those close to the status quo). In turn, as territory increases in value, the relative cost of fighting declines and, it follows, war becomes more likely. As territory decreases in value, the relative cost of fighting increases and war becomes less likely. This is illustrated in Figure 6.3. This produces our primary hypothesis: as states increase in size, war is more likely and should, all else being constant, be more frequent; as states decrease in size, war is less likely and, therefore, should be less frequent. The null hypothesis, by contrast, is that there is no systematic relationship between the average territorial size of states and interstate conflict.

We are emphatically not predicting that particular territorial disputes are likely to result in war, or that states that repeatedly engage in war necessarily place greater value on territory. Rather, we predict only that the same sources that lead states on average to expand their territories are likely to produce greater conflict throughout the system as states try to accommodate themselves to their evolving environment. Areas with acute and persistent interstate conflict may contain states trying to expand unsuccessfully to seize the benefits of larger territories; the

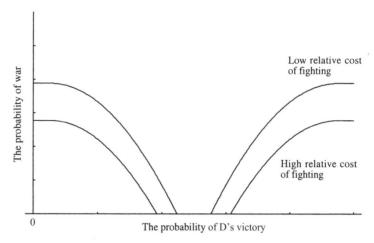

Figure 6.3. The effects of an increase in the relative cost of fighting
Source: Adapted from Powell (1999, 112, Fig. 3.8).

absence of particular territorial changes does not count against our predictions about the incentives of states. Conversely, areas with lots of territorial changes may not experience unusual levels of interstate conflict; weaker parties may simply foresee inevitable defeat and concede. Yet we expect that, on average, as economies of scale increase and states respond by attempting to acquire more territory, they will produce on average more interstate conflict. Conversely, as economies of scale contract and states become willing to shed territory, we predict a smaller number of interstate wars. Thus, we predict specifically that levels of interstate war will be higher in the nineteenth than in the twentieth century. In offering this prediction, we recognize that the process of state change is slow and episodic, and that in a noisy environment states may have difficulty in drawing conclusions about trends in the value of territory. Thus, we allow for states to update their expectations slowly, suggesting that changes in territorial size will be reflected in trends in interstate war only with some lag.

Patterns of state size and conflict

Our principal research strategy is really quite simple, which is to examine levels and changes in average territorial size and interstate wars over time. This is a variant of an interrupted time series design (Cook and Campbell 1979, 207–32).[3] The narrower the "treatment window" around an event, of course, the more confidence we can have in our estimate of the relationship between territory and conflict. We allow for a substantial (but somewhat arbitrary) lag of up to twenty-five years between changes in the average size of states and conflict levels. Although this limits confidence in our inferences, it seems appropriate, as noted above, given the ambiguous and slowly evolving nature of the environment to which states are responding. Since both territorial change and conflict are relatively rare events, in all the figures below we fit a third-degree polynomial to the decade average data to highlight better the long-term trends in average state size and conflict.

Although economies of scale are often universal, and we treat them as such throughout the analysis above, they may nonetheless vary by region. Investments in technology differ widely, with railroads spreading across the several continents at very different times and to very different degrees. Similarly, openness to trade is a political decision that, although it may cluster by region, is nonetheless reached at different times by different countries. Although regime type also appears to cluster spatially and temporally (K. S. Gleditsch 2002b), this too is a national decision that will exhibit substantial regional variation. Thus, there may be important regional variations in state size and, in turn, conflict propensities. In addition to testing the above hypothesis at the system level, we also examine it at the regional level in those areas where a sufficient percentage of the territory is incorporated into states such that a) we can get a robust measure of average state size and b) states have an opportunity to come into conflict with one another. In Africa, Asia, and the Middle East, most of the territory for most of the period covered in this study is either held by colonial powers or "uncounted" in our census of sovereign states. With in some cases only one or two states considered sovereign in the region, we hesitate to infer anything about the "average" states in these areas. In practice, we thus restrict our regional sample to Europe and the Western hemisphere.

Data

We have recently reconstructed the standard data sets on state size to create more accurate estimates of home territory for the period 1815 to the present. As we began to work with the existing data, we quickly realized that they were deeply flawed, requiring that we rebuild them from "scratch."[4] The data set we have constructed identifies all sovereign states during this period, applying an essentially juridical definition of sovereignty that focuses on recognition by other states.[5] Territory is defined as home or national land mass, generally a contiguous area governed as a single political unit (as noted, thereby excluding colonial territories), and is measured in square kilometers. Our system begins in 1815 with 35 states, and grows to 46 states in 1890, 63 in 1920, and 154 in 1998. There is, of course, a substantial amount of missing data here. There are currently 191 members of the United Nations, for instance, but we possess territorial data for their complete histories on only 80 percent of them.

We measure interstate war using the Correlates of War Project's data on militarized interstate disputes, examining the 102 cases occurring between 1822 and 1992 that the Correlates of War Project codes as wars. To test our hypotheses, we must transform these data into a "count" measure that captures the number of conflicts that occur in each period. The simplest measure is the number of new wars begun in any year divided by the number of countries in the system. We then aggregate this measure by decade to reduce the noise created by an annual measure. As the number of states grows rather dramatically over the last two centuries, it is important to adjust for this change: 5 wars in a system of 15 states represents a very different level of conflict than 5 wars in a system of 150 states. We refer to this indicator as interstate war onset. Our regional measures are created in an identical fashion, simply replacing the total number of wars in the system with the number of wars in each region and the total number of countries in the system with the number of countries in the region. Our second measure is the number of war years per decade divided by the number of countries in the system at the end of that decade. This captures in an intuitive way not only the number of wars occurring within a given decade but the intensity or magnitude of conflict as well. Wars that last longer, creating a larger number of war years, are more difficult to resolve (almost by definition) and, more importantly, reflect more intense preferences over goals by the belligerents. We refer to this second measure as ongoing wars or war years. We find that war onset and war years track one another quite well, with the latter simply exacerbating swings in the trend.

Results

At the system-wide level, there is a strong correlation between state size and the pattern of interstate war (see Figure 6.4). As state size increases over the nineteenth century, levels of interstate conflict also grow, with a particularly noteworthy spike in wars during the period of most rapid state expansion between 1850 and 1870. Once state size begins to decline after 1900, interstate conflict also decreases – although World Wars I and II form dramatic conflict peaks well after the system-wide trend in size has turned. At the system-wide level, the long-term trend

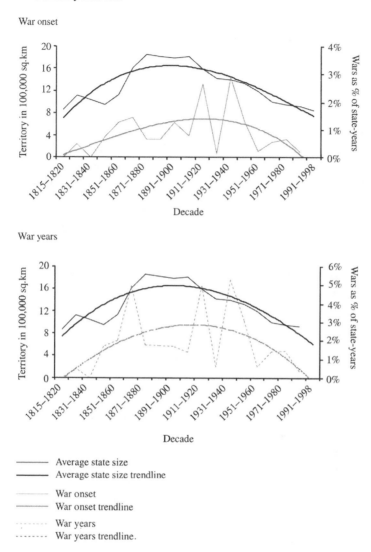

Figure 6.4. State size and conflict.

in both size and conflict, represented by the third-degree polynomial trendlines, form inverted Us, with the peak level of war years lagging the peak in territorial size by two decades. While closely mirroring the trend in war years, the peak in war onset occurs twenty-five years after the peak in territorial size, pushing the outer edge of our treatment window. We attribute this difference to the large number of individual disputes that comprised the two world wars, to which the war onset variable is particularly sensitive. Overall, our expectations about territorial size and interstate conflict are generally confirmed at the system-wide level.

There is more variance in the relationship at the regional level, of course, where the numbers of states, territorial changes, and wars are smaller and more episodic. In both sets of regional graphs, we present average state size in the region and the level of interstate conflict in the region by decade. With the largest number of countries and wars, Europe closely mirrors the system-wide trends already described above, providing support for our hypothesis (see Figure 6.5). Throughout almost the entire period, Europe's states were relatively small compared to those in other regions, but otherwise the pattern over time is the same. State size increases until approximately 1900, and then begins to decline thereafter – although the decrease is less dramatic in Europe than in the system as a whole. Levels of conflict, as measured by both war onset and war years, also peak around the time of World War I, lagging state size by about one decade.

The Western hemisphere is a slightly more complicated case. States in North and South America start the nineteenth century considerably larger than those elsewhere, largely Europe during this period (see Figure 6.6). They decline in size, then rebound, closely tracking the system-wide average at its peak. Although average size falls slightly after 1900, states in the Western hemisphere remain well above the system mean thereafter. In turn, the greatest period of conflict in the Western hemisphere is in the 1860s, when state size is once again growing from its historic lows in the 1840s. Once state size stabilizes after 1870, the level of interstate conflict drops and then oscillates around a mean of 1.8 percent for war years and 0.6 percent for war onset for the period 1880 to the present. The slight uptick in the polynomial in the final decades of the twentieth century is, in our view, largely an artifact of the fitting method. Despite the relative lack of change in average state size since 1870, the Western hemisphere still largely confirms our expectations.

In general, the relationship between state size and interstate conflict confirms our expectations both at the system-wide and regional levels. As states become larger on average interstate conflict increases, and as states become smaller on average interstate conflict decreases.

Conflict issues

In this section, we examine patterns in the issues that led to interstate war between 1815 and 1989. Following the rationalist model of war

War onset

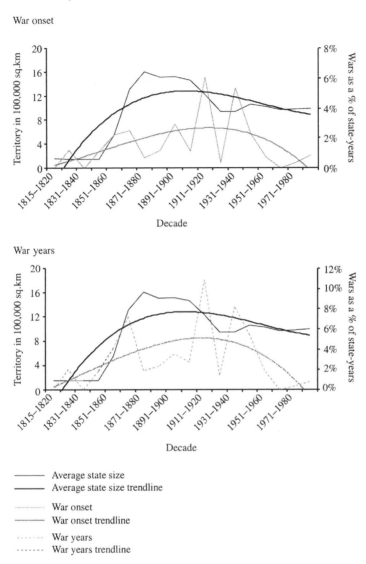

Figure 6.5. Europe: state size and conflict.

discussed above, we do not posit that these issues led directly to war. Rather, we claim only that these issues were central to the disputes that eventually led to larger bargaining failures. Nonetheless, tracking the distribution of issues over time can help reveal the salience of territory to

War onset

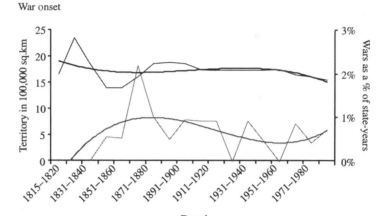

War ongoing

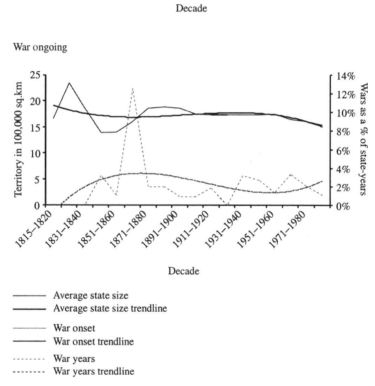

Figure 6.6. Western hemisphere: state size and conflict.

interstate wars. Our primary hypothesis here is that issues of territory were more frequent in disputes that led to interstate war during the period of expansion in average state size, and that territorial issues have been less frequent in disputes that led to war during the period of decline in average state size. Specifically, we expect the salience of territory to decline after approximately 1900.

We employ a "pattern-matching" non-equivalent dependent variables research design in this test (Trochim 2001, 231–34). The power of a NEDV design comes from the predicted effects of a treatment on some outcome variables but not others. The other outcomes serve as controls for alternative causes. Thus, we predict that the rise and then decline in average state size will affect the frequency of territory as an issue in disputes, but will not be correlated with the frequency of other types of issues that led to war. Although not commonly employed in political science, NEDV designs have strong internal validity.

Holsti (1991) has coded all interstate wars in this period for the issues that were salient for the original combatants. His method is inductive, building from what diplomats of the period and subsequent scholars have identified as the key issues in the dispute. Unfortunately, Holsti does not define his issues very completely. Rather, he creates inductively broad common categories that are left purposely open-ended. Lacking formal definitions for the various issues he identifies, before analyzing the data we each separately coded Holsti's issues into four broad categories: territory-related, foreign interests, economic interests, and realpolitik. We concurred on almost all coding, and then resolved the few differences through discussion. There is, no doubt, room for argument on some of our coding. Our classification of the issues is presented in Table 6.1, along with Holsti's findings on the distribution of issues that generated wars. Since there can be multiple issues involved in any war, the number of issues in any period is greater than the number of wars.

We aggregate the distribution of issues by category in Table 6.2. As we predict, the frequency of territory as an issue in interstate wars declined significantly between the nineteenth and twentieth centuries. Although Holsti's periods do not align exactly with ours, the trend nonetheless supports expectations. In the period 1815–1914, territory-related issues constituted 51 percent of all issues that led to war, declining to 43 percent between 1918 and 1941 and 38 percent between 1945 and 1989. Importantly for our NEDV design, there is no evident relationship between the trend in average state size and the frequency of other, non-territorial issues. This suggests, as we expect, that the trend in average state size is related to territorial issues but not others.

Table 6.1. *Distribution of issues that generated interstate wars, 1815–1989, as a percentage of all wars*

Issue	1815–1914	1918–1941	1945–1989
Territory-related			
Territory	42	47	24
Territory (border dispute)	—	—	7
Strategic territory	13	30	21
Empire creation	10	20	—
Colonial competition	3	—	—
National unification/consolidation	26	—	17
Maintain integrity of state/empire	55	30	28
Ethnic/religious unification/irredenta	6	17	12
Colonialism	—	—	7
Foreign interests			
National liberation/state creation	29	13	28
Secession/state creation	—	—	7
Ethnic liberation/state creation	—	—	—
Protect ethnic/religious confreres	26	7	9
Dynastic/succession claims	10	—	—
Government composition	13	17	28
Ideological liberation	10	10	14
Population protection/peacekeeping	—	—	9
Prevent population movement/refugees	—	—	5
Economic interests			
Commerce/resources	—	20	9
Compensation/reparation for incident	—	7	—
Protect nationals/commercial interests	3	17	9
Commerce/navigation	13	—	3
Realpolitik			
National security/immediate threat	—	—	7
Balance of power	3	1	—
Regime/state survival	6	37	21
Test of strength	3	—	—
Maintain regional dominance	10	7	5
Autonomy	6	7	7
National/crown honor	6	—	—
Defend/support ally	—	10	16
Revise treaty terms	—	10	—
Meet treaty obligations/enforce treaty terms	—	—	7
Preserve alliance unity	—	—	3
Enforce treaty terms	3	30	—

Source: Holsti 1991; Tables 7.2, 7.3, 9.2, 9.3, 11.2, and 11.3.

Table 6.2. *Distribution of issues that generated interstate wars, 1815–1989, as a percentage of all issues*

Issue categories	1815–1914	1918–1941	1945–1989
Territory-related	51	43	38
Foreign interests	28	14	32
Economic interests	5	13	9
Realpolitik	12	31	21
Total (varies due to rounding errors in Holsti)	96	101	100

Source: Compiled by categories defined in Table 6.1 and from Holsti 1991, Tables 7.2, 7.3, 9.2, 9.3, 11.2, and 11.3.

Table 6.3. *Percentage of all wars in which one or more "territory-related" issues were present, 1815–1989*

Period	Percentage of all wars in which territory was an issue
1815–1914	84
1918–1941	77
1945–1989	74

Source: Compiled by categories defined in Table 6.1 and from Holsti 1991, Tables 7.1, 9.1, 11.1.

By Holsti's construction, wars can involve more than one territory-related issue, thus the evidence in Table 6.1 contains "double-counting." In Table 6.3, we recalculate Holsti's war-by-war codings and present the percentage of all wars in which one or more territory-related issues were at stake. In 1815–1914, 84 percent of all wars involved at least one territory-related issue. Between 1945 and 1989, only 74 percent of all wars involved one or more such issues. As others have claimed, territory is still obviously an important issue in many wars – indeed, it is the most frequent issue leading to war (Vasquez 1993 and 1995; Hensel 2000; Huth 2000). But as we expect, territory is less often an issue today than it was in the past.

The evidence here also supports expectations. The distribution of issues that led to war reinforces our earlier finding that the rise and decline in the average territorial size of states appears to be related in important ways to the level of interstate conflict in the international system. As the average size of states in the system has declined, territory has become less salient as a cause of war.

This trend in recent decades is also evident in the empirical analyses undertaken in the Gartzke and Buhaug and Gleditsch contributions to this volume. Although both chapters focus on globalization rather than territorial size as an explanation for the declining importance of territorial issues in post-World War II interstate conflicts, both analyses suggest that territorial disputes now play a smaller role in interstate conflict than was the case in the nineteenth century. For Gartzke, while globalization in the post-World War II era has had little to no effect on the incidence of interstate conflict, he finds that globalization has led to a shift away from conflict over territorial issues. Similarly, Buhaug and Gleditsch's analysis of all militarized interstate disputes between 1875 and 1998 provides inconclusive but suggestive support for their hypothesis that globalization reduces the political value of territory, thereby reducing the likelihood that territorial disputes will result in interstate conflict. While both analyses point to increased economic interdependence to explain this trend, the fact that the high levels of economic interdependence that existed in the nineteenth century coincided with an increase rather than a decline in the percentage of territorially motivated interstate disputes suggests that while globalization may mute interstate conflict over territory, globalization by itself is insufficient to explain the salience of territorial disputes as a cause of war.

Conclusion

The average territorial size of states and interstate conflict appear to be related, as we expected, at the macro-historical level. As state size on average increased and then decreased over the last two centuries, interstate conflict rose and fell as well. A similar pattern is found across Europe and the Western hemisphere. Moreover, territorial issues were more frequently associated with war during the period of state expansion and less frequently associated with war during the period of contraction. The evolution in state size is a slow, incremental process, but one that nonetheless appears to be associated with the overall pattern of interstate war.

The findings in this chapter support a recurrent theme in this volume, specifically, that states and individuals have only an instrumental attachment to territory. As Barbara Walter argues in the concluding chapter, "individuals will embrace a particular piece of land when it benefits them socially, economically, politically or defensively, and increasingly disregard it when it does not. Thus, once this function disappears, so too should the attachments and the conflicts that may arise as a result."

While our analysis demonstrates at the macro-historical level that this appears to be true, a systemic-level analysis is insufficient to predict when and how the salience of territorial attachment will weaken in any particular state. One finding that shines through most of the chapters in this volume is that not all territory is equally likely to change hands. A compelling state-level explanation for territorial change would address how territorial attachments change as a function of the characteristics of the territory, broadly conceived – including, for example, the productive and symbolic value of the territory, and its importance as a domestic and international focal point.

Starting from societal or state-level analyses, other contributions in this volume provide a good foundation for undertaking such an analysis. Focusing on the informational role played by clearly delineated state control over territory, Goemans' exposition on the importance of focal points for creating a credible commitment between the ruler and the ruled, and Simmons' evidence that stable, uncontested borders greatly increase the value of interstate economic relations, suggest that states have a strong preference for managing changes in their territorial holdings that do not erode the domestic and international bargains that rest upon the state's unquestioned commitment to fight for its own territory.

Turning to the changing symbolic importance of territory, Newman and Robbins demonstrate how globalization can have radically different outcomes on groups' territorial attachments. With the decline in the productive importance of territory associated with globalization (Gartzke), the symbolic value of territory may increase, as in the case of Israeli–Palestinian conflict (Newman), or decline, as in the case of the Urapmin in Papua New Guinea (Robbins). Similarly, Lyons demonstrates that globalization also affects which groups mobilize around which pieces of territory. With the rise of politically oriented diaspora networks, the resources domestic groups can bring to bear with the support of their international compatriots in the defense of their territory have increased.

Long-term changes in the value of territory have contributed to levels of interstate conflict over the last two centuries. Even though we cannot, as yet, explain particular conflicts, the link between territory and conflict appears strong at the aggregate, macro-historical level. As Rosecrance (1986) has argued, the territorial state has given way to the trading state. However, this need not suggest a permanent change. Globalization has waxed and waned before, and it could certainly do so again in the future. Economies of scale can shift for exogenous reasons, openness to trade is a political decision subject to the whims and vicissitudes of domestic politics, and the world has seen waves of democracy come and, unfortunately, go. Territory could, once again, become more valuable and an object of renewed struggle. Understanding territoriality and its relationship to conflict remains an important topic of continuing debate and research.

NOTES

1   In full information, war is seldom an equilibrium outcome. For exceptions to this rule, see Slantchev (2003).

2   Von Neumann-Morgenstern preferences are unique up to a linear transformation, which means the payoffs can be multiplied by any positive number or summed with any number without changing any results. In effect, this means we can simplify by setting two of the payoffs to convenient numbers. In the bargaining model, the payoff to controlling all of the territory is normally set equal to 1 and the payoff to controlling none of the territory is set equal to zero. Let the un-normalized payoffs to winning everything, losing everything, and the cost of fighting for the status quo state S be v, b, and s. (We can do the same normalization for the dissatisfied state.) The normalized payoffs are then given by subtracting b from everything and dividing by $v - b$. This gives normalized payoffs of $v' = 1$, $b' = 0$, and $s' = (s - b)/(v - b)$. The equilibria with un-normalized payoffs are identical to those with the normalized payoffs. We thank Robert Powell for his assistance and clarity on this point.

3   In an interrupted time series design, an exogenous change in the "treatment variable" is predicted to lead to a change in the outcome variable within some specified "treatment window." In our case, we expect changes in the trend in average state size will produce a change in the trend in interstate conflict. Thus, a change in the trend in average state size (that is, a change in the sign of the first derivative) is our "treatment," which is expected to have a directed impact on the trend in conflict within a 25-year period. Because it relies upon multiple observations of the outcome variable before and after the treatment, an interrupted time series design has high internal validity: in essence, past observations of the outcome variable serve as "control variables." In our analysis below, the system and each region form separate series, so we essentially perform the same test multiple times, providing us with additional opportunities for confirmation or disconfirmation of our hypotheses.

4   Territorial data in Banks (1976) and apparently used in the Correlates of War (Singer and Small 1994) and Polity IV (Marshall and Jaggers 2000) data sets do not capture all known territorial changes. We began with Banks (1976) and current World Bank (2001) territorial estimates as our starting point. We reconciled these two territorial size estimates using Goertz and Diehl's Territorial Change data set (see Goertz and Diehl 1992) to highlight the timing and magnitude of territorial changes, relying upon the *Statesman's Yearbook* to confirm and elaborate upon each entry in the Goertz and Diehl (1992) data set. Although there is undoubtedly some measurement error remaining in the data, we expect that it is essentially random; but since this is an ongoing series

we nonetheless face the risk that whatever errors do exist compound themselves over time. However, this is, we believe, the most complete and accurate series on territorial size now available.

5 We compiled the list of sovereign states from Arthur S. Banks' Cross National Times Series data set, the Correlates of War project, the Polity IV database, and K. S. Gleditsch and Ward (1999). Disagreements between "birth" and "death" dates for states were settled by reference to the *Statesman's Yearbook*, which provides concise explanations for the historical events in question. As to whether mergers of states created new entities (for example, Germany and Italy in the nineteenth century) or simply larger but continuing entities (for example, the Federal Republic of Germany after reunification), we followed the coding decisions used in the above sources. In using a juridical notion of sovereignty, we thereby include some "semi-sovereign" states, such as Canada or Australia, that might otherwise be excluded and some "divided states," such as China in the early twentieth century, that might be disaggregated.

7 Globalization, economic development, and territorial conflict

Erik Gartzke

Introduction

In a world of finite resources, states occasionally use or threaten force to coerce what they cannot obtain more expediently through bargain or barter. Historically, territory has been a particularly potent source of interstate friction (Vasquez 1993). Land, and the resources in and under territory, traditionally served as the basis for sovereign wealth and power. Big states were naturally stronger, and often attempted to co-opt their smaller neighbors (Fazal 2002; Alesina and Spolaore 2005; Lake and O'Mahony 2004). Warfare ensued as sovereigns sought to take or hold territory, or to acquire or retain resources and populations tied to the soil. A variety of arguments and anecdotes suggest ways in which the incentives to compete over territory have diminished among advanced industrialized economies. Two main forces characterize economic changes thought to be associated with a decline in the propensity toward territorial conflict: economic development and globalization. Economic development involves specialization of labor, technological innovation, the concentration of capital, and other measures that substantially increase productivity beyond levels in traditional societies. Globalization consists of the integration of markets and the decentralization of production networks.

Students of international politics have long been interested in the role of economic development in curbing, or augmenting, the impetus to take up arms. Still, how economic processes relate to interstate conflict is as yet poorly understood. Elsewhere, I point out that contrasting claims about economic development and conflict can be reconciled by recognizing that development differentially affects competition over different "goods." Increases in state capacity associated with economic development potentially allow sovereigns to project power, while also making the conquest of certain economic factors – such as land, minerals, and unskilled labor – less desirable and more expensive. Development enhances the ability of states to engage in disputes over international policies, while decreasing interest in resource conflicts, particularly with a state's neighbors (Gartzke 2004).[1]

Here, I extend this research to a comparison of the effects of globalization and development on territorial conflict. There exists considerable diversity of opinion about how globalization and development influence political competition and conflict. It is unclear, for example, whether economic forces lead to a domestic "pull" dampening willingness to fight or a foreign "push" limiting opportunity. By distinguishing between initiators and targets of militarized conflict, I can adjudicate among theories asserting a decline in the utility of aggression to states owing to higher direct or indirect costs of conquest and other theories asserting reduced benefits of occupation brought about by changes in the nature of production. There also exist profound differences between the two economic processes. However, most of the same arguments about conflict are applied equally to both globalization and development. I show that differences between the two economic processes are relevant to how each impacts territorial disputes: development diminishes the impetus toward territorial conquest and the capture of resources through force while it actually increases policy conflict among both economically advanced initiators and targets. Globalization has little or no effect on territorial disputes, while its impact on non-territorial conflict is conditioned by interdependence. Two integrated states are least likely to fight, while the most disputatious dyads combine globalized and non-globalized countries.

In the next section, I review arguments relating development and globalization to territorial conflict.[2] I then develop hypotheses that allow me to evaluate alternative theoretical claims and compare the influence of each economic process on the probability of war and peace. The results of these analyses are both informative and non-intuitive. The effects of globalization variables seem most consistent with their role as international linkages and mechanisms for signaling. States exposed to mobile capital are as a consequence more transparent in their political dealing. It is difficult for these states to bluff given the contrasting incentives of sovereigns to both calm markets and compel foreign opponents. Economic development increases the physical ability of non-contiguous or distant states to engage in disputes, but also decreases the interest of initiators in fighting neighbors, particularly over territorial possessions. This does not mean that developed countries are unwilling to defend existing territory, however, as there is no decrease in the probability of conflict associated with the economic status of targets. The logic behind these findings is complex, as are the findings themselves. I conclude with a discussion of the implications of the research.

Studies of development, globalization, and conflict

Globalization and development are substantially different economic processes, though the two appear related.[3] Globalization is international, while economic development can be largely domestic in origin and benefit. Globalization involves the promise (but certainly no guarantee) of prosperity, while development represents actual prosperity, if only of the narrow material kind, and possibly only for some in society. An empirical comparison of these two processes makes sense because they have already been associated through parallel accounts of their effects on war and peace. Arguments that have been developed in the context of economic development have been applied in the same manner to globalization, sometimes by the same author. Whether this theoretical equivalence is appropriate is a question best adjudicated empirically. The comparison also stands to offer new insights about each of these processes, insights that may in turn spur additional theory building.

Economic development: grand panacea or dangerous storm?[4]

Debates about the determinants of competition and violent conflict suffuse modern social thought.[5] Liberals have long associated a variety of environmental conditions with a cessation of warfare.[6] Kant famously argued that "a republic must be more inclined to perpetual peace by its nature" (1957, 28). Kant also claimed that "the spirit of commerce, which is incompatible with war, sooner or later gains the upper hand in every state" (1957, 32).[7] These ideas were not new even to Kant's contemporaries.[8] As Ceadel notes, "the argument that 'republican' regimes are necessary for peace . . . was already a near-commonplace of Anglo-American radicalism" (2000, 16).[9] That, in addition to regime type and trade, Kant saw international organizations, political stability, and the habit of peace as pacifying is merely to note that he was not immune to piling on.

Liberal theories are multi-hued, exhibiting different foci depending on the nature of the times. Explanations linking economic development to peace rapidly gathered steam with the industrial revolution.[10] Writing in 1835, Cobden shifted the emphasis in the standard liberal argument:

There is no remedy for [interventionism] but in the wholesome exercise of the people's opinion in behalf of their own interests. The middle and industrious classes of England can have no interest apart from the preservation of peace. (Cobden 1903, 34)

Cobden's version of liberal peace privileges income. The interests of the middle classes derive from their pocket books. Kantian liberal institutions and practices are not enough. Indeed, democracy is incidental in this view, facilitating the pass-through of liberal preferences, but not by itself ensuring fortuitous effects. Peace occurred because the voting middle classes could not derive benefit from war, and because wise men (such as Cobden) enlighten the citizenry about the public interest.[11]

Intellectual history, to say nothing of politics, would be less interesting without friction.[12] Where liberals saw the march of progress and peace, others heard the drumbeat of war. Hobson (1938), in particular, identifies capitalist development with imperialism. As Cobden had done before him, Hobson modified the standard liberal argument, emphasizing the distribution of income and control over capital, rather than historic prosperity. Capital accumulation and the resulting thirst for markets would lead to disaster. "Imperialism – whether it consists in a future policy of expansion or in the rigorous maintenance of all those vast tropical lands which have been earmarked as British spheres of influence – implies militarism now and ruinous wars in the future" (1938, 130).[13]

Hobsonian imperialism tied in nicely with Marxist theory and helped to address a troubling empirical inconsistency. With the revolution slow to materialize, Lenin (1965) and others sought to associate industrial development with economic and political subjugation outside Europe.[14] Imperialism temporarily delayed the dialectic, but the inevitable was just around the corner; the continuing thirst for markets would lead to war and the proletarian revolution.[15] Writing in 1907, Karl Liebknecht anticipated the Great War in the colonial machinations of the European powers.

This tension is a necessary consequence of the ever-growing economic rivalry between England and Germany on the world market, i.e., a direct consequence of unbridled capitalist development and of international competition.

(Liebknecht 1969, 13)[16]

Not to be outdone by the Marxists in their disdain for the "starry" ideals of liberals, realists offer a different conception of the role of development in precipitating violence. Carr (1939) in particular mounts an emphatic, almost visceral attack on liberal theories of peace.[17] Development increases the resources available to states, allowing them to buy more weapons.[18] The struggle for markets also has an analog in the realist preoccupation with the zero-sum struggle for power.[19] The two "isms" part company, however, in how they order events, and which events they emphasize. For Marxists, economic forces dominate politics.

Leaders simply follow the lead of capitalists. Realists reverse the causal arrow, arguing that politics trumps economic interests (or at least that it should). Thus, while orthodox Marxism claims that capitalist development inevitably descends into warfare, the realist view is conditioned by how states play their capitalist cards.[20] While realists predominately reject the idea that economic development promotes cooperation among nations,[21] development itself need not increase the frequency of conflict, even if growing state capacity raises the economic costs associated with whatever wars actually occur (Morgenthau 1948).[22]

Paradigmatic debates are cyclical, or possibly helical.[23] Circumstances during the Cold War emphasized relative, rather than absolute, power, diminishing the importance of development as a direct determinant of war and peace. Arms racing, deterrence, and balancing supplanted imperialism and growth as the focus of most scholarly attention in the study of international relations. Still, one can discern the familiar dialectic over the consequences of development in discussions between neorealists and neoliberals (Keohane and Nye 1989; Mearsheimer 1983 and 2001; Waltz 1959 and 1979).[24]

A number of scholars bucked the Cold War trend, retaining development in the driver's seat of history. As before, optimists (Kuznets 1966 and 1973; Rosecrance 1985 and 1996) and pessimists (Choucri and North 1975 and 1989; Kennedy 1987)[25] coexisted in a common analytical universe.[26] The challenge was to find ways of adjudicating contrasting claims, given that anecdotal support was ubiquitous. Even in earlier debates, the quantification of key variables had been widely practiced, though researchers seldom went further than using data in tabular form for descriptive purposes.[27] Unfortunately, when statistical methods were applied, it was generally discovered that there existed no empirical basis for accepting any relationship between development and interstate conflict (Richardson 1960; East and Gregg 1967; Rummel 1967; Thompson 1982; Maoz and Russett 1992).[28]

In contrast to findings for interstate conflict, the level of economic development has been shown to be one of the most robust predictors of intrastate conflict (Collier and Hoeffler 2002; Elbadawi and Hegre 2004; Elbadawi and Sambanis 2002; Ellingsen 2000; Fearon and Laitin 2003; Hegre et al. 2001). Fearon and Laitin find that GDP/population "is strongly significant in both a statistical and substantive sense" even when controlling for a wide variety of other factors including region, ethnicity, religion, prior conflict, territory, regime type and stability, and foreign involvement" (2003, 83). Wallensteen et al. note that "It has been repeatedly observed that the onset of internal wars is related to the level of economic development" (2001, 21).

A closer look at arguments linking development to war or peace helps to explain the dearth of systemic support for either relationship even as it suggests a way to reconcile the enigma of contrasting domestic and international results. Rosecrance (1985) offers an optimistic vision of development and peace reminiscent of Cobden, Bastiat, and other nineteenth-century liberals. "Land, which is fixed, can be physically captured, but labor, capital, and information are mobile and cannot be definitively sized; after an attack, these resources can slip away like quicksilver" (Rosecrance 1996, 48).[29] In contrast, Ashley claims that "war is mainly explicable in terms of differential growth" (1980, 3).[30] The incompatibility of the two claims is largely only apparent. The declining value of territory relative to other factor inputs to production should discourage territorial conquest. It does not follow that development eliminates all motives for conflict. Development can lead to an increase in the probability of some kinds of disputes (particularly those over policy) and a decrease in other types of conflict (territorial aggression).[31] If these tendencies are roughly equivalent and opposing, then they will cancel each other out. A naive interpretation of the empirical record will suggest that both development optimists and pessimists are wrong when in fact both are (partially) correct. Gartzke (2004) provides evidence suggesting that this is the case: disputes decrease with economic development among contiguous states, and increase among noncontiguous or distant states. Since most territorial disputes occur among neighbors – between 80 and 90 percent of all territorial disputes involve contiguous states – the shift in conflict propensity from near to far appears to stem from a decline in territorial conflicts and a resulting increase in non-territorial disputes.

Globalization: integrating force or impetus for conflict?

In contrast to the economics, the politics of globalization and development involve natural bedfellows, intellectually and in practice. Proponents and critics of each seem to pool, favoring or opposing similar policies, logrolling, or forming coalitions. Development shifts the economic emphasis from productive factors that are tied to land (land itself, minerals, and some forms of labor) to factors that are more mobile (intellectual and financial capital). Globalization makes factors more mobile, particularly those that were relatively mobile to begin with. The essential element of interpretation thus involves how changing factor mobility is likely to influence whether states fight.

Angell (1933) offers a particularly eloquent interpretation of the liberal view of the consequences of international factor mobility.[32] Witness to dramatic growth in economic livelihood, banking, trade, and travel at the end of the nineteenth century, Angell argued "that it is impossible for one nation to seize by force the wealth or trade of another – to enrich itself by subjugating, or imposing its will by force on another; that, in short, war, even when victorious, can no longer achieve those aims for which peoples strive" (Angell 1933, 59–60). Global capital markets allowed money to flee conflict. Conquered states could not be looted for anything of real value. Indeed, continued productivity depended on enticing mobile inputs to production with good government and the honoring of contracts, behaviors that were at odds with conquest. Even if one could get the economy running, global markets made occupation a relatively expensive form of production.[33]

Since Marxists tie capitalist development and globalization together in the form of imperialism, their position on economic integration should be clear. Prominent non-Marxist critics of Angell and other early globalization optimists included Alfred Thayer Mahan (1987 [1890] and 1915) and Halford Mackinder (1962).[34] The most famous advocate of sea power, Mahan is often compared with Clausewitz in terms of his influence on military doctrine. Mahan saw the productive regions of the world as those connected to oceans. Trade (and, by extension, empire) was critical to national wealth. Control of the sea thus meant control of productive resources. Mackinder, the most distinguished student of geopolitics, famously argued that the key to international power lay in the "heartland," the center of the Eurasian landmass (that is, Russia).[35] Control of strategic geography (territory that ensures control of other territory) is critical to prosperity, or even survival, in Mackinder's view of world politics: "The great wars of history . . . are the outcome, direct or indirect, of the unequal growth of nations" (Mackinder 1962, 1–2).[36] These two great figures, one on land and one at sea, both advocated the control of physical space as a means to power, though each offered opposing claims about which space was preeminent. Spykman (1942) offers something of a synthesis, arguing that sea power is of significant but declining importance while valuable territory involves the coastal regions where productivity is highest ("rimlands"). Production for war purposes is essential because "total war is permanent war" (1942, 40).

There is strikingly little contemporary research on the systematic effects of globalization on war and peace. Students of conflict have tended to focus narrowly on trade, limiting analysis to economic interdependence.[37] As Schneider et al. (2003a) note in an edited volume titled *Globalization and Armed Conflict*, "the impact of foreign direct investment and similar facets of globalization on the likelihood of conflict has almost disappeared from the research agenda" (5).[38] One could argue that this inattention reflects the general sense that globalization coincides with a reduction in interstate violence, but this is tantamount to acknowledging that peace, when it actually happens, is not interesting.[39] Why states are fighting less today, and whether this will continue, should be of intense interest to international relations scholars, and possibly to others as well.[40]

A small amount of work has begun to arrive from military strategists and tacticians on the consequences of globalization for fighting wars, when and if they happen (Pegg 2003; Kugler and Frost 2001; Tangredi 2002).[41] Other research focuses on the consequences of global markets for civil conflict (Gissinger and Gleditsch 1999; Hegre et al. 2002; Bussmann and Schneider 2003; Mason 2003). Finally, two studies (Gartzke et al. 2001; Gartzke and Li 2003c) examine the impact of integrated global markets on interstate conflict.[42] They find that globalization variables (foreign direct investment, portfolio investments, an index of economic policy liberalization) reduce dispute propensity while making trade statistically insignificant as a predictor of conflict. The authors argue that global markets act as a barometer of the credibility of leaders' international threats or demands. Sovereigns wish to keep markets satisfied, but they also desire to pressure other governments into making diplomatic concessions. Since these two objectives are in tension (one cannot simultaneously scare foreign politicians and soothe foreign investors), how leaders respond to the dilemma posed by global capital mobility is informative. Bluffing in international politics is more difficult for leaders of globalized states, allowing more effective bargaining and less fighting.

The most common argument about globalization and politics has been that of declining state power (Kindleberger 1969; Rodrik 1997; Strange 1996 and 1998; van Creveld 1999; Vernon 1971). A related set of claims has to do with extraterritoriality and the formation of a world without borders (B. Cohen 1998; Ohmae 1995; Ruggie 1993).[43] Globalization traditionalists argue that, for sovereign states, it is business as usual, or at least that claims of the demise of the state are greatly exaggerated (Kapstein 1994; Krasner 1999; Wade 1996; Waltz 1999 and 2000). Among economists, there is some division of opinions, though the bulk of academic economists favor liberalizing markets eventually and with proper regulatory controls in place (Rodrik 1999; Stiglitz 2002; Bhagwati 2004). Broader approaches to globalization include Friedman (1999), an enthusiast, and Barber (1992 and 1996), Inglehart and Norris (2001), Kaplan (1994 and 2000), and Kennedy and Connelly (1994), all skeptics.[44] Huntington (1993b and 1996), possibly the most rabid of the skeptics, argues that conflict will be common among different "civilizations."[45] Huntington's thesis is contradicted by all existing systematic work (Russett et al. 2000; Henderson 1997; Henderson and Tucker 2001; Chiozza 2002; Gartzke and Gleditsch 2005).[46] Still, in terms of opinion, the deck is stacked against globalization.

Brooks (1999) makes a valuable contribution to the "globalization is good" perspective, clarifying existing arguments about development and extending them to the subject of globalization. Brooks examines how global market forces reshape the price of empire. He presents four accounts of why modern economies constitute a "bitter pill" for occupiers. First, labor mobility allows workers with globally marketable skills to flee conquered territories. Second, conquered assets may be difficult to repatriate to the homeland. Third, invaders scare away investment, leading to capitalization problems for industries with short product cycles (technology, consumer, media). Fourth, coercion tends to stifle the innovation and entrepreneurialism that are essential engines of modern economies. The inability of occupiers to credibly commit not to steal from investors and firms makes it difficult for markets in occupied countries to prosper (Olson 1993; McGuire and Olson 1996).

Each of the four explanations seems plausible, but argumentation alone cannot decipher their relative impact. Nor does Brooks offer evidence that any version of the four explanations is necessarily correct. Indeed, the lack of a statistical association between development and conflict suggests that at least part of Brooks' argument must be questioned. The fact that rich states are not generally less likely to fight implies that the labor mobility, intellectual capital, and possibly capital mobility arguments are empirically suspect. Further, Brooks (1999) does not directly address the possibility that development and/or globalization increase the ability of states to engage in conflict. The Hobbesian war of all against all is limited by logistics; in nature, most individuals are unable to project force much beyond their immediate surroundings. The jet age made reaching out to touch distant countries relatively easy (at least in historical terms), fast, and often decisive.[47]

There may be other reasons to question elements of Brooks' (1999) argument. For example, repatriation of assets may actually be easier as a result of modernity. Land cannot be moved. Infrastructure and even human populations are movable, but only with great difficulty. Ideas, however, have ready mobility. The Soviet Union and the United States competed after World War II to round up Nazi documents and scientists. The Soviet Union, China, and other countries made significant use of industrial espionage during the Cold War and after. One might even claim that repatriation of valuable industrial know-how is too easy. In the information age, the rate of technological change, and the ease with which competitors can "reverse engineer" products makes innovation the only really effective competitive strategy. Technological innovation in turn requires trust in government and allied institutions (credible enforcement of intellectual and financial property rights, and so on).

Brooks argues that the decentralization of production networks makes it difficult for sovereigns to conquer all stages of production. An occupier could find itself in possession of an assembly plant, but not the factories supplying parts. The portion of the surplus captured by a given producer is a function of market power. Vertical integration (ownership of the entire production chain) is only one method for acquiring more of the surplus. Horizontal integration (ownership of much of a single stage of production) can also be used to capture more of the available profits. Natural resources such as minerals and water are assumed to be contributors to international conflict since they are excludable (property rights can be enforced) and demand is inelastic (consumers cannot easily substitute other goods or means of production).[48] Salt mines were traditional sources of wealth and a convenient repository of political prisoners, though few monarchs expected to bake the bread. Saddam Hussein's attempts in the 1980s and early 1990s to capture much of the world's known supplies of crude oil were threatening to Western powers, even though he would still not control petroleum distribution and marketing networks. Appealing targets for conquest need not be autarkic. Interdependent production networks may even increase the appeal of conquest, where nodes in the production process are essential, easily coerced, and difficult to replace.[49]

Like Angell (1933) and other students of development, globalization, and conflict, Brooks (1999) assumes that states fight over territory or resources. While resource competition is one motive for conflict, states also compete over sovereign prerogatives.[50] What a state is entitled to decide or impose on others can often be as valuable as where it is able to collect taxes. The absence of a discussion about how modernity affects the policy sphere in international politics suggests that at most only part of the impact of globalization and development has been addressed. Similarly, the profitability of invasion is assumed to be an attribute of targets rather than attackers. Potential attackers may have domestic economic reasons for avoiding aggression. Brooks' (1999) argument implies that conquest should be less likely only when the target is less economically viable if occupied. Globalized states should remain about as likely to fight over policy differences as non-globalized states.

While studies of economic modernization offer rich context and salient debate within each subject area, there has been relatively little effort to directly compare the effects of globalization and economic development. In particular, these two sets of processes may involve different, but related, causal logics. I explore this possibility in the next section.

How globalization and development influence conflict

Given the mélange of arguments, it seems essential to do some clarifying and sorting out of claims. The task is complicated by the diversity of theoretical logics, and by the fact that resulting hypotheses point in almost every conceivable direction. Conventional accounts can be improved by examining them through three overlapping sets of relationships: territorial versus non-territorial effects, incentives for initiator or target, and development versus globalization.

Territorial versus non-territorial conflict

Proponents of a link between globalization or economic development and a reduction in interstate disputes generally identify the declining value of occupation, the increasing cost or risk of invasion, or the lack of necessity for conquest given the relatively free availability of goods. These claims are not supported by the quantitative literature. Proponents of theories linking modern economic processes to a reduction in militarized conflict have been overly categorical in their claims, arguing in effect that modernity reduces all motives for militarized violence. In most instances, however, to the degree that optimists are correct, their claims involve the demise of, or de-emphasis on, a particular kind of interstate conflict. Territory (and the resources in and on land) has been a major source of warfare, but land is not the only item over which states fight. Sovereign powers also use force to impose their will on other states or populations. Since in most cases, the argument made by advocates of a link between economic processes and peace only impinges on the economic value of territory, other reasons for fighting should not be reduced by development or globalization.

Hypothesis 1: Developed and/or globalized states are less likely to experience territorial disputes.

Pessimists, on the other hand, argue that development or globalization increases disputes among states. Again, existing quantitative work clearly rejects this claim. However, one can modify the economic pessimist argument in light of the distinction between resource competition and conflict over policies. If development and/or globalization augment the wealth available to sovereigns, then these economic processes also stand to enhance power projection. States that benefit from economic modernization should be more likely to use force in more instances where they remain invested in the stakes. In other words, globalization and/or development should be associated with an increase in conflict behavior in the realm of policy and regime change, while not, perhaps, over territory.

Hypothesis 2: Developed and/or globalized states are more likely to suffer non-territorial disputes.

Initiators and targets

Explanations anticipating relative peace from economic modernization suggest variously that globalization and/or economic development make it harder to generate profit from occupied territory (call this "bitter pill"), or that potential initiators with advanced or integrated economies stand to suffer domestic economic hardship as a consequence of any attack (call this "problems at home"). Distinguishing between opportunity (bitter pill) and willingness (problems at home) effects is important in understanding how modern economic processes influence disputes and in refining existing claims (Most and Starr 1990). Brooks makes a bitter pill argument when he emphasizes the difficulty in maintaining modern economies under occupation: "[I]t is almost certain that conquest will significantly reduce the available pool of risk capital within the conquered territory" (1999, 657). Angell, on the other hand, is imagining problems at home when he notes that German invaders looting the Bank of England would produce "a damage in credit and security so serious as to constitute a loss immensely greater than the value of the loot obtained" (1933, 107).[51]

Bitter pill arguments stress characteristics of the potential target of conflict. If bitter pill versions of the economic optimist argument are correct, then developed or globalized states should be less likely to be attacked than other states. Conversely, the problems at home rationale suggests that initiators with globalized or developed economies should be reluctant to initiate the use of force.

Hypothesis 3: Developed and/or globalized states are less likely to initiate territorial disputes.

Hypothesis 4: Developed and/or globalized states are less likely to be targets of territorial disputes.

A variety of critics emphasize that the effect of capitalism should be to increase dispute behavior. The arguments posed by Marxist and Marxist-inspired writers are typically about motive. Economically developed or globalized capitalists are more likely to use force.[52] Again, the systematic evidence rejects the claim that development or globalization generally increases dispute propensity. However, a version of the argument can be used to examine whether potential initiators that are developed or globalized are more likely to resort to force in non-territorial disputes.

Hypothesis 5: Developed and/or globalized states more often initiate non-territorial disputes.

If instead we focus on the broader claim made by realists and others about the opportunity for states to enhance power projection, allowing increased fighting farther from home, then development or globalization should increase disputes for either initiators or targets (Hypothesis 2).

Differences between globalization and development

Existing research does not make much of the distinctions between globalization and development as economic processes. The most important of these differences is potentially the sphere in which each operates. Globalization links countries, increasing interdependence and creating feedback effects between states. For this reason, globalization is likely to influence states at the dyadic level. The effect of development on conflict does not need to be as directly affected by the behavior of other states. Bargaining theories of interstate conflict emphasize the jointly strategic nature of conflict processes. In many cases, factors that influence the appeal of resorting to force for one state will not alter the probability of disputes if these variables are common knowledge, and if the states are free to bargain over the terms of settlements that preempt a contest (Fearon 1995). Variables that increase the appeal of one state resorting to force simply encourage its opponent to make additional concessions. Competitors must often be uncertain about some relevant aspect of a looming contest in order to fight. An important exception would occur if some values of a variable preclude a contest, while other values make the contest possible. The bargaining approach implies that, while not sufficient in itself, development is a facilitating condition that is likely to function independently in each state. Two poor and distant states are unlikely to fight, for example, even if they have tense relations and are uncertain about the likely outcome of a contest. The physical limitations of distance enforce peace. Conversely, if one of the two states becomes richer, the developing state may then be physically able to dispute with the other state, even though the two states will still need to have different interests and will have to fail in bargaining in order to fight.

Hypothesis 6: The effects of development should appear largely at the monadic level.

The international nature of globalization suggests that its most significant impact on conflict will be at the dyadic level. States become integrated globally only to the extent that they stop isolating their own economies from other national economies. At the extremes are two separate (autarkic) economies and one common (integrated) economy. Thus, globalization should involve the interaction, rather than just the action, of state economic policies. More specifically, globalization ties states together in ways that facilitate some forms of (minor) conflict behavior and discourage other forms of (more major) conflict. Globalization may discourage direct or intense military violence, but may also allow for additional nonmilitarized competition. Occasionally, this competition may spill over into militarized threats as the game of brinkmanship ("chicken") is played out, but we should expect globalized economies of pairs or groups of states to be less disputatious at the level of militarized disputes. There may not be much of a monadic effect, as globalization is not a monadic process, though existing measures poorly represent cross-border effects.

Hypothesis 7: The effects of globalization should appear largely at the dyadic level.

Research design

I assess the effects of economic development and globalization on militarized conflict using a sample of all directed dyads in the period (1950–2001). Directed dyads make it possible to differentiate initiators and targets in militarized disputes, which is essential in evaluating the hypotheses. I examine the post-World War II period for three reasons. First, this is the period during which the most substantial changes in economic development occur and over which the greatest variation in globalization is present. Second, this is the largest period for which reliable data quantifying elements of globalization and development is generally available. Third, the sample is well documented in numerous other studies. I begin with a statistical model of conflict based on Oneal and Russett (1999). Adopting many of the features of this canonical research program allows for ready comparison of results and diminishes the possibility that my findings are the product of idiosyncratic coding decisions or model specifications. I estimate coefficients using probit in Stata (v. 8) with Huber/White robust standard errors. Independent variables are lagged by one year to limit the effects of endogeneity. I use the Beck et al. (1998) method of splines to control for duration dependence.[53] I review the data below, and then discuss the results.

Data

Dependent variable   The dependent variable is based on the militarized interstate disputes (MIDs) data set, representing militarized threats, deployments, uses of force, or wars (Gochman and Maoz 1984; Jones et al. 1996). MIDs are by far the most widely used data in studies of this type. Given the role of motive in some arguments, it seems important to identify whether a state precipitates, or is the target of, a dispute. A dummy for MID "initiation" is defined in the data management software EUGene (Bennett and Stam 2000 and 2001), where 1 is a dispute initiated by state A, and 0 is either no dispute, an ongoing dispute, or one initiated by state B in a given dyad. Some hypotheses are also applicable to joining, so that it is appropriate to evaluate these hypotheses against all disputes.

Key independent variables   *Economic development:* The consensus measure of average national wealth, gross domestic product per capita (GDP/population), has yielded mixed and inconclusive results in other studies (Richardson 1960; East and Gregg 1967; Rummel 1967; Thompson 1982). Statistical research on the democratic peace initially included per capitized GDP, but the variable was found to be insignificant and was dropped from later studies (Maoz and Russett 1992). I show elsewhere that the insignificance of per capita GDP is due to the contrasting effects of development on disputes (Gartzke 2004). I code two variables to measure the effects of development. Development measures the monadic population weighted gross domestic product per capita statistic for each state in a dyad. These data come from K. S. Gleditsch (2002b), who in turn obtained them from the Penn World Tables (v. 5.6). I take the natural log of the Development variables to control for heteroskedasticity common in economic time series. Dev. × Contig. captures the interaction between average national income and proximity. The bulk of territorial conflicts involve neighbors (Vasquez 1993; Tir et al. 1998). The interaction term thus isolates the effect of wealth on likely participants in territorial disputes and should be associated with a lower likelihood of a MID. I also conduct analyses by breaking down the dependent variable into samples for territorial and non-territorial disputes.

Globalization: The International Monetary Fund (IMF) provides several indicators of market size, robustness, and liberalization. The IMF publication *Annual Reports on Exchange Arrangements and Exchange Restrictions* (AREAER) lists a series of variables measuring economic openness. I use an index from previous studies that takes the difference between eight and the sum of eight types of government restrictions on foreign exchange, and current and capital accounts (Gartzke et al. 2001; Gartzke and Li 2003a). Missing values are a problem, but actually bias against significance for the variable. The IMF sample only includes member countries (no Warsaw Pact members) and only begins in 1966 at the earliest. I also have to extrapolate values after 1996, as the data have not been coded after this date.[54] I include linear terms for each state in the directed dyad (Capital), the interaction between contiguity and each linear term (Cap. × Contig.), and an interaction between the linear terms (Cap. A × Cap. B) to reflect the synergistic effects of globalization at the dyadic level.[55]

Additional variables Democracy: The Polity project provides the standard indicators of democracy for statistical studies of interstate conflict (Jaggers and Gurr 1995). Polity data provide two eleven-point indexes of regime type based on formal constraints on the executive (AUTOC) and institutional support for democracy (DEMOC) (Gurr et al. 1989). I prepare monadic values by combining Polity democracy (DEMOC) and autocracy (AUTOC) scales as follows, $[(\text{DEMOC}i - \text{AUTOC}i) + 10]/2$, (where $i \in [A,B]$). This construction differs from Oneal and Russett in that I add 10 to make all values non-negative and divide by 2 to yield the 0–10 range of Polity variables. I also include an interaction term between the monadic variables.

Geographic contiguity and distance: Neighbors fight more than states that are geographically distant. In part, this can be explained by opportunity. Neighbors have easier access to fight one another. Yet, there is a greater likelihood of fighting among contiguous dyads independent of distance. This suggests that neighbors also develop greater animosity or motives for conflict. Contiguity is a dichotomous variable for dyadic partners that are contiguous (shared land border or separated by less than 150 miles of water). I also include a variable measuring the metric distance between states in a dyad. Distance is the natural logarithm of the great circle distance between state capitals (in some cases other cities or ports are used).

Major power status: Major powers tend to be more active internationally, resulting in more frequent conflict behavior. Since major powers also tend to be relatively prosperous, there is a danger that the hypotheses involving development and conflict might be confounded by major power behavior. I include a dummy variable, Maj. Power, coded "1" for the five post-World War II major powers (China, France, United Kingdom, United States, and the USSR).

Allies: Alliances are formed with the intention of influencing interstate conflict, by deterring aggression and encouraging intervention. Alliance is a dichotomous variable for the presence of a defense pact, neutrality pact, or entente in the dyad based on the Correlates of War (COW) Alliance Dataset (Singer and Small 1966; Small and Singer 1990).[56]

Capabilities: Capabilities determine the ability of states to project power and conduct warfare independent of national income. I assess capabilities in the dyad using the Correlates of War (COW) Composite Indicators of National Capabilities (CINC) score. CINC scores are computed as the weighted average of a state's share of total system population, urban population, energy consumption, iron and steel production, military manpower, and military expenditures. CINC represents the CINC score for each state in the directed dyad.[57]

Dyad longevity: A variety of factors associated with the duration of the dyadic relationship may mistakenly be attributed to development. Culture, politics, and the sampling problem in the MIDs data associated the notion of "sovereignty," while not modeled here directly, are at least partially addressed by including a variable Dyad Dur., representing the duration of the dyad, or at least its recognition by the COW project.[58]

Temporal dependence: Finally, I control for temporal dependence using the Beck et al. (1998) technique. I construct three spline variables, interpolated from a dummy matrix coding the lag between conflict dyad years (or militarized conflict dyad years) in the dependent variable using a Stata batch file created by Tucker (1999).

Results

Findings for the study are presented in two tables and three figures. Table 7.1 reports the effects of economic development on militarized disputes. Table 7.2 presents the results for globalization in a similar manner. Each table contains four regressions, two of all MIDs in which state A was or was not the initiator, and two regressions distinguishing between territorial and non-territorial MIDs.

Model 1 in Table 7.1 lists the probit coefficient estimates for a model of the monadic effects of development on all dispute initiations by state A. As can be seen, development by itself is not a significant predictor of either initiator or target behavior. The coefficient estimates on Development A and Development B are not statistically different from zero. This is consistent with previous research and serves as a baseline for subsequent regressions. It may also be useful to review the results for the control variables.

Note that both Democracy variables are positive and significant, increasing the probability of a dispute. The overall effect of the three democracy variables including the interaction term, however, is negative.

Table 7.1. *Directed dyads, probit models of development, and MIDs*

D.V.: MID	Model 1 Initiator	Model 2 Initiator	Model 3 Terr. Initiator	Model 4 Non-Terr. MIDs
Development A	−0.007	0.083***	−0.257***	0.059***
	(0.020)	(0.023)	(0.068)	(0.017)
Dev. × Contig. A		−0.193***		
		(0.048)		
Development B	0.006	0.064***	0.041	0.059***
	(0.020)	(0.020)	(0.076)	(0.017)
Dev. × Contig. B		−0.065		
		(0.047)		
Democracy A	0.041***	0.039***	0.014	0.041***
	(0.008)	(0.008)	(0.026)	(0.007)
Democracy B	0.047***	0.046***	0.066**	0.040***
	(0.008)	(0.008)	(0.022)	(0.007)
Dem. A × Dem. B	−0.009***	−0.009***	−0.006	−0.013***
	(0.001)	(0.001)	(0.004)	(0.001)
Contiguity (dummy)	1.029***	3.207***	1.132***	0.710***
	(0.105)	(0.366)	(0.269)	(0.111)
Distance (ln)	−0.059***	−0.049***	−0.108***	−0.079***
	(0.013)	(0.013)	(0.032)	(0.014)
Maj. Power A	0.311***	0.270**	−1.012*	0.284***
	(0.092)	(0.086)	(0.404)	(0.086)
Maj. Power B	0.216*	0.198†	−0.325	0.291***
	(0.110)	(0.106)	(0.495)	(0.086)
Alliance (dummy)	−0.072	−0.053	−0.205†	−0.020
	(0.055)	(0.052)	(0.111)	(0.053)
CINC A	2.042**	2.126***	7.556**	1.868**
	(0.698)	(0.629)	(2.508)	(0.694)
CINC B	2.204**	2.191**	3.559	1.806**
	(0.834)	(0.807)	(3.400)	(0.697)
Dyad Dur.	0.004***	0.004***	0.008***	0.005***
	(0.001)	(0.001)	(0.002)	(0.001)
N	739230	739230	739230	739230
Log-likelihood	6071.816	6029.687	526.773	9640.606
χ^2 (17,19,17,17)	2091.03	2161.594	398.105	2696.477

Notes: Significance: † = 10%; * = 5%; ** = 1%; *** = 0.1%. Values in parentheses are standard errors.

The monadic democracy variables do not report statistical significance in the absence of the interaction term. This reinforces the argument in the democratic peace literature that it is the interaction, and not just the action, of democracies that is critical in differentiating democratic behavior. *Ceteris paribus*, state A is more likely to initiate an MID with a contiguous neighbor, and less likely to fight with a distant state. Major power status increases conflict for both the potential initiator and target. Alliances slightly diminish the prospects of an MID, though often this variable is not statistically significant. Similarly, power measured as CINC scores increases dispute propensity, but only marginally. Old dyads are much more disputatious than new ones, though the reason for this is complex and is not addressed here.

Model 2 adds the two interaction terms between monadic development and contiguity. Three of the four variables for development now become highly statistically significant. Both monadic Development variables are now positive, indicating that average national income increases the propensity toward dispute initiation. The Dev. × Contig. A interaction term for the potential initiator is also significant, but in the opposite direction. Prosperity reduces the propensity to target one's neighbors. Interestingly, the interaction term for the target state is not statistically significant. These results indicate that the effect of development differs substantially between contiguous and noncontiguous states. Development increases disputes for both initiators and targets for non-contiguous states, and decreases disputes only for initiators for contiguous states. If my previous speculation is correct, then this is because of the difference between opportunity and willingness. Development increases the opportunity for disputes by both initiators and targets, while it decreases the willingness of states to behave aggressively with neighboring states over territory.

Models 3 and 4 explore whether the relationships identified in Model 2 hold after breaking up the sample into territorial and non-territorial disputes. Model 3 shows that development decreases the propensity to initiate disputes over territory. Exactly as expected, it is only the characteristics of the initiator that are significant determinants of variation in dispute behavior. The development of the target is not relevant to the initiator's decision, independent of capabilities, major power status, and so on. If developed states can be subdued by less developed countries, then the status of the target state's economy is not a deterrent to aggression. Conversely, developed potential initiators seem reluctant to pursue territorial aggrandizement regardless of the characteristics of the target. Prosperous states appear unwilling to use superior power projection capabilities to seek territory.

Developed countries do not appear reluctant to use militarized aggression for other purposes. In fact, as Model 4 shows, developed countries are much more likely to be both the initiators and targets of such aggression. This may at first appear confusing. Why don't developed countries initiate conflicts more often against undeveloped countries?

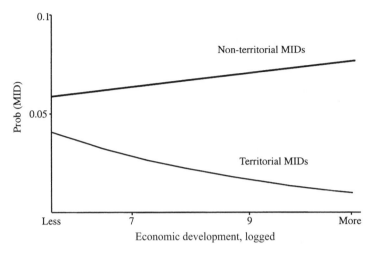

Figure 7.1. Probability of MID as function of development.

In fact, they do. Both monadic development coefficients (which are virtually identical) are positive and significant, meaning that there are equivalent, independent contributions from each. Developed states A are more likely to initiate a dispute regardless of the characteristics of state B, but are most likely to experience an MID with other developed countries. The dependent variable codes MID onset, regardless of whether state A is the initiator. Many of the disputes in which developed countries are more likely to participate involve joining or patron-client relationships. In fact, MID behavior appears to be driven by the development characteristics of one's partner. Coding the dependent variable for all of state B's non-territorial MIDs leads state A's development variable to become positive and significant, and vice versa. This is fascinating and confusing, and as yet I have no explanation.

Figure 7.1 plots the probability of territorial (Model 3) and non-territorial (Model 4) MIDs as a function of economic development. The figure helps to make clear why it is that the overall effect of development on conflict appears nonexistent. Development increases non-territorial conflict in about the same proportion as it decreases territorial conflict. The two effects literally cancel each other out. One should keep in mind, however, that disputes over territory are commonly the most intense, leading not infrequently to wars, while non-territorial MIDs usually involve few or no casualties. The contribution of development is thus one of shifting conflict away from the most casualty-producing forms of warfare, to conflicts that, if not peaceful, are at least relatively small.

Table 7.2. *Directed dyads, probit models of globalization, and MIDs*

D.V.: MID	Model 5 Initiator	Model 6 Initiator	Model 7 Terr. Initiator	Model 8 Non-Terr. MIDs
Capital A	0.008	0.066***	−0.009	0.107***
	(0.009)	(0.016)	(0.019)	(0.016)
Cap. × Contig. A	−0.044*			
	(0.017)			
Capital B	−0.006	0.066***	−0.022	0.107***
	(0.008)	(0.016)	(0.018)	(0.016)
Cap. A × Cap. B		−0.018***		−0.025***
		(0.003)		(0.003)
Democracy A	0.031***	0.033***	0.020	0.034***
	(0.008)	(0.008)	(0.015)	(0.007)
Democracy B	0.033***	0.033***	0.018	0.034***
	(0.007)	(0.008)	(0.017)	(0.007)
Dem. A × Dem. B	−0.012***	−0.012***	−0.005*	−0.011***
	(0.001)	(0.001)	(0.003)	(0.001)
Contiguity (dummy)	0.754***	0.516***	0.941***	0.532***
	(0.150)	(0.126)	(0.190)	(0.133)
Distance (ln)	−0.116***	−0.128***	−0.084***	−0.104***
	(0.016)	(0.016)	(0.022)	(0.017)
Maj. Power A	0.347***	0.357***	0.087	0.335***
	(0.110)	(0.112)	(0.211)	(0.105)
Maj. Power B	0.366***	0.357***	0.307	0.337***
	(0.111)	(0.112)	(0.253)	(0.105)
Alliance (dummy)	−0.112*	−0.101[†]	−0.027	−0.033
	(0.053)	(0.054)	(0.111)	(0.050)
CINC A	2.247*	2.290*	4.089*	1.742[†]
	(1.070)	(1.092)	(2.006)	(0.996)
CINC B	2.289*	2.289*	0.387	1.712[†]
	(1.096)	(1.092)	(2.718)	(0.997)
Dyad Dur.	0.007***	0.007***	0.007***	0.007***
	(0.001)	(0.001)	(0.001)	(0.001)
N	539040	539040	539040	539040
Log-likelihood	−9202.035	−9174.141	−1109.005	−5942.470
χ^2 (18,18,17,19)	2498.12	2618.44	1250.48	3313.03

Notes: Significance: [†] = 10%; * = 5%; ** = 1%; *** = 0.1%. Values in parentheses are standard errors.

The effects of globalization on dispute behavior are detailed in Table 7.2. Model 5 attempts to mimic Model 2, replacing the Development and Dev. × Contig. variables with Capital and Cap. × Contig. variables based on the index of economic liberalization discussed in the data section. However, this effort is clearly unsuccessful. The results in Model 5 are quite different. Only Cap. × Contig. A is modestly statistically

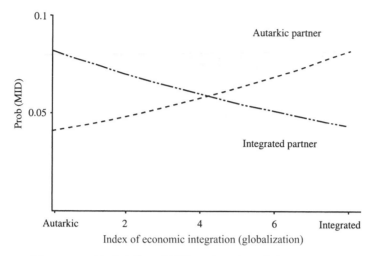

Figure 7.2. Probability of MID as function of globalization.

significant. In fact, Cap. × Contig. B is dropped from the model due to multicollinearity. All four variables are highly collinear. There is not much difference between the role of the capital variables in influencing the initiator or target, or in contiguous versus noncontiguous dyads.

A better way to model the effects of liberalization on conflict appears in Model 6. In a similar way to the democracy variables, globalization has a monadic linear effect and a dyadic non-linear effect. Actually, the monadic effects are quite weak, as removing the interaction term leads the two linear variables to become insignificant (this result can be seen in Model 7). Globalization has relatively little effect on territorial disputes, perhaps because these involve conflicts of an intensity where integration is neither an effective deterrent nor a particularly useful signal of resolve. States that are willing to incur a thousand battle deaths will also be willing to sacrifice a degree of economic prosperity, but so will many states that are not willing to lose hundreds or thousands in war. Economic integration is most likely to allow signaling as an effective alternative to militarized violence in situations where the likely intensity of violence is low to begin with. Model 8 shows that most of the impact of globalization on conflict behavior is on non-territorial conflicts.

Figure 7.2 plots the effects of the globalization variables on non-territorial disputes from Model 8. The upward-sloping dashed line assumes that state B is not globalized (autarkic), while the downward-sloping dashed and dotted line represents the interaction of an increasingly integrated state A with a globalized (integrated) state B. It is clear

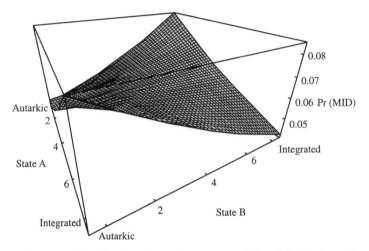

Figure 7.3. The interdependent nature of the globalization effect on conflict.

that the similarity of economic system influences the level of conflict. There are a variety of possible reasons for this relationship. Given the similarity in data structures, one can use arguments that parallel those about the democratic peace, except of course that globalization is occurring between states rather than within them.

Figure 7.3 offers a more detailed representation of the interaction of the monadic and dyadic globalization variables with non-territorial disputes. Except for the most autarkic states (which are presumably also the poorest), symmetric globalization has the effect of reducing conflict behavior, while asymmetric globalization ether reflects or creates additional friction between states.

Conclusion

I began by noting that territory has traditionally been a major impetus for interstate war. The historical record provides numerous examples of big states gobbling up their smaller neighbors. Yet, small states still existed throughout history. What kept big states from eliminating small states altogether? While there are several factors, including use as buffers (Fazal 2002), norms of appropriate international behavior (Bull 1995; Wendt 1999, 283–84), and adept diplomacy (Fox 1959), one should also acknowledge the role of material constraints in thwarting unlimited expansion. From time immemorial, states have failed to extend their domains because they could not. Rome stopped at the Rhine, not because its leaders had misgivings about the moral content of (more) empire, but because Rome's legions could stretch themselves no further (Wells 2002).[59] Similarly, for Britain empire flowed, then ebbed, because, as one historian puts it, "we had a comparative advantage as an island sea power. It was then enlarged and sustained because we secured the further comparative advantage of being the world's first industrial nation. These advantages first shrank and then disappeared" (Low 1991, 6).

Today we witness the United States at the apogee of its power, or somewhere near it, frequently resorting to force, but seldom in the pursuit of territory. What is different about the "American empire" is its reluctance to gather up the supposed fruits of victory that came with empire in the past. Where the insatiable thirst for territory was kept in check historically by the limits of power, the United States, with unprecedented capabilities, does not want to keep what it conquers. Development reduces the utility of territorial theft. It is now cheaper in most cases for the most advanced countries to leave government to local authorities and to purchase what they need through global markets. This is not a characteristic of the land itself. Indeed, after controlling for the effects of power and proximity, developed states as potential targets are no less likely to be the subject of territorial aggression. Rather, development works on the willingness of potential initiators of territorial conflict, reducing their interest in taking through force what can be had through exchange. Trade is cheap. War is expensive.

This does not mean that development is synonymous with peace. As previous statistical studies make clear, average national income has no simple monotonic effect on militarized conflict. In particular, by increasing state capacity, economic development expands the ability of prosperous states to impose themselves on their neighbors. The evidence here suggests that developed states do engage in more of certain kinds of aggressive behavior with other states. Development increases non-territorial conflict. Further, developed states fight over disputed policies more often regardless of whether development is a characteristic of the initiator or target. Developed countries concern themselves with more of the world's problems, and are thus drawn in as participants in a wider array of policy- or regime-oriented conflicts far from home. As is clear from the literature, however, deadly disputes are overwhelmingly territorial (Vasquez 1993). As I show elsewhere, developed states have fewer casualties in their disputes and are less likely to escalate to the most intense forms of warfare over policy conflicts (Gartzke 2004). Thus, though it does not decrease the overall level of militarized conflict among states, economic development is associated with a shift from the deadliest form of conflict (territorial) to more benign forms of conflict (non-territorial).

Globalization variables generally reduce the dispute propensity of states, working most effectively in the interaction, rather than action, of states. Two globalized countries are much less likely to fight each other than are a globalized country and a non-globalized country. In this sense, globalization is both simpler and more complex as a process affecting dispute propensity. The effects of globalization are about the same for contiguous and noncontiguous states. While there is no statistically significant relationship between globalization variables and territorial disputes, it is also the case that globalization does not generally increase conflict behavior, at least among symmetrically integrated states. The impact of globalization does differ between territorial and non-territorial issue areas. Globalized states are less likely to experience non-territorial disputes, while the effect of globalization variables on territorial disputes is not robust. This is partly due to sample size (there are relatively few territorial disputes), but the more important reason probably has to do with how globalization operates to influence conflict.

So what have we learned? The world is both reassuringly consistent with elements of theories that made sense but were confounded by the apparent lack of statistical evidence, and at the same time strikingly complex. Even minimally adequate explanations for the effects of economic modernization on conflict require considerable nuance and contingency. We learn more about the world, but at the price of explanations that are difficult to easily digest. Unlike physics, there may be no grand unified field theory of international relations that allows all the bits and pieces to fold back into one. Social processes just appear complex, even at the preliminary and minimalist level explored here. Much more remains to be done, but at times it is useful to poke a light into a forgotten passageway, to show that something worth looking at remains to be explored.

NOTES

1 Gartzke (2004) offers an initial assessment of the argument using non-directed dyads and limiting the analysis to economic development. The directed-dyads approach used here is more appropriate for assessing different causal claims about development and globalization. This study also focuses more narrowly on territorial disputes.

2 Symbolic, or other immaterial, aspects of territory are ably covered elsewhere in this volume (see Goemans, Robbins, Newman, and Lyons). Material and

immaterial factors may coincide, and certainly appear to do so. My position is that, *ceteris paribus*, a lack of material incentive for territorial aggrandizement diminishes the likelihood of pursuing conquest, while even apparently strong identification with territory may be overcome. Serb attachment to Kosovo did not survive a few nights of NATO bombing, in spite of the fact that Kosovo is deeply enmeshed in Serb identity and NATO itself was ambivalent about its own military campaign.

3 Development can occur without globalization and globalization without development. Experts agree that development is spurred by open markets (cf. Ray 1998; Rostow 1998; Seligson and Passe-Smith 1998; Easterly 2001).

4 "Commerce is the grand panacea, which, like a beneficent medical discovery, will serve to inoculate with the healthy and saving taste for civilization all the nations of the world" (Cobden 1903, 36). "The growth of capitalism, spreading out rapidly over a reconstituted Europe . . . reaching an unnatural zenith in the prosperity of the 1890s opened up a new period of storm and danger among the nations of Europe" (Luxemburg 1971, 128).

5 Malthus, for example, peppers his work with anecdotes about environment and war: "Among the Tartars, who from living in a more fertile soil are comparatively richer in cattle, the plunder to be obtained in predatory incursions is greater than among the Arabs. And as the contests are more bloody from the superior strength of the tribes, and the custom of making slaves is general, the loss of numbers in war will be more considerable" (1958, 82).

6 A Ph.D. dissertation by Boehmer (2001) offers a detailed analysis of the effects of economic growth on conflict.

7 Mill claims that "[i]t is commerce which is rapidly rendering war obsolete, by strengthening and multiplying the personal interests which are in natural opposition to it" (1864, book III, ch. XVII, para III.1714). I distinguish trade theory (Montesquieu 1989 [1748]; Viner 1937; Polanyi 1957) from arguments about liberal development.

8 Plans for perpetual peace were a virtual cottage industry among Enlightenment thinkers. Proposals by the Abbé de Saint-Pierre, Rousseau, and Bentham all preceded Kant's *Perpetual Peace*. Bentham, in particular, lays the blame for war on territorial aggression in the form of colonial conquest and maintenance. Texts appear in Jacob (1974).

9 Ceadel (1980, 1987, and 1996) is the undisputed authority on peace movements in Enlightenment and modern Britain.

10 See Blainey (1988, 18–32) for a lucid description of Manchester School theories of liberalism and peace.

11 Cobden also offers the often-repeated claim that development makes war more expensive. "Should war break out between two great nations I have no doubt that the immense consumption of material and the rapid destruction of property would have the effect of very soon bringing the combatants to reason or exhausting their resources" (Cobden 1903, 355). The argument is peculiar given that development has the effect of increasing state resources.

12 Etherington (1984) reviews the intellectual evolution of imperialism in the United States and Britain.

13 For Hobson, imperialism can be thwarted by democracy. "The power of the imperialist forces within the nation to use the national resources for their private gain, by operating the instrument of the State, can only be overthrown by the establishment of genuine democracy" (1938, 360). Long (1996) also shows that Hobson was pivotal in redirecting liberalism away from laissez-faire economic theory and toward a focus on international organizations.

14 Most Marxists reject the notion that capitalism can be revived; "imperialist wars are absolutely inevitable under [monopolist capitalism], as long as private property in the means of production exists" (Lenin 1965, 5).

15 Rowe (1999) offers a twist on expansionist war theory. Rising factor prices in periods of heated development lead to a general sense of relative decline, insecurity, and preventive war. However, military innovation could also adjust factor utilization in response to changes in supply. Gartzke (2001) shows that rich states use more capital in their armed forces and proportionately less labor. Factor allocations do not seem to be influenced by regime type.

16 "[T]he capitalist policy of expansion and colonial policy have placed countless mines under the edifice of world peace. The fuses are held by most varied hands, and the mines may easily and unexpectedly explode" (13–14).

17 "What confronts us in international politics to-day is, therefore, nothing less than the complete bankruptcy of the conception of morality which has dominated political and economic thought for a century and a half . . . The synthesis of morality and reason, at any rate in the crude form in which it was achieved by nineteenth-century liberalism, is untenable" (Carr 1939, 62). Carr's commentary, of course, leaves open the possibility of refining liberal theory.

18 Underlying these arguments are assumptions about the nature of state capacity (Kugler and Arbetman 1997).

19 One may also draw parallels about growth.

> Marxists and realists share a sense of the importance of contracting frontiers and their significance for the stability and peace of the system. As long as expansion is possible, the law of uneven growth (or development) can operate with little disturbing effect on the overall stability of the system. In time, however, limits are reached, and the international system enters a period of crisis. The clashes among states for territory, resources, and markets increase in frequency and magnitude and eventually culminate in hegemonic war.
> (Gilpin 1981, 201)

> However, while Marxists clearly see growth as the critical dynamic in the timing of crisis, the relationship for realists is ambiguous. One might stave off crisis through internal and external balancing.

20 Karl Kautsky concluded that World War I was not an imperialist war, and that the war could prolong capitalism by encouraging cartels among imperialist powers.

> The violent competition of great concerns led to the formation of trusts and the destruction of small concerns. Just so there may develop in the present

war a combination of the stronger nations which will put an end to the competitive building of armaments. From a purely economic point of view, therefore, it is not impossible that capitalism is now to enter upon a new phase, a phase marked by the transfer of trust methods to international politics, a sort of super-imperialism. (Kautsky 1914, 286).

This view, and Kautsky's increasingly pointed criticism of Bolshevism, prompted Lenin to polemic,

Kautsky the "historian" so shamelessly falsifies history that he "forgets" the fundamental fact that pre-monopoly capitalism – which actually reached its zenith in the seventies – was by virtue of its fundamental economic traits, which found most typical expression in Britain and in America, distinguished by a, relatively speaking, maximum fondness for peace and freedom. Imperialism, on the other hand, i.e. monopoly capitalism, which finally matured only in the twentieth century, is, by virtue of its fundamental economic traits, distinguished by a minimum fondness for peace and freedom, and by a maximum and universal development of militarism. To "fail to notice" this in discussing the extent to which a peaceful or violent revolution is typical or probable is to stoop to the level of the most ordinary lackey of the bourgeoisie. (Lenin 1978,15–16)

See Salvadori (1979, 251–84) for a discussion of the intellectual battles between the two.

21 A few realists advocate trade (Copeland 1996 and 1999; Papayoanou 1996 and 1999; Papayoanou and Kastner 1999).

22 An exception might be nuclear proliferation, associated with a certain level of economic development. See Sagan and Waltz 1995. Realist power transition theories offer an explicitly dynamic alternative to balance of power theory in which differential growth is the critical determinant of conflict (Kugler and Organski 1989; Kugler and Lemke 1996; Lemke 2002; Organski 1958; Organski and Kugler 1980). Conflict is most likely precisely where neorealists say it is least likely.

23 Long cycle theorists argue that fluctuations in growth (business cycles) account for variable conflict (Toynbee 1961; Gilpin 1981; Modelski 1987; Goldstein 1988; Thompson 1988; Sayrs 1993). For a critique, see Beck (1991).

24 Keohane and Nye (1989) are credited with reviving liberal internationalist theory. It is important to note, however, that the study is descriptive rather than analytical, since the authors assume by definition the relationship between economic variables and peace that is the basis of contention among liberals and their critics (1989, 20–25).

25 Zuk (1985) finds no support for the thesis that resource shortages act as a catalyst for major power expansion. Tir and Diehl (1998) report a weak increase in militarized disputes associated with population growth, but find no evidence that population density is responsible for interstate conflict. They conclude that "there are substantial limits to the validity of extending overcrowding arguments to the context of interstate relations" (1998, 336).

26 One could generate optimistic or pessimistic claims using other conceptual frameworks. For example, Mueller (1989) argues that populations have simply changed their attitude about war, no longer finding fighting acceptable.

27 For a series of readings reflecting Cold War perspectives on imperialism, see Boulding and Mukerjee (1972).

28 Quincy Wright (1942) is an exception, attempting to demonstrate that development increases deadly warfare. Numerous studies show that states with greater military capabilities are more likely to use force (Bremer 1980 and 1992; Small and Singer 1982), but this could be the result of motivation (states planning to fight would do well to invest in armaments).

29 Rosecrance (1996) makes a developmental distinction between "trading states" and globalized "virtual states."

30 The claim is heard from a diverse community of researchers. Realists, for example, argue that balancing brings peace. Thus, rapid or differential economic development can threaten international stability. "Great powers need money, technology, and personnel to build military forces and to fight wars" (Mearsheimer 2001, 55).

31 Boehmer and Sobek (2005) apply the Most and Starr (1990) opportunity and willingness framework to argue (and then demonstrate) that development has contrasting effects on military disputes at the level of individual states. Hegre (2000) shows that development conditions the behavior of liberal democracies. See Lemke (2003) for a review.

32 In the United States, the leading exponent of liberal peace was Nicholas Murray Butler (1934 and 1940), a prominent politician, recipient of the Nobel Prize for Peace in 1931 (Angell received the peace prize in 1933), and president of Columbia University.

33 Olson (2000) argues that liberal government possesses advantages in a globalized world, including competence and enforcement of property rights. For an entertaining discussion of the origins of government, see Olson (1993).

34 Fettweis (2003) offers a comparison of Mackinder and Angell. "Nearly a hundred years of evolution from the time that these two men wrote have rendered Mackinder's theories, and the worldview from which they sprang, as obsolete as major power war itself. At the dawn of the twenty-first century, long-discredited Norman Angell has emerged triumphant" (2003, 109–10). Gray (2004) offers an apology for Mackinder and the theory of geopolitics.

35 Mackinder is best known for the statement "Who rules East Europe commands the Heartland: Who rules the Heartland commands the World-Island: Who rules the World-Island commands the World" (1962, 150).

36 The comment closely parallels Ashley (1980), quoted above, though in other respects their views are incompatible.

37 For an informative analytical literature review and discussion of economic interdependence, see Polachek (2002).

38 Only three of sixteen chapters in Schneider et al. (2003b) deal primarily with globalization and conflict.

39 "My argument is that War makes rattling good history; but Peace is poor reading" (Hardy 1936, 87).

40 Several studies find that warfare is decreasing (Woods and Baltzly 1915; Levy 1983; Luard 1986 and 1988; N. P. Gleditsch et al. 2002; Sarkees, Wayman, and Singer 2003). "There has been a general decline in the significance of economic issues as sources of international conflict" (Holsti 1991, 316). Holsti and Huth and Allee (2003) show that fighting over territory is less prevalent. Cioffi-Revilla (2004) notes that, while wars are less frequent, the number of battle deaths in the biggest wars has increased over time. In fact, we appear to be decades overdue for the next big war.

41 For an analysis of long cycles in the context of sea power, see Modelski and Thompson (1988).

42 Weede (2003) argues that there is a case to be made for a "capitalist peace" among globalized states. Gartzke and Li (2003b) provide a case study of the effects of economic globalization on conflict across the Taiwan Straits.

43 Herz (1957) was one of the first scholars to argue that modernity leads to permeable borders. The notion of dissolving boundaries is myopic, however. International borders have seldom proven impervious, or even particularly well defined. The idea of exercising total control over borders really only arrives in Europe in the eighteenth century. Earlier, sovereigns built bridges across rivers and walls around cities as much to capture tax revenues as to facilitate movement and protect inhabitants (Keene 1996; Lilley 2002). Tariffs nominally due at the border were uncollectible, as merchants could always transit around border stations on their journey to market. Merchants could not avoid going to market, however, and here the sovereign intervened. Populations were treated as subject, but until relatively recently this was achieved through an association with territory, rather than through being able to identify and track individuals themselves (Torpey 1998 and 2000). Even today, in the United States, with passports, controlled access through major points of entry, a heavily patrolled southern border, and heightened concerns about terrorism, the US government estimates that over 5 million "undocumented immigrants" reside within its borders, mostly from Latin America (USCIS, Department of Homeland Security. Estimate as of 1996, with estimated annual growth at 275,000. See http://uscis.gov/graphics/shared/aboutus/statistics/illegalalien). See also Andreas and Snyder (2000).

44 On the tendency toward pessimism in international relations (and the fact that times are relatively good, at least in the West), see Maynes (1995) and Mueller (1995). N. P. Gleditsch (1995b) provides a clarification on Mueller (1995).

45 A number of writers take Huntington (1993b and 1996) to task rhetorically. See Heilbrunn 1998; Kaplan 1997; Kirkpatrick et al. 1993; Said 2001; Walt 1997. See Huntington (1993a) for a reply to Kirkpatrick et al. (1993).

46 See Huntington (2000) for a reply to Russett et al. (2000). Huntington appears not to understand the critique.

47 Buhaug and Gleditsch (this volume) offer evidence of continuity: "Major powers fight conflicts at longer distance, but their power is not exempt from distance decay." Kay (2004) argues that globalization can increase state power.

48 A large set of arguments posit that resource scarcity (or abundance, take your pick) lead to increases in conflict (Homer-Dixon 1991, 1994 and 1999). De

Soysa (2000, 123–24) finds that "the incidence of civil war is completely unrelated to the per capita availability of natural resources, defined as the stocks of both renewable resources . . . and nonrenewables." Conversely, "the higher the per capita availability of . . . mineral wealth, the greater the incidence of conflict" (2000, 124). See also De Soysa (2002). Much remains to be done. N. P. Gleditsch (1998, 395) finds that he must offer "a fairly pessimistic assessment of the state of the study of environmental causes of conflict."

49 Montague, for example, chronicles the theft of the mineral coltan by rebel groups and foreign armies operating in the Democratic Republic of Congo (DRC). "International competition for scarce resources in general, and for coltan in particular, is a key factor in the lack of state stability and the continuation of war in the DRC" (2002, 104).

50 Angell debunks the argument that control of raw materials (through colonization or territorial conquest) gives industrialized nations an advantage: "the outstanding fact about the producer of material anywhere is that above all he desires to get rid of it" (1936, 12). Angell claims that colonies offer no advantage. Still, he fails to draw the obvious policy implication: Great Britain should willingly cede its colonial territories to Germany to avoid war.

51 Angell, like other optimists, offers both problems at home and bitter pill arguments. "As the only feasible policy in our day for a conqueror to pursue is to leave the wealth of a territory in the possession of its occupants, it is a fallacy, an illusion to regard a nation as increasing its wealth when it increases its territory" (1933, 91).

52 Marxists emphasize that it is capitalist development, and not all development, that leads to expansion and war. I ignore the distinction for two reasons. First, I test the arguments of a variety of pessimists together, only some of whom make this distinction. Second, this is effectively a claim about the size of the coefficient. In some instances development leads to increased dispute behavior while in others it does not. I should observe some relationship even in the larger sample. For discussion of a socialist peace, see Peceny et al. (2002); Oren and Hays (1997).

53 I have prepared a Stata "do" file that replicates all aspects of data construction and quantitative analysis.

54 The extrapolated values do not alter results. Use of other indicators produces the same substantive results.

55 I examined an interaction between the monadic Development variables, finding no significant relationship.

56 I also examined an alliance dummy coded only for defense pacts. See Gartzke (2004) for further robustness checks.

57 An interaction term between the CINC variables is seldom significant and does not alter the results.

58 See Daxecker (2004) for a discussion of the contrasting implications of the "age" of a dyad for dispute behavior.

59 Tolerance of buffer states may be endogenous. Both Ancient Rome and the series of Chinese empires adopted explicit strategies of creating buffer polities by "civilizing" and co-opting settled tribal groups on their borders.

8   The death of distance? The globalization of armed conflict

Halvard Buhaug and Nils Petter Gleditsch

Interaction

Interaction is the exchange of value or information between two parties. While trade, mail, and diplomatic ties transmit positive value, war and other forms of armed conflict are examples of the exchange of negative value.[1] Interaction – positive as well as negative – is determined by opportunity, motive, and identity. An interacting party needs a motive to engage in interaction, such as the desire to gain, financially or otherwise. Secondly, a transaction must be practically feasible. Finally, each party needs to have sufficient identity or coherence to be considered as an actor. In order to join the European Union and NATO, for instance, the motivation to become a member is not sufficient. Cooperation also depends on the opportunity to join as determined by the good will of the organization and the right timing. The prospective member also needs to be identified as an actor. Greenland can leave the European Union, while Occitania cannot. Likewise, negative interaction, including the use of military force, is unrealistic unless all three factors are present. Features that promote peaceful interaction may also constitute a foundation for conflict.

Various models of internal conflict are related to this three-factor model, whose origins are usually credited to Gurr (1970). In their work on interstate war, Most and Starr (1989, 23) posit that decisions to go to war require opportunity and willingness. Willingness refers to "the choice (and process of choice) that is related to the selection of some behavioral option from a range of alternatives," in other words what we call "motivation" in this article. Opportunity is a shorthand term for "the possibilities that are available within any environment." Identity is not part of their model, probably because for interstate war it is assumed that the group formation is defined by the nation-state.

In this chapter, we focus on the opportunity element in interstate conflict, and geographic opportunity in particular. Political scientists traditionally have a very narrow view of geography. Quantitative IR studies rarely go beyond simple indicators of contiguity and proximity, which has led some geographers to criticize the political science literature for being "blinded by an equation of geography and distance" (O'Loughlin 2000, 131). Conversely, geographers tend to be preoccupied with the concept of "place." This chapter seeks to bridge this gap by studying elements of both space (distance) and place (location).[2] The main research question is to what extent the processes attributed to globalization have affected the relationship between the incidence of militarized disputes and the relative location of the states. We test three alternative operationalizations of geographic opportunity: minimum interstate distance, direct land contiguity, and neighborhood effects. Particular emphasis is placed on the temporal dynamics of the geography–conflict nexus. The empirical findings strongly contradict the popular belief that globalization involves the death of distance – some results even suggest that proximity may have gained importance in explaining why some states fight while others don't. Finally, we ask whether our findings can be reinterpreted in terms of willingness, specifically the territorial motive for war, but we reject this interpretation.

The distance factor

Theoretically, distance is related to interaction in three different ways (N. P. Gleditsch 1995a, 298). The first is economic cost. The transmission of value and information depends on human effort, physical infrastructure, and means of transportation. All of these require investment and operating costs, from the education of a railway engineer or an airline pilot to the consumption of fuel and the building of transportation terminals. The relationship between cost and distance is complicated by special geographical factors like mountains, land and water interfaces, or changes from one means of communication to another (as when a letter goes from an aircraft to a post-office van to a post-office employee who hand-delivers the mail). Therefore, we cannot assume that the costs are proportional to the distance, but we assume that – everything else being equal – costs tend to increase monotonically with distance. The bulk of the relevant literature supports such a linkage (Maurseth 2003).

The association between distance and costs applies to negative interaction as well. Projecting force to distant parts of the world is much more costly than attacking one's neighbor:

Great distances between home bases and operational areas reduce opportunities for timely employment of military responses in emergencies. Lengthy lines of supply and communication increase requirements for long-haul transportation and, if vulnerable to enemy interdiction, make users divert combat forces to protect them. (Collins 1998, 14–15)

Kennan (1962, 261) argues that "the effectiveness of the power radiated from any national center decreases in proportion to the distance involved." Such considerations are incorporated into a formal model of conflict proposed by Boulding (1962). Two factors are essential for projecting force. One is a nation's power at the point of origin. The other is the rate at which this power diminishes over distance because of transportation costs, the "loss-of-strength gradient" (LSG).[3] In its deterministic form, this model cannot account for war, only for conquest. Where the weaker party realizes that it has less power at home than the projected power of the opponent, it should yield to invasion rather than resist. However, if we introduce uncertainty about the aggressor's power preponderance or about the LSGs, war becomes possible because both parties may see themselves as likely winners.

As in the case of positive interaction, distance decay in conflict is unlikely to be linear and involves substantial discontinuities (Wohlstetter 1968). The costs of land transportation are usually higher than those of sea transportation. The worst bottlenecks are often local factors such as climate, terrain, availability of harbors, and so on. Large jumps in the loss-of-strength curve may occur at the switching points. Wohlstetter argued that in some cases the relationship between war-fighting potential and distance might even be reversed. In the case of nuclear warfare, forward bases are both vulnerable and costly. The optimal alternative may be the intercontinental missile located on the home territory and with no need for refueling once set on its way to the target. But on the whole Wohlstetter accepted the generally negative relationship between war-fighting capability and distance.

The general argument about distance and interaction reveals an apparent paradox. If both positive and negative interaction is facilitated by geographical opportunity, we should have a positive correlation between cooperation and conflict. To some extent this is true. Previous positive interaction influences the willingness to go to war, precisely because it provides an arena where disagreements may arise and lead to conflict. A study by Bearce and Fisher (2002) concludes that some of the same factors that promote trade may also encourage military conquest. Likewise, Polachek et al. (1998) demonstrate that geographic distance reduces both conflict and cooperation. Indeed, most of the large, destructive wars in the twentieth century – from World War I to the Iran–Iraq War – started out as wars between neighbors with high levels of pre-war interaction. Countries that conduct no peaceful transactions are unlikely to find any reason – or have the opportunity – to fight.

A second theoretical basis for the relationship between distance and interaction is time. Generally, it is faster to communicate at short distances, although comparing across the military services the link is not always straightforward. The forward movement of a rifle company at 4 km per hour is proportional to time, and so is the deployment of airmobile troops. But it takes longer to move the rifle company 30 km by foot than to airlift troops across the Atlantic Ocean. Time differences may also exercise a delay factor on interaction in the East–West direction, as when business partners or academic associates find that their e-mail correspondents have already left work or have not arrived yet when they try to communicate with them in normal working hours (N. P. Gleditsch 1974).[4]

A third theoretical justification for the distance–interaction relationship originates in what Stouffer (1940) called intervening opportunity, a model originally developed for migration and later applied to numerous forms of interaction (for examples, see Black et al. 2002; Guldmann 1999). Stouffer assumed that interaction would be limited by interaction opportunities encountered along the way to the original target. For instance, a migrant from A, who finds himself in transit in C while on his way to B, may find that the living conditions in C are acceptable and may decide to stay there rather than move on to a more uncertain future in his original destination. Given certain additional assumptions, Dodd (1950) and Coleman (1964, 470) have demonstrated a formal equivalence between the interaction opportunity model and the so-called gravity model, which posits that interaction between two units is proportional to the product of the populations and inversely proportional to the distance between them (or some function of distance).[5] Applying the idea of intervening opportunity to negative interaction means that hostilities between two noncontiguous countries are likely to involve intermediate countries as well. When Poland was carved up by Germany and the Soviet Union in September 1939, this may be seen as a prelude to the war between the two major rivals, which in fact occurred less than two years later. But since Poland was allied with France and the United Kingdom, attacking Poland quickly came to involve Germany in war with its largest neighbor on the other side.

Yet another link between distance and interaction may arise from shared resources along boundaries, whether territory (Vasquez 1993) or water resources (Toset et al. 2000; Furlong et al. 2005). Such resources have the potential to ignite interstate contestation, but they may likewise lead to increased cooperation. We return later to the territorial interpretation of the relationship between proximity and war. Our first hypothesis, then, is simply

H1: The incidence of armed conflict is negatively related to the distance between the parties.

Location

A less frequently explored element of geography in studies of international relations is the importance of location. By contrast, studies of individual behavior, such as voting patterns, have a long tradition for controlling for contextual effects (see O'Loughlin 2004). Yet, the role of location, or context, is not undisputed. Some scholars argue that the context should not matter, once the model includes all relevant socioeconomic factors (King 1996). In this spirit, Collier and Hoeffler (2002) argue that there is nothing peculiarly African about conflicts in Africa: the continent simply harbors an accumulation of factors that make for violence anywhere. Similarly, Sørli et al. (2005) found that conflict in the Middle East is quite well explained by a general theory of civil war, with no need to invoke a pattern of "Middle Eastern exceptionalism." Nevertheless, in the absence of more or less perfect explanatory models we should expect context to matter, at least on the national or regional scale. Anselin and O'Loughlin (1992) find strong evidence of clustering patterns of conflict as well as cooperation, trade, and economic development in Africa. In fact, the spatial clustering of conflict partially overlapped with the cooperation cluster. They conclude that African states interact (positively and negatively) "predominantly with first-order neighbors" (1992, 73). There is little reason to believe that the rest of the world should be systematically different. Ward and Gleditsch (2002) demonstrate that the conflict proneness of a state is affected by the recent conflict history of proximate states, which may reflect regional characteristics but also suggests contagious behavior. Earlier studies on the diffusion of war include Most and Starr (1980) and Siverson and Starr (1990). In their work on democratic diffusion, O'Loughlin et al. (1998) provide evidence for spatial as well as temporal clustering of democratization. Analyses of economic growth (Murdoch and Sandler 2002 and 2004) reveal substantial spillover effects from nearby civil wars, where the impact of a conflict on neighboring economies is positively associated with the relative length of the common border and negatively related to the distance between the states (for noncontiguous pairs of states). Collier et al. (2003, ch. 2) also report a neighbor effect in the consequences of civil war.

Thus, the likelihood of conflict should not only be affected by the dyadic combination of state-level attributes and the distance between the aggressor and the potential target, but also by characteristics of the neighborhood. States in democratic regions are less likely to be involved in a military conflict because their most likely opponents enjoy pacific norms and institutional restraints to state power, and because there are fewer nearby conflicts with contagious effects. Therefore, states in unstable regions will have a higher likelihood of conflict at any given time than otherwise similar states in developed, democratic regions. Our second hypothesis, then, is

H2: The incidence of armed conflict is positively related to the conflict incidence of neighbor states.

Globalization

The globalization debate has revitalized the position that distance and location are less important than they used to be, and that the integrity of territorial units – notably the nation-state – is being undermined. These are not new ideas. Wright (1942, 1241, n. 4) noted that geographical distance had declined in relative importance for cultural contact between groups "with the invention of new means of transport and communication." And Herz (1957) argued vigorously that the basis of the territorial state was about to vanish. The territorial state had arisen when the immunity of the knight in his castle (and the medieval city within its walls) was broken by radical developments in military technology, notably the invention of gunpowder. The large-area state took the place of the castle or fortified town as the "unit of impenetrability" (477). However, by the middle of the twentieth century, Herz argued, the territorial state had been left without walls or moats, through four factors in increasing order of effectiveness: economic blockade, ideological-political penetration, air warfare, and atomic warfare. The last two had already demonstrated the penetrability of territorially based power, particularly in World War II.

A major characteristic of globalization is technological innovation. Technological innovation reduces the cost of interaction, increases its speed, and increases the range of the vehicles of interaction. The exchange of goods, money, or information can be achieved at lower cost, but so can the exchange of "bads" such as bombs or invading soldiers. The decline of interaction cost is familiar to any middle-aged traveler. Based on IMF data, the Global Policy Forum has compiled information which shows a sharp decline in average sea-freight charges (reduced by 70 percent from 1920 to 1990), average revenue per passenger mile

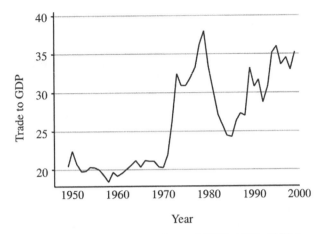

Figure 8.1. World trade as a share of GDP, 1950–2000 (percent).

(reduced by about 84 percent from 1930 to 1990), and the cost of a three-minute phone call from New York to London (reduced by about 99 percent from 1930 to 1990).[6] The decline in the time required to interact at a distance is illustrated in Wolfe (1963, 120), who details the approximate speed in miles per hour, ranging from an army moving long distance on foot (0.5) via early steamships (10) and propel-driven planes (200) to orbiting satellites (18,000). Not all of these vehicles of transportation are equally relevant to all forms of interaction – for instance, exotic ideas about mail delivery by decommissioned intercontinental missiles have not come to fruition. No form of transportation, however, is unaffected by the revolution in speed.

The decline in transportation cost and time is a long-term phenomenon; yet, the concept of "globalization" has only been around for about two decades.[7] The term is usually interpreted to mean the rapid increase in trade, foreign investment, and other forms of economic interaction that the world has witnessed since the end of World War II and particularly in the most recent decades (Figure 8.1). As a response to this development, a best-selling book about the communication revolution announces "the death of distance" in its title (Cairncross 2000). Similarly, a book about financial integration trumpets "the end of geography" (O'Brien 1992).

Travel and trade are obvious sectors that are facilitated by falling transaction costs and increasing speed, but the consequences of globalization may be substantially more far-reaching. In a classic study, Svalastoga (1956) found that most murders are committed by people who know each other. In today's globalized societies – dominated by extensive travel and commuting, providing interaction with a higher number of people – some crime statistics suggest that this trend may be on the decline. In the United States, the number of murders committed by intimates between 1976 and 1998 decreased by 4 percent per year on average for male victims and 1 percent per year for female victims. The total number of murders also declined, but less substantially, from 18,870 to 16,974 per year, representing an annual decline of a mere 0.4 percent.[8] The number of ongoing armed conflicts has also declined in the most recent decade, and if the analogy holds, we should expect conflicts with neighbors to decline more than average.

The view of globalization as undermining the territorial nation-state is strongly reinforced by the emergence of electronic communication, which is virtually time-invariant and where cost does not depend on distance (Cairncross 2000). It costs no more to send an e-mail to the other side of the world than to the house next door, nor does it take any longer. This has not only facilitated globalization, but has also – paradoxically – served to unite antiglobalization activists across national boundaries.[9] Electronic infrastructure (communication and navigation, as well as information collection, processing, and dissemination) plays an increasingly crucial role in modern warfare. Defense strategy is now as much about information technology and computer skills as about building better bombs. Hence, even states that do not possess long-range ballistic weapons may overcome the tyranny of distance by initiating jamming, propaganda, and electronic attacks on military infrastructure. Ironically, the more technologically advanced the society, the more vulnerable it is to electronic attacks. In 1987, Ronald Reagan became the first US president to acknowledge the potential problem of cyber attacks, signing the "Computer Security Act" to protect federal computer data.[10] Some have even speculated that so-called cyber warfare will become the main – perhaps the only – form of future combat (CNN, 2003).

The removal of trade barriers and the establishment of global markets imply that, in theory, citizens of any state can acquire any desired commodity at a competitive price. The uneven distribution of natural resources may no longer be a curse for the rich or for the poor. This should reduce the strategic importance of territory, which for various reasons is claimed to be the main cause of armed interstate conflict (see Vasquez 1995; Hensel 2000). For example, the establishment of the European Coal and Steel Community in 1952, the forerunner to the European Union, was motivated primarily by a need to secure peace and stability between two of Europe's major rivals: France and Germany.

According to the preamble of the ECSC Treaty, the six member states were resolved

to substitute for age old rivalries the merging of their essential interests; to create, by establishing an economic community, the basis for a broader and deeper community among peoples long divided by bloody conflicts; and to lay the foundations for institutions which will give direction to a destiny henceforward shared.[11]

Further, if relatively fewer wars are fought between neighboring states, as theorized above, we should expect to see a declining ratio of territorial conflicts. The main motivation behind most territorial disputes is a desire to gain control over a specific territory, be it for security reasons, due to valuable natural resources, or based on historical or nationalistic claims. Disregarding colonial holdings, distant states are not likely to start fighting over such issues. Although empirical support for a declining role of territory is sparse, Holsti (1991) suggests that territory has been a less prominent conflict issue after 1945.

Globalization may also affect armed conflict through the global proliferation of (Western) norms, ideas, and cultures, including the recent wave of democratization (Huntington 1991). Democratic peace theory suggests that this should make the world a safer place (N. P. Gleditsch and Hegre 1997). Thus, Cairncross (2000, xvii) may well be right in her prediction that globalization will "foster world peace," but since this argument does not relate clearly to territoriality we do not pursue it further here.

Summing up the globalization perspective, technological innovation reduces transaction cost by lowering the absolute cost of shipping and by reducing the time of transaction. The declining cost and time of international interaction will gradually undermine the relationship between distance and interaction, resulting in a lower impact of distance on interaction over time. Similarly, the pacifying or hazardous effect of neighborhoods will decrease, given that an increasing share of international interaction will be interregional. Finally, the development of global trade markets reduces the strategic importance of borders and territory, lowering the motivation for territorial expansion by military means (see Gartzke and Simmons, both this volume, for related arguments). The resulting globalization hypotheses are

H3: Globalization weakens the relationship between distance and the incidence of armed conflict.

H4: Globalization weakens the relationship between the incidence of armed conflict and the incidence of armed conflict of neighbor states.

H5: Globalization decreases the number of territorial conflicts relative to other armed conflicts.

But it ain't necessarily so

Some of the arguments for the death of distance thesis are hard to test empirically because they refer mainly to the future. However, there are several bases for skepticism. First, much of the globalization literature confuses the absolute cost of interaction with the relative cost. Absolute cost may decline with little or no impact on relative cost. If relative cost is what matters to interaction, the distance–interaction relationship should continue to hold up. Most studies of globalization fail to acknowledge these mechanisms and rather focus on changes in absolute costs of trade. On the other hand, econometric studies of trade and globalization, using the standard gravity model, have noted as one of the big puzzles of macroeconomics that there is no evidence of a decline in the distance coefficient over time (Obstfeld and Rogoff 2001).[12]

Even for forms of interaction with little or no cost, the death of distance argument is suspect.[13] The interaction capacity of an actor is not unlimited. If interaction ever became fully independent of cost, it would expand to a level where it strains the capacity of the actors to process the value exchanged. E-mail provides an example. Even disregarding spam (which is a problem precisely because it costs virtually nothing to distribute), the principle that anyone can contact anyone else in the world directly will inevitably lead to information overload. What rationing principle can be invoked in order to cope with this information flow? Users may be forced to filter away incoming e-mails that seem suspicious or, more drastically, do not come from a limited group of recognized users. This user community is likely to be derived from past interaction, which did depend on distance, and from other forms of interaction (such as personal interaction) which still do. Similarly, even though there are few physical barriers and even fewer structural obstacles to extensive trade between, say, Italy and Ireland, both continue to trade more with their neighbors, both because the costs are relatively smaller and because of established regional cooperation.

For most forms of exchange of goods, the costs appear to decline only up to a point. Although the transportation costs have declined drastically over a period of 60–70 years, most of the decline occurred in the early part of that period (see Masson 2001). Shipping costs, according to the same statistics, declined only marginally from 1950 to 1990, and revenue per passenger mile in aviation has remained constant since the 1980s. This stands in stark contrast to developments in other technologies, most notably within telecommunication, suggesting that not all kinds of interaction are equally affected by the processes attributed to globalization. In fact, some types of interaction may hardly be affected at all. In particular, this seems to apply to states' military reach.

Deciding whom and when to fight is a matter of high national priority, which is less likely to be influenced by mundane factors such as fluctuations in transportation costs. When the stakes are high, for example when the jurisdiction over a territory is challenged by another state, lesser issues are likely to be neglected. Therefore, we do not expect states in general to be more belligerent simply because transportation costs have fallen. Nor do we expect states to initiate hostilities toward more distant targets just because it is cheaper to do so. In this respect, we argue, globalization should not affect the relationship between distance and conflict. However, globalization may work through another channel: technological development.

Throughout most of modern history, military planners and the arms-producing industry have focused on speed, range, and power, that is, the physical performance of weapons. Each new manufactured item, be it a catapult, a steam-driven frigate, an armored fighting vehicle, or a combat aircraft, had to be faster, better armed and armored, and have a longer range than its predecessor. These virtues now seem devalued in favor of "modern" criteria like agility, precision, and battlefield reliability. The fastest combat aircraft in the world is still the Soviet-built MiG-25, nearly forty years after its first of several record-breaking flights.[14] Likewise, the world's most widely distributed tactical surface-to-surface missile, the SS-1 "Scud," dates back to the mid-1950s. There are numerous upgrades and derivatives of this missile, but attempts to increase its range (such as the Iraqi al-Hussein version designed to reach Israel) have been made at the expense of payload and accuracy (Bokhari 1999). The recent breakthroughs in military technology are the development of stealth technology, satellite navigation, night capability, and precision-guided munitions ("smart bombs"). These inventions are undoubtedly progressive from a military point of view, but that does not necessarily imply that armies equipped with such weapons are capable of fighting at longer distances than less advanced ones. They will, however, have a larger probability of winning the battle, *ceteris paribus*, given the superior reliability and precision of state-of-the-art weaponry. They also reduce the number of battle deaths (Lacina and Gleditsch 2005).

Modern weapons are extremely expensive and this has resulted in an increasing technological gap between the haves and the have-nots. Even today, most armed forces rely exclusively on unguided rockets and "iron" bombs, old-fashioned artillery, and outdated tanks as their offensive striking force. With the exception of cruise missiles and in-flight refueling, also technologies unavailable to all but a few armed forces, the average striking range of ground- and air-launched weapons does not appear to have increased markedly since the 1960s.

The main factor to limit the military reach of armed forces is not the range of the artillery or the combat radius of attack planes, though. The largest obstacles to remote military operations relate to transportation and logistics. If an aggressor decides to attack a noncontiguous rival state, he must either force his way through a third party (such as Poland in the wars between Germany and Russia), or ship his forces by air or sea to the target territory. Either way, shortage of transportation vehicles and lengthy lines of supply quickly become the largest hindrance to sustaining the battle and winning the war.[15] Most countries have very limited capabilities for shipping or airlifting mechanized troops to foreign soil. For example, Germany, a major NATO country, had to lease Ukrainian transports when sending its troops to assist the United States in Afghanistan, and European troops were painfully slow to deploy in Kosovo because of transport restraints. Most armies have been designed for defensive purposes, where national infrastructure is sufficient for mobilization. In reality, these states are only capable of fighting their neighbors.

Even though electronic warfare is gaining ground, a country cannot conquer territory just by jamming and transmitting electromagnetic pulses. Cyber wars with the objective of overthrowing another government also seem to belong to a distant future. Hence, the degree to which a state's military deployment capacity has improved over time is to a large extent dependent on the purchase of additional transport vehicles (aircraft, ships) and advanced weapons (cruise missiles, ICBMs), rather than on technological innovation or lowered fuel prices. If globalization affects the military reach of states, it appears to do so only indirectly, through economic development that is accompanied by increased military spending.

In short, while distance may no longer be a tyranny in terms of imposing absolute barriers to positive or negative interaction, its death has probably been prematurely announced.[16] Indeed, after only a decade Herz (1968, 13) pronounced himself "doubtful of the correctness" of his own thesis. He still saw traditional territoriality as threatened by the factors that he had enumerated, but he saw a "new territoriality" emerging in international relations. Specifically, regarding the use of military force there is little reason to expect that recent advances in technology and reductions in transportation costs per se have contributed to increasing the average striking range.

Perhaps we should even expect the relationship between distance and conflict to be strengthened in the future. Globalization is likely to

weaken the regional, colonial, and alliance-based special relationships in favor of more universal forms of interaction, where distance
exercises a monotonic restraint on interaction at all levels. The most
important of these special relationships, which disappeared during
the most recent period of globalization, is, of course, the Cold War.
With its ideological alliances between geographically distant countries,
the Cold War led to several "unrealistic" conflict dyads, including
Cuba's involvement in Africa on behalf of the Soviet Union and New
Zealand's participation in Vietnam in solidarity with the United States.
However, since only a fraction of our data represent the post-Cold War
period, we do not expect the current empirical investigation to capture
this trend.

The interaction hypotheses are

*H6: Globalization has not affected the relationship between distance and the
incidence of armed conflict.*

*H7: Globalization has not affected the relationship between the incidence of
armed conflict and the incidence of armed conflict between neighbor states.*

Research design

We used Version 3.04 of the EUGene data management program (Bennett and Stam 2000) to construct a non-directed dyad year data set for
all system members in the period from 1875 to 1998. The interstate
conflicts under study are from Correlates of War's Militarized Interstate
Disputes data set Version 3.0 (Ghosn and Palmer 2003). Some 4,083
dyad years of disputes are recorded in this period, including 1,045 dyad
years of war (MID hostility level 5). Overall, the dyadic data set contains
587,042 units of observation. In addition, we generated a comparable
monadic data set, since some of the hypotheses pertain to the conflict
involvement of states rather than pairs of states. The monadic data set
contains 10,467 observations, including 3,582 country years of dispute
and 671 country years of war.

Our main proxy for geographic opportunity, interstate distance, was
constructed by combining the K. S. Gleditsch and Ward (2001) minimum distance data for proximate states with measures of intercapital
distance, generated by EUGene. For states that are separated by less
than 950 km we relied on the Gleditsch and Ward data, while intercapital distances are given for states that are further apart.[17] The period
covered by the minimum distance data set (1875–1998) defines the
temporal domain of our study. To estimate the effect of land contiguity,
we include a dummy variable from Version 3.0 of the Correlates of War's
direct contiguity data (Stinnett et al. 2002). A third proxy for geographic

opportunity is neighboring conflict. The neighborhood (spatial lag) variable is assigned a unique value to each observation by multiplying a binary conflict incidence variable for all other system members with their corresponding value on an inverse distance weights matrix for the given country.[18] The variable has a theoretical range from 0 (no disputes in the system the given year) to 1 (all other system members involved in disputes the given year), where proximate conflicts count more than distant ones.[19]

Most models of the relationship between distance and interaction (for instance the gravity model and the LSG model) posit that larger countries have a longer reach. We control for the size of countries by including the monadic/lowest dyadic capability score (CINC score[20]) as well as a dummy for major powers. We additionally control for dyadic democratic peace, alliances, and other standard control variables used in studies of interstate conflict. Finally, we control for system-level economic openness – a binary indicator originally defined by Wallensteen (1984) and later updated by Vasquez and Henehan (2004) – and time (coded as number of years since 1875, the initial year in our analysis).

Generally, the extent of globalization is assumed to increase over time, if not necessarily in a linear fashion. Almost all states are more internationally integrated today than they were half a century ago. However, not all regions of the world are equally globalized, and states globalize at different rates. Hence, time (year) may not be the best proxy for globalization. As a better operationalization, we relied on COW's trade and capability data (Barbieri 2002; Singer et al. 1972) to construct a measure of (log) total combined exports and imports divided by (log) population size. In the dyadic data set, the globalization proxy gives the lowest trade-to-population ratio in the dyad. The variable distinguishes between trading states and more closed regimes – a central aspect of globalization. By controlling for time, we also rule out general temporal trends that might otherwise be captured by the trade-to-population measure. This is by no means a perfect approximation: for example, it hardly captures the technological level of a society and ignores other forms of interaction. The globalization proxy also introduces sample selection bias, owing to substantial missing data.[21] To assess the extent of the bias, we run parallel models with and without the globalization variable.

All models are estimated by logit regression with robust standard errors. To account for temporally correlated error terms, an inherent problem of time-series cross-sectional data, the models include a "peace years" count variable and a natural cubic splines function with three interior knots (see Beck et al. 1998).

Empirical results

Hypothesis 1 states that the dyadic conflict incidence should be negatively related to the distance between the states. Figure 8.2 presents an initial test of this hypothesis by showing the smoothed share of noncontiguous dyads involved in conflict as a function of distance. With regard to all types of disputes, the figure presents strong evidence in favor of the proposition. The risk of MIDs falls monotonically with the distance between states, with the exception of a local peak at about 6,000 km.[22] In fact, the initial distance decay is even stronger than the smoothed line suggests. Noncontiguous dyads that are separated by less than 100 km of land or water are about twenty times as likely to quarrel at any given time (p = 0.07) as states that are at least 1,000 km apart (p = 0.003), *ceteris paribus*. For wars, the picture is more blurred. Figure 8.2 suggests a weak U-curved relationship between interstate distance and war, where the lowest war probability is found at around 8,000 km. However, the extreme right tail of the war curve is driven by some unusual war dyads, many of which never saw action on any battlefield. No less than 70 of the 127 dyadic war years with intercapital distance above 10,000 km involve Australia or New Zealand during World War II. Because of such outliers, and because it seems reasonable to assume that an additional kilometer becomes less vital the further apart a pair of states are, the dyadic regression models include a log-transformed distance variable.

In Table 8.1 we estimate the effect of logged distance on both MID and war incidence, controlling for a number of dyadic and systemic attributes. The results for the distance variable correspond well with Figure 8.2 and provide further support for Hypothesis 1. According to Model 1, two states separated by the 5th percentile value (412 km) are

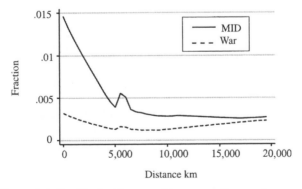

Figure 8.2. Conflict incidence and interstate distance for noncontiguous dyads, 1875–1998.

Table 8.1. *MID and war incidence, 1875–1998: the basic dyad-year model*

	MID incidence		War incidence	
	Model 1	Model 2	Model 3	Model 4
Interstate distance (log)	−.322***	−.315***	−.215***	−.214***
	(.005)	(.006)	(.013)	(.014)
At least one major power	1.700***	1.732***	2.121***	2.227***
	(.043)	(.046)	(.083)	(.087)
Lowest capability score	.016***	.015***	.021***	.021***
	(.001)	(.001)	(.001)	(.001)
Jointly democratic	−1.276***	−1.367***	−2.488***	−2.723***
	(.085)	(.103)	(.284)	(.367)
Allied	.033	−.027	−.022	−.154
	(.062)	(.066)	(.158)	(.165)
Open economic system	−1.256***	−1.267***	−2.651***	−2.701***
	(.065)	(.067)	(.140)	(.150)
Lowest globalization score		−.002		−.983***
		(.122)		(.205)
Time	.014***	.016***	.022***	.031***
	(.001)	(.001)	(.002)	(.002)
Peace years	−.616***	−.604***	−.999***	−.977***
	(.015)	(.016)	(.047)	(.048)
Intercept	−.973***	−1.147***	−2.254***	−2.271***
	(.079)	(.085)	(.153)	(.177)
N	500,216	423,397	500,216	423,397
Pseudo R^2	.381	.374	.398	.396

Robust standard errors are in parentheses. The models also include three natural cubic splines to correct for temporally correlated residuals (estimates not reported).
*** $p < 0.01$; ** $p < 0.05$; * $p < 0.1$

more than three times as likely to be in a dispute as a dyad with the 95th percentile value (15,835 km), all other variables held at their median value. In fact, the impact of interstate distance in the MID models is comparable to that of dyadic democracy, and only a little weaker than the effect of the involvement of at least one major power. Distance is less powerful as an explanatory variable of war but still plays a substantial role (the probability of war increases by a factor of 2.6 when the distance variable shifts from the 5th to the 95th percentile value). The very strong effect of proximity is also robust to choice of indicator. An alternative model with a dummy for direct contiguity instead of dyadic distance produces comparable findings. Evidently, geographical distance is a vital factor in interstate conflict.

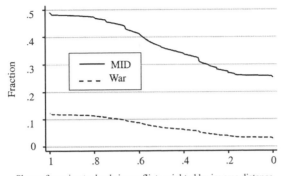

Figure 8.3. Conflict incidence and proximate conflicts, 1875–1998.

Apart from the allied dummy, all control variables have statistically very significant effects in all models, and the results compare well to findings from similar investigations. Dyads that include at least one major power and dyads with comparably high military and economic capabilities are more often involved in conflict than weaker dyads. The models also confirm the dyadic democratic peace. Adding joint democracy to the median dyad reduces the likelihood of an MID by about 75 percent. In the war model, the effect of joint democracy is four times as large (in terms of magnitude of change of probability for conflict), and now is the most influential covariate. In line with liberal theory, globalized dyads are substantially less often at war than less advanced pairs of states. For less severe disputes, the level of globalization does not appear to affect the risk of conflict. We also see that the general risk of conflict has increased over time. This is not because of the enlargement of the system as such, but rather reflects the growing number of poor, unstable states in the system and the increasing tendency to form coalitions and engage in multiparty conflicts.[23] The positive effect of time on MID incidence may also in part be an artifact of reporting bias of the MID data toward more recent events. Finally, rivals and dyads with a turbulent recent past also suffer from enlarged risk of conflict.

Following the second hypothesis, we expect the incidence of conflict to be positively associated with the conflict involvement of nearby states. Again, we evaluate this in two steps. Figure 8.3 shows the share of states involved in MIDs and wars as a function of the weighted proportion of neighboring disputes, and provides strong support for Hypothesis 2. The likelihood of conflict is clearly affected by the degree of hostility in the neighborhood. A country with conflicts on all borders is about twice as likely to be involved in an MID as a country located in a peaceful neighborhood. The relative effect of the neighborhood appears to be even larger for wars.

Next, we consider the impact of the neighborhood in logit models of monadic MID and war incidence. In addition to including spatially lagged measures of disputes, we include a similarly constructed distance-weighted measure of democratic neighborhood as a control. We expect the share of proximate democracies to be negatively associated with the conflict likelihood for state *i*, since democratic clusters tend to be less antagonistic and thus provide fewer opportunities for hostile interaction (K. S. Gleditsch 2002b). Table 8.2 presents the results. The estimate for the spatially lagged conflict component is positive and very significant in all models. The rate of disputes in the neighborhood has a strong impact on the general conflict propensity. Holding everything else at the median value, the likelihood of an MID is more than doubled when we change the weighted conflict rate of the neighborhood from the 5th to the 95th percentile. The spatial diffusion mechanisms are even more apparent in the war models. When all contiguous neighbors are involved in a militarized dispute (95th percentile value), a country's risk of war is about five times higher than when no contiguous neighbors are in conflict. This finding compares very well to similar work by Most and Starr (1980) and Siverson and Starr (1990). The effect of the neighborhood is further enhanced by the distribution of democratic regimes. States in democratic regions experience fewer conflicts, presumably because there are fewer nearby conflicts that might spread and because the most likely adversaries, the contiguous countries, share norms and institutions for peaceful conflict resolution. In other words, a favorable neighborhood may to a large extent compensate for disadvantageous country attributes.

There are several notable differences between the MID and war models. First, we find that a parabolic relationship between democracy and MID incidence is reduced to a positive and linear democratic effect on the risk of war. Second, the war models fail to reproduce Richardson's (1960) observation that states tend to engage in armed conflict in proportion to their number of borders. Table 8.2 further indicates that an open economic system only contributes to reduce the risk of wars, not of low-level disputes.[24] Globalization only weakly reduces the monadic risk of war, despite the strong dyadic findings reported above. However, the trade-to-population variable also affects the impact of some other covariates, in particular the democratic neighborhood variable in the war model (Model 8), suggesting that the missing observations are not randomly distributed. The difference between the models caused by

Table 8.2. *MID and war incidence, 1875–1998: country-year model with neighborhood effects*

	MID incidence		War incidence	
	Model 5	Model 6	Model 7	Model 8
Conflicting neighborhood	1.213***	1.161***	1.740***	1.761***
	(.081)	(.087)	(.155)	(.165)
Major power	.695***	.634***	.971***	1.031***
	(.139)	(.147)	(.213)	(.233)
Capability	.010***	.009***	.004***	.003**
	(.001)	(.001)	(.001)	(.002)
Democracy score	.010**	.010**	.020**	.022**
	(.005)	(.005)	(.009)	(.010)
Democracy squared	−.003***	−.003***	−.0002	.0004
	(.001)	(.001)	(.002)	(.002)
Democratic neighborhood	−.392***	−.273**	−.629***	−.353
	(.111)	(.121)	(.224)	(.237)
Number of borders	.059***	.055***	−.002	−.023
	(.013)	(.014)	(.022)	(.024)
Open economic system	−.128	−.095	−.737***	−.697***
	(.083)	(.085)	(.143)	(.154)
Globalization score		−.302		−.672*
		(.185)		(.356)
Time	.007***	.008***	.008***	.014***
	(.001)	(.001)	(.002)	(.003)
Peace years	−.831***	−.842***	−.792***	−.763***
	(.036)	(.039)	(.050)	(.050)
Intercept	−.656***	−.530***	−1.510***	−1.446***
	(.097)	(.122)	(.175)	(.228)
N	8,838	7,682	8,838	7,682
Pseudo R^2	.246	.244	.340	.340

Robust standard errors are in parentheses. The models also include three natural cubic splines to correct for temporally correlated residuals (estimates not reported).
***$p < 0.01$; **$p < 0.05$; *$p < 0.1$

the missing observations of the globalization variable is nevertheless less than we feared. Hence, we only report the results for models that include this measure in the remaining tests.

The remaining hypotheses consider the impact of globalization on the opportunity–conflict nexus. Hypothesis 3 asserts that globalization should reduce the general relationship between interstate distance and armed conflict. Conversely, Hypothesis 6 expects the relationship to hold up in the face of globalization. Figure 8.4 does not provide strong support for either hypothesis, but is less at odds with the interaction argument. While the mean distance between all states has increased at a

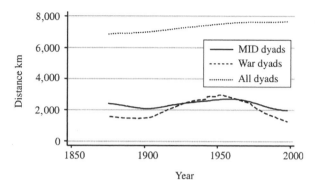

Figure 8.4. Mean interstate distance by year, 1875–1998.

steady rate during the period, the mean distance for conflicting dyads assumes a third-degree polynomial shape. Apparently, the average disputing distance reached its maximum value in the mid-twentieth century, and has since declined to the level of the initial period.[25] At no time, of course, did the average distance between the conflict dyads approach even close to the average dyadic distance, as predicted by the death of distance argument.

Models 9 to 12 in Table 8.3 are extensions of the first dyadic models where we have added interactions between distance or land contiguity and the dyadic globalization score. In line with the interaction argument and reflecting the impression of Figure 8.4, the results demonstrate that distance is indeed as much an impediment to conflict involvement for globalized dyads as it is for less liberal pairs of states. While the interaction between distance and globalization shows a weakly negative effect on MID incidence (Model 9), the interaction terms fail to make a difference in the other models.[26] However, the coefficient for globalization again demonstrates that dyads with higher trade-to-population ratios are overall substantially less likely to engage in war. Consequently, Hypothesis 3 must be rejected in favor of Hypothesis 6. The effects of the remaining variables as well as the fit of the models are almost identical to the initial models in Table 8.1. Major power, dyadic democracy, type of economic system, and proximity are the most influential factors in all models.

Our fourth hypothesis expects globalization to reduce the hazardous effect of conflicting neighbors. Hypothesis 7, on the other hand, predicts the neighborhood effect to be unaffected by globalization. The first test of these conjectures is presented in Figure 8.5, which shows the smoothed correlation between dyadic MID incidence and the

Table 8.3. *MID and war incidence, 1875–1998: model with interaction effects*

	MID incidence		War incidence	
	Model 9	Model 10	Model 11	Model 12
Interstate distance (log)	-.284*** (.018)		-.207*** (.039)	
Interstate distance × globalization	-.047* (.026)		-.013 (.064)	
Land contiguity		2.460*** (.055)		1.867*** (.148)
Land contiguity × globalization		.075 (.235)		.234 (.600)
At least one major power	1.728*** (.046)	1.801*** (.045)	2.226*** (.088)	2.253*** (.086)
Lowest capability score	.015*** (.001)	.017*** (.001)	.021*** (.001)	.022** (.001)
Joint democratic	-1.382*** (.105)	-1.354*** (.104)	-2.726*** (.339)	-2.698*** (.367)
Allied	-.041 (.067)	.104 (.071)	-.156 (.165)	-.135 (.171)
Open economic system	-1.269*** (.067)	-1.273*** (.066)	-2.702*** (.150)	-2.682*** (.148)
Lowest globalization score	-.115 (.130)	.039 (.127)	-1.001*** (.206)	-1.088*** (.206)
Time	.016*** (.001)	.016*** (.001)	.031*** (.002)	.031*** (.002)
Peace years	-.604*** (.016)	-.610*** (.015)	-.977*** (.048)	-.981*** (.048)
Intercept	-1.316*** (.138)	-3.699*** (.084)	-2.325*** (.344)	-4.031*** (.136)
N	423,397	423,609	423,397	423,609
Pseudo R^2	.374	.358	.396	.392

Robust standard errors are in parentheses. The models also include three natural cubic splines to correct for temporally correlated residuals (estimates not reported).

*** $p < 0.01$; ** $p < 0.05$; * $p < 0.1$

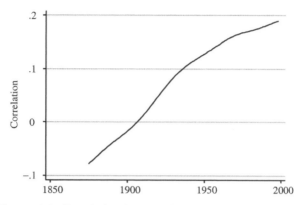

Figure 8.5. Correlation between MID incidence and proximate conflict incidence, 1875–1998.

distance-weighted incidence of neighboring disputes. Although the correlation varies greatly from year to year, the general trend is unmistakable. From a decreasing relationship in the initial period (the correlation approaches 0), the effect of the neighborhood has increased throughout most of the twentieth century. This finding is directly incompatible with the globalization perspective and more radical than the interaction perspective. Apparently, contemporary conflicts are more prone to spread to nearby states, although the figure is also consistent with increased joining behavior of neighbors. However, since we have argued that the processes of globalization rarely mirror the linear evolution of time, and since the figure ignores potentially important third factors, such as regional democratization, we need to conduct an additional analysis to fully evaluate the diffusion hypotheses.

Table 8.4 presents extended versions of the monadic models in Table 8.2, where we include an interaction term between weighted neighboring conflicts and the globalization proxy.[27] Again, we have to reject the globalization perspective. Regardless of conflict intensity, globalized states are neither more nor less affected by a belligerent environment than less liberal states. Due to high multicollinearity, globalization in and of itself also appears to be irrelevant, but the parameter estimate regains a significant and negative effect on war incidence when the interaction term is dropped.

According to Hypothesis 5, globalization is associated with a devalued political importance of territory, which should lead to a relative decline of territorial conflicts. Figure 8.6 provides a test of this proposition.

Table 8.4. *MID and war incidence, 1875–1998: interaction and neighborhoood effects*

	MID incidence	War incidence
	Model 13	Model 14
Conflicting neighborhood	1.162*** (.087)	1.717*** (.165)
Conflicting neighborhood × globalization	.052 (.359)	−1.056 (.713)
Major power	.635*** (.147)	.998*** (.232)
Capability	.009*** (.001)	.003** (.002)
Democracy score	.010** (.005)	.021** (.010)
Democracy squared	−.003*** (.001)	.0003 (.002)
Democratic neighborhood	−.273** (.121)	−.345 (.238)
Number of borders	.056*** (.014)	−.022 (.024)
Open economic system	−.094 (.086)	−.707*** .154
Globalization score	−.308 (.188)	−.431 (.362)
Time	.008*** (.001)	.014*** (.003)
Peace years	−.842*** (.039)	−.763*** (.050)
Intercept	−.529*** (.122)	−1.560*** (.245)
N	7,682	7,682
Pseudo R^2	.244	.340

Robust standard errors are in parentheses. The models also include three natural cubic splines to correct for temporally correlated residuals (estimates not reported).
***$p < 0.01$; **$p < 0.05$; *$p < 0.1$

The plots illustrate the annual share of MIDs that deal primarily with territorial issues, based on all and the 50 percent most globalized dyads, respectively. In this respect, an MID is defined as a territorial dispute if at least one participating actor is coded with territory as the primary revision issue. The general picture is inconclusive, even though the slight decline since 1950 in both plots offers some support for the hypothesis. However, this is to some extent offset by the upsurge in territorial disputes in the 1990s, so it remains to be seen whether the trend has been reversed. Similar plots for the incidence of war (not shown) offer even less support for the hypothesized relationship: the overall trend here is in fact toward a slight increase in the relative share of territorial wars over time. Therefore, we reject the hypothesis that globalization reduces the salience of territory.

Is it really territory?

The persistent role of distance and location in shaping interstate conflict is consistent with the interaction perspective, which draws on relative

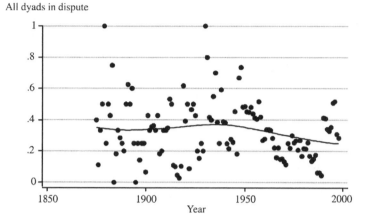

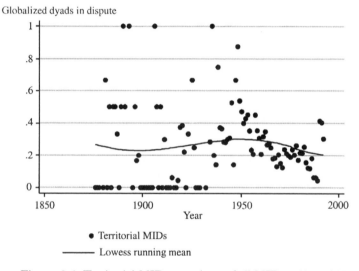

Figure 8.6. Territorial MIDs as a share of all MIDs, 1875–1998.

cost arguments to explain why geography should remain a vital factor in militarized disputes, even if globalization may have reduced the role of distance with respect to other forms of interaction. But these findings are also consistent with alternative theories in the literature. One such perspective is the so-called territorial explanation of war.

In a discussion of why neighbors fight, Vasquez (1995) distinguishes between what he calls the proximity, the interaction, and the territorial interpretations. By proximity Vasquez appears to mean reachability in an absolute sense. He discards this perspective with reference to an unpublished paper by Gochman (1990). The increasing absolute range of war has also been demonstrated by N. P. Gleditsch (1995a, 309) and is confirmed for the MIDs in our data set.[28] The interaction perspective refers to conflicts of interest between the two parties to a conflict. As interaction increases, so do the potential conflicts of interest. Vasquez finds that this explanation fails to account for the fact that interaction moves some dyads in the direction of cooperation while others end up in conflict, and argues that this is contrary to the neoliberal view of inter-state conflict and fails to account for Gochman's findings. Instead, Vasquez (1995, 281) sees war as "arising from specific territorial dis-putes between states that have been unable to be resolved by other means." While proximity provides an opportunity for war, "territorial disputes provide the willingness to go to war." It is not clear why this explanation is theoretically more satisfying. It immediately raises the question of why some territorial disputes are settled and others are not. Potential territorial disputes abound, and could arise from historically disputed settlements, or from the lack of congruence between national boundaries and ethnic and religious dividing lines. One-third of Hun-garians live outside Hungary, indicating a powerful potential for territor-ial disputes between Hungary and its neighbors, yet no serious disputes have arisen since World War II. Besides, less than half of the MID years for contiguous states are territorial disputes, so there are certainly other mechanisms at play.

Vasquez (1995, 281) questions the idea that "greater interaction should lead to both greater cooperation and conflict" but suggests that this has not been systematically tested because of a lack of long-term data on diplomatic interaction. However, there are a number of indicators of positive interaction that can be used to test this relation-ship. In fact, early studies of trade and conflict (such as Russett 1967) that did not correct for distance showed a positive relationship between the two. In our sample, total dyadic trade and the incidence of MIDs are positively correlated (r = .016, p < .01). When we correct for the logarithm of interstate distance, the sign of the correlation changes (r = −.009, p < .01). This is consistent with the view we have argued, that geographical opportunity influences both cooperation and conflict.

Also, if Vasquez were correct, we would expect contiguity to be the decisive factor rather than geographical distance. Territorial disputes are most likely to occur between immediate neighbors over land rather than between countries separated by other countries. In fact, Vasquez (1995,

279) argues that the earlier finding that intercapital distance is related to war "is probably a function of the fact that most wars are fought between neighbors." This is incorrect. In Figure 8.2 we showed the relationship between minimum distance and interstate disputes for countries that are not geographically contiguous. The figure showed that even for non-contiguous countries there is clear distance decay. When we divide this into different periods, the result remains the same, even for the most recent period. In fact, the land contiguity dummy fails to make a significant impact if added to the models in Table 8.1. In some of their work on the liberal peace, Oneal and Russett (1999a; see also Russett and Oneal 2001), too, find intercapital distance to be related to disputes, even after controlling for contiguity (and other realist and liberal factors).

There is another reason for skepticism about the territorial argument: whatever the initial reason for starting a conflict, the actors in most armed conflicts will at some point acquire a territorial base to fight from. For instance, the Cold War-related conflicts were ideologically inspired, but were nevertheless fought over territory. And the ongoing military operations by the United States and allies in Iraq and Afghanistan were hardly motivated primarily by ambitions of territorial gains. War – particularly interstate war – is a form of activity inevitably tied to the loss or gain of territory.

Walter (2003, 137) also views territorial conflicts as the most intractable, with combatants far less likely to initiate peace negotiations than combatants fighting ethnic or ideological civil wars. She rejects the idea that the economic, strategic, or psychological value of the land is decisive in the willingness to compromise and favors the explanation that the low rate of negotiation in such conflicts results from the government's fear that one territorial concession will lead to another. Refusal to negotiate is therefore part of building a reputation. She finds some empirical support for this interpretation in an analysis of domestic conflicts, but speculates that it should also apply to interstate territorial conflicts. Countries with a large number of neighbors should be less willing to settle boundary disputes. She claims (2003, 150) that this offers an alternative to the hypothesis that neighbors tend to fight more frequently because of geographical opportunity. This argument does not seem entirely convincing. International territorial disputes can more easily be settled in a symmetric fashion than internal disputes. A territorial loss in one place can be compensated for by a gain somewhere else. Disputes over secession (or even regional autonomy) are by definition one-sided. The rebels have nothing to yield in terms of territory – their only bargaining point is to end their opposition to the government.

Conclusions

Popular views hold that globalization contributes to the demise of national and cultural boundaries, reduces time and costs of transaction, and consequently makes distance increasingly irrelevant in shaping interaction patterns. However, not all forms of interaction are equally affected by technological development and electronic communication. According to what we label the interaction argument, interstate interaction should be determined by relative, rather than absolute, costs. Hence, whereas the globalization perspective expects the impact of proximity and neighborhood characteristics on interstate behavior to decline in a globalizing world, the interaction perspective predicts distance to hold up as an impeding factor, and that states will continue to interact predominantly with their neighbors. To test these propositions in a systematic fashion, we conducted a number of large-N analyses of the empirical association between globalization and an extreme type of interstate interaction – interstate conflict. The results indicate that globalization (measured as trade per capita) reduces the conflict involvement of states only weakly, if at all. However, the dyadic models presented robust evidence that globalized pairs of states are much less likely to meet on the battlefield, even after controlling for joint democracy and other relevant factors. These results compare very well to Gartzke (this volume). Most importantly, we found no evidence of a declining importance of distance. States continue to fight their proximate counterparts, presumably because neighbors interact more overall, and because projecting force to distant locations is still relatively costly. We also found little evidence that globalized states are less impeded by distance or neighborhood characteristics than less liberal states. Finally, we found no evidence that territory is becoming less salient in a globalized world.

Overall, the analysis provides overwhelming support for the interaction argument. Geographical opportunity remains a pervasive determinant of international interaction. Does this imply that distance will always constitute an impediment to international interaction and that territoriality will persist as a major motive for interstate aggression? Only the future will tell, but we are confident that the physical transaction of goods and "bads" will continue to be affected by the distance to the target, where actors are more concerned with relative than absolute costs. Moreover, despite never-ending technological developments, most states are not able to reach noncontiguous states by military means, and most will not be able to do so in the foreseeable future. The art of war – as we know it – will continue to be conducted predominantly by neighbor states and their allies. In that sense, the world may never become truly globalized.

NOTES

Work on this article was supported by the Research Council of Norway, in separate grants to NTNU and PRIO and from the Carnegie Foundation through a grant to the University of California, San Diego. We are grateful to Indra de Soysa, Charles Gochman, and John A. Vasquez for help with the literature. We also thank Miles Kahler, Barbara Walter, Angela O'Mahony, and participants in the Globalization, Territoriality, and Conflict project at UCSD for valuable comments and suggestions on an earlier draft.

1 We use the term "transaction" for the action of one of the interacting parties, and the term "interaction" for the intersection of two transactions. We view interactions in a limited time frame, rather than as sequences of action and reaction, as in Richardson's arms race models or enduring rivalries in the conflict literature.

2 As noted by a referee, the concept of "place" is frequently interpreted more widely than just "location" (O'Loughlin 2000), but we find these wider aspects of place hard to pin down.

3 Loss-of-strength gradients are also part of models of regime change, such as Gilpin (1981) and Cederman and Gleditsch (2004).

4 In the North–South direction, climate difference may act as a deterrent to interaction. A recent example is the suggestion that the death rate of Europeans in hostile African climates had an immediate effect on the forms of interaction – long-term settlement occurred only where the climate was relatively benign, whereas hostile conditions restricted the interaction to looting (Acemoglu et al. 2001). Climatic difference generally is related to distance by an inverted U-shaped relationship, while the "hostile climate" variable suggested by Acemoglu et al. has a more complicated relationship to distance.

5 The term "gravity model" was first used by Zipf (1949). For an early application to international trade, see Linnemann (1966) and for an application to international airline connections, see N. P. Gleditsch (1969).

6 See www.globalpolicy.org/globaliz/charts/trnsprt2.htm. Downloaded 30 December 2003.

7 Fischer (2003, 2) notes that the word "globalization" never occurred in *The New York Times* in the 1970s and less than once a week in the 1980s. In 2000 it occurred on average once a week. The idea of being "anti-globalization" did not occur until around 1999.

8 Source: US Department of Justice, crime statistics, available at www.ojp. usdoj.gov.

9 For instance, the demise of the Multilateral Agreement on Investment (MAI) draft treaty in 1997 has been attributed to the ability of an advocacy group in Washington, D.C., to post the draft treaty on the web and to use the internet to mobilize the opposition (Capling and Nossal 2001, 447).

10 The latest of a long list of similar initiatives is "The National Strategy to Secure Cyberspace" (2003), available at http://www.whitehouse.gov/pcipb/cyberspace_strategy.pdf.

11 See *Treaty Establishing the European Coal and Steel Community.* Downloaded from http://europa.eu.int/abc/obj/treaties/en/entr30a.htm#Article_1, 28 April 2004.

12 Using a non-linear specification of the gravity model, Coe et al. (2002) dissent from this conclusion. They find that "the declining importance of geography made its mark in the 1990s" (25).

13 Here and in what follows, we use "cost" in a broad sense, incorporating not just economic cost but also time and intervening opportunity.

14 The current world record speed of Mach 3.2 was set in 1978, eleven years after the MiG-25 first captured the prestigious title of "the fastest aircraft in the world." The MiG-25 also holds the record for highest altitude reached by a combat aircraft (118,898 feet) (*Guinness Book of World Records*, available at www.guinnessworldrecords.com/).

15 Numerous military campaigns have failed at least partly as a result of over-stretched supply lines. The collapse of the Roman Empire, the failed attempt of the Crusaders to conquer Jerusalem, and Napoleon's and later Hitler's unsuccessful operations on the Eastern Front have all been interpreted from this perspective. On a grander scale, Kennedy (1987) views the fall of empires as a result of "overstretch."

16 Or perhaps, as harried e-mail consumers may be tempted to conclude, it is precisely the death of distance that is the new tyranny.

17 The main argument for mixing intercapital distance and minimum distance in this way is that it seems unreasonable to assign a high score on the distance variable to immediate neighbors just because their capitals are far apart. An example is provided by Norway and Russia, which share a 196-km land boundary in Norway's northeast, while the capitals are 1,644 km apart.

18 The distance weights matrix is given by $wij = 1/dij\sum j = 1n1/dij$ and measures the inverse of the distance between state i and any state j as a share of the sum of the inverse distances (1/d) between i and all js.

19 In our sample, the distance-weighted MID incidence variable has a range of {.000036, .99981}. Ironically, Bolivia, 1924, enjoyed the safest neighborhood but was itself involved in a dispute with Paraguay; the nearest and only other dispute in 1924 was Italy–Turkey. Of the 1,409 observations that experienced disputes on all borders within a single year, 743 managed to remain peaceful.

20 The CINC score (Composite Indicator of National Capability) is based on the values for total population, urban population, iron and steel production, energy consumption, military personnel, and military expenditure (from the Correlates of War Project).

21 Roughly 18 percent of the observations in the dyadic data set lack trade data for at least one state. The baseline probability of MID for the missing dyads is only two-thirds of the probability for the valid sample.

22 This peak reflects the numerous conflict years during World Wars I and II between North American and European countries.

23 An additional test with a square term indicates that the relationship between time and risk of conflict is parabolic, with a downward trend at the end. This is consistent with what Lacina, Russett, and Gleditsch (2005) find about the long-term trend in battle deaths, but contradicts the claim made by Sarkees, Wayman, and Singer (2003: 49) about "a disquieting constancy of warfare." We also tested a "number of dyads in system year" count measure as an alternative to controlling for time. Despite the very high correlation between the two (r = 0.92), the correlation with conflict no longer holds up. In fact, the size of the system is weakly negatively associated with the baseline risk of conflict. This corresponds well to Lake and O'Mahony (this volume), who find a positive correlation between average state size and frequency of interstate conflict at the system level.

24 The dyadic effect, however, is always negative and significant (see Table 10.1 and Table 10.3). The relative distribution of the units over time is likely to have some influence. In the monadic data set, the median year is 1965 – in the dyadic data set it is 1978. In other words, a larger share of the results in the dyadic models is driven by the units in the last couple of decades, which incidentally were atypically peaceful. Since 1978, only 0.4 percent of the dyads are involved in an MID at any time; the corresponding figure for the pre-1978 period is 1 percent. In the monadic data set, the difference between the pre- and post-median year period is minimal (35 percent versus 33 percent). When the model additionally controls for other factors that are also likely to vary temporally (such as democracy), the marginal impact of the economic system diminishes.

25 We generated similar graphs based on Maoz's (2001) dyadic MID data, which excludes several of the "irrelevant" war dyads, but these differed only marginally from Figure 8.4 and are not shown here.

26 If distance and contiguity interact with time rather than with the crude globalization measure, we find that the geography increases in importance during the investigated period. The interaction between distance and time is strongly negative (supporting H3), whereas the interaction between land contiguity and time is positive and significant (in contrast to both hypotheses). The joint inference from these findings is that relatively fewer states today engage in disputes with noncontiguous rivals but those who do are less concerned about the distance to the target than they used to be.

27 To avoid problems of multicollinearity, the interaction term is based on centered versions of the spatial lag and globalization measures.

28 These results are not reported in detail for space reasons.

Part III

Territorial regimes in an era of globalization

9   The evolution of territoriality: international relations and American law

Kal Raustiala

Assumptions about territory permeate legal systems. American law is no exception. Territoriality is a defining attribute of the Westphalian state, the model upon which the framers of the US Constitution based their aspirations for a new nation. Under Westphalian principles the scope of a sovereign's law corresponds to the geographic boundaries of the sovereign's territory, what Miles Kahler, in his introduction to this volume, calls "jurisdictional congruence."

Yet it is increasingly common to assert that Westphalian territorial sovereignty is breaking down – that we are entering a borderless world in which international forces permeate the once-hard shell of the state.[1] Globalization, many argue, is rapidly eroding the significance of territorial boundaries (for example, Ohmae 1990; Held et al. 1999). Capital, labor, goods, and ideas are said to move largely without regard for political borders, radically transforming our polities and economies. These claims are controversial and have spawned fierce debate in economics and political science. Within legal scholarship, by contrast, the domestic impacts of globalization have received less sustained attention.[2] Yet legal rules and practices provide an important and overlooked window on the alleged impacts of globalization, particularly with regard to territoriality.

All legal systems presuppose some relationship between law and territory. I call these rules of *legal spatiality*. This chapter charts the evolution of legal spatiality in the United States, and offers several causal arguments about this evolution and its connections to shifts in international security and economics. In the nineteenth century the dominant rule of legal spatiality was strict territoriality: law and land were understood to be tightly and fundamentally linked.[3] The general, though uneven, trajectory over the last century has been to loosen these geographic restraints and increasingly assert domestic law beyond sovereign borders. To be sure, Westphalian territoriality is not dead. Territoriality is broadly respected today for all states, whereas in the past only a handful of Western powers enjoyed full territorial sovereignty. Spatial location also continues to be a critical rule of decision in some areas of American law, as the continuing litigation over non-citizen detainees held in the US naval base at Guantanamo makes clear. Even citizens within the sovereign territory of the United States but outside the fifty states – such as residents of Puerto Rico – enjoy less robust constitutional rights simply because they are located in a different *kind* of American territory.[4]

Despite these areas of persistence, it is indisputable that territoriality is decreasingly important as a jurisdictional principle. US domestic rules of jurisdiction long ago deemphasized strict territoriality in favor of more flexible, functional concepts such as "interests analysis" and "minimum contacts." Since the 1940s, federal statutes in a wide range of areas – antitrust, securities, criminal law, intellectual property, to name just a few – have frequently been understood to have extraterritorial effect. Similarly, the protections of the Bill of Rights, once believed to apply only within US territory, now extend across the globe with regard to US citizens. In short, territoriality has been slowly unbundled from sovereignty.

What explains the evolution of legal spatiality? The second-image reversed tradition in political science argues that international relations play an important and understudied causal role in domestic institutional and political change (Gourevitch 1978). Most work in this tradition looks at domestic political, rather than legal, factors. Even there, however, "the degree and character of influence exercised by international factors on American political development remains remarkably unprobed" (Katznelson 2002, 4). The impact of world politics on domestic law is nearly untouched.[5] In this chapter I explore how international factors have shaped the transformation of legal spatiality in the United States. While internal, doctrinal evolutions in discrete areas of the law are undoubtedly an important factor in this shift, I argue that legal rules, like other domestic policies, are influenced by the constraints and opportunities presented by the international system. This is especially likely for doctrines of jurisdiction, since jurisdictional notions draw so deeply from international concepts such as sovereignty and statehood.

My primary claim is that the existing pattern of legal spatiality reflects power and interest. The contingencies of history of course play an important role. But US courts, litigants, Congress, and the Executive have all engaged in instrumental assessments of the benefits and detriments of a reliance on territorial location as a legal principle in particular instances. As world politics has changed, these benefits and detriments have also changed. One such change is a focus of this volume:

globalization. While globalization is often said to reduce the centrality of territory to states, I argue that globalization *vel non* cannot adequately explain the decline of territorial doctrines of jurisdiction. Globalization was highly significant during the nineteenth century – the height of jurisdictional congruence. Rather, it is the particular nature of the post-war wave of globalization, coupled to the rise of the modern regulatory state, that has increased the incentives for states – in particular the United States – to assert their domestic law beyond their sovereign borders.

Equally, if not more, important are major changes in global security structures that have facilitated such assertions. The United States is far more powerful today than it was a century ago. While in the past rules of legal spatiality reflected the fear that extraterritorial claims could provoke significant conflict with other states, three features of the post-war era – the extent of US hegemony, the strengthening of the democratic peace, and the decline of territorial wars – have dampened these fears considerably. Likewise, the unprecedented forward projection of American force initiated by the Cold War raised the stakes of maintaining a spatially delimited constitutional jurisprudence. While these factors help to account for the transformation of rules of legal spatiality, territoriality exhibits persistence in several areas of the law. Most notably, concerns about the negative effects of interdependence – concerns heightened after the attacks of September 11 – have strengthened assertions of territoriality with regard to individual aliens abroad, with the detention of foreign nationals in overseas US bases the most prominent example.

In this chapter I first describe the conceptual linkage between law and territory, and chart the broad evolution of US doctrines of spatiality from the mid-nineteenth century to today. I next show that the period of strict territoriality in US law in fact coincided with an early, strong wave of globalization. As a result, simplistic causal connections between globalization and legal spatiality are not tenable. But there are important differences between the current wave and the earlier wave that do help account for the decline of territoriality in US law. Moreover, there are important differences in the wider international context that play important roles as well. I close with four broad hypotheses about the evolution of legal spatiality in the United States and its connection to overall trends in the international system. These claims in turn reflect the more general argument that rules of legal spatiality in American law derive from configurations of power and interest, not from any overarching normative theory of legal geography.

Westphalia and territoriality

The Treaty of Westphalia is commonly, if mythically, taken to denote the birth of territorially based state sovereignty (Krasner 1999). The medieval order, broadly characterized, comprised multiple layered power centers as well as diverse sources of legitimation, allegiance, and status (Spruyt 1996; Bull and Watson 1984). The Westphalian conception of the state represented a break with the past because it drew all legitimate power into a single sovereign, who controlled absolutely a defined territory and its associated population. These ideas in turn provided the bedrock principles for the development of international law in the post-Westphalian era. As Herz writes, territoriality begat "the concepts and institutions which characterized the interrelations of sovereign units, the modern state system . . . [O]nly to the extent that it reflected their territoriality and took into account their sovereignty could international law develop. For its general rules and principles deal primarily with the delimitation of the jurisdiction of countries" (Herz 1957, 480–81). State power was rendered territorial in the Westphalian revolution, so as to limit conflict and clearly demarcate sovereign power. Thus territoriality can be seen as a response to conflict – an attempt to cabin it by delimiting sovereign jurisdiction. Jurisdictional concepts in turn flow from territory; as Oliver Wendell Holmes famously stated, "the foundation of jurisdiction is physical power" (*McDonald v. Mabee* 243 US 90, 91 (1917)).

Westphalian territorial sovereignty became supreme in Europe throughout the eighteenth and nineteenth centuries, and spread slowly and unevenly to the rest of the globe. Each sovereign state, according to the nineteenth-century view of international law, possessed and exercised "exclusive sovereignty and jurisdiction throughout the full extent of its territory . . . No state can, by its laws, directly affect, bind, or regulate property beyond its own territory, or control persons that do not reside within it, whether they be native-born subjects or not" (Wheaton 1936 [1866]). International law thus contained rules about jurisdiction – technically, prescriptive jurisdiction – that limited the reach of a sovereign's law to its territorial base. In short, Westphalia introduced a conception of legal spatiality that was no longer status-based but instead place-based. Legal rules primarily corresponded to places, not to people.

Empire and extraterritorial courts

In the nineteenth century not all polities were sovereign. The "standard of civilization" kept out of international society many political entities.

One important manifestation of the divide between sovereign states and other political units was imperialism. Ascendant in the nineteenth century, imperialism was fueled by many factors, but one was the desire to control valuable territory. In an era in which tangible resources – rather than human capital and intellectual property – determined wealth and power, territory was often thought worth fighting for, and it formed the basis of much conflict in this period. This stands in marked contrast with the current era, in which territorial conquest is virtually nonexistent (Zacher 2001). Sometimes domestic legal systems were fully extended throughout an empire (French colonies are departments of France), but often not (the Philippines were US territory through 1946 but Filipinos were not citizens, only American nationals). Nineteenth-century international law aided the process of imperialism. A leading treatise of the time asked "Is there a uniform law of nations? There certainly is not the same one for all the nations and states of the world. The public law, with slight exceptions, has always been, and still is, limited to the civilized and Christian people of Europe or to those of European origin" (cited in Anghie 1999, 23). This viewpoint made the coercive acquisition of territory easier to accept while simultaneously illustrating the profound divide that many in the West believed lay between them and the rest of the globe.

Though not an expression of imperialism in the strict sense, as great powers increasingly traded with non-Western entities they created extraterritorial courts in these "uncivilized" nations. These courts, discussed below, had jurisdiction over disputes involving Westerners in nations such as China and Turkey, nations that were too powerful to colonize but nonetheless provided rich commercial opportunities. As a result of such courts US citizens were not subject to local law, but instead to an array of American laws. While seemingly inconsistent with then-prevailing norms of legal spatiality, these courts actually reflected the limited nature of the circle of sovereign states. They existed only in those polities that were not sovereign, precisely because they did not meet the "standard of civilization" (Gong 1984). The practice of extraterritorial jurisdiction reinforced the centrality of territory to the Westphalian conception of sovereignty. Extraterritoriality in this form was a vestige of the personal status relations that marked the feudal era. Sovereign states, of course, did not permit extraterritorial courts on their territories. Thus extraterritorial courts reinforced the norm that strict territoriality prevailed among juridical equals.

These courts can also be understood as products of the first wave of globalization. Nineteenth-century extraterritorial courts were reactions to the growing presence of merchants and missionaries in foreign jurisdictions and the felt need to protect those citizens from barbaric, arbitrary, discriminatory, and unfamiliar legal systems. Imperialism entailed conquering foreign territory and ruling it; extraterritoriality meant doing nearly the same, though the sovereignty of polities like China – such as it was – remained nominally present. In some cases, even that was missing: so-called international zones, such as the International Zone of Tangier, were created by treaty and carved out of non-Western territory.[6] At the turn of the last century, the United States established extraterritorial jurisdiction in many non-Western countries. In China, Congress went so far as to create the "U.S. District Court for China" (Scully 2001). (It similarly established a court for the Panama Canal Zone.) By the 1940s the normative backdrop that permitted extraterritorial courts had changed. Ideas of sovereign equality, self-determination, and anti-imperialism brought extraterritorial courts to an end.[7]

A vestigial version of extraterritorial jurisdiction continues, however, for armed forces members stationed abroad, via the various "Status of Forces Agreements," or SOFAs, negotiated with host states. Typically, SOFAs decree that US military courts will handle certain infractions, and even when local courts take command some special rules may apply. The SOFA with Japan, for instance, requires the United States to hand over American service members to Japanese authorities only after they have been charged with a crime, a right Japanese citizens do not enjoy.

The dominance of jurisdictional congruence

In short, prior to the twentieth century jurisdiction was "defined in international law exclusively in territorial terms" (Currie et al. 2001, 732). American law drew on this tradition. The notion that US territory could not be subject to the control of another sovereign was strongly held: as Chief Justice Marshall wrote at the time of the War of 1812, "the jurisdiction of the nation within its own territory is necessarily exclusive and absolute. It is susceptible of no limitation not imposed by itself" (*Schooner Exchange v. M'Faddon*, 11 US (7 Cranch) 116, 136 (1812)).

Yet even during the height of strict territoriality the geographical scope of US law was not perfectly coterminous with sovereign borders. "Anomalous zones" existed, geographic locations that were, and still are, treated differently from other American territory (Neuman 1996a). Puerto Rico and Guam, for example, come fully within the sovereignty of the United States, yet are constitutionally distinct from the mainland. Military bases as well as embassies and occupied territories are yet further manifestations of the complex pattern of legal spatiality.[8] And overlaying the Westphalian conception of territoriality embodied in the US Constitution has often been a distinction between insiders – non-citizens – and outsiders. As I describe more fully below, the rights of aliens, unlike those of citizens, remain quite dependent on spatial location even today.

Territoriality and sovereignty in the nineteenth century

The dominant assumptions of legal spatiality have been challenged and transformed over the last century. Jurisdictional congruence has given way to a more layered approach to the connection between sovereignty and territory. This uneven evolution is charted below.

Constitutional rights abroad

In 1880, on an American ship docked in Yokohama Bay, a sailor named John Ross killed a crewmate (*In re Ross*, 140 US 453 (1891)). Ross was convicted of murder by an extraterritorial US court in Japan, and later challenged his conviction before the US Supreme Court. Ross' case directly raised the question of the geographical reach of the Constitution and the rights of US citizens abroad at a time when the United States' connection to foreign markets was rising rapidly. US extraterritorial courts did not employ the full panoply of protections guaranteed by the Constitution. There was no indictment by a grand jury, and no trial by a petit jury. Ross argued "that so far as crimes of felonious character are concerned, the same protection and guarantee against an undue accusation or an unfair trial, secured by the Constitution to the citizens of the United States at home, should be enjoyed by them abroad" (*Ross* 1891, 463).

Reflecting the prevailing conception of legal spatiality, the Supreme Court roundly rejected Ross' argument. The view that the Constitution was unfettered by territorial boundaries was incorrect. As the majority wrote,

By the Constitution a government is ordained and established "for the United States of America," and not for countries outside of their limits. The guarantees it affords . . . apply only to citizens and others *within the United States*, or who are brought there for trial for alleged offences committed elsewhere, and not to residents or temporary sojourners abroad. The Constitution can have no operation in another country. (*Ross* 1891, 464)

In this passage the Court laid out a clear vision of legal spatiality, one that claimed to respect other sovereigns in their respective territories and limited the Constitution's reach to US territory. Of course, the very extensive jurisdiction of the American extraterritorial court was a "violation" of Westphalian sovereignty. But, since Japan was not yet a fully sovereign member of international society, this was not seen as aberrational.

Ross is frequently held to be a defining case for the strict territoriality of the nineteenth century (Neuman 1996b, 82). The decision's language – that the Constitution can have no force outside the territory of the United States – is forceful, blunt, and widely cited. Seventy years later the Supreme Court would overrule *Ross* and its conception of legal spatiality, calling the case "a relic from another era."[9]

The reach of the regulatory state

Just as constitutional rights were seen as territorially delimited, ordinary statutes were generally believed to correspond to a state's geographic borders. An influential example involved the early efforts of American antitrust regulation. While the primary focus of the Sherman Act was the anticompetitive activities of US firms in US markets, in 1909 the American Banana Company sued the United Fruit Company, arguing that it had been injured by actions undertaken at the behest of United Fruit. The twist was that these actions had occurred in Panama. This case raised a similar question to that in *Ross*: did statutes like the Sherman Act apply beyond US territory?

The Supreme Court in *American Banana* (213 US 347 (1909)) argued that US courts lacked jurisdiction over such acts because US law did not reach into the territories of other sovereign states. The majority said that "no doubt in regions subject to no sovereign, like the high seas, or to no law that civilized countries would recognize as adequate, such countries may treat some relations between their citizens as governed by their own law, and keep to some extent the old notion of personal sovereignty alive."[10] The court thus argued that extraterritorial courts – like the one that convicted Ross – were distinguishable because they involved uncivilized countries and inadequate law. In such aberrant situations a state could extend its law into the territory of another sovereign. But, the Court said,

The general and almost universal rule is that the character of act as lawful or unlawful must be determined wholly by the law of the country where the act was done . . . For another jurisdiction, if it should happen to lay hold of the actor, to treat him according to its own notions rather than those of the place where he did the acts, not only would be unjust, but would be an interference with the authority of another sovereign, contrary to the comity of nations, which the other state concerned justly might resent.[11]

This statement encapsulates the legal spatiality of the period. The Sherman Act did not apply to the actions of the United Fruit Company, the Court held, simply because those actions took place outside the territorial borders of the United States and hence beyond the geographical reach of American law. This principle was grounded in concern with sovereignty and the conflict that might arise if sovereign borders were not respected.

Colonies and possessions

The United States was expansionist for most of its history – devastatingly so, to the native tribes of North America – but it was not a colonial power in the traditional sense. The United States did acquire new territories on the continent, but these were geographically contiguous rather than overseas possessions and were generally settled and granted statehood quickly. That pattern changed dramatically in the 1890s, when the United States rapidly acquired extensive overseas territories. The United States annexed Hawaii in 1898. Then the defeat of Spain in 1898 left Puerto Rico, Cuba, and the Philippines in the hands of the United States. "Abroad as well as at home . . . 1898–99 marked the emergence of the United States as a great power" (May 1991, ix).

This newfound empire raised difficult questions about the spatial scope of US law. Did the Constitution apply to these new and distant territories? The former Spanish colonies had tropical climates which many believed made them unsuitable for immigration by peoples of Northern European descent. They would likely remain non-Anglo-Saxon indefinitely. Many Americans were thus chary about embracing these new territories as their own, and opposed to statehood for them. But the fever for imperialism was high in 1898, and granting them immediate independence was unpopular.

Legally, the important question was what the precise status of these new possessions was. It did not take long to come before the Supreme Court, and when it did it capped a surprisingly heated and bitter controversy. The rapidity with which the United States embraced the European practice of empire may have partly accounted for the utter confusion over how to integrate these colonies into the constitutional framework. But in a series of cases running through the early 1920s, known as the *Insular Cases*, the Supreme Court laid down the principle that some American territory is distinct from other American territory (Burnett and Marshall 2001). The notion they used was "incorporation." For territory that was acquired with the intent of incorporating into the union – that is, territory destined for statehood – the

Constitution operated much as it did in the states. But territories not so incorporated – in other words, colonies intended to be held as such indefinitely – were distinctive. Only "fundamental constitutional rights" applied in this territory, despite US sovereignty being absolute. This holding has proved critical to much of the jurisprudence of legal spatiality throughout the twentieth century. Despite seeming increasingly archaic, it remains the law to this day.

The decline of strict territoriality

The *Insular Cases* demonstrated conclusively that there was daylight between the Constitution and the sovereign territory of the United States. The Constitution followed the flag but, as Elihu Root quipped, never quite caught up. The Constitution had full force within the confines of the various states, but territories could be held by the federal government, as California was, and ruled by a military government. And colonies could be held, as Puerto Rico was, without the Constitution applying fully. This set of beliefs was consistent with the prevailing nineteenth-century Westphalian vision which took territoriality seriously, accepted conquest as legitimate, and paid obeisance to the notion that one sovereign's laws could not intrude in the space of another.

This worldview began to change in the mid-twentieth century. Change in legal spatiality was exhibited in several contexts. Within the United States, the law governing the jurisdiction of a state over nonresidents underwent marked change, increasingly permitting the assertion of personal jurisdiction against actors that caused harm from outside state borders. Second, the regulatory laws that governed the growing administrative state were increasingly found to have extraterritorial effect. While United States courts maintain to this day a doctrinal "presumption against extraterritoriality," that presumption is easily rebutted in several key regulatory areas. Third, at the height of the Cold War the Supreme Court reconsidered the extraterritorial scope of the Constitution itself. In the landmark case of *Reid v. Covert*, which involved the trial of an American in the United Kingdom by US military authorities, the Court held that the full panoply of constitutional rights applied to Americans abroad, notwithstanding any treaty to the contrary. In so doing it directly overruled *Ross*.

The rise of extraterritoriality: regulatory law

American Banana, decided at the height of the first wave of globalization, laid down a rule of jurisdictional congruence clearly in line with that of

Ross. Like *Ross*, this decision would be overturned during the twentieth century, but in the case of statutory extraterritoriality change came much more quickly. Several cases in the 1920s and 1930s chipped away, in perhaps inadvertent but ultimately significant ways, at the view that US statutes were territorially bounded. And in *Bowman v. US* the Supreme Court held that "criminal statutes which are, as a class, not logically dependent on their locality for the Government's jurisdiction" do not run afoul of any presumption against extraterritorial application (260 US 94 (1922), 98). *Bowman* involved a fraud claim relating to an international steamship company (and was thus an example of how increasing global trade challenged the functionality of strict territoriality). For regulatory law the chief signpost in the doctrinal evolution is the 1945 case of *US v. Aluminum Co. of America* (148 F2d 416 (2nd cir. 1945); known as *Alcoa*). With *Alcoa*, the federal courts began in earnest to move to an "effects" test for asserting prescriptive jurisdiction, in which effects on domestic markets was sufficient to trigger jurisdiction over foreign conduct. This was seen as a "startling projection" of existing doctrine by European observers (for example, Jennings 1957, 165). Under an effects test, the spatial location of the underlying activity was not the key criterion: the location of economic impact was.

Alcoa in part reflected larger moves afoot in American law. Federalism had led to numerous domestic jurisdictional rules that reflected territoriality, and indeed flowed directly from Westphalian principles. But across a range of areas of the law assumptions of legal spatiality were undergoing transition by the 1940s. The year 1945, when *Alcoa* was decided, was also the year of *International Shoe* (23 326 US 310 (1945)), which decisively rejected the strict territorial underpinning of the law of personal jurisdiction in the United States. In *International Shoe*, the notion of minimum contacts with the forum state as sufficient for personal jurisdiction "displaced the entire conceptual structure of the strict territorial theory" (Rutherglen 2001, 347). As the US economy nationalized, it became increasingly dysfunctional to rely on the older territorial theories of jurisdiction. Growing international interdependence created similar incentives. Reliance on functional interests such as the effects of activities on local markets, rather than the spatial location of the actors or acts, was soon accepted in a number of areas of the law. By the 1950s, for example, the Supreme Court applied the effects-based justification for extraterritoriality of *Alcoa* to trademark law and maritime law (*Steele v. Bulova Watch*, 344 US 280 (1952); *Lauritzen v. Larsen* 345 US 571 (1953)). By the 1970s, extraterritorial applications of regulatory law were common.

The "presumption against extraterritoriality" remained, however, as a canon of statutory construction and reappeared occasionally – making for a complex, even inconsistent pattern of case law involving the territorial reach of the law. Federal courts were particularly eager to invoke assumptions of territoriality in cases involving the reach of American labor laws, for example. In 1991, the Supreme Court held that the Civil Rights Act did not apply to American employers operating overseas.[12] That case treated the presumption against extraterritoriality as quite strong and seemed to find the notion that Congress meant to extend civil rights law abroad implausible. In so doing the Court, in Larry Kramer's words, "slipped back to the nineteenth century, seemingly unaware that it was doing so" (Kramer 1991, 202). But such cases were the exception – and Congress quickly acted to rewrite the statute to make clear that it did apply extraterritorially. In most regulatory areas, especially antitrust regulation, the executive branch, Congress, and the courts rapidly embraced the idea that US law applied globally. The Department of Justice, for example, began to aggressively pursue cartels abroad. Where firms were located was irrelevant; what mattered was whether they impacted US markets.

Deterritorializing the Constitution

In 1956 Clarice Covert, an American civilian, killed her husband, a US military officer, at an airbase in England and was convicted by a court-martial of murder. Like Ross in 1891, she argued that she had been denied the full protection of the Constitution. (Courts-martial do not follow the procedures that ordinary criminal trials do.) The Supreme Court had upheld courts-martial for military dependents just a few years before, in *Madsen v. Kinsella* (343 US 341 (1952)), a case also involving the murder abroad of a US soldier by his wife. In *Madsen* the murder occurred in postwar occupied Germany; *Reid v. Covert*, by contrast, involved peaceful forward deployment in the United Kingdom. The Eisenhower administration argued that the Constitution could not possibly have effect in the United Kingdom, citing the principles of legal spatiality declared in *Ross*. Now, however, the Supreme Court rejected jurisdictional congruence, arguing, "When the Government reaches out to punish a citizen who is abroad, the shield which the Bill of Rights and other parts of the Constitution provide . . . should not be stripped away just because he happens to be in another land."[13]

To make the point sharply, the Court heaped scorn on the *Ross* vision of territoriality, calling it a "relic from another era."[14] To Justice Black, the US consular court that convicted Ross blended powers in a manner that represented "the very acme of absolutism."[15] *Ross*, the Court said, could not be understood outside its peculiar setting. That setting was a nineteenth-century world divided into civilized and uncivilized states, with great-power war frequent, conquest endemic, and imperialism at its height. The mid-twentieth century and the Cold War were clearly different.

In *Reid* the Court also sought to discredit the underlying notion that the Constitution did not fully follow the flag. *Reid* was nearly as dismissive of the *Insular Cases* as it was of *Ross*. The decision did not challenge the existence of status of forces agreements that guaranteed US service members greater protections abroad in nations hosting US bases than US civilians in the same nation would enjoy. Extraterritorial in a sense – they mandated practices common to the United States, though often uncommon to the local jurisdiction – these agreements typically offered more, rather than less, protection than local law did. Likewise *Reid* did not question the right of the United States to try service members in a parallel justice system that offered weaker constitutional protections – regardless of where these individuals were physically located. Rather, it made clear that the US government cannot, as far as civilians are concerned, distinguish its treatment of them based on *where* that treatment occurs. Geography, in the view of the majority, did not determine justice.

Reterritorializing the Constitution

Reid involved an American citizen. It is important to underscore that the global view of legal spatiality enunciated in *Reid* did not straightforwardly extend to non-citizens. Yet in the postwar period aliens were increasingly in contact with US officials abroad, and the United States continued to have a major military presence abroad throughout the Cold War, including the occupation of Berlin. The unusual *Tiede* case grew out of this occupation. *Tiede* was a criminal proceeding that arose in the US Court for Berlin during the 1970s (US v. *Tiede*, 86 FRD 227 (US Court of Berlin 1979)). The question in *Tiede* was, as in *Reid*, the right to a jury trial; the larger question was the applicability of the Constitution to a proceeding against a non-citizen by the US government beyond the territorial bounds of the United States. The United States argued bluntly that the US presence in Berlin "grows out of conquest, *not the consent of the governed*."[16] Consequently, the government argued, whatever rights the defendant had stemmed not from the Constitution, but from an affirmative grant by the Executive. This argument was rejected wholesale by the Berlin court, echoing *Reid*. It is a "first principle of American life – not only life at home but life abroad – that everything American public officials do is governed by, measured against, and must be authorized by the US Constitution."[17] The Court nonetheless took care to limit the impact of its ruling:

> This Court does not hold that jury trial must be afforded in occupation courts everywhere and under all circumstances; the Court holds only that if the United States convenes a United States court in Berlin, under the present circumstances, and charges civilians with non-military offenses, the United States must provide the defendants with the same constitutional safeguards found in any other United States court.[18]

Tiede, while fascinating, was on all dimensions an aberrational case – and not only because it declared that non-citizens abroad had constitutional rights. Much more common were cases involving US agents acting against criminals abroad. The expansion of policing across sovereign borders raises many issues related to the geographic scope of constitutional protections, both on the high seas and in foreign territory. As global markets for licit goods grew over the postwar era, so did global markets for illicit goods (Raustiala 1999). Narcotics trafficking was the most salient example, and in the postwar period the United States increasingly prosecuted the drug war abroad as well as at home.

US v. Verdugo-Urquidez (494 US 259), decided in 1990, involved drug trafficking and illustrates the continuing power, and even retrenchment, of territorial assumptions with regard to non-citizens. *Verdugo* concerned the search by US agents of a suspected Mexican drug smuggler's home in Mexico. The defendant challenged the search as a violation of his Fourth Amendment right against unreasonable search and seizure. The Supreme Court rejected, holding that the Fourth Amendment does not apply to searches of non-citizens abroad. Citing the *Insular Cases*, the Court maintained that spatial distinctions were permissible and citizens and aliens distinct. Outside the borders of the United States the Constitution applies to each in dramatically different ways. The interesting twist was that in *Verdugo* the defendant was actually *within* US territory at the time of the search. Having been arrested and detained in San Diego, he was unquestionably within the border. His property, however, was not. For the court this spatial fact was critical. Had the property been in San Diego, but he in Mexico, there is no doubt a warrantless search would have run afoul of the Fourth Amendment. Thus it was the location of Verdugo's home, not his person, that ultimately determined the outcome of the case – despite the (incorrect) claim by the Court that previous cases "establish only that aliens receive constitutional protections when they have come within the territory of the [United States] and developed substantial connections with this country."[19] The "substantial connections" principle predicts that a first-time visitor, in the United States only briefly, would enjoy the barest minimum of protection by the Fourth Amendment. Yet that is not the result: a Japanese tourist stopping over in Seattle en route to Canada enjoys the full protections of the Fourth Amendment. The rationale for this protection is simply spatial: location within the United States is deemed fully sufficient to invoke the Fourth Amendment. A pure spatiality principle – rather than a substantial connections principle – is also reflected in both *Eisentrager* and *Quirin*, the World War II precedents upon which the Bush Administration relied in the recent Guantanamo litigation. Both suggest that even enemy aliens captured abroad but brought back to the United States for detention and trial would enjoy access to US courts on territorial principles alone.[20]

The verdict in *Verdugo* was significant because US law has long held that aliens in the United States enjoy many of the same rights as citizens. To be sure, US law at times looks to formal entry into the United States rather than pure spatial location. And the exact location of the territorial borders of the United States is occasionally unclear. In 1953 for example, the Supreme Court held that "harborage on Ellis Island is not an entry into the United States," despite the fact that Ellis Island is incontrovertibly American territory (*Mezei*, 345 US 206, 213 (1953)). The rationale for the continuing commitment to strict territoriality for aliens is unclear, but it is perhaps best understood as a combination of two ideas: a vestigial commitment to jurisdictional congruence – held over from the nineteenth-century era of strict territoriality – coupled to the idea that the alien is a sort of guest when she is within the borders of the United States. As a result, aliens enjoy the constitutional protection while within the borders of the United States, but only while within those borders. Prior to the decision in *Reid* the guest theory made more sense, since for all individuals – citizen or alien – the Constitution was spatially delimited. Post-*Reid*, continued adherence to a guest theory is on far weaker conceptual ground.

Rehnquist's opinion in *Verdugo* was bolstered by an extensive discussion of the policy consequences of a territorially unbounded jurisprudence. According to Chief Justice Rehnquist, extraterritorial constitutional protection for aliens

would have significant and deleterious consequences for the United States in conducting activities beyond its boundaries . . .The United States frequently employs Armed Forces outside this country – over 200 times in our history – for the protection of American citizens or national security. Application of the Fourth Amendment to those circumstances could significantly disrupt the ability of the political branches to respond to foreign situations involving our national interest . . . For better or for worse, we live in a world of nation-states in which Government must be able to "function effectively in the company of sovereign nations." (*Verdugo*, 273–75)

This vision of international relations is one of Hobbesian conflict and anarchy. "Situations threatening to important American interests may arise halfway around the globe, situations which in the view of the political branches of our Government require an American response with armed force" (*Verdugo*, 275). In this dangerous setting, the court claimed, US law enforcement agents, no less than US armed forces, cannot be fettered by constitutional restrictions that other states lack and that, moreover, were intended for a setting of relative peace and community.

In short, since *Reid* spatial location has been irrelevant to the constitutional rights of American citizens. But that principle has not been extended to non-citizens. Indeed, the Supreme Court has recently stated that "it is well established that certain constitutional protections available to persons inside the United States are unavailable to aliens outside of our geographic borders."[21] To be sure, a handful of cases have argued that non-citizens abroad enjoy certain protections of the Constitution. The Ninth Circuit has held that the Fifth Amendment due process clause applies to aliens prosecuted for drug smuggling on the high seas.[22] Most recently, a federal court held that foreign suspects interrogated abroad by the FBI must receive *Miranda* warnings.[23] These cases are outliers, however, and to date their reasoning has not been endorsed by the Supreme Court.

Globalization, territoriality, and the international system

The preceding sketched the contours of the evolution of legal spatiality in American law. In this account territoriality – a defining attribute of the Westphalian state – gradually weakened and legal jurisdiction was increasingly understood in nonspatial, functional terms. Casual empiricism suggests that globalization has driven the United States to relax doctrines of legal spatiality as interdependence has risen in the postwar era. Globalization is frequently said to produce an "'unbundling' of the relationship between sovereignty, territoriality, and state power" (Held et al. 1999, 8). Globalization reflects "the sense that activities previously undertaken within national boundaries can be undertaken globally or regionally – to some extent 'deterritorialized'" (Woods 2000, 5; see also Agnew 1994). Looked at more closely, however, the relationship between globalization and the evolution of territoriality in American law is not clear.

Though contemporary globalization is often framed as an unprecedented development, in fact the world has seen at least two waves of globalization. The first ran from the late nineteenth century through 1914. The pre-World War I world was in several ways more tightly integrated than it is today (Baldwin and Martin 1999, 1; Held et al. 1999, 5). In an oft-cited passage, John Maynard Keynes wrote

What an extraordinary episode in the progress of man that age was which came to an end in August 1914! . . . The inhabitant of London could order by telephone, sipping his morning tea in bed, the various products of the whole earth . . . he could at the same time and by the same means adventure his wealth in the natural resources and new enterprise of any quarter of the world . . . he could secure forthwith, if he wished it, cheap and comfortable means of transit to any country or climate without passport or other formality.

(Keynes 1919, quoted in Sachs and Warner 1995).

Overall trade levels were high. As a share of GDP, exports from the United States were roughly the same in 1989 as they were in 1889 (Irwin et al. 1999, 43). Inventions such as the telephone and transoceanic cables linked markets at breathtaking speed, and financial movements intensified enormously. The gold standard made currency risk minimal and capital highly mobile (Baldwin and Martin 1999, 23). Immigration levels were as high or higher than today. With regard to financial liberalization and mobility – two allegedly signal aspects of contemporary globalization – it has been said that "the only real debate among informed observers is whether we have returned to 1914 levels of financial integration."[24] In short, across many dimensions the pre-Great War era was as globalized as our own.

This historical pattern raises an empirical puzzle: why does the current wave of globalization correlate with a decoupling of territory from sovereignty in American law, while the first wave correlated with the height of legal spatiality?

International influences on the decline of strict territoriality

The evolution of legal spatiality has not been previously studied in a systematic fashion.[25] Nor have scholars theorized much about the causes of this evolution even in the discrete areas of the law that have been examined. Existing causal claims have largely revolved around doctrinal changes within particular legal rules, idiosyncratic statutory developments, and the like.[26] These local, specific factors are undoubtedly important. My claim in this chapter, however, is that the evolution of legal spatiality, because it is intrinsically tied up with conceptions of the Westphalian territoriality, cannot be understood solely through reference to domestic causal factors. Rather, broad shifts in international relations, both economic and political, have influenced legal conceptions of territoriality in the United States. Shifts in globalization and in interstate conflict have shaped territorial conceptions of domestic law and the incentives of the Executive, Congress, the courts, and litigants. Nonetheless, the influence of these changes cannot be crisply demonstrated and thus my arguments are suggestive rather than conclusive.

Below I present four broad hypotheses about the connection between the evolution of the international system and the evolution of spatiality in US law. Each is consistent with a core argument that rules of legal spatiality reflect American power and interests rather than normative ideals. When claims of jurisdictional congruence benefit important US interests, Congress, the president, and the judiciary cling to, or revive, older territorial principles. When functional pressures demand a more global approach, spatiality has been altered in favor of extraterritoriality. As US power has grown, and the scope of US interests abroad has grown, the United States has been increasingly willing and able to assert its law extraterritorially. Adherence to principle is an allegedly signal aspect of the legal process. But adherence to principle is conspicuous by its absence here. With few exceptions, extraterritoriality has been asserted to benefit the United States, and spatial limits to the law have been used to limit the rights and powers of outsiders. I offer four arguments about the causes of this uneven evolution in legal spatiality.

Globalization past and present

I have already cast doubt on the simple claim that globalization is the key force eroding legal spatiality. The first wave of globalization correlates with the high point of strict territoriality in US law. However, the first wave of globalization and the second, while sharing important similarities, also exhibit major differences. Considering these differences sheds light on what precisely about the process of globalization has influenced changes in territorial doctrines.

One difference is the rise of the regulatory state during the twentieth century and the distinctive nature of contemporary trade. *Greater scope and scale of domestic regulation creates more scope for regulatory divergence and hence greater incentives for unilateral extraterritorial assertion. The current era of globalization promotes such assertions because it exhibits more extensive intraindustry trade and multinational production chains.* Because domestic firms are more likely today to be directly competing with foreign firms facing differential regulatory terrain, the rise of intraindustry trade creates greater political incentives to use domestic law extraterritorially to regulate economic activities abroad.

It is indisputable that we have a much more elaborate domestic regulatory apparatus today than in 1900. And unlike the pre-1914 era, contemporary societies expect government intervention in the economy and punish leaders who fail to deliver growth and stability. This is the "compromise of embedded liberalism," in John Ruggie's famous phrase. Greater intervention is true throughout the advanced industrial democracies. Extensive intervention yields extensive rules, and one result is cross-national divergence in specific regulatory rules. While many efforts at regulatory harmonization exist, and global convergence in regulatory policy is certainly occurring, important differences remain. These differences create incentives for extraterritorial assertions: if regulatory rules were globally uniform, as long as each state enforced their rules even-handedly (for example, provided national treatment) there would be little incentive for State A to assert its law against actors located in State B. Regulatory rules are not uniform, however, and thus states often have good reasons to seek to enforce their laws against extraterritorial actors who affect their markets. These firms have, owing to increased liberalization and openness, the ability to access markets that were once closed or were at least more delimited. Extraterritorial assertions of jurisdiction thus follow increases in regulation coupled to economic liberalization. The post-war spread of American multinationals adds to this dynamic. As former Deputy Secretary of the Treasury Kenneth Dam testified before Congress, "as more American firms have established more subsidiaries and branches abroad, the possibility arises that they will enter into conspiracies with local firms concerning local markets. Since those conspiracies, even where they concern local production in that country, could be found to affect U.S. exports, there is a surface argument for sustaining U.S. jurisdiction over them."[27]

A second key difference between the two waves of globalization is the rise of intraindustry trade. Pre-World War I integration was characterized by *inter*-industry trade: that is, trade of one kind of good (steam engines) for something completely different (rubber). Contemporary globalization is distinctive in that we see items such as disk drives constructed in many different countries: firms based in the United States assemble the devices in Thai factories with precision parts coming from Japan. This multinationality of production is new and a product itself of the tremendous decline in transportation costs, as well as the large inequalities in local labor costs that make such production patterns profitable. The current wave of globalization is also distinct in that firms from many states now directly compete in tightly integrated markets. Japanese cars vie with German, American, Swedish, and Korean cars for dominance in the global market. These varied firms thus face a direct incentive to demand "level playing fields" for their competitors. One way to achieve such a level playing field is to negotiate global rules through new international agreements. Another is to lower domestic law to match the more lax standards of competitor states – the so-called race to the bottom. A third is to assert domestic law extraterritorially. The first is a multilateral, consensus-based solution; the second and third are unilateral solutions. While multilateralism is often favored, extraterritorial extensions of regulatory law – particularly for powerful states – can be very effective. As a state's relative economic power rises, moreover, unilateralism will be more available and hence, all else equal, more likely to be used.

This broad explanation for the rise of extraterritoriality is consistent with some aspects of the empirical record. The rise and consolidation of the regulatory state in the first half of the twentieth century created the potential for regulatory conflict, conflict which was realized as the global economy progressively integrated in the postwar era. As intraindustry trade rose, firms increasingly sought to export their home regulatory frameworks through multilateral, but also unilateral, action. It is noteworthy that antitrust and securities law have been two of the most intensive areas of extraterritorial assertion. Both lack broad multilateral legal frameworks. Attempts at multilateral solutions have been made in the area of antitrust in particular, but these attempts have been blocked by the United States, which prefers to extend its regime unilaterally and extraterritorially rather than compromise its rules multilaterally. The economic dominance of the United States in the postwar era made this strategy viable. The fact that US regulatory extraterritoriality appears to have peaked in the 1970s is consistent with my argument: the US share of global GDP declined over the postwar era as Europe and Japan rebounded from the devastation of the war.

One problem with this argument is its comparative reach. The United States was a pioneer in regulatory extraterritoriality. Only in recent years have its chief economic competitors, in particular the EU, begun to embrace extraterritoriality aggressively. Given the incentives to assert regulatory law against foreign actors, why did only the United States do so consistently and strongly until the 1990s? It is not that European powers lacked legal doctrines permissive of extraterritoriality – indeed,

French law permits French plaintiffs to sue anyone in French courts whether or not the dispute has any connection with France (Juenger 1983–84). One answer is suggested by the earlier characterization of extraterritoriality as a unilateral solution to regulatory divergence. US economic dominance in the postwar era – especially in the 1950s and 1960s – was overwhelming. Hence the United States had the greatest economic power to act unilaterally. Most importantly, the United States possessed the functional ability to enforce its laws against foreign firms because those firms were often trading in US markets or had seizable assets in US markets. The current wave of extraterritorial assertions by the EU is consistent with this argument: as the EU's economic strength has grown, the EU has been more willing to assert its law extraterritorially.

But why did European states not assert extraterritoriality vis-à-vis each other (or against middle powers such as Canada or Australia) as Europe gained economic strength during the 1960s and 1970s? The same question arises with regard to Japan. This pattern remains a puzzle. It is possible that a concern with rule consistency played a role, making it difficult for courts and regulators to countenance assertions of extraterritoriality against an economically weak state but not against a strong one. Courts and regulators also may have been inhibited from asserting domestic laws outside their territories by the difficulty of keeping such assertions from impacting relations with the United States. Only once the EU approached economic parity with the United States could Europe embrace the United States' assertive extraterritoriality.

The liberal peace and the decline of territorial war

One of the more striking findings in the study of international relations is the liberal peace: the existence of a general state of peace among liberal or democratic states (Oneal and Russett 1999a; Gowa 1999; Doyle 1983a and 1983b).While often disputed in the details, the claim that liberal states rarely wage war on one another – though they do wage war on non-liberal states – has proved fairly robust. Liberal states enjoy a distinct politics among one another, one in which raw military power is present but rarely utilized. What Karl Deutsch termed "a pluralistic security community" now seems emergent among the advanced industrial democracies of the West (Deutsch et al. 1957, 58). The United States and Canada, for example, share the longest unprotected border in the world. Germany twice in twenty-five years waged total war on France, but these states now share not only a supranational legal and political system but also a common currency and central bank. While economic competitors, the advanced industrial democracies are not significant security competitors; indeed, the West has largely ceded unchallenged military supremacy to the United States, which spends more on defense than the next fifteen states combined. These varied changes are striking when compared to the state of affairs among Western nations a century ago.

What are the implications of these considerations for changes in legal spatiality? Reduction of military conflict does not mean the reduction of conflict; instead, it can enable increased economic conflict. This yields a second argument about the causes of change in legal spatiality: *the United States is less constrained in asserting extraterritorial jurisdiction vis-à-vis economic competitors in the postwar era because conflict with other Western states is less dangerous and thus less troubling.* Westphalian territorial sovereignty – a consequence of the bloody Thirty Years' War – was predicated on the need to inhibit warfare by sealing off states from one another's rule and jurisdiction. This conflict-minimization rationale animated the development of sovereign territoriality throughout the subsequent centuries. Yet the risk of spillover – of economic or legal conflict leading to military conflict – has been at an historic low with regard to other advanced industrial democracies since the end of World War II. In this low-risk environment, Congress, the executive branch, and the courts face stronger incentives to assert extraterritoriality even in the face of strong opposition from other states (or, alternatively, face weaker incentives to refrain) because the risks of significant conflict are low. These extraterritorial assertions are most likely to arise with regard to regulatory laws because of the deep economic links that developed among these states, particularly as contemporary globalization has accelerated.

By contrast, in the nineteenth century extraterritorial assertions of law were frequently seen as dangerous incursions into the sovereignty of another state. This was true even if in particular cases – such as *American Banana* – the sovereigns in question hardly posed a threat, because the *principle* could not be readily contained such that it only applied to weak states. As the Supreme Court wrote in that case: "For another jurisdiction, if it should happen to lay hold of the actor, to treat him according to its own notions rather than those of the place where he did the acts, not only would be unjust, but would be an interference with the authority of another sovereign, contrary to the comity of nations, which the other state concerned justly might resent."[28] The implication is that this resentment may well give rise to international conflict, conflict which juridical notions like comity were meant to forestall. The federal courts in the United States understood sovereignty through the nineteenth-century prism of conflict minimization. Sovereignty was total: "The very meaning of sovereignty is that the decree of the sovereign makes law."[29] Hence an extraterritorial assertion of jurisdiction over acts taking place on another state's territory was truly an interference with another sovereign's prerogative. Given the propensity in this era for war among great powers, interference with the authority of another sovereign was readily and unsurprisingly viewed as no trifling matter. As the Supreme Court stated as late as 1963, the presumption against extraterritoriality was designed "to protect against unintended clashes between our laws and those of other nations which could result in international discord" (*McCulloch v. Sociedad Nacional de Marineros de Honduras*, 372 US 10, 20–22, 83 S.Ct. 671, 9 L.Ed.2d 547 (1963)).

Starting in the Cold War the need for such protection against clashes – or at least the concern on the part of the United States about the implications of clashes – diminished markedly. European states huddled under the US nuclear umbrella, brought together both by the paramount Soviet threat and by rising levels of economic interdependence. At the same time, formerly warlike Europe embarked on a novel project of integration. The West coordinated policies extensively through such forums as the OECD and NATO and through a diverse array of multilateral agreements and institutions. International relations became highly institutionalized. In this setting, the likelihood of economic conflict spilling over to military conflict is extremely low.

The effects of the liberal peace are magnified by the marked decline in territorial wars in the postwar world. Territorial conquest was legion in the pre-World War II period, yet in the postwar era only two plausible examples exist: South Vietnam and Kuwait. The reasons for this shift are contested, but it is clear that in the contemporary economy, where human capital and innovation are primary engines of economic growth, control over territory is no longer as economically advantageous as it once was. Indeed, some states prosper with virtually no territory at all, Singapore being an extreme example.[30] Regardless of cause, it is uncontested that territorial war underwent a strikingly rapid decline during the twentieth century (Zacher 2001). This phenomenon, unlike the liberal peace, applies to all types of states, though it is arguably more robust among liberal states.

Thus shifts in patterns of conflict can yield shifts in territoriality. States, most strikingly the United States, appear to have embraced more aggressive extraterritoriality in response to the reduction in the prevalence of interstate war among the advanced industrial democracies. That decline has eliminated one of the key rationales of the nineteenth century for constraints on extraterritorial assertions: the fear that such acts will be seen as belligerent and hence dangerous encroachments on state sovereignty. To be sure, extraterritorial assertions of legal jurisdiction by the United States have continued to deeply upset other states, leading to the enactment of blocking and claw-back statutes and significant diplomatic protests. But the United States can be reasonably secure that this conflict will not fundamentally rupture relations – and after several decades, and many provocations by the United States, it has not. In short, today there is much less need for deference to the territorial jurisdiction of other sovereigns when those sovereigns are part of the broad liberal peace. This creates a permissive cause of the expansion of opportunistic extraterritorial jurisdiction, especially in areas characterized by economic competition.

Global power pojection and the territoriality of rights

A third argument similarly relates to changes in international security, but focuses instead on the uneven evolution of legal spatiality with regard to constitutional rights. Here the particular nature of military conflict influences changes in rules of territoriality. One of the signal facts of the postwar period was that the United States became a superpower with global reach. The United States' superpower status – and the totalizing conflict of the Cold War – meant that the United States actively projected force around the world. One result was a tremendous increase in US troop deployments abroad as the policy of containment was implemented. These troops brought many dependents. *The vastly larger number of American citizens stationed abroad in the mid-twentieth century, compared to the nineteenth century, made the costs of maintaining strict territoriality with regard to civil rights far higher.*

Reid v. Covert radically changed the territorial scope of constitutional rights in American law. Until 1957 the United States maintained a rigidly territorial conception of constitutional rights. The 1890 *Ross* decision clearly articulated a Westphalian vision. And the early twentieth-century *Insular Cases* made clear that the Constitution did not necessarily or fully follow the flag, even when US sovereignty over its imperial acquisitions was unquestioned. Yet *Reid* decisively overturned the rule that the Bill of Rights was spatially bound for citizens. Why this abrupt change in the understanding of territoriality? The Cold War plainly presented a radically different context for the decision the Supreme Court faced in *Reid* – which was, on its facts, quite similar to that faced seventy-five years earlier in *Ross*. Unlike the late nineteenth century, in 1957 nearly 1 million US military personnel were stationed around the globe in some sixty-three countries.[31] With them were over 250,000 dependent civilians. This represented a massive deployment of military force and of civilian dependents, one without historical precedent. Perhaps most striking, on average there were 435 trials a year of dependent civilians in the 1950s – more than one a day. The large number of trials meant that the *Ross* precedent was not subject simply to occasional invocation. Rather, it might arise persistently and in a wide array of cases.

Consequently, reinforcement of territorial limits on constitutional rights would have denied those rights indefinitely to a quarter of a million citizens – *simply as a result of their presence on foreign soil*. By comparison, prior to the Iraq war and occupation the United States had less than one-quarter of the number of troops stationed outside US territory, despite an overall population twice the size. Thus a large fraction of the citizenry of the time was implicated by the decision in *Reid*, either directly or through familial ties. Moreover, there was no reason in 1957 to believe that the global projection of US military power and personnel would decrease. If anything, the Soviet threat seemed to be growing. (Indeed, Sputnik was launched in October of 1957, the year *Reid* was decided.) In short, for the United States as a society, an unprecedented number of citizens were living abroad. Continued territorial limits on rights would have a major and unparalleled impact on civil liberties.

Undoubtedly, rising consciousness of civil rights in the United States played an important role in *Reid* as well as in subsequent decisions extending its framework. But it is highly implausible that the Court was influenced solely by general civil rights concerns. The briefs and argument made clear that extensive extraterritorial justice meted by the US government was now going to be a fact of life. As the US government itself argued in the case,

> In the troubled circumstances of our time, our national security requires that we station in many foreign nations large military and naval establishments. Sizable civilian contingents closely accompany, live with, and form integral parts of these establishments . . . equally significant to the armed forces is the need to sustain the morale of troops stationed in many and remote corners of the earth – morale which, even apart from the calls of humanity, promotes stability of the complement by permitting longer periods of overseas assignments and encourages reenlistments. To this end, the services have transported at military expense hundreds of thousands of dependents.[32]

In other words, given the vast numbers of citizens abroad, there would be many future Clarice Coverts.

Of course, it is hardly the case that the United States failed to engage in extraterritorial justice in the era of *Ross* – as the creation of the US District Court for China makes clear. But the number of individuals who fell within the China court's jurisdiction was extremely small, of the order of a few hundred.[33] In addition to stark numerical differences, the Justices in *Reid* may also have viewed the situation of the defendant differently than had the *Ross* court. US citizens hauled before the US District Court for China were usually present in China for economic gain.[34] Women like Clarice Covert were accompanying their husbands to the frontlines of the Cold War. This was, as the US government conceded, not for their pleasure but for the assistance and morale of the troops.[35] They were, in sum, innocent victims of the Cold War struggle.

The justices in *Reid* never presented a theory of legal spatiality that explained why the Constitution was to be read globally for citizens but not for aliens. And to be sure, some members of the court worried about how the decision to extend constitutional protections for citizens extraterritorially might inhibit the United States' new role as superpower. One justice noted that "Our far-flung foreign military establishments are a new phenomenon in our national life, and I think it would be unfortunate were we unnecessarily to foreclose . . . our future consideration of the broad questions involved in maintaining the effectiveness of these national outposts, in the light of continuing experience with these problems."[36] Nonetheless, the tenor of the decision was unequivocal. Previous territorial limitations on constitutional protections are outdated in the new postwar world of global military struggle – "relics from another era."[37]

Territoriality, aliens, and transboundary bads

Despite the varied changes described above, territory retains great importance in some areas of US law. This is particularly true with regard to such transboundary "bads" as narcotics and terrorists. The great increases in technology of travel associated with globalization have rendered states far more vulnerable and sensitive to transboundary flows of persons and goods – the attacks of September 11 being a salient example. One result is strong assertions by the executive and judiciary in the United States of territoriality in areas involving potentially dangerous influences from abroad – what might be called the dark side of globalization. Most notable are military and police actions by US agents against overseas aliens. It is in these areas that the executive branch, Congress, and the courts are most willing to maintain or revive older conceptions of legal spatiality. Thus *security threats by aliens give rise to strong assertions of traditional territoriality*.

For example, the Bush administration chose to place foreign enemy combatants in Guantanamo Bay and not a military base on the US mainland primarily for legal reasons. The administration asserted – and many lower courts endorsed – the claim that foreign nationals held abroad lacked any constitutional rights. *Rasul v. Bush*, the 2004 case in which the Supreme Court held that the federal *habeas* statute permitted aliens abroad to challenge their detention in federal court, did not squarely reject this claim, though it did cast some doubt on it.[38] Similarly, the Supreme Court's decision in *Verdugo*, which held that the Fourth Amendment did not apply to an alien's property outside the United States, is replete with language suggesting that we continue to live in a dangerous world with serious threats lurking beyond our borders. The claim seems to be that the protections of the Constitution, though well designed to safeguard liberty at home, cannot realistically be extended abroad without endangering the United States. While *Verdugo* reinstates jurisdictional congruence for the Fourth Amendment, what is perhaps most striking about the case is a feature that receives little attention: the fact that US government agents were engaged in criminal search and enforcement actions within the sovereign territory of Mexico. Increasingly, the United States is projecting both its police forces and its military forces abroad in an effort to stanch the flow of narcotics and immigrants into US territory. Policing across borders is on the rise precisely because globalization has made it far easier for all goods – licit and illicit – to move rapidly and freely around the globe. Thus the United States is extending not only its criminal law but also its criminal law enforcement apparatus extraterritorially (Nadelmann 1993), but it refuses to extend extraterritorially the protections that ordinarily accompany that domestic criminal law and procedure.

Terrorism, narcotics, weapons, and refugees move rapidly around the world and across US borders. In these situations, the world of today appears more, rather than less, dangerous than the world of the nineteenth century. Hence the executive branch and the courts frequently argue that strict territoriality needs to be maintained, not dismantled. Both the executive branch and the judiciary have sought to maintain traditional territorial limitations on constitutional rights for individual aliens, even as – arguably especially as – US substantive law is increasingly wielded abroad. The result is that spatial location has been deemed constitutionally irrelevant for citizens, but highly relevant for aliens.

Power and purpose

The preceding section presented four broad claims about the relationship between the international system and change in legal spatiality.

Globalization is undoubtedly an important driver of the erosion of jurisdictional congruence in American law, just as economic integration among the states of the United States heralded the demise of strict territoriality in personal jurisdiction as a matter of domestic law. But economic change is not the sole driver of jurisdictional change. Rather, military conflict – which has diminished in some areas of the globe but continues in others – has also driven the articulation and rearticulation of legal rules about sovereignty and territory. The striking reduction in conflict among liberal states has facilitated assertions of extraterritorial jurisdiction as the fear of spillover from legal to military conflict has abated. At the same time, the persistent threat of armed conflict during the Cold War led to extensive projection of force abroad by the United States, which in turn helped sway the Supreme Court to extend constitutional protections for citizens globally. And continued conflict over the dark side of globalization – sex traffickers, drug smugglers, money launderers, and especially terrorists – has only bolstered the willingness of Congress, the courts, and the executive branch to fortify the principle that aliens abroad lack constitutional protections against the US government even as they increasingly are held to fall within American prescriptive jurisdiction.

What explains the broad evolution of legal spatiality I have sketched? Legal scholars sometimes claim that law evolves toward normative principles oriented around conceptions of justice, and reflects principled commitments within a society and a legal tradition. Legal rules are also said to change as the result of discrete doctrinal developments that accrete over long stretches of time. Does the evolution of legal spatiality – away from jurisdictional congruence and toward more flexible understandings of jurisdiction – reflect clear normative commitments grounded in American constitutional theory? It is difficult to see how. The jurisdictional congruence of the nineteenth century did rest on an overarching principle – strict territorial sovereignty. The application of strict territoriality was fairly, though not wholly, consistent in this era. Even the major exception – the extraterritorial courts of the time – did not so much undermine the principle as support it, by highlighting the centrality of the principle for sovereign states (who never had to face extraterritorial jurisdiction in their own territories). The evolution of legal spatiality over the last century, however, reflects no clear set of principles. The persistent disjuncture in the constitutional rights accorded aliens and citizens abroad, for example, has never been explained in a manner consistent with the strong protection of aliens' rights within the sovereign borders of the United States. There is no overarching normative principle that can fit this pattern.

A more compelling account of the development of rules of legal spatiality rests on the broad interests and power of the United States. This account is instrumental and power-based, and argues that the rule evolution I have charted tracks shifts in underlying political incentives and capabilities. Territorial sovereignty delimits US legal rules when such limits are useful to US policymakers, but leaves rules geographically unfettered when that too is useful. US regulatory and criminal law, for example, has been held to apply globally because in a globalized economy the United States generally benefits from the extension of its law abroad. During the twentieth century, the incentives to extend US law abroad grew as clashes developed between emerging regulatory systems and as rising inter-industry trade created political pressure to ensure level playing fields. The evolution of legal doctrine reflects these incentives. American power – both economic and military – made it possible for the United States to assert such claims. Legal protections that might constrain the exercise of US power, however, have rarely followed such substantive extensions.

This account is broadly consistent with power-based theories of state behavior. Over the last century, executive actions, judicial decisions, and congressional lawmaking with regard to territoriality have all reflected the perceived interests of the United States in the field of foreign relations and, of course, the direct interests of the litigants that appear before the federal courts. In many of the relevant cases the US government was the key litigant. The executive branch thus was well positioned to argue that particular conceptions of territoriality would aid or hinder particular geopolitical aims. Federal judges are not immune to political and economic context. Particularly in the field of foreign relations law, US courts are notoriously deferential to the executive branch, which faces direct incentives to seek the most advantageous legal rules regarding extraterritoriality.[39] It thus no surprise that the evolution of territoriality in American law reflects shifting assessments of American interests toward jurisdictional congruence and, most fundamentally, the shifting geopolitical and economic contexts that give rise to these new assessments. In a time in which US unilateralism is receiving increasing attention and censure, it is worth noting that extraterritoriality – particularly the à la carte extraterritoriality of the last fifty years – is equally unilateralist.

Conclusion

In the early 1990s, John Ruggie declared that it is "truly astonishing that the concept of territoriality has been so little studied within international relations" (Ruggie 1993, 174). This statement is equally true with regard to legal doctrines of territoriality. It is within law – both international and domestic – that conceptions of territory are most clearly and strikingly instantiated. Thus rules of legal spatiality present an unparalleled window on the evolution of territoriality. As this chapter has shown, conceptions of territoriality have changed radically over the last century. Once tightly fettered to sovereign soil, law is now increasingly disconnected from land.

Change in legal rules and institutions is rarely considered in light of international influences. My contention is that we can understand the broad path of American legal doctrine regarding territory not by looking within the law, narrowly, but by looking without at the far-reaching economic and military shifts that have transformed world politics during the twentieth century. While globalization has plainly influenced territorial doctrines, the influence is less direct than commonly supposed. It was only as the nature of globalization itself changed – as well as the nature of the state and its place in the national and global economy – that extraterritoriality became ever more attractive as a legal principle. Yet, as this chapter has made clear, not all states embraced extraterritorial jurisdiction at once or evenly. The United States was the leader, both because of its hegemonic economic and political role but also owing to its unique military reach. Increasingly, however, other states are asserting domestic laws extraterritorially, leading to numerous legal conflicts and complex jurisdictional questions.

Yet these conflicts are less numerous than they might be, because there are clear alternatives to extraterritorial assertions of substantive law: most commonly, multilateral treaties and institutions but also, more and more frequently, transgovernmental networks and "soft law." Both traditional multilateralism and contemporary transgovernmentalism permit states with diverse regulatory and constitutional regimes to harmonize or mutually recognize the rules of other states. Extraterritoriality remains possible, but it is not always the optimal choice. Nevertheless, extraterritorial assertions of domestic law have the virtue of unilateralism: states need not engage in the often nettlesome process of compromise demanded by multilateral negotiations. As resistance to new efforts at regime negotiation persists, extraterritoriality will undoubtedly continue to seem attractive to policymakers facing an ever more interdependent and complex world.

NOTES

I thank participants in workshops at Princeton, UCLA, Temple, Hofstra, Columbia, UC San Diego, and Chicago for comments on earlier drafts. In particular

I thank Alex Aleinikoff, David Currie, Michael Doyle, David Golove, Miles Kahler, Eugene Kontorovich, Andy Moravcsik, Gerry Neuman, Eric Posner, Beth Simmons, Anne-Marie Slaughter, Detlef Vagts, Barbara Walter, and John Yoo for helpful discussions, and Tom Hale and Lindsey Carlson for excellent research assistance. The Program on Law and Public Affairs at Princeton provided financial support.

1 The "hard-shell" metaphor is from Herz 1957.
2 Exceptions include "Symposium" 2003; Berman 2002; Spiro 2002.
3 As Johnson and Post argue, "We take for granted a world in which geographic borders – lines separating physical spaces – are of primary importance in determining legal rights and responsibilities" (1995–96, 1368).
4 As the Supreme Court once asserted, Puerto Rico is "foreign in a domestic sense." This phrase, almost a Zen koan, neatly captures the paradoxes of colonial territoriality (Burnett and Marshall 2001).
5 One prominent exception is Mary Dudziak's (1988) work on desegregation.
6 The Tangier Zone was established in 1926 (Bederman 1996).
7 The last example of US consular jurisdiction, in Morocco, ended in 1956.
8 Aside from the recent occupation of Iraq, officially terminated on 28 June 2004, the United States militarily occupied parts of West Berlin until 1990 and Okinawa until 1971.
9 *Reid v. Covert* (354 US 1 (1957)), 12.
10 *American Banana*, 355-56.
11 *American Banana* 358.
12 *EEOC v. Arabian American Oil Co.* (499 US 244 (1991)).
13 *Reid v. Covert*, 5–6.
14 *Reid v. Covert*, 12.
15 *Reid v. Covert*, X.
16 *Tiede*, 239.
17 *Tiede*, 244.
18 *Tiede*, 260.
19 *Verdugo*, 271.
20 In other words, it is not the place of the capture but rather the place of *detention* that is germane to the *habeas* claim.
21 *Zadvyads v. Davis* (533 US 678 (2001), 693).
22 *US v. Klimavicius*, 144 F2d 1249 (1998). Other courts disagree: see *US v. Suerte*, 291 F3d 366, 5th Circ. (2002).
23 *US v. Bin Laden*, 91 F. supp. 2d 600, 621 (SDNY 2000).
24 Baldwin and Martin (1999, 7–8).
25 An exception is Neuman (1996b).
26 For example, Kramer (1991), explaining extraterritorial assertions of regulatory law in terms of changes in conflicts doctrine.
27 Testimony, 12 October 1995. Available at http://www.ftc.gov/opp/global/dam_kw.htm.
28 *American Banana*, 358.
29 Ibid.
30 State size has on average been shrinking in the postwar era. See Lake and O'Mahony, this volume.

31 See the oral argument in *Reid I*, in *Landmark Briefs*. The sixty-three figure comes from the US government's oral argument in *Reid II*.
32 Brief in *Reid I*, 98.
33 Personal communication, Eileen Scully, May 2004.
34 Missionaries were the other large category.
35 Oral argument in *Reid II* in *Landmark Briefs of the Supreme Court*, 824.
36 *Reid II* (354 US 1 (1957)), 72.
37 Ibid., 12.
38 Indeed, the Bush administration continues to argue that the detainees held in Guantanamo and other locations abroad lack any *constitutional* rights whatsoever. The decision in *Rasul* rested solely on statutory grounds.
39 On the extent of deference, see Franck 1992.

10 Trade and territorial conflict in Latin America: international borders as institutions

Beth A. Simmons

More than three decades ago, Richard Cooper stated that "the trend toward economic interdependence between countries will require substantial changes in their approach to foreign policy in the next decade or so" (1972, 159). A wide range of studies has since been premised on the proposition that interdependence has significantly raised the costs to governments and the economies they govern of taking unilateral action. One solution to problems of coordination and collaboration among states has been to develop international institutions that reduce transactions costs and uncertainty, allowing states to enjoy greater mutual gains than would have been possible in the absence of such institutions.

The institutional paradigm has informed a broad range of studies in international political economy (Simmons and Martin 2002). The same cannot be said of international conflict studies. Scholars looking at interstate disputes have typically bypassed institutional theory, focusing instead on the basic constellations of state power. The irony is that war and peace often revolve around the most ubiquitous international institution of the modern age: sovereign authority over delimited territorial space.

This chapter argues for a reconceptualization of international borders as they have come to be understood in the international relations literature. One branch of that literature has emphasized the extent to which disputes over territory, more than any other issue, have spurred interstate rivalry, military confrontation, and all-out war. Borders as territorial divisions are then analyzed as zero-sum manifestations of state competition for power, prestige, lebensraum, or an imagined historical identity. Hein Goemans' contribution to this volume has a creative take on the security dimensions of territorial borders, viewing them as focal points for collective defense, group cohesion, and, ultimately, survival.

Yet the globalization literature continually reminds us that we live in a world in which territory matters less, and human capital matters more, to national power. It also entreats us to believe that national boundaries matter less now than they ever have in the past. Markets override national boundaries, causing some commentators to suggest that our world is increasingly "borderless" (Ohmae 1990).

Neither of these conceptions is useful for understanding the role of international boundaries in a world of potentially highly interdependent nation-states. In such a world, international borders are more important than ever, but they are increasingly inappropriate objects of interstate competition. The best way to understand this irony is to theorize about international borders as international political–economic institutions that produce not only divisible benefits, but mutual benefits as well. As I will show, thinking about borders in this fashion is not only plausible; it also resolves a number of issues that from the traditional realist and the globalization perspectives are puzzling.[1]

This study proceeds in three sections. The first section sets out the argument that international borders that are accepted by adjacent states as legitimate should be thought of as international institutions that enhance certainty, reduce transactions costs, and provide mutual gains that are eroded or lost if the legitimacy of the border is in dispute. I concede that, from an economic point of view, a world of separate jurisdictions is less efficient than one of distinct nation-states. But given a state system, settled territorial boundaries allow governments to realize important economic and political benefits that are very difficult to achieve in the absence of a well-accepted international border agreement. I will demonstrate this in a very concrete fashion by showing that there are substantial opportunity costs to disputing the accuracy or legitimacy of a particular territorial division.

The second and third sections develop the methodology and demonstrate this claim empirically. Using a gravity model of trade, and controlling for a broad range of likely alternative explanations, I show that the mere fact of disputing a border has a significant negative impact on contiguous countries' bilateral trade. This is true even when we control for the effects of the actual threat or use of force. In short, I show that there is a high opportunity cost to disputing an international boundary. The argument is *not* that globalization and post-industrial technological advances have made territory per se less important, an idea Erik Gartzke effectively refutes in his contribution to this volume. Rather, it is that borders as *institutions* for organizing understandings about jurisdiction over territory are increasingly important as the potential for economic interdependence increases. I conclude in section four that settled borders are an important international institutional arrangement that, as long as we live in a world of nation-states, is helpful to further economic integration. The consequences for our understanding of international conflict and cooperation in this area are profound.

Borders as institutions

Geographers usually define international boundaries as spatial manifestations of political control displayed in the landscape (Rumley and Minghi 1991). As such, international boundaries separate areas subject to different political control or sovereignty. They represent the physical line of contact between states, and afford opportunities for both cooperation and discord (Prescott 1987, 5).

It is the latter feature of international boundaries that has received so much attention in the international relations literature. Borders place physical limits on the exercise of state authority, as well as providing the physical space available for the provision of national security. For these reasons, they are a primary concern of scholars in the realist tradition who view power and the search for security as the central features of international relations. Hans Morgenthau, who was remarkably eclectic in this regard, placed geography and natural resources – elements closely associated with territory – right at the top of the list of elements of national power (Morgenthau 1985, 127–36). Moreover, he emphasized territorial reallocation as a central way to preserve the balance of power, a process he characterized as achievable by "diminishing the weight of the heavier scale or by increasing the weight of the lighter one" (Morgenthau 1985). Yet one ought not to portray his approach as unduly mechanistic. Morgenthau was also willing to consider national character, national morale, and the problem of popular support as important determinants of national power.[2] Each of these, of course, can be closely linked with the prospects of territorial loss or accretion.

Realist thinking overlapped with conceptions of the state and territoriality developed by early twentieth-century scholars of geopolitics (Mackinder 1904). Robert Gilpin's claim that "throughout history" states have had as a principal objective "the conquest of territory in order to advance economic, security, and other interests" (Gilpin 1981, 23) is not radically different from the claims of classical nineteenth-century scholars, whose theories treated states as "competitive territorial entities vying with one another for control over parts of the earth's surface" (Murphy 2001).

For those who draw inspiration from realist theory, an international boundary is typically conceived of in zero-sum terms. Gary Goertz and Paul Diehl provide the clearest contemporary expression of this general assumption:

Because a territorial dispute is primarily zero-sum (usually only one entity can control a piece of land) it may appear surprising that the vast majority of all territorial changes over the last 165 years have been completed peacefully.
(Goertz and Diehl 1992, 51)

The assumption has informed a good deal of research that shows disputes over territory are much more prone to degenerate into violent interstate conflict than are disputes over other issues (Brecher 1993; Gochman and Leng 1983; Hensel 1999; Senese 1996). Disputes over territory have been linked to ongoing violent rivalries between states, as well as to the frequency and intensity of war (Goertz and Diehl 1992; Holsti 1991; Huth 1996; Mandell 1980; Vasquez 1993; Vasquez 1995). Studies that focus on the resolution of territorial disputes almost always focus on external security variables, though in light of the literature on the "democratic peace" more attention has been given to domestic regime type and international norms (Huth 1996; Kacowicz 1994).

The realist approach to territorial issues has not quite figured out what to do with a few stubborn facts. The first is highlighted in the quote by Goertz and Diehl above. If control over territory is truly zero-sum and so closely connected to issues of national security, why has territory so often been transferred peacefully? Immediately one thinks of imposed solutions where resistance may have been deterred, but there are other apparent anomalies from a realist perspective. Paul Huth cites evidence that in all of the years since World War II, less than one-third of all international borders have been disputed (Huth 1996, 8). The best empirical analysts merely flag these as "null cases" for purposes of statistical controls, but they are of serious theoretical import. Why are so many borders accepted as legitimate and uncontested? Even in the Middle East, usually perceived as a hotbed of territorial contention, formal mutually accepted treaties exist for 80 percent of the region's land boundaries (Blake 1992). Realists do not have a clear answer for why so much of the world should have been in apparent equilibrium for the past half-century. Institutionalism on the other hand provides insights, which we discuss below.

Moreover, it is difficult to articulate (and to my knowledge, no one has attempted) a realist account for the decline in the use of force in cases of territorial disputes. Yet there is an emerging scholarly consensus that disputes are less and less often resolved through violence. One revealing statistic is that territorial change as a result of violence dropped from 33 percent before World War II to 16 percent afterwards (Goertz and Diehl 1992, 52). Edward Morse attributed this development to the forces of modernization, including the rise of economic interdependence (Morse

1976). Mark Zacher has proposed a more normative explanation, arguing that growing acceptance of an "anti-territorial revisionism norm" discourages the use of violence in border disputes (Zacher 2001).

While realists are working out empirical explanations of the hows and whys of boundary disputation and territorial transfer, the globalists are telling us that none of this should matter. Though not all go as far as Ken'ichi Ohmae, who asserts that the world is now "borderless" (Ohmae 1990; Ohmae 1995), it is rather commonly accepted that borders are declining in economic significance (Herz 1957; O'Brien 1992) as well as social–cultural significance (Agnew and Duncan 1989; Appadurai 1996). Richard Rosecrance has long argued that trade increasingly trumps territory as a source of national power (Rosecrance 1986; Rosecrance 1996). John Stopford and Susan Strange have argued extensively that competition for world markets, for example, has replaced competition for territory, or for control over the natural resources of territory, as the "name of the game" between states (Stopford and Strange 1991; Strange 1996). Geographers as well as political scientists in the 1990s have argued that the control of networks of finance, information, and transportation are much more important than control over territory per se (Agnew and Knox 1994; Kobrin 1997; Luke 1991; Murphy 1999; Ruggie 1993).

The evidence for these claims is in most cases episodic, but where it has been systematic, it has not been especially supportive of the irrelevance of international borders. Although internationalization in today's "global era" is no doubt real and important, national boundaries continue to have significant influences on international economic relations. Globalists are at a loss to explain why international investment is not *more* globalized than it is: why is there such a "home bias" when it comes to investing (Goldstein and Mussa 1993; Sobel 1994)? John McCallum's study of bilateral trade between the United States and Canada was the first to show empirically that a "borderless" North America does not yet exist: as of 1990, trade between Canadian provinces was on average almost 22 times trade between a similar Canadian province and a US state, all other factors being held equal (McCallum 1995, 617). This study served as the foundation for a more complete and comprehensive study by John Helliwell, who not only confirmed McCallum's findings, but also found that even after the Free Trade Agreement (FTA) of 1990, US–Canada border effects were still in the tenfold range (Helliwell 1998, 21). Furthermore, Helliwell extended the analysis to trade between all countries in the 1986–96 period, showing that border effects were an international phenomenon, and particularly acute for developing countries (Helliwell 1998, 59). Departing from

McCallum and Helliwell's trade-centered analyses, Charles Engel and John Rogers confirmed the importance of borders using the "law of one price." They showed that even after holding all other factors equal, price divergences between cities in different countries are much greater than between cities in the same country (Engel and Rogers 1996). Borders, they claim, are indeed still quite "wide."

What is needed is a way to think about international boundaries that is neither prisoner to realism's zero-sum approach to traditional concerns of state security, nor falls prey to claims that borders do not matter. It is instructive to return to the description by Prescott (a geographer) of an international boundary and to notice how much it has in common with the conditions which international relations scholars have associated with those giving rise to "interesting" issues with respect to cooperation (Keohane 1984). International boundaries involve "mixed motive games" which Schelling characterized as having elements of "mutual dependence, and conflict, of partnership and competition" (Schelling 1980, 89). Realists have spelled out quite well the competitive elements in boundary determination and acceptance: territory may have symbolic, political, historical, or other kinds of significance that make it difficult for states to give it up. On the other hand – and this is rarely emphasized in the literature on territory and boundaries – well-accepted international border arrangements provide *mutual* benefits for states that may be very difficult for either to realize through unilateral policies.

Governments may want to maximize their territorial authority, but like players in a game of battle of the sexes they may place a good deal of importance on capturing the value associated with agreeing on the line. Governments may in some cases be relatively indifferent to where the exact line is drawn (at least over the range of territory that is being negotiated), and may place far more value on settlement itself. I argue this is because an institutionalized border arrangement provides benefits that each country can only enjoy if it cooperates with its neighbor in resolving the border dispute. Primarily, these benefits flow from the certainty and the reduction in transactions costs associated with a normalization of relations regarding the border.

Just what are some of these benefits that require mutual acceptance of the border? In this chapter I focus on the economic benefits. All of the economic literature suggests that trade is highly sensitive to the risk and transactions costs involved among even the friendliest of trade partners (the studies cited above found significant effects to the border between countries as friendly as the United States and Canada). Now insert contention over the extent of territorial authority. There are good theoretical reasons to believe that such a dispute would inject marked uncertainty and risk into developing cross-border trade links. Most obviously, the dispute could become active, and most studies have shown that war reduces bilateral trade volumes (Anderton et al. 1999; Anderton and Carter 2001).[3] More subtly, the disputing governments may be more likely to interfere with trade at the border (customs hassles) or to develop explicit policies to reduce their mutual dependence out of mutual suspicion of one another's motives and intentions stemming from the territorial dispute (Hirschman 1945). In some cases, the border might simply be closed for security reasons. In any case, a heavy military or police presence of a hostile state around the border itself is unlikely to be very inviting to traders.

But the broader reasons for stagnant trade will have to do with the general uncertainty surrounding property rights (broadly conceived) when two countries' governments dispute territorial jurisdiction. Should an investment be made in developing relationships with suppliers or marketing to consumers in a country with which relations are so uncertain? Subjection to hostile propaganda campaigns is another potential problem. In short, traders face costs and risks of developing business links in countries with which their government has a dispute.[4] The territorial dispute over the Kurile Islands, for example, has caused economic relations between Japan and Russia to stagnate, even while those between Russia and Korea have continued to expand (Akaha 1996; Linge 1995; Meyer 1998).[5]

Historically, the link between settling an outstanding territorial claim and improving bilateral trade has often been manifest in the nearly simultaneous conclusion of territorial agreements and treaties of "friendship, commerce, and navigation." For example, Argentina and Bolivia addressed border issues in a Friendship, Commerce, and Navigation Treaty in 1868; Chile and Argentina settled the Beagle Channel dispute and signed a friendship and commerce treaty in 1984; Brazil and Peru signed a series of boundary treaties that also addressed commerce and navigation (1841, 1851, 1909) (Ireland 1938; Ireland 1941). Governments have historically been willing to facilitate international economic relations once disputes over territory have been settled.

International investors may be even more wary than traders of cross-border contracts involving jurisdictional disputes over the border. In the case of the Saudi–Yemeni border dispute (settled by treaty, 12 June 2000), the expectation that the region was well-endowed with hydrocarbons drove attempts to negotiate a boundary settlement (Schofield 1997). But even if we consider the broader decision to invest away from the border, investors are likely to run risks of a sovereign-induced nature if they sink assets in countries that have a fundamentally hostile posture to their home country. Finally, despite the inherent attractions of some border regions (Timothy 1995), tourists can hardly be expected to flock to border regions that may be heavily armed, or that lack basic infrastructural investment owing to the dispute over the border. Though we rarely consider this impact, tourism is increasingly significant to the economies of many countries. These are opportunities forgone for the lack of clearly accepted understandings about the international border.

There is another reason why unsettled borders are potentially costly to governments: they may stand in the way of regional economic integration. The prospect of Turkey or Cyprus joining the European Union, for example, has run up against the territorial claims of the former over portions of the latter, as well as other disputes involving Greece in the Aegean Sea (Joseph 1996; Theophylactou 1995). Leaders in both Peru and Ecuador viewed regional economic integration primarily emanating from Mercosur as an incentive to settle the border. The alternative was to risk getting left behind as the rest of Latin America developed stronger trade relations. Exclusion from regional arrangements in some cases is another opportunity cost of territorial disputes.

If we view settled international boundaries as valuable international institutions that provide joint benefits to adjacent governments, then we can understand some findings that from a realist perspective appear quite anomalous. Goertz and Diehl, for example, expect that "the greater the intrinsic value of the territory involved, the more likely military conflict is to be a part of the transfer" (Goertz and Diehl 1992, 88). Yet Paul Huth found that "when economic issues are predominantly at stake then compromise settlements are quite likely" (Huth 1996, 153). How can a realist, especially one concerned with relative gains (Grieco 1988; Mearsheimer 1994–95) explain such an outcome? It is easily explicable in institutionalist terms: without a settlement, these would have been economic gains largely forgone for lack of investment – the result of uncertainty and transactions costs for private actors associated with governmental territorial disputing. (It is interesting to note, however, that Huth explains the propensity to settle where economic issues are at stake as flowing from the ease of *dividing*, rather than the institutional potential for *generating*, economic benefits.)[6]

There are good reasons for accepting this paradigm shift with respect to borders. The traditional geopolitical concept of security as defense of territory and containing or neutralizing threats to a nation's sovereignty has come to be regarded as narrow and even self-defeating.[7] Governments are often willing to expand the parameters of security to include inputs of economic development, social reconstruction, and empowerment of human rights.[8] In the case of the Peru–Ecuador conflict, governments were increasingly aware of the opportunity costs they pay in terms of domestic social development and lost international trade and investment (Simmons 1999). In that case (finally resolved in 1998) Peruvian and Ecuadorian leaders were motivated to build agreements on joint development into the border agreement, and then marketed the package to the broader community of international investors (Simmons 2005).

To summarize: international border arrangements can be fruitfully analyzed in institutionalist terms. Settled borders signal to private economic agents that military conflict is less likely, that economic development is a higher value than territorial acquisition, that hostile harassment at the border is much less likely, and that property rights will not be subject to jurisdictional controversies. In short, settling territorial disputes is a costly signal that a state has made the conversion from a territorial state to a trading state. In the next section, some plausibility is provided for these arguments by demonstrating just how costly territorial disputes can be. There is no denying that such disputes can be costly in terms of human life, military expenditures, and lost trade when these conflicts become hot. But what I seek to show is that, *even when controlling for the threat or use of force and other sources of bilateral tensions, merely disputing the border is a costly drag on bilateral trade.*[9] These costs are documented using a gravity model, to which is added the presence of a territorial dispute. The results suggest that institutional arrangements that reduce uncertainty and transactions costs go a long way toward supporting the conditions under which economic integration may flourish.

Data and methodology

Establishing a baseline for trade: border effects using a gravity model of bilateral trade

The strategy of this section is to isolate the effects of a disputed border on the bilateral trade between two countries.[10] The central hypothesis is that disputed borders involve tremendous economic opportunity costs, which are conceptualized for purposes of empirical testing as bilateral trade forgone. The problem is how to estimate the size of this "lost opportunity," controlling for other plausible determinants of trade.

I employ a gravity model of trade, which has been widely used to examine bilateral trade flows since it was pioneered in the 1960s (Linnemann 1966; Poyhonen 1963; Tinbergen 1962). The basic gravity model is a very simple empirical model that explains bilateral trade between countries as proportional to their "mass" (usually captured by gross domestic product) and inversely proportional to the distance between countries. This simple baseline model has a remarkably consistent history of success as an empirical tool. The response of bilateral trade to income and distance regularly produces large, correctly signed, and statistically significant coefficients (Davis et al. 1997; Frankel et al. 1997; Helpman 1984; Leamer and Levinsohn 1995; Linnemann 1966).

Gravity models of trade now have a clear and convincing link to international trade theory (J. E. Anderson 1979; Oguledo and MacPhee 1996). Constant-returns Hecksher-Ohlin trade models can generate the basic gravity equation, in the presence of large factor endowment differences between countries that support trade specialization and inter-industry trade (Deardorff 1998; Evenett and Keller 1998; Leamer 1974). This theory has been especially useful for analyzing the volume of north–south trade (Marcusen and Wigle 1990). On the other hand, increasing returns models can also generate the specialization required for gravity models to make conceptual sense, but are more likely to apply to trade within regions and to generate high proportions of intra-industry trade (Bergstrand 1989; Helpman 1984; Helpman 1987). Since the relationships specified in the gravity equation are basically consistent with more than one theoretical tradition, scholars have emphasized that it is less useful for discriminating between theories of trade than for making empirical predictions about the volume of trade itself (Deardorff 1998).

The empirical robustness and theoretical foundations that have been drawn make the gravity model highly useful for exploring the impact of a broad range of factors on a baseline model of trade. For example, by including a variable for regional trade institutions, a number of scholars have used this approach to study the extent to which regional trade arrangements are trade-creating or trade-diverting (Bayoumi and Eichengreen 1995; Frankel and Wei 1993; Hamilton and Winters 1992; Polak 1996). Andrew Rose uses a gravity model as a baseline to measure the impact of currency union on international trade (Rose 1999). Rebecca Summary examined the effects of political rights on arms trade using this approach (Summary 1989). Brian Pollins includes membership in free trade agreements such as NAFTA, LAFTA, and the EU, as well as a "conflict and cooperation index," in order to study the relationship between foreign policy and trade (Pollins 1989). Gravity models have been used to explain patterns of trade in sectors from wheat to apparel to mobile communication flows (Christerson 1994; Koo and Karemera 1991; Matthes 1994). It is employed here to ask: how much does a border dispute detract from expected bilateral trade volumes?

Gravity models of bilateral trade typically take the following form

$$T_{ab} = f(Y_{ab}, D_{ab}, R_{ab})$$

T represents the trade flow between countries; a and b; **Y** represents the economic size of the two countries; **D** represents the physical distance from country a to b; and finally, **R** represents other factors that may resist or encourage trade between a and b. Because we are interested in the effects of a settled, mutually accepted border on bilateral trade flows, we use the following specification of the gravity model:

$$\log(T_{ab}) = \beta_0 + \beta_1 \log(Y_a + Y_b) + \beta_2 \log(D_{ab}) + \beta_3(BD) + \beta_4(controls) + \epsilon$$

The dependent variable **log(T_{ab})** represents the logged total flow of dyadic trade expressed in millions of US dollars.[11] **Log(Y_a+Y_b)** represents the combined economic size of the two trading nations, measured as the logged gross domestic product. The expected coefficient is positive. **Log(D_{ab})** represents distance between capitals of the country dyad, expressed in logged kilometers. The expected coefficient is negative, as greater distance represents greater transportation costs that should add "economic distance" and thus decrease trade volume. **BD** represents the existence of a border dispute, coded as 1 if there is a dispute between the two countries, otherwise 0. The expected coefficient is negative; our central expectation is that disputes reduce bilateral trade.

The primary explanatory variable: defining territorial disputes

A crucial question is how one identifies a territorial dispute. Conceptually, we are interested in overlapping territorial claims that can be expected to instill uncertainty regarding jurisdictional authority, even in the absence of the overt use of military force. Paul Huth has developed a useful set of criteria for selecting cases that fit our concern. He coded territorial disputes as cases of governments' disagreement over the location of a border (whether or not a treaty has attempted to spell this out); when one country occupies the national territory of another and refuses to relinquish control or withdraw; when one government does not recognize the sovereignty of another over some portion of territory within the border of that country; or when a government does not recognize the independence and sovereignty of another country (or colonial territory), and seeks to annex some or all of its territory (Huth 1996, 19–23).

In Huth's study, disputes are considered "resolved" when these conditions are reversed.[12] I favor Huth's rather stringent definition of resolution – involving governments' formal acknowledgment of the legitimacy of a particular border arrangement – because the argument turns precisely on institutions' role in reducing transactions costs and uncertainty. Publicly articulated arrangements of a formal nature are more likely to produce the confidence in resolution upon which our theory turns.[13] I therefore use Huth's list of cases, updating them where necessary (see Appendix 1; disputing dyads are also listed in Table 10.2, discussed below).

Controls

I also include a set of control variables that could influence bilateral trade levels. First, it is important to control for policies that *independently* could improve bilateral trade. Certainly it is possible that each country's general trade posture (its commitment to protection to enhance self-sufficiency, its overall development strategy) could be a central determinant of bilateral trade levels as well. I include total exports plus imports to and from the rest of the world as a proportion of GDP for each country (multiplied and logged) to control for general trade posture. The expectation is that bilateral trade is partially a function of two countries' general trade policy. The more open generally, the more positive the effect on bilateral trade. I also control for the effects of common membership in preferential trade arrangements. Independent of whatever effects one might want to ascribe to a territorial dispute, we would expect preferential trade agreements to have a positive effect on bilateral trade among members. I code each country-pair as 1 when both parties are members of the same agreement or arrangement. I control for time as well. The expectation is that all trade is increasing over time, and thus that we should see a strong positive correlation of bilateral trade with the passage of time.

A second cluster of controls is designed to reduce the possibility that territorial disputes and trade are both driven by deeper bilateral tensions. If bad underlying relations both drive border disputes and deter trade, the link between trade and border institutions could be spurious. Since the argument revolves around settled boundaries per se, non-territorial sources of conflict must be taken into account.

As a first cut, I distinguish my argument about stable territorial institutions from arguments about the consequences of war or the threat of military force for commercial relations. Empirical studies suggest that war between countries reduces their bilateral trade. Admittedly, this is likely to be true, but here it is argued that the prolonged uncertainty of an ongoing dispute over territory is a more pervasive detriment to trade than actual cases of the use of force. Countries need not actually brandish their military might or engage in armed conflict to incur the opportunity costs of disputing their borders.[14] We are more interested in negative externalities associated with unsettled borders for cross-border trade, though we would expect the actual use of force to reduce trade as well.

Another way to isolate border disputes is to distinguish them from other kinds of bilaterally disruptive political claims. Surely one of the most significant sources of bilateral conflict flows from challenges to the legitimacy of another government's rule. "Regime claims" involve instances in which one government has publicly called for the removal of another government from office. Disputes over the legitimacy of governance might fan the flames of a territorial dispute and simultaneously reduce the willingness to permit or facilitate bilateral trade. We should expect a strong negative effect on trade when such challenges have been issued.

At a more subtle yet possibly more pervasive level, one might suspect that both bilateral trade patterns and territorial disputing are jointly influenced (and hence only spuriously related) by a more basic underlying disagreement or divergence in policies, interests, or outlook between two governments. Far short of serious disputes that would elicit military threats, governments may have significant policy differences that serve to throw sand in a range of harmonious bilateral relations. If underlying political conflict explains both meager trade *and* hostile border policies, the empirical case for an institutional theory of borders is weakened. Measuring underlying comity is difficult, but one approach is to control for similarity of positions on foreign policy issues. I experiment by controlling for the extent of similarity within each country-pair on votes on the United Nations General Assembly. While hardly a perfect measure, on average (and despite occasional strategic voting) it captures the underlying degree of "affinity" between country-pairs on a range of issues in world politics.[15] Conversely, a low or falling index should indicate the potential for underlying tensions within a country-dyad. Additionally, I try to control for a propensity for underlying conflict by controlling for those dyads with at least one nationalistic government.[16] If the link between territorial disputes and lower than expected bilateral trade is spurious, the common cause could be nationalism.

Since so much of the literature suggests its importance in other contexts, I control for the possibility that certain regime types are simply more likely to enjoy cordial bilateral relations than are others. More democratic countries may simply tend to be more liberal economically and may very well have more intense bilateral trading relationships. I use a dichotomous indicator for a democratic pair – coded 1 when *both* countries score above 5 for democratic governance on the Polity scale of −10 (low) to 10 (high). Nationalist governments might be more willing to exploit and even manipulate public sentiments to revive dormant disputes as well as to protect domestic producers from international trade competition. Controlling for these regime characteristics should therefore reduce the possibility that we are incorrectly attributing a causal impact to settled international borders.

A third set of variables controls for the possibility that the uncertainty that I argue follows from unsettled boundaries is actually domestic in origin. After all, a host of internal conditions could in theory discourage economic actors from making the investments necessary for profitable bilateral trade. My argument rests on the uncertainty generated by the unsettled border itself. I therefore control for two sources of domestic uncertainty: domestic armed violence and domestic political instability. Their inclusion raises the probability that a theory of international borders as uncertainty-reducing institutions has some empirical traction.

Since, as described below, a fixed-effects model is used, over-time variance in these explanatory variables is important. Appendix 2 indicates how the incidence of military disputes, the regime type of each pair, and the level of overall trade openness have varied for each country-pair over time (see Appendix 1 for all data measures and sources).

Case selection and estimation methods

These ideas are tested using territorial disputes from Latin America between 1964 and 2000. This region of nearly half a billion people affords a good opportunity to assess claims about the importance of settled borders for trade. Most importantly, it is a region in which the boundary conditions of our theory are likely to hold. That is, evidence suggests that for the most part governments in this region are likely to value trade, as past experiments with import substitution have been set aside and conscious efforts over the last two decades to develop regional trade through such institutions as Mercosur, the Andean Pact, and the Central American Common Market have accelerated. Figure 10.1 illustrates the growth in share of GDP in Latin American that is traded intra-regionally and with the rest of the world.

Focusing on Latin America also holds some variables constant: language, culture, and highly charged ethnic conflicts are not likely to be at play in border and trade relations in this region. This region is also appropriate because of its long history of political independence. Unlike areas which have more recently been under foreign administration, trade is less likely in Latin America to be distorted by colonialism. More

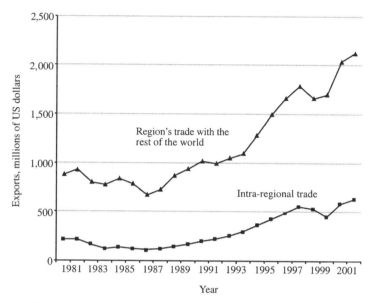

Figure 10.1. Latin American and Caribbean trade with the rest of the world.

generally, there are good reasons to believe that regions are highly heterogeneous and that to pool them at this point in our research would be premature. While border disputes are likely to distort trade generally, the most appropriate model is very likely to differ across regions.

The choice of Latin America does provide a good degree of variance with respect to territorial disputes across countries. For the time period examined here,[17] twenty-three contiguous country-pairs have had no territorial disputes, eight country-pairs have settled their disputes,[18] three are still disputing,[19] and one dispute seems to have developed during the period of observation.[20] Finally, because we are only interested in those cases in which there is a *possibility* of a territorial dispute, I focus here on contiguous country-pairs, with one exception for a case regarding islands involving noncontiguous countries.[21]

Time-series cross-sectional data are used for the years 1960–2000 for thirty-six country-pairs (where possible),[22] and the data are analyzed using ordinary least squares and robust standard errors for clustered samples.[23] Because we are analyzing time series, autocorrelation is a concern, and to address this issue I present models with and without a lagged dependent variable for easy comparison. There are strong theoretical reasons for using a fixed effects model: certainly, we are offering a quite spare model of bilateral trade, and have explicitly decided to set aside a number of plausible influences on bilateral trade unique to each pair.[24] Country-pair dummies absorb many of the crucial aspects of geography (mountains, waterways, Amazonian jungle) that obviously influence the transactions costs of transportation, but are not picked up in our distance measure. These dummies are also likely to absorb other disturbances or dislocations of a domestic nature that affect demand and production (civil conflicts, for example). In all of the specifications below country-pair dummies are included and most are highly significant, but are not reported.[25]

Findings

The results of the analysis are reported in Tables 10.1a and 10.1b, and 10.2. Tables 10.1a and b differ by the inclusion of a lagged dependent variable in the latter. The two primary elements of the gravity model, distance and size of economy, work precisely as anticipated: distance reduces trade and the combined economic size of the trading partners increases it. The most important result for our purposes, however, is that the existence of a territorial dispute almost certainly puts a serious drag on bilateral trading relations. Note that the strong negative effect of disputing holds for all models in Tables 10.1a and b. The results associated with territorial disputes are always negative and twice statistically significant even when a lagged dependent variable is included (Table 10.1b).

For the period as a whole, the effect of disputing is to reduce bilateral trade by about 36 percent each year the dispute is not settled.[26] For Peru and Ecuador, Model 1 estimates an average loss of about $35 million in forgone bilateral trade for every year those two countries continued to dispute their borders. More dramatically, the model estimates that Argentina and Chile lost potentially an average of some $326 million per year until their (multiple) territorial disputes were settled in 1995.

In order to give a clearer idea of the estimated impact of territorial disputes on trade for particular country-pairs at particular points in time, Table 10.2 shows what effect our most basic model (Model 5 Table 10.1a) would expect a territorial dispute to have had on trade during our period of observation.[27] Each of the country-pairs in this table had an unresolved dispute over territory during the period under observation. Estimates of bilateral trade assuming disputes compared with no disputes are presented first. The difference between these estimates represents forgone bilateral trade attributed by this model to disputes over territory. This can be compared with actual observed trade averages for both disputed and undisputed years.

Table 10.1a. *The effect of territorial disputes on bilateral trade volume: result of a fixed effects gravity model; coefficients (robust standard errors)*

Explanatory variables	Model 1 Basic gravity	Model 2 Openness controls	Model 3 Dyadic controls	Model 4 Uncertainty controls[†]	Model 5 Reduced form
Log of combined GDP	2.62***(.451)	2.61***(.475)	2.59***(.460)	1.91***(.506)	2.55***(.467)
Log of distance between capitals	-.830***(.185)	-.834***(.190)	-.617***(.156)	-.859***(.198)	-.632***(.158)
Territorial dispute	**-.400***(.202)	**-.417***(.208)	**-.512****(.213)	**-.507****(.208)	**-.457****(.209)
Year	.015(.018)	.011(.019)	.014(.018)	.028*(.014)	.011(.019)
Alternative explanations for trade openness:					
General trade openness	—	.240*(.138)	—	—	.283**(.130)
Preferential trade arrangement	—	.135(.164)	—	—	—
Alternative explanations for the nature of bilateral relations:					
Militarized interstate dispute	—	—	.171(.158)	—	—
Joint democracy	—	—	-.165(.189)	—	—
Policy affinity	—	.—	1.24*(.638)	—	1.25*(.697)
Regime claims	—	—	-.065(.259)	—	—
Alternative explanations for uncertainty:					
Armed domestic conflict	—		—	-.094	—
Institutional instability	—		—	-.023	—
Number of obs.	1329	1272	1300	807	1260
R-squared	.889	.887	.887	.901	.888

Notes: ***significant at .01 level
**significant at .05 level
*significant at .10 level
[†] Inclusion of instability reduces observations significantly (data only go back to 1976). If instability is removed and only domestic armed conflict included, the territorial dispute coefficient is -.407 (p = .054), and armed conflict remains insignificant (N = 1329).

Table 10.1b. *The effect of territorial disputes on bilateral trade: result of a lagged dependent variable fixed effects gravity model; coefficients (robust standard errors)*

Explanatory variables	Model 1	Model 2	Model 3	Model 4	Model 5
Log of combined GDP	.795*** (.150)	.699*** (.157)	.766*** (.149)	1.08*** (.267)	.694*** (.158)
Log of distance between capitals	-.833*** (.150)	-.253*** (.050)	-.261*** (.054)	-.501*** (.115)	-.254*** (.050)
Territorial dispute	-.125* (.069)	-.096 (.071)	-.154* (.072)	-.117 (.101)	-.084 (.071)
Lagged log of bilateral trade	.723*** (.053)	.715*** (.058)	.732*** (.053)	.643*** (.089)	.717*** (.055)
General trade openness	—	.190*** (.058)	—	—	.189*** (.058)
Preferential trade arrangement	—	.100** (.050)	—	—	.097* (.050)
Militarized interstate dispute	—	—	-.212* (.117)	—	-.185 (.131)
Joint democracy	—	—	-.051 (.073)	—	—
Policy affinity	—	—	.040 (.173)	—	—
Regime claims	—	—	-.117 (.090)	—	—
Armed domestic conflict	—	—	—	-.049 (.065)	—
Institutional instability	—	—	—	-.053 (.045)	—
Number of obs.	1315	1260	1290	803	1260
R-squared	.953	.952	.952	.945	.952

Notes: ***significant at .01 level
**significant at .05 level
*significant at .10 level
† Inclusion of instability reduces observations significantly (data only go back to 1976). If instability is removed and only domestic armed conflict included, the territorial dispute coefficient is -.121 (p =. 085), and armed conflict remains insignificant (N = 1315).

Table 10.2. *Estimated effects of territorial disputes on trade, 1967–2000[#] (yearly averages and cumulative totals, millions of US dollars)*

	Date settled	Estimated average yearly trade		Estimated cumulative impact of disputing	Actual average yearly trade	
		Dispute	No dispute		Dispute	No dispute
Argentina–Uruguay	1974	154.51	242.32	614.67	*33.6*	*506.50*
El Salvador–Honduras	1992	52.30	82.03	718.25	*12.96*	*138.70*
Argentina–Chile	1995	573.54	899.49	9126.60	*501.55*	*2730.44*
Brazil–Uruguay	1995	440.15	690.29	7003.92	*395.51*	*1550.67*
Guyana–Suriname	1995	1.38	2.18	15.20	*1.46*	*3.16*
Bolivia–Chile	1996	40.12	62.92	663.32	*43.84*	*174.70*
Ecuador–Peru	1998	59.21	92.86	1043.15	*74.94*	*182.67*
Belize–Guatemala	unsettled	2.29	3.59	23.40	*4.96*	*1.10*
Colombia–Nicaragua	unsettled	4.88	7.66	50.04	*8.90*	*2.75*
Guyana–Venezuela	unsettled	32.67	51.24	603.8	*22.52*	*—*

Notes: [#] Estimates calculated based on Table 10.1a, Model 5.

The final column shows how much bilateral trade may have been reduced for each country-pair for the period as a whole. When we cumulate the effects of disputing territory between Argentina and Chile for the period under observation, for example, the total bilateral trade forgone (1967–94) is estimated to total over $9 billion. The cumulative total for Ecuador and Peru is estimated to be over a billion dollars. To put these quantities in perspective, this is more than a third of Ecuador's and about a sixth of Peru's total overseas development assistance received during the same period.[28]

In most cases, country-pairs traded less on average while disputing over territory than our model predicts, and more on average than our prediction once the dispute was settled. Clearly, there is more volatility in trade than this spare model is able to detect. The model does a better job predicting the level of bilateral trade under disputes than for dispute-free years, because of the greater volatility and the smaller number of data points for dispute-free years among these pairs. Actual trade figures between Colombia–Nicaragua and Belize–Guatemala go against expect-ations because they begin the period without disputes, but conclude under the cloud of territorial contestation. A few partners have managed to maintain high trade levels in spite of their disputes. Ecuador and Peru, for example, had levels of actual trade that were above those predicted

Colombia and Nicaragua

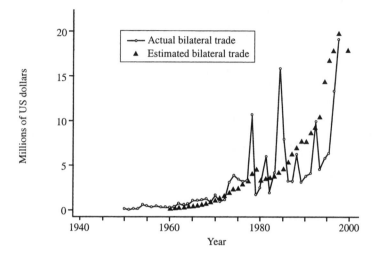

Ecuador and Peru

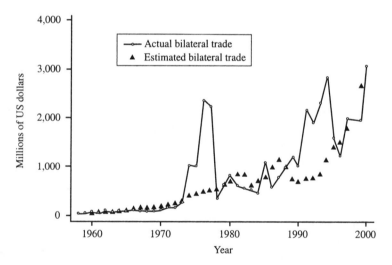

Argentina and Uruguay

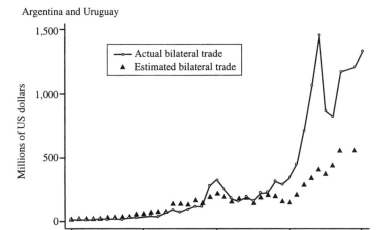

Argentina and Chile

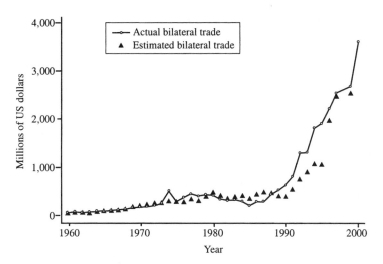

Figure 10.2. Comparison of estimated and actual trade.

under both conditions by Model 5. Overall, however, the table shows how costly it has been to bilateral economic relations – in terms of lost economic opportunities – for Latin American countries to actively contest their boundaries.

Figure 10.2 takes a closer look at how the estimations of Model 5 square with reality. It plots actual versus predicted bilateral trade for four country-pairs based on Model 5. In the case of Colombia and Nicaragua, the model simply could not cope with the extreme volatility in trade over the last two decades. Ecuador and Peru have had two distinct spikes in their trade that the model misses. We can see actual trade tumble in 1995, though, which is what we would expect with the deterioration that year in relations around the border. In the case of Argentina and Uruguay, we see actual trade trend upward in the 1990s in what is likely the effect of Mercosur (though the effects of preferential trade agreements could not generally be detected without a lagged dependent variable; compare Model 5 across both tables). Nonetheless, trade does clearly pick up after 1974 – the year these countries' territorial claims were resolved. Finally, the model does extremely well predicting the actual trade of Argentina and Chile. The 1990s have been a boom period for bilateral economic relations between these two erstwhile territorial competitors.

It is possible that these results are simply a function of countries' developmental strategies rather than the consequence of an open diplomatic wound involving territory. Bilateral trade might be low because of a general commitment to import substitution or a policy of self-sufficiency. To account for this possibility, Models 2 and 5 include a measure of general openness. Unsurprisingly, the pairs' general export orientation is positively reflected in higher bilateral trade levels and trade increases; the latter effect is especially convincing in models containing a lagged dependent variable (Models 2 and 5). But the important observation for our purposes is that overall trade orientation does not wash out the bilateral effects of disputing; in fact in Table 10.1a, its inclusion enhances them somewhat. Model 2, Table 10.1a, also indicates that bilateral trade levels have not been significantly affected by preferential trade arrangements: the coefficient is statistically insignificant and the impact of disputing is unaffected. Preferential trade agreements probably have contributed to bilateral trade growth however, as this variable is statistically significant when a lagged dependent variable is included (Models 2 and 5, Table 10.1b).

Nor is there much consistent evidence that the uncertainty I am attributing to unsettled borders is essentially attributable to strained underlying bilateral relations. Models 3 and 5 (Table 10.1a) show that while highly coherent positional affinities on foreign affairs within a dyad has a positive effect on trade levels, the basic finding with respect to territorial disputes is unaffected, possibly even strengthened. Controlling for regime claims had no impact on trade. Nor are regime type effects significant. It is highly unlikely that bilateral trade can be explained by processes of democratization and regime liberalization in the region. Joint democracy – a condition we might have associated with economic liberalization – is unlikely to impact bilateral trade, according to these data (Model 3 both tables).[29] Indeed, in every test, joint democracy seemed to be associated with less bilateral trade, although the results are never statistically significant. The results regarding nationalist regimes were never statistically significant and since the use of this variable eliminated observations prior to 1975 I dropped this control from the analysis.

What is most fascinating about the effect of disputing territory is that it persists even when controlling for actual militarized disputes. Model 3 (both tables) Controls for the active threat, show, or use of force between the countries of a pair, and this variable has no significant impact on bilateral trade levels for these countries in this time period, though it may slow trade growth (Table 10.1b).[30] Of course, the actual number of militarized disputes between Latin American countries during this time period is relatively small (see Appendix 2). Still, these results are extremely interesting for our theory of borders: beyond any damage done by the actual or imminent use of military force, the uncertainties surrounding border disputes continue to cumulate opportunity costs in terms of forgone bilateral trade. Whether or not foreign relations come to blows, trade is diminished by the exertion of contradictory sovereignty claims over the territory of a trading partner. This brings us closer to isolating the effect of territorial uncertainty *itself* on economic opportunity losses that cumulate over time and put a drag on the economy.

Finally, because globalization has tended to trend upward over the course of the postwar years, it would seem appropriate to control for the passage of time on bilateral trade. Surprisingly, including a variable to capture time had no significant effect on any of the variables in the analysis, nor was it significant in explaining bilateral trade (with a partial exception in Model 4, Table 10.1a). This raises our confidence that we are capturing the real effects of disputing and not simply time-related globalization trends. A check for robustness to outliers found that removing one country-pair from the sample at a time had no significant impact on the results of Model 5.[31]

Do territorial disputes have a constant effect on trade over time? One possibility is that as long as governments do not act *forcibly* to stake their claims, economic actors become adjusted to the ambient level of uncertainty and develop economic links to the best of their ability under the tenuous circumstances. Informal norms to "agree to disagree" may develop, effectively reducing the impact of the formal dispute on trade.

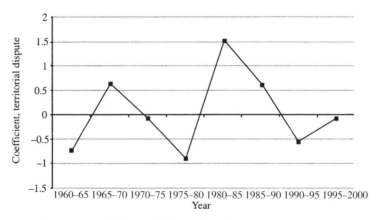

Figure 10.3. Estimated effects of territorial disputes on trade, by half-decade.

If this is the case, we should see a trend upward in the coefficient for territorial disputes over time. Figure 10.3 displays the coefficients estimated separately for five-year periods using the specification in Model 5 (Table 10.1a).[32] These five-year cross-sections produce volatile estimates (a few of which are not statistically significant) of the effects of disputing. While this period analysis returns both negative and positive coefficients, there is no clear trend in these coefficients over time. Five periods had negative coefficients (four of which were statistically significant) and three periods had positive coefficients (one of which was highly statistically significant). It is not easy to conclude that there has been a secular change in the relationship between territorial disputes and bilateral trade over the last forty years.

Finally, it is reasonable to ask whether territorial disputes have resulted in lost or merely diverted trade. If territorial disputes have simply resulted in trade diversion, then we would expect disputes to have positive effects in countries *other than those whose borders are under dispute*. As a first cut, we can assume that trade that might have taken place with a neighboring country, but for a territorial dispute, has been diverted to other countries in the region. Table 10.3 explores this hypothesis in two ways. First, it examines the (weighted) effect of a territorial dispute on all countries within the region with the exception of the disputing pair itself. If diversion is taking place we should expect these weighted disputes to have a *positive* impact on non-disputing countries.

Table 10.3. *Trade forgone or trade diversion? The effect of territorial disputes on bilateral trade with non-disputing countries (includes country-pair fixed effects, not reported)*

Explanatory variables	Model 1a	Model 1b (Lagged d.v.)	Model 2a	Model 2b (Lagged d.v.)
Log of combined GDP	2.71** (1.02)	.676** (.314)	2.79*** (.709)	.766*** (.244)
Log of distance between capitals	-1.71 (1.36)	-.390 (.341)	-2.05** (.955)	-.478* (.238)
General trade openness	.043 (.181)	.102** (.050)	.109 (.163)	.132*** (.048)
Military dispute	-.021 (.403)	-.361*** (.080)	.083 (.121)	.392*** (.047)
Territorial dispute	-.420 (.290)	-.122* (.054)	-.401 (.257)	-.114 (.112)
Cumulative weighted disputes elsewhere			-.00087 (.0017)	-.00057 (.00046)
Argentina–Chile, Bolivia–Chile	.003 (.003)	.010** (.004)	—	—
Argentina–Uruguay	-.022 (.009)	-.006 (.004)	—	—
Belize–Guatemala	-.007 (.008)	-.009** (.004)	—	—
Brazil–Uruguay	.011 (.009)	.005 (.004)	—	—
Colombia–Nicaragua	.009 (.005)	.002 (.003)	—	—
Ecuador–Peru	.002 (.003)	.004* (.002)	—	—
El Salvador–Honduras	.010* (.006)	.0002 (.002)	—	—
Guyana–Suriname	-.0004 (.007)	-.010*** (.194)	—	—
Guyana–Venezuela	.001 (.014)	.004 (.005)	—	—
Honduras–Nicaragua	.001 (.008)	.001 (.005)	—	—
Lagged log of trade		.732*** (.070)		.720*** (.070)
No. of obs.	925	925	925	916
R-squared	.884	.950	.881	.949

Notes: ***significant at .01 level
**significant at .05 level
*significant at .10 level

The first two columns of Table 10.3 contain little support for the diversion hypothesis. There are only two disputes that plausibly might have resulted in some trade diversion, according to these results. The first involves Chile's border resolutions with both Argentina and Bolivia. (Both of these were resolved in 1995, and they are analytically impossible to distinguish in this model.[33]) Model 1b, using a lagged dependent variable, suggests that trade to other countries in the region may have grown faster when these Chilean borders were under dispute than once they were resolved. The Peru–Ecuador conflict may also have resulted in some trade diversion to the rest of the region, resulting in slower trade growth elsewhere once this dispute was resolved. Nonetheless, it is difficult to find any cumulative effect of trade diversion on balance. Model 2 (a and b) shows that a cumulative measure of territorial disputes (weighted by log of GDP) had no systematic effect on countries that were not party to those disputes.

Some plausible examples

These numbers may sound abstract, but there is good evidence that governments depress trade by pressing their territorial claims. For example, while regional trade was growing, the dispute between Ecuador and Peru stunted bilateral economic relations significantly: Peru exported more to Bolivia than to Ecuador ($166 million compared with $147 million between 1992 and 1994), despite the fact that Ecuador's gross domestic product is almost three times the size of Bolivia's. Moreover, Ecuador bought $684 million worth of exports from Colombia between 1992 and 1994, and only $147 million from Peru, even though Peru's economy is only slightly smaller than Colombia's.[34] The territorial dispute between these two states likely contributed to this distorted trade relationship.

Ecuador and Peru's approach to the resolution of their conflict in 1998 demonstrates the perceived economic value of settlement. The resolution of this dispute led to a treaty on trade and navigation,[35] a liberalized border regime,[36] programs for binational border development projects,[37] and a memorandum of understanding on tourism cooperation (Simmons 2005). The United States, as one of four guarantor states, was actively involved in facilitating the 1998 peace accord between Peru and Ecuador and remains committed to its implementation, having pledged $40 million to the Peru–Ecuador border integration project.[38] While not on track to meet the $6 billion bilateral trade goal announced by the two countries' presidents in 1998,[39] bilateral trade between these two countries has soared from $119 million in 1995 (the year of active hostilities at the border) to $232 million in 2000.[40]

Meanwhile, those governments that continue to dispute their borders continue to lose out on economic opportunities. In Central America, the Common Market arrangement collapsed when Honduras and El Salvador went to war over territorial issues in 1969. Integration efforts in the region weakened due to the renewed severity in the 1990s of Central American territorial disputes. Both Guyana and Belize suffer from deterred investment in their countries, largely owing to the uncertainty surrounding the territorial claims of Venezuela and Guatemala, respectively. In 2000 for example, Guyana suffered a direct economic loss when Beal Aerospace Technologies canceled its planned development project because of Venezuelan threats on Guyana were the project to go forward (Serbin 2001).[41] Investment in Guyana further suffered that year when Venezuela commenced oil exploration in the controversial offshore exclusive economic zone, in retaliation for Guyana's granting of licenses to Exxon and Century for oil exploration in the disputed Essequibo region.[42] Venezuela's effort to punish Guyana by excluding it from preferential access to Venezuelan oil has only been avoided by the intercession of CARICOM members.[43] The ongoing dispute between Nicaragua and Colombia provides another example of institutional uncertainty for transnational business relations. In December 1999, according to the United States Trade Representative, Nicaragua imposed a punitive 35 percent tariff on all goods from Honduras and Colombia as a retaliatory measure for Honduras' signing of a maritime border delineation agreement with Colombia, which Nicaragua claims infringes on its territory.[44] These are hardly the conditions under which traders and investors feel secure in developing external economic relations.

Conclusions

Border disputes have led to serious economic opportunity costs, even in cases where trade partners have never exchanged an explicit military threat. Notwithstanding a few excruciating exceptions, far from living in a "borderless" world, we live for the most part in a *well-bordered world*; one in which humans have accepted the boundaries of jurisdiction and sovereignty and have gone on to trade, invest, travel, and communicate across well-established political jurisdictions. The central claim of this chapter is that we are able to do these things precisely where governments have accepted as settled the first-order question of who is formally sovereign over what geographical space. The most permeable political boundaries in the world tend to be those that are taken for granted by both of the bordering political authorities, as well as by other governments in the region. The Canadian–US border comes to mind, as do borders between the countries of Western Europe. The razor wire separating Israeli and Palestinian settlements provides a tragic contrary example. David Newman's contribution to this volume reminds us that in many cases territorial attachments remain profound and, effectively, non-negotiable.

Nonetheless, political boundaries are human institutions. Just as people who are in love in most modern cultures tend to get married (which provides them with a set of clearly defined rights that love outside of marriage does not), countries who want to benefit fully from cordial relations settle their territorial disputes and go on to enjoy *joint gains* from the set of recognized rights that exclusive jurisdiction affords. I have framed these joint gains in this research in terms of lost trading opportunities. But they include as well the economic joint gains of investment, travel, tourism, as well as a host of positive externalities associated with friendly bilateral diplomatic relations with a neighbor. Of course, once territorial disputes turn violent the human suffering and the costs associated with the use of military force mount and potentially create humanitarian crises that far outweigh the economic considerations analyzed here. But I have been at pains to demonstrate that *even non-military disputes over territory* – by virtue of the uncertainty and ill will they sow – entail costs that have rarely been explicitly considered.

Nor are the results I have attributed to territorial disputes likely to be a mere reflection of uncooperative bilateral relations that have led both to disputing and to underdeveloped trade. One advantage of the fixed country-pair effects model is its ability to control for constant features of the dyad that otherwise might lead to spurious conclusions about the border settlement–trade link discussed here. In addition, several models controlled for conditions that could reflect changes in the general cordiality of the bilateral relationship over time (the rise and fall of nationalist governments, conditions of joint democracy, challenges to the legitimacy of governance, changes in the compatibility of outlook with respect to foreign affairs generally). These controls ameliorate (but of course do not eliminate) the possibility of spurious correlation.

A simple gravity model of bilateral trade suggests that the costs associated with border disputes are likely to be significant. Ecuador and Peru likely missed out on hundreds of millions of dollars of bilateral trade owing to their long-running controversy over a large tract of undeveloped Amazonian jungle. The same can be said for Argentina and Chile with their multiple disputes over the Beagle Channel, Patagonia, and the Ice Fields. A fraction of these flows may have been diverted to other regional trade partners; nonetheless, case studies suggest that in negotiating a settlement leaders in these countries were indeed cognizant of these costs, and viewed them as one reason for hastening agreement over the legitimate location of the international border (Simmons 1999). Jorge Dominguez has argued that in Latin America, the greater the developmental objective of the government, the more likely it will engage in a grand strategy that ends in the resolution of territorial disputes (Dominguez 2001). Colombia and Nicaragua are two countries that would do well to pursue such a strategy, as they have lost a total estimated $50 million in bilateral trade since their dispute over a cluster of Caribbean islands erupted in 1980. Perhaps this is one reason Nicaragua has recently decided to initiate settlement proceedings at the International Court of Justice.

The theoretical implications of these findings are profound. Realist lenses have provided the focus for the mainstream study of territorial disputes and their resolution in the field of international relations. Territory is viewed in zero-sum terms, and theories about peace and conflict, disputation and resolution have revolved around traditional problems of dividing the territory, its strategic importance, its resource endowment, and other power considerations. Very few studies have considered the possibility of joint gains, and none have considered joint gains beyond joint natural resource exploitation.

Institutionalist theory provides a natural way to think about political boundaries. Governments create them and accept them as legitimate in order to overcome uncertainty, high transactions costs, and other negative externalities that flow from contentious territorial claims. Such a paradigm shift would lead us to investigate the extent to which growing opportunity costs (alongside more traditional considerations) provide an impetus for governments to settle their disputes, even turning at times, contrary to realist expectations, to authoritative third parties to render legally binding rulings (Simmons 2002). As regional trade intensifies, governments should be increasingly willing to settle their territorial disputes so as not to get left behind as the regional integration train pulls away from the station. Theories of the settlement of territorial claims have much to gain from the institutional literature on cooperation generally.

Appendix 1: Data

Dependent Variable

Bilateral trade. The logged sum of imports into Country A originating from Country B plus the sum of imports into Country B originating from Country A, in millions of US dollars. *Source:* International Monetary Fund, *Direction of Trade Statistics*, various years.

Explanatory Variables

Combined GDP. The log of the sum of gross domestic product of Country A and Country B, in millions of US dollars. *Source:* World Bank, *World Development Indicators*, at http:devdata. worldbank.org.ezp2.harvard.edu./dataonline/.

Distance between capitals. The log of the distance in kilometers between capital cities. Because it is not Brazil's major city, Brasilia was replaced with Rio de Janeiro. *Source:* http://www. indo.com/distance/index.html.

Territorial dispute. Whether (1) or not (0) incompatible claims over territory are made by government officials. For a discussion of the criteria see text and footnote 12. *Source:* Huth 1996. Updates to these cases were made using newspaper reports and various country-specific sources.

Military dispute. Whether (1) or not (0) either government of the disputing pair engaged in the threat or use of force against the other member of the pair. *Source:* Militarized interstate disputes (MIDs) data set.

Year. Calendar year.

Joint democracy. Whether (1) or not (0) *both* countries in the pair score above a 5 on the polity score. Range: 10 (highly democratic) to −10 (completely non-democratic). *Source:* Polity IV data set.

General trade openness. Log of the product of Country A's and Country B's total imports and exports as a proportion of each country's GDP. *Source:* World Bank, *World Development Indicators*.

PTA membership. Coded 1 if both countries in the pair are members of the same PTA, 0 otherwise. *Sources:* WTO website (http: www. wto.org) and http://www.sice.oas.org.

Affinity index. Index of the cohesion for each country-pair year on UN General Assembly votes. The index ranges from a low of 0 to a high of 1. *Source:* Erik Gartzke and Dong-Joon Jo, "The Affinity of Nations Index, 1946–1996," available at http://www.columbia.edu/~eg589/datasets.htm. The average from the preceding year was used to bring the data up to 2000.

Nationalist government. Coded 1 if the party of the chief executive was nationalist, 0 otherwise. *Source:* World Bank.

Regime claims. Case is coded 1 if there is at least one regime claim in a given year, 0 otherwise. A regime-based claim involves explicit contention between two or more states over a regime's control of the governing apparatus of one of the states. Essentially, one government issues a verbal challenge to the other state's regime, calling for its removal. Official representatives of the state's government must support the regime claim – an unambiguous statement calling for the removal of another regime. See Tures 2000. *Source:* Obtained from Paul Hensel's website: http://garnet.acns.fsu.edu/~phensel/icowdata.html#territory. Accessed 10 December 2003.

Appendix 2: *Explanatory variables: militarized disputes, joint democracy dates and general trade openness*

Country-pair	Militarized dispute	Joint democracy dates		General trade openness within each country-pair		
		Polity cut-off 5:	Polity cut-off 7:	Mean	Std.Dev.	Range
Argentina–UK	1976, 1982	1973–75; 1983–2000	1983–88	6.66	.29	6.12–7.19
Argentina–Chile	1964–65, 1967–68, 1977–81	1990–2000	—	6.57	.48	5.67–7.24
Bolivia–Chile		1989–2000	1989–98	7.83	.26	7.18–8.27
Brazil–Colombia		1985–2000	1988–94; 1999–2000	6.26	.25	5.60–6.88
Colombia–Ecuador		1979–2000	1979–94; 1999–2000	7.34	.32	6.70–8.04
El Salvador–Guatemala		1996–2000	—	7.72	.31	7.17–8.25
Belize–Guatemala		1996–2000	1996–98	8.43	.20	7.91–8.67
Dominican Rep.–Haiti		1990; 1996–2000	—	7.61	.32	7.04–8.16
El Salvador–Honduras	1976	1984; 1989–2000	—	8.27	.34	7.62–8.84
Guatemala–Honduras		1996–2000	—	7.93	.35	7.21–8.46
Guatemala–Mexico		1997–2000	—	7.04	.52	6.34–8.04
Belize–Mexico		1997–2000	—	8.40	.31	7.95–8.88
Colombia–Nicaragua		1990–2000	1999–2000	7.62	.46	6.64–8.54
Costa Rica–Nicaragua		1990–2000	1995–2000	8.48	.46	7.45–9.42
Honduras–Nicaragua		1990–2000	—	8.44	.55	7.11–9.43
Colombia–Panama		1989–2000	1989–94	7.79	.18	7.44–8.06
Costa Rica–Panama		1989–2000	1989–98	8.66	.20	8.35–9.05
Argentina–Paraguay		1992–2000	—	6.57	.57	5.77–7.44
Bolivia–Paraguay		1992–2000	—	7.83	.31	7.24–8.36
Brazil–Paraguay		1992–2000	—	6.67	.46	5.77–7.41
Bolivia–Peru		1982–91	1990–91	7.49	.27	6.94–8.04
Brazil–Peru		1985–91	1990–91	6.33	.24	5.79–6.75
Chile–Peru		1989–91	1990–91	7.34	.33	6.50–7.85
Colombia–Peru		1980–91	1990–91	6.93	.16	6.56–7.27

Appendix 2: (cont.)

Country-pair	Militarized dispute	Joint democracy dates[#]		General trade openness within each country-pair		
		Polity cut-off 5:	Polity cut-off 7:	Mean	Stnd.Dev.	Range
Ecuador–Peru	1977–78, 1981, 1995	1980–91	1990–91	7.41	.23	7.01–7.82
Argentina–Uruguay	1969, 1973	1985–2000	1985–88	6.57	.29	5.97–7.13
Brazil–Uruguay		1985–2000	1988–2000	6.67	.24	6.13–7.10
Brazil–Venezuela		1985–2000	1988–98	6.67	.24	6.13–7.10
Colombia–Venezuela		1966–2000	1974–94	7.27	.26	6.59–7.65
Guyana–Venezuela	1966, 1969–70, 1976, 1981–81	1992–2000	2000	8.86	.41	8.13–9.66
Brazil–Guyana		1992–2000	2000	6.42	.32	5.76–6.94
Brazil–Suriname		1985–2000	1988–2000	7.09	.616	5.37–8.09
Guyana–Suriname	1976, 1978	1992–2000	2000	7.86	.59	6.05–8.54
Argentina–Bolivia		1983–2000	1983–88	6.72	2.07	6.29–7.11
Argentina–Brazil		1985–2000	1988, 2000	5.56	.31	4.97–6.24
Bolivia–Brazil		1985–2000	1988–2000	6.82	.21	6.40–7.43

NOTES

1 These issues were, to my knowledge, first explored empirically by Albert Hahn in "Borders, Conflict, and Money: The Effect of Territorial Disputes on Bilateral Trade from 1950 to 1990." MA thesis, UC Berkeley Department of Political Science, 2000.
2 Morgenthau was also willing to recognize the reduced importance of territory in the nuclear age (Biersteker 2002).
3 But see Barbieri and Levy 1999; Barbieri and Levy 2001.
4 Brian Pollins, for example, found that "importers (regardless of the level of analysis we choose) take account not only of price and quality of goods and services but of the place of origin of these products and the *political relationship between the importing and the exporting nation*" (Pollins 1989, 738). Pollins also notes that exporters are subject to the same considerations.
5 But see Carlile 1994.
6 Yarbrough and Yarbrough suggest that demands for sovereign control over territorial resources should be related to transactions costs. They argue that economic agents are likely to want to change international boundaries in order to reduce transactions costs by bringing resources under a single governance structure (Yarbrough and Yarbrough 1994).
7 This point has long been recognized by liberals such as Norman Angell (1911) who, on the eve of World War I, was highly skeptical of the idea that sovereign territorial acquisition would provide a basis for prosperity and influence (Angell 1911).
8 This point is made with respect to South Asia by Gupta (1997).
9 The effect of a territorial dispute on a country's total trade is not explicitly tested here. There is some possibility that disputes divert a portion of potential bilateral trade to third countries. Such diversion is not likely to absorb all of the potential trade between disputants, and in any case is not likely to be as efficient as trade between contiguous neighbors.
10 Certainly, other kinds of international disputes may also affect bilateral trade. Political or ideological disputes, such as that between the United States and Cuba, are also candidates for reducing trade. The effect of foreign policy posture on trade has been analyzed by Pollins (1989). The purpose here is to focus explicitly on territorial disputes as a way to motivate a theoretical re-orientation of international boundaries.
11 When trade is zero, the value zero was kept instead of allowing it to fall out after the log function.
12 Huth (1996, 23) defines the end of a dispute as:

  a The occupation and assumption of control over disputed territory by the challenger being formally recognized by the target in a treaty, an international agreement, or in an official statement by the political leadership of the target.
  b The signing of a bilateral agreement with a target or an official statement by the challenger in which its territorial claims are either renounced or are satisfied with a compromise settlement.
  c The challenger agreeing to abide by a ruling issued by the ICJ [International Court of Justice] or an international arbitration panel.

13 On the value of formal arrangements (usually treaties) for signaling an intention to comply, see Abbott and Snidal 2000; Lipson 1991.

14 There is a mild positive correlation between territorial disputes and military disputes of .258 in this data set.

15 Erik Gartzke and Dong-Joon Jo, "The Affinity of Nations Index, 1946–1996." Available at http://www.columbia.edu/~eg589/datasets.htm.

16 Tests including nationalist governments drop all observations prior to 1975.

17 Reliable GDP data – essential for the gravity model – are difficult to assemble in a consistent time series for some of these countries prior to the early 1960s.

18 Honduras and Nicaragua (1960), El Salvador and Honduras (1992), Argentina and Uruguay (1973), Guyana and Suriname (1994), Brazil and Uruguay (1994), Argentina and Chile (1995), Bolivia and Chile (1995), and Ecuador and Peru (1998).

19 Belize and Guatemala, Guyana and Venezuela, and Colombia and Nicaragua.

20 The dispute between Nicaragua and Colombia seems to have opened in 1980 with Nicaragua's assertion of a claim to the islands of Providencia, San Andres, and Santa Catalina, which are claimed also by Colombia.

21 The noncontiguous case is that of Colombia and Nicaragua. The use of contiguous pairs necessitates the use of distance between capitals as our measure of distance. In Brazil's case, Rio de Janeiro is used instead of Brasilia.

22 The following countries do not enter the data set until the date of their independence: Guyana (1966), Suriname (1975), and Belize (1981).

23 Robust to deviations from ordinary assumptions of independent, identically distributed errors. The purpose is to adjust standard errors taking into account non-independent observations within country-pairs.

24 For a discussion of the use of fixed effects, see Green et al. 2001.

25 Full results including coefficients on country-pair dummies are available from the author upon request.

26 Using the coefficient for logged bilateral trade in Model 5, Table 10.1a, this is calculated as $1 - e^{-.45}$.

27 I choose to present the substantive results using Model 5, Table 10.1a because it returns a mid-range estimate of the impact of trade disputes.

28 Ecuador received about $2.83 billion and Peru about $6.1 billion in official overseas development assistance during the period of their territorial dispute. Figures are from the World Bank's *World Development Indicators* CD-ROM.

29 This result is robust to varying specifications of joint democracy. While the above results relate to a mutual cut-off point of 5 on the combined democracy–autocracy index (ranging from −10 to 10), a similar coefficient results from a mutual cut-off at 7 (−.123, with s.e. of .248).

30 Moreover, when military disputes are inserted into Model 1 and territorial disputes are removed, military disputes alone have no apparent effect on bilateral trade (coefficient .072, standard error .157). This raises our confidence further that the institutional uncertainty of a border conflict rather than military conflict per se puts a drag on trade.

31 Territorial disputes remained highly statistically significant in each case. The estimated coefficient ranged from a high of −.650 when Bolivia and

Chile were removed, to a high of −.412 when Guyana and Suriname were removed.

32 Using the coefficients from Model 2 produces substantially the same results.

33 As was Argentina's dispute with the United Kingdom over the Falkland Islands.

34 All figures are from the Inter-American Development Bank.

35 The two presidents signed a Trade and Navigation Treaty that spelled out the rights and responsibilities of both countries with respect to Ecuador's guaranteed (but nonsovereign) access to Amazonian shipping routes. This treaty begins by re-emphasizing all of Ecuador's rights as enumerated in Article 4 of the Protocol of Rio de Janiero (1942). Article 2 of the Trade and Navigation Treaty gives Ecuador explicit access to an (unnamed) river through Peruvian territory that will permit them to connect their shipping directly with the Amazon. The agreement also gives Ecuador the right to enjoy free land transit by the public access roads, and the use on a nondiscriminatory basis of dock services available as specified points on the river. Article 2 states that "These rights will be exercised freely, without cost, continuously and forever." Several articles in the Treaty provide for national treatment of Ecuadoran shipping and cargoes. In order to facilitate storage and transshipment, Article 22 provides for the creation for fifty years (renewable) of two "trade navigation centers" financed, constructed, operated, and administered by a private Ecuadoran firm, appointed by the Ecuadoran government, subject to Peruvian regulations. Article 24 provides that goods shipped through Peruvian territory (though not goods destined for Peru) are to pass duty free, while Article 35 reciprocally grants Most Favored Nation status. Finally, the Trade and Navigation Treaty contains provisions for the resolution of future disputes. It establishes an "Ecuadorian-Peruvian Trade and Navigation Commission," which is to be in charge of addressing controversies arising from the Treaty (Article 37). If the Commission cannot resolve any controversies arising from the agreement within sixty days, it is to be referred to the Ministries of Foreign Affairs of both countries, to be handled through diplomatic means (Article 38). For a summary and discussion of the Treaty, see http://www.asil.org/ilib/ilib0111.htm 02.

36 A new border regime was agreed in order to enhance commercial and tourist traffic, through the opening of new and more liberal border crossings. Presidential Act of Brasilia (1998), Arts. 12–15.

37 Title V of the Comprehensive Agreement signed in 1998 envisaged a ten-year plan, to be developed by a Bilateral Executive Board and an International Advisory Committee, to develop programs to encourage social, economic, and environmental infrastructure, as well as to promote private sector investment in these areas in the border regions (Arts. 18–20). A highway linking Mendez, Yaupi, and Borja – to be completed by 2005 – was for example considered a top priority (Art. 21). These projects are to be financed by direct contributions of the governments of Peru and Ecuador, a Bilateral Fund for Peace and Development, monies raised by an International Peru–Ecuador Financial Consulting Group, a Bilateral Group for the Promotion of Investment, "and others" (Art. 22). The agreement envisages support for the larger projects from the Inter-American Development Bank, the Andean

Development Corporation, specialized agencies within the UN system, and "governments of friendly countries" (Art. 28).

38 *CIA World Factbook* 2004, US Dept. of State Country Background Notes.
39 Robert Taylor, "Peru/ Ecuador: A Peaceful Year." *World Press Review*, January 2000, 18. See also Susana Madera, "Ecuador-Peru Peace Could Boost Trade to Six Billion Dollars Next Decade." EFE News Services, 25 October 1999.
40 International Monetary Fund, Direction of Trade Statistics.
41 Beal also announced that it was folding in that same year.
42 *Stabroek News* (Guyana), 6 August 2000. http://www.landofsixpeoples.com/gynewsjs.htm
43 Guyana has been able to benefit from Caracas Energy Cooperation Agreement (CECA) following agitation by its CARICOM partners and the Foreign Ministry. Guyana was initially excluded by Venezuela when it made the offer to the Caribbean Community. "Guyana/Venezuela Activate Energy Accord," *Stabroek News*, 30 November 2002.
44 See http://www.ustr.gov/html/2001_nicaragu.pdf.

Conclusion

Barbara F. Walter

One of the surprises in our increasingly globalized world is that the attachments to territory of individuals, ethnic groups, and governments have not appeared to weaken significantly. Governments have remained vigilant about the exact demarcation of their territorial boundaries even as goods and people move ever more seamlessly across these borders. Governments have also continued to fight for territory even as their wealth and security have become increasingly disconnected from it. Indonesia, for example, spent millions of dollars fighting to retain East Timor even though this was more than they could ever hope to recoup from any offshore oil reserves. And emigrants from places like Eritrea and Ireland continue to maintain close political and economic ties with their homelands even though many of them know they will never return. Territorial boundaries may have become more permeable, and the material and strategic value of land may have become less significant, but people's attachment to particular pieces of territory does not seem to have declined.

This paradox has been the focus of this volume. In the book, we have attempted to explain how territorial attachments are constructed, why they have remained so powerful in the face of an increasingly globalized world, and what effect continuing strong attachments may have on conflict. Each of the chapters has examined a different element of the inter-relationship between territoriality, globalization, and conflict, yet one common conclusion stands out. Territorial attachments and people's willingness to fight for territory appear to have much less to do with the material value of land and much more to do with the symbolic role it plays in constituting people's identities and providing a sense of security and belonging.

This suggests that the puzzle initially posed by the editors – the fact that territoriality has persisted in the face of an increasingly globalized world – may not be a puzzle at all. Globalization, at least defined in terms of greater economic integration and the greater movement of goods and capital across borders, should not have a significant effect

288

on the perceived value of territory if its value is derived primarily from its symbolic role in helping people define their identity and determine their immediate and intimate social relationships. One of the main contributions of this volume, therefore, is to carefully delineate what we mean by globalization, territoriality, and conflict and in the process determine the distinct effects of each. Only by separating these rather vague and abstract concepts into their component parts can we begin to trace the exact causal links that may exist between and among them, and begin to understand what is really going on.

The remaining chapter is divided into three parts. The first part examines the findings that have emerged from this project regarding the sources of territorial attachments and the effect globalization appears to have had on the value of territory over time. The second discusses what these findings suggest to scholars interested in territorial conflicts and to policymakers given the task of resolving or managing these conflicts. The final part identifies important questions left unanswered by this particular study and points to potentially new and productive avenues for future research.

The findings

Sources of territorial attachments

The chapters in the first part of the book carefully delineate some of the processes by which territorial attachments emerge and change. Goemans, Robbins, Newman, and Lyons are not of one mind about how attachments to these territories are constructed or why they persist, but they agree that these attachments serve very instrumental purposes. Territory is important, not so much because land contains important natural resources that can be translated into tangible assets, but because it plays the more important role of defining one's social, spiritual, and communal world.

According to Robbins, for example, the deep attachment to territory of the Urapmin of Papua New Guinea stemmed from two underlying sources. The first was a religion based on territorially rooted gods, where the worship of trees, rocks, and other physical features instilled a deep appreciation for the land. The second was a social system based on gift giving. Land was valuable, but only in so far as it housed one's gods and produced the goods necessary to build and sustain social connections within the group. Once the Urapmin embraced Pentecostal Christianity with its emphasis on the "non-physical, non-territorial . . . sense of community," land was no longer needed for religious grounding. And once the group's social circle expanded beyond its immediate members, the nature of the goods needed to trade and foster relationships also changed, further disconnecting them from the land. It was the Urapmin's unique religious beliefs, and the nature of their social ties, that made land valuable, not any of the land's tangible features.

Other groups develop a deep attachment to a particular piece of territory because it serves as a focal point around which individuals can organize for collective defense. According to Goemans, a particular border helps to delineate who is to be protected, what is to be protected, and who is responsible for providing that protection. Defining a group territorially serves to promote cohesion and overcome collective action problems that might otherwise arise when individuals are called to defend each other in a time of crisis. This does not mean that all territory and all borders will be equally valuable in the eyes of citizens and their governments. In fact, one of the puzzles that Goemans attempts to explain in his chapter is why governments fight so hard for some pieces of territory, but let other pieces go. Territory in this case is not valuable because it contains mountains or rivers that have strategic value per se, but because they represent natural focal points around which individuals can organize. The value is in the information these features provide, not in the material they may contain.

Territory can also serve a third, related purpose. One of the puzzles surrounding people's attachment to land is that it sometimes persists even after individuals have permanently left their homeland. In fact, diaspora communities that have fled a country because of war are notorious for refusing to compromise on issues related to the "homeland" and for steadfastly demanding that the original boundaries of this territory be preserved. During the lengthy conflict over Northern Ireland's political status, for example, Irish Americans were less willing to make concessions than the Irish themselves. The result was a longer, bloodier conflict.

Lyons addresses this puzzle in chapter 5, arguing that this almost fanatical attachment to the "homeland" serves an important social function for emigrants attempting to re-establish themselves in a new country. Having a common tie to the mother country, and in particular a common enemy against which to fight, helps to bring otherwise unconnected immigrants together. For Eritreans in the United States, for example, the fight for the territorially defined homeland of Eritrea serves as an important focal point around which the diaspora can mobilize. It is precisely because stateless migrants no longer have a state to defend their rights that they must create strong diaspora networks to do this for them. Mobilizing around a common connection to one's homeland, even if it is a homeland to which most members cannot or will not return, provides a sense of security and belonging in an otherwise foreign world.

But territorial attachments can also be created from the top down, by elites who have their own self-interested reasons for linking subjects to a particular piece of land. Both Goemans and Newman agree that territory can take on important symbolic value at the local level, but they argue that these attachments may also be manipulated by political leaders for their own purposes. Goemans, for example, emphasizes that political leaders may consciously create a group identity around a piece of land as a way to delineate who their subjects are and the extent of their own state power. This helps to provide security for the state, but also enables leaders to credibly signal their own territorial ambitions. Newman, on the other hand, argues that territorial attachments can be exploited by political leaders who wish to cement a particular power base, as Slobodan Milosevic appeared to do when he invoked the idea of a greater Serbia. The deep emotional attachment many individuals feel for a particular piece of land, therefore, may be very real, but is also often the result of carefully designed state policies. Jews and Arabs, for example, clearly have strong symbolic attachments to Jerusalem and the West Bank. But the residential segregation of Jews and Arabs and the unequal distribution of resources within these territories is the result of specific policies that are supported by the Jewish majority and carefully implemented by state planning authorities.

The first four chapters in this book looked at quite different phenomena. Goemans attempted to explain why countries have deep attachments to pieces of territory deemed "homelands." Robbins sought to explain why a small tribe in Papua New Guinea came to reject the very land that had sustained it socially and spiritually over time. Lyons asked why certain emigrant groups have remained so involved in the political affairs of their mother country while others have not, and Newman looked at strong local attachments to neighborhoods, streets, and cultural spaces. Their answers all converge on the intangible or symbolic dimensions of territory, and on the role these play in constituting people's identities and providing a sense of community and security. Attachments rise and fall, not with changes in trade and capital movement, but with factors that affect focal principles, perceptions of homeland conflicts, myths and narratives, and everyday facts on the ground. Thus, globalization may have an effect on the value people attach to territory, but only if we look at the more expansive definition of globalization that includes the movement of people, norms, and ideas, as well as money and goods.

Globalization's effect on territoriality and
conflict: the empirical results

The chapters by Lake and O'Mahoney, Gartzke, Buhaug and Gleditsch, and Simmons look more closely at any empirical relationships that may exist between globalization and territorial conflict. At first glance the results appear to be mixed. Gartzke and Buhaug and Gleditsch both find that globalization does not appear to affect a government's willingness to fight for territory. Using a data set of all dyad years for all states between 1875 and 1998, Buhaug and Gleditsch find no support for the idea that globalization has made it easier for states to fight each other at great distances, and little or no support for the idea that globalization has reduced the number of territorial conflicts around the world. Similarly, using a data set of all dyad years between 1950 and 2001, Gartzke finds that globalization appears to be unrelated to the incidence of territorial conflict.

But the findings by Lake and O'Mahoney and Simmons suggest that something else may be going on. In their study of all interstate disputes between 1815 and 1998 Lake and O'Mahoney find that as the size of states has declined over the last century, so too has the number of interstate wars. They hypothesize that a combination of economic openness and democratization has made the control of large land masses less important and thus less worthy of war. And in a study of all territorial disputes in Latin America between 1967 and 2000, Simmons finds a significant relationship between border disputes and a loss in interstate trade, suggesting that countries should have decreasing incentives to fight over international boundaries as trade increases.

If trade makes border disputes more expensive, and economic openness makes large land masses less vital, why do countries continue to fight over territory? The chapter by Gartzke presents a fascinating answer to this question. Gartzke takes the relationship between globalization and territorial conflict one step further and asks whether a difference exists between the effects of globalization (defined as a country's level of economic openness) and the effects of economic development (defined as wealth). If you disaggregate the openness of markets from wealth, do you see a difference in whether or not governments fight for territory? Gartzke finds that you do. Although the level of openness has no effect on the outbreak of territorial conflict, countries that are more economically developed, and therefore wealthier, are far *less* likely to engage in territorial disputes.

Gartzke's study, therefore, presents a more nuanced evaluation of the relationship between globalization and conflict, and highlights the

importance of carefully defining which element or elements of globalization are being examined. A study that measures globalization in terms of
levels of trade is likely to have different results from a study that measures the same concept in terms of wealth, foreign direct investment,
government restrictions, or factors such as travel and internet usage. His
study also reveals that a concept as broad as globalization may be
endogenous to other, more important, causal processes. It is possible,
for example, that greater democratization causes both economic openness and a decrease in territorial conflicts. If this is true, it would appear
as if open markets were influencing the likelihood of territorial conflicts,
when in fact it was democratization that was doing much of the work.

A related problem is addressed in Raustiala's study on territory and
law. In his chapter, Raustiala challenges the argument that globalization
is the main driver behind the decoupling of territory from sovereignty.
Tracing the evolution of US legal jurisdiction, he shows that extraterritorial jurisdiction is more a product of changes in the nature and structure of the military and of increases in global levels of democracy and
economic development than any effects of globalization. Thus, while it
may appear as if territory has become more and more separated from
legal rules and practices as globalization has increased, this is only
because globalization has developed simultaneously with the causally
more important processes of democratization and development.

Implications for theory and policy

Theoretical implications

At the start of this project, the authors acknowledged that they did not
fully understand why particular territorial attachments have persisted, or
why territorial conflict remains so prevalent even as various aspects of
the material and strategic value of land have declined. What we have
attempted to do is to draw out the causal links by which attachments to a
particular territory are created and sustained, and the ways in which
certain processes may create incentives or disincentives to fight for
territory. We have learned that the concept of territoriality is broad,
encompassing the attachments individuals have to land, the value they
associate with it, and the role it may play in organizing their world. We
have also learned that territory and territorial boundaries include both
symbolic and tangible dimensions, and that the symbolic dimensions
play a much larger role in people's individual lives and in their willingness to retain or relinquish territory should disputes arise. Once we
understand that particular pieces of territory can serve as important focal

points around which groups organize, and as an integral feature of a group's identity, then it becomes clear why territorial conflict would persist in a world of increasingly open markets. It is only when we distinguish the symbolic from the material that the absence of any connection between territorial disputes and economic forms of globalization begins to make sense.

Policy implications

The chapters in this volume also offer at least two main insights for policymakers facing longstanding territorial disputes. The first is that measuring the value of land strictly in terms of its tangible assets and making these assets the basis of a settlement is unlikely to bring long-term peace. To date, policymakers have tended to focus disproportionately on issues related to border length and placement, and the distribution of natural resources, rather than dealing with the deep psychological bonds that may exist among individuals at the local level. But one of the things we have learned from this book is that the cases that break out in violence, such as the conflict between the Israelis and Palestinians, are likely to be those cases where symbolic lands are at the heart of the conflict. The outbreak of war, therefore, is likely to be an indicator that the conflict has already been defined in zero-sum terms due to the nature of the stakes. Thus, "for conflict resolution to be attainable," argues Newman, "it is necessary to deal with the symbolic and emotional dimensions of the territorial attachment . . . before bartering can take place at the level of the tangible."

But how does one deal with the symbolic? History offers both good and bad news about our ability to resolve these conflicts. The good news is that even though territorial attachments may appear fixed and even innate, Goemans, Robbins, Lyons, and Newman all agree that these attachments can change over time. Robbins, for example, shows that individuals can have an extremely strong attachment to territory rooted in religion and mythology, and still willingly give up their territory if religious beliefs and social interactions have been transformed or replaced with something else. For Goemans, a change in military technology or the rise of a new ideology can create incentives to change a focal point, freeing up a disputed piece of territory for a negotiated settlement. Lyons believes that third parties can work with conflict-generated diaspora groups to reframe categorical perceptions about a conflict, and encourage a shift in support away from the most militant leaders toward those seeking peace. And Newman argues that conflict resolution can take place by changing the discourse by which individuals understand their relationship to a particular piece of land. Shift the discussion about Jerusalem, for example, away from its importance as the "eternal city" and focus instead on the reality of neighborhoods and social services, and people's perceptions about it will slowly change as well.

None of these solutions, however, is particularly easy or straightforward. The bad news, therefore, is that most territorial conflicts will continue to be difficult to resolve. Disputes that happen to arise over deeply symbolic territory will not lend themselves to a quick division of the physical stakes. Simply identifying disputes as expensive and showing governments how they might creatively divide up the land, therefore, will often not be sufficient to obtain successful settlements. Governments fighting these wars do not care that they are expending a disproportionate amount of money fighting for land that has little material value. Argentina and Chile were willing to give up hundreds of millions of dollars in trade per year in order to avoid making any concessions on their international border. This does not mean that negotiated solutions to these conflicts are impossible, only that it will take far more than economic incentives to obtain the support and acceptance of populations whose emotional ties to the land are intangible but real.

Conclusion

This book represents a first step on the road to understanding the interrelationship between globalization, territoriality, and conflict. What we have shown is that exploring the symbolic side of territoriality offers considerable leverage in understanding why globalization has not produced either a borderless world or a world where attachments to territory have disappeared or declined. At least three tasks, however, remain. The first is to uncover the many additional ways in which territory may have symbolic value. This volume explored at least four ways in which attachments may take hold, but this is far from an exhaustive list. Individuals, groups, and governments continue to fight for territory for reasons that have little to do with focal principles, conflict diasporas, religion, or social relationships. Why has it been easier, for example, for governments to move some populations off their land than others? Why do some ethnic groups fight for their land in the midst of a war, while others flee? What sort of relationship do nomads such as the Bedouin of the Middle East or the Berbers of North Africa have with the land, and how is their relationship different from those of more stationary populations? All of these questions address the same basic puzzle: namely, why do some individuals and groups appear to be tied to a particular piece of land more than others? Understanding these questions and the nature of these attachments is an important subject for future study.

A second task has to do with theorizing in greater detail about the effect of different economic, political, and social processes on territoriality and conflict. If one expands the definition of globalization to include the movement of people, political ideas, and cultural norms and practices, what effect do these trends have on people's attachment to territory and their willingness to fight for it? The chapter by Robbins has shown how the spread of Pentecostal Christianity can loosen the ties traditional peoples have to their land, but this is just one small change taking place around the world. The movement of goods and capital is important, but it is the movement of immigrants, democratic ideals, and cultural and religious values that are likely to have far greater consequences.

The final task is empirical. This book has attempted to define and measure the difficult concepts of globalization, territoriality, and conflict, but our proxies remain rough, and our answers incomplete. One of the biggest challenges that remains, therefore, is to begin to systematically test the relationship that exists between symbolically valuable land and war. Most statistical studies of interstate territorial conflicts include no measure of symbolic value because it is so difficult to pin down. The authors in this volume have convincingly argued that territorial conflicts are more likely to be driven by symbolic attachments to land, and they have convincingly shown that economic factors such as economic openness have little effect on conflict over land. But until we are able to include information on the more intangible aspects of territory, policymakers will continue to focus disproportionately on the material side of territorial conflict to the detriment of more appropriate and lasting solutions.

References

Abbott, Kenneth W., and Duncan Snidal. 2000. "Hard and Soft Law in International Governance." *International Organization* 54 (3): 421–56.

Acemoglu, Daron, Simon Johnson, and James A. Robinson. 2001. "The Colonial Origins of Comparative Development: An Empirical Investigation." *American Economic Review* 91 (5): 1369–401.

Acharya, Amitav. 2000. *The Quest for Identity: International Relations of Southeast Asia*. Oxford: Oxford University Press.

Adamson, Fiona B. 2002. "Mobilizing for the Transformation of Home: Politicized Identities and Transnational Practices." In *New Approaches to Migration? Transnational Communities and the Transformation of Home*, edited by Nadje al-Ali and Khalid Koser. London: Routledge.

Adler, Emmanuel, and Michael Barnett, eds. 1998. *Security Communities*. Cambridge: Cambridge University Press.

Agnew, John A. 1994. "The Territorial Trap: The Geographical Assumptions of International Relations Theory." *Review of International Political Economy* 1 (1): 53–80.

2000. "Territory." In *The Dictionary of Human Geography*, 4th edn, edited by R. J. Johnston et al. Oxford: Blackwell.

Agnew, John A., and James S. Duncan. 1989. *The Power of Place: Bringing Together Geographical and Sociological Imaginations*. Boston: Unwin Hyman.

Agnew, John A., and Paul Knox. 1994. *The Geography of the World Economy: An Introduction to Economic Geography*. New York: Routledge, Chapman, and Hall.

Akaha, T. 1996. "Russia and Asia in 1995: Bold Objectives and Limited Means." *Asian Survey* 36 (1): 100–08.

Albert, Mathias. 1998. "On Boundaries, Territory and Postmodernity: An International Relations Perspective." *Geopolitics* 3 (1): 53–68.

Albert, Mathias, David Jacobson, and Yosef Lapid, eds. 2001. *Identities, Borders, Orders: New Directions in International Relations Theory*. Minneapolis: University of Minnesota Press.

Alesina, Alberto, and Enrico Spolaore. 1997. "On the Number and Size of Nations." *Quarterly Journal of Economics* 112 (4): 1027–58.

2003. *The Size of Nations*. Cambridge, Mass.: MIT Press.

2005. "War, Peace, and the Size of Countries." *Journal of Public Economics* 89 (7): 1333–54.

Alesina, Alberto, Enrico Spolaore, and Romain Wacziarg. 1997. "Economic Integration and Political Disintegration." NBER Working Paper 6163. Cambridge, Mass.: National Bureau of Economic Research, September.

Alexander, Lewis M. 1963. *World Political Patterns.* 2nd edn. Chicago: Rand McNally.

Anderson, Benedict R. O'G. 1991. *Imagined Communities: Reflections on the Origin and Spread of Nationalism.* New York: Verso.

1992. "The New World Disorder." *New Left Review* 193: 3–13.

1994. "Exodus." *Critical Inquiry* 20 (winter): 314–27.

Anderson, James. 2001. "Theorizing State Borders: 'Politics/Economics' and Democracy in Capitalism." Working Paper CIBR/WP01-1. School of Geography and Centre for International Borders Research, Queen's University, Belfast. Available at http://www.qub.ac.uk/cibr/WorkingPapers2001.htm.

Anderson, James E. 1979. "A Theoretical Foundation for the Gravity Equation." *American Economic Review* 69: 106–16.

Anderson, Malcolm. 1996. *Frontiers: Territory and State Formation in the Modern World.* Oxford: Blackwell.

Anderton, C. H., and J. R. Carter. 2001. "The Impact of War on Trade: An Interrupted Times-Series Study." *Journal of Peace Research* 38 (4): 445–57.

Anderton, C. H., R. A. Anderton, and J. R. Carter. 1999. "Economic Activity in the Shadow of Conflict." *Economic Inquiry* 37 (1): 166–79.

Andreas, Peter, and Timothy Snyder, eds. 2000. *The Wall around the West: State Borders and Immigration Controls in North America and Europe.* Lanham, Md.: Rowman and Littlefield.

Anene, J. C. 1970. *The International Boundaries of Nigeria.* London: Longman.

Angell, Norman. 1911. *The Great Illusion: A Study of the Relation of Military Power in Nations to Their Economic and Social Advantage.* 3rd edn. New York and London: G. P. Putnam's Sons.

1933. *The Great Illusion.* New York: Putnam.

1936. *Raw Materials, Population Pressure, and War.* New York: World Peace Foundation.

Anghie, Antony. 1999. "Finding the Peripheries: Sovereignty and Colonialism in Nineteenth-Century International Law." *Harvard International Law Journal* 40 (1): 1–81.

Anselin, Luc, and John O'Loughlin. 1992. "Geography of International Conflict and Cooperation: Spatial Dependence and Regional Context in Africa." In *The New Geopolitics,* edited by Michael D. Ward. Philadelphia, Pa.: Gordon and Breach, 39–76.

Appadurai, Arjun. 1996. *Modernity at Large: Cultural Dimensions of Globalization.* Minneapolis: University of Minnesota Press.

Aradom, Tesfay. 1990. "Issues of Social Adjustment Potentially Relevant to the Eritrean Immigrant Community in the United States." *Journal of Eritrean Studies* 4, 1–2 (summer and winter): 12–27.

Ardrey, Robert. 1966. *The Territorial Imperative.* New York: Atheneum.

Armstrong, Karen. 1997. *Jerusalem: One City, Three Faiths.* New York: Ballantine Books.

Arthur, Paul. 1991. "Diasporan Intervention in International Affairs: Irish America as a Case Study." *Diaspora* 1, (2) (fall): 143–62.

Ashley, Richard K. 1980. *The Political Economy of War and Peace*. New York: Nichols.

Avant, Deborah. 2000. "From Mercenary to Citizen Armies: Explaining Change in the Practice of War." *International Organization* 54 (winter): 41–72.

Bakker, Piet. 2001. "New Nationalism: The Internet Crusade." Paper presented at the Annual Meeting of the International Studies Association, February, Chicago, Ill.

Baldwin, Richard E., and Philippe Martin. 1999. "Two Waves of Globalization: Superficial Similarities, Fundamental Differences." NBER Working Paper 6904(January).

Baldwin, Thomas. 1992. "The Territorial State." In *Jurisprudence: Cambridge Essays*, edited by Hyman Gross and Ross Harrison. Oxford: Clarendon Press, 207–30.

Banks, Arthur S. 1976. "Cross-National Time Series, 1815–1973." Electronic resource. Ann Arbor, Mich.: Inter-University Consortium for Political and Social Research, University of Michigan.

Barber, Benjamin. 1992. "Jihad Versus McWorld." *Atlantic Monthly* 269 (3): 53–65.

    1996. *Jihad Versus McWorld: How Globalism and Tribalism Are Reshaping the World*. New York: Ballantine Books.

Barbieri, Katherine. 2002. *The Liberal Illusion: Does Trade Promote Peace?* Ann Arbor: University of Michigan Press.

Barbieri, K., and J. S. Levy. 1999. "Sleeping with the Enemy: The Impact of War on Trade." *Journal of Peace Research* 36 (4): 463–79.

    2001. "Does War Impede Trade? A Response to Anderton and Carter." *Journal of Peace Research* 38 (5): 619–24.

Barrett, D. B., and T. M. Johnson. 2002. "Global Statistics." In *The New International Dictionary of Pentecostal and Charismatic Movements*, edited by S. M. Burgess and E. M. van der Maas. Grand Rapids, Mich.: Zondervan, 283–302.

Barrington, Lowell W., Erik S. Herron, and Brian D. Silver. 2003. "The Motherland is Calling: Views of Homeland among Russians in the Near Abroad." *World Politics* 55 (January): 290–313.

Bayoumi, Tamim, and Barry Eichengreen. 1995. "Is Regionalism Simply a Diversion? Evidence from the Evolution of the EC and EFTA." NBER Working Paper No. 2583. Cambridge, Mass.: National Bureau of Economic Research.

Bearce, David H., and Eric O'N. Fisher. 2002. "Economic Geography, Trade, and War." *Journal of Conflict Resolution* 36 (3): 365–93.

Beck, Nathaniel. 1991. "The Illusion of Cycles in International Relations." *International Studies Quarterly* 35 (4): 455–76.

Beck, Nathaniel, Jonathan Katz, and Richard Tucker. 1998. "Taking Time Seriously: Time-Series Cross-Section Analysis with a Binary Dependent Variable." *American Journal of Political Science* 42 (4): 1260–88.

Bederman, David. 1996. "The Souls of International Organizations." *Virginia Journal International Law* 36: 275–377.

Bennett, D. Scott, and Allan C. Stam. 2000. "EUGene: A Conceptual Manual." *International Interactions* 26 (2): 179–204.

2001. "EUGene: Expected Utility and Data Management Program, version 2.250." Computer program. The Pennsylvania State University and Dartmouth University.

Benveniste, Meron. 2000. *Sacred Landscape: The Buried History of the Holy Land since 1948.* Berkeley: University of California Press.

Bergstrand, Jeffrey H. 1989. "The Generalized Gravity Equation, Monopolistic Competition, and the Factor-Proportions Theory in International Trade." *Review of Economics and Statistics* 71 (February): 143–53.

Berman, Paul. 2002. "The Globalization of Jurisdiction." *University of Pennsylvania Law Review.* 151: 311–545.

Bhagwati, Jagdish N. 2004. *In Defense of Globalization.* Oxford: Oxford University Press.

Biersteker, Thomas J. 2002. "State, Sovereignty, and Territory." In *Handbook of International Relations,* edited by W. Carlsnaes, T. Risse, and B. A. Simmons. London: Sage, 157–76.

Biger, Gideon, ed. 1995. *The Encyclopedia of International Boundaries.* New York: Facts on File.

Binkley, Robert C. 1941. *Realism and Nationalism 1852–1871.* New York: Harper and Row.

Black, John A., A. Paez, and Putu A. Suthanaya. 2002. "Sustainable Urban Transportation: Performance Indicators and Some Analytical Approaches." *Journal of Urban Planning and Development–ASCE* 128 (4): 184–209.

Blainey, Geoffrey. 1988. *The Causes of War.* New York: Free Press.

Blake, G. H. 1992. "International Boundaries and Territorial Stability in the Middle East: An Assessment." *GeoJournal* 28 (3): 365–73.

Boehmer, Charles. 2001. "Economic Growth, Strategic Interaction, and Interstate Conflict." Paper presented at the 42nd Annual Meeting of the International Studies Association, February 20–25.

Boehmer, Charles, and David Sobek. 2005. "Violent Adolescence: State Development and the Propensity for Militarized Interstate Conflict." *Journal of Peace Research* 42 (1): 5–26.

Bokhari, Eas. 1999. "The Scud Missile Syndrome." *Defence Journal* 3 (5). Available at http://www.defencejournal.com/may99/scud-missile.htm.

Boulding, Kenneth. 1962. *Conflict and Defense.* New York: Harper and Row.

Boulding, Kenneth E., and Tapan Mukerjee. 1972. *Economic Imperialism: A Book of Readings.* Ann Arbor: University of Michigan Press.

Brawer, Moshe. 1990. "The Green Line: Functions and Impacts of an Israeli–Arab Superimposed Boundary." In *International Boundaries and Boundary Conflict Resolution,* edited by Carl Grundy-Warr. Durham, UK: International Boundaries Research Unit, 63–74.

2002. "The Making of an Israeli–Palestinian Boundary." In *The Razor's Edge: International Boundaries and Political Geography,* edited by Clive Schofield et al. London: Kluwer Academic Publishers, 473–92.

Brecher, Michael. 1993. *Crises in World Politics: Theory and Reality.* Oxford: Pergamon.

Bremer, Stuart. 1980. "National Capabilities and War Proneness." In *The Correlates of War II: Some Realpolitik Models,* edited by J. David Singer. New York: Free Press, 57–82.

1992. "Dangerous Dyads: Conditions Affecting the Likelihood of Interstate War." *Journal of Conflict Resolution* 36 (2): 309–41.

Brooks, Stephen G. 1999. "The Globalization of Production and the Changing Benefits of Conquest." *Journal of Conflict Resolution* 43, 5 (October): 646–70.

Brown, Elizabeth A. R. 1973. "Taxation and Morality in the Thirteenth and Fourteenth Centuries: Conscience and Political Power and the Kings of France." *French Historical Studies* 8 (1): 1–28.

Bulcha, Mekuria. 2002. *The Making of the Oromo Diaspora: A Historical Sociology of Forced Migration.* Minneapolis, Minn.: Kirk House Publishers.

Bull, Hedley. 1995. *The Anarchical Society: A Study of Order in World Politics.* 2nd edn. New York: Columbia University Press.

Bull, Hedley, and Adam Watson, eds. 1984. *The Expansion of International Society.* Oxford: Oxford University Press.

Burghardt, Andrew. 1973. "The Bases of Territorial Claims." *Geographical Review* 63 (2): 225–45.

1988. "Marxism and Self-Determination: The Case of Burgenland, 1919." In *Nationalism, Self-Determination and Political Geography,* edited by R. J. Johnston, David B. Knight, and Eleonore Kofman. London: Croom Helm, 57–69.

Burnett, Christina, and Burke Marshall, eds. 2001. *Foreign in a Domestic Sense: Puerto Rico, American Expansion, and the Constitution.* Durham, N.C.: Duke University Press.

Burnett, D. Graham. 2000. *Master of All They Surveyed: Exploration, Geography, and a British El Dorado.* Chicago: University of Chicago Press.

Burridge, Kenelm. 1969. *Tangu Traditions: A Study of the Way of Life, Mythology, and Developing Experience of a New Guinea People.* Oxford: Oxford University Press.

Bussmann, Margit, and Gerald Schneider. 2003. "The 'Peace Dividend' of Globalization: Foreign Economic Liberalization and Internal War." Paper presented at the 44th Annual Meeting of the International Studies Association, Portland, Oregon, February 25–March 1.

Butler, Nicholas Murray. 1934. *Between Two Worlds: Interpretations of the Age in Which We Live, Essays and Addresses.* New York: Scribner.

1940. *Why War? Essays and Addresses on War and Peace.* New York: Scribner.

Byman, Daniel L., Peter Chalk, Bruce Hoffman, William Rosenau, and David Brannan. 2001. *Trends in Outside Support for Insurgent Movements.* Santa Monica, Calif.: RAND Corporation.

Cairncross, Frances. 2000. *The Death of Distance: How the Communications Revolution is Changing Our Lives.* Revised edn. Cambridge, Mass.: Harvard Business School Press.

Camarota, Steven A., and Nora McArdle. 2003. "Where Immigrants Live: An Examination of State Residency of the Foreign Born by Country of Origin in 1990 and 2000." Washington, D.C.: Center for Immigration Studies Backgrounder no. 12–03, September.

Capling, Ann, and Kim Richard Nossal. 2001. "Death of Distance or Tyranny of Distance? The Internet, Deterritorialization, and the Anti-globalization Movement in Australia." *Pacific Review* 14 (3): 443–65.

Carlile, L. E. 1994. "The Changing Political Economy of Japan's Economic Relations with Russia: The Rise and Fall of Seikei Fukabun." *Pacific Affairs* 76 (3): 411–32.

Carneiro, Robert L. 1970. "A Theory of the Origin of the State." *Science* 169 (21 August): 733–38.

Carr, E. H. 1939. *The Twenty Years' Crisis: 1919–1939*. London: Macmillan.

Casanova, Jose. 2001. "Religion, the New Millennium, and Globalization." *Sociology of Religion* 62 (4): 415–41.

Castellino, Joshua, and Steve Allen. 2003. *Title to Territory in International Law*. Aldershot: Ashgate.

Ceadel, Martin. 1980. *Pacifism in Britain 1914–1945: The Defining of a Faith*. Oxford: Clarendon Press.

    1987. *Thinking about Peace and War*. Oxford: Oxford University Press.

    1996. *The Origins of War Prevention: The British Peace Movement and International Relations, 1730–1854*. Oxford: Clarendon Press.

    2000. *Semi-Detached Idealists: The British Peace Movement and International Relations, 1854–1945*. Oxford: Oxford University Press.

Cederman, Lars-Erik, and Kristian S. Gleditsch. 2004. "Conquest and Regime Change: An Evolutionary Model of the Spread of Democracy and Peace." *International Studies Quarterly* 48 (3): 603–29.

Central Intelligence Agency. 2004. *CIA World Factbook*. Available at http://www.cia.gov/cia/publications/factbook/.

Chaliland, Gérard, ed. 1989. *Minority Peoples in the Age of Nation-States*. London: Pluto.

Chester, Lucy. 2002. "Drawing the Indo-Pakistani Boundary during the 1947 Partition of South Asia." Ph.D. diss., Department of History, Yale University.

Chiozza, Giacomo. 2002. "Is There a Clash of Civilizations? Evidence from Patterns of International Conflict Involvement, 1946–97." *Journal of Peace Research* 39 (6): 711–34.

Chisholm, Michael, and David M. Smith, eds. 1990. *Shared Space, Divided Space: Essays on Conflict and Territorial Organization*. London: Unwin Hyman.

Choucri, Nazli, and Robert C. North. 1975. *Nations in Conflict: National Growth and International Violence*. San Francisco: W. H. Freeman.

    1989. "Lateral Pressure in International Relations: Concept and Theory." In *Handbook of War Studies*, edited by Manus I. Midlarsky. Boston, Mass.: Unwin Hyman, 289–326.

Christerson, Brad. 1994. "World Trade in Apparel: An Analysis of Trade Flows Using the Gravity Model." *International Regional Science Review* 17 (2): 151–66.

Chwe, Michael Suk-Young. 2001. *Rational Ritual: Culture, Coordination, and Common Knowledge*. Princeton, N.J.: Princeton University Press.

Cioffi-Revilla, Claudio. 2004. "The Next Record-Setting War in the Global Setting: A Long-Term Analysis." *Journal of the Washington Academy of Sciences* 90, 2 (summer): 61ff.

Cizre, U. 2001. "Turkey's Kurdish Problem: Borders, Identity, and Hegemony." In *Right-Sizing the State: The Politics of Moving Borders*, edited by B. O'Leary, I. Lustick, and T. Callaghy. Oxford: Oxford University Press, 222–52.

CNN. 2003. "Fierce Cyber War Predicted." Posted 3 March. Available at http://edition.cnn.com/2003/TECH/ptech/03/03/sprj.irq.info.war.ap/.

Coakley, John, ed. 1993. *The Territorial Management of Ethnic Conflict.* London: Frank Cass.

Cobden, Richard. 1903. *The Political Writings of Richard Cobden,* Vol. I. 4th edn. London: T. Fisher Unwin.

Coe, David T., Arvind Subramanian, and Natalia T. Tamirisa, with Rikhil Bhanavnani. 2002. "The Missing Globalization Puzzle." IMF Working Paper 171. Washington, D.C.: International Monetary Fund.

Cohen, Benjamin. 1998. *The Geography of Money.* Ithaca, N.Y.: Cornell University Press.

Cohen, Robin. 1997. *Global Diasporas: An Introduction.* Seattle: University of Washington Press.

Cohen, Saul B., and Nurit Kliot. 1981. "Israel's Place Names as Reflection of Continuity and Change in Nation Building." *Names* 29: 227–46.

1992. "Place Names in Israel's Ideological Struggle over the Administered Territories." *Annals of the Association of American Geographers* 82: 653–80.

Coleman, James S. 1964. *Introduction to Mathematical Sociology.* New York: Free Press.

Collier, Paul, and Anke Hoeffler. 2000. "Greed and Grievances in Civil War." Policy Research Working Paper 2355. Washington, D.C.: World Bank.

2002. "On the Incidence of Civil War in Africa." *Journal of Conflict Resolution* 46 (1): 13–28.

2004. "Greed and Grievance in Civil War." *Oxford Economic Papers New Series* 56, 4 (October): 563–95.

Collier, Paul, Lani Elliot, Håvard Hegre, Anke Hoeffler, Marta Reynal-Querol, and Nicholas Sambanis. 2003. *Breaking the Conflict Trap: Civil War and Development Policy.* Oxford: Oxford University Press and Washington, D.C.: World Bank. Available at http://econ.worldbank.org/prr/CivilWarPRR/.

Collins, John M. 1998. *Military Geography for Professionals and the Public.* Washington, D.C.: Brassey's.

Congleton, R. D. 1995. "Ethnic Clubs, Ethnic Conflict, and the Rise of Ethnic Nationalism." In *Nationalism and Rationality,* edited by A. Breton, G. Galeotti, P. Salmon, and R. Wintrobe. Cambridge: Cambridge University Press, 71–97.

Cook, Thomas D., and Donald T. Campbell. 1979. *Quasi-Experimentation: Design and Analysis Issues for Field Settings.* Boston: Houghton Mifflin.

Coon, Anthony. 1992. *Town Planning under Military Occupation.* Aldershot, UK: Dartmouth Press.

Cooper, Richard. 1972. "Economic Interdependence and Foreign Policy in the Seventies." *World Politics* 24 (2): 159–81.

Copeland, Dale C. 1996. "Economic Interdependence and War: A Theory of Trade Expectations." *International Security* 20 (4): 5–41.

1999. "Trade Expectations and the Outbreak of Peace: Detente 1970–1974 and the End of the Cold War 1985–91." *Security Studies* 93: 15–58.

Copper, John F. 1996. *Taiwan: Nation-State or Province?* 2nd edn. Boulder, Colo.: Westview Press.

Cox, Michael. 1999. "The War that Came in from the Cold: Clinton and the Irish Question." *World Policy Journal* 16, 1 (spring): 59–67.

Currie, David, H. H. Kay, and Larry Kramer. 2001. *Cases and Materials on Conflict of Laws.* St. Paul, Minn.: West.

Cutts Dougherty, Katharine, Margaret Eisenhart, and Paul Webley. 1992. "The Role of Social Representations and National Identities in the Development of Territorial Knowledge: A Study of Political Socialization in Argentina and England." *American Educational Research Journal* 29 (4): 809–35.

Daniel, Tim. 2000. "African Boundaries: New Order, Historic Tensions." In *Borderlands under Stress*, edited by Martin Pratt and Janet Allison-Brown. London: Kluwer Academic Publishers, 211–26.

Davies, W. D. 1994. *The Gospel and the Land: Early Christianity and Jewish Territorial Doctrine.* Sheffield, UK: Sheffield University Press.

Davis, D., D. Weinstein, S. Bradford, and K. Shimpo. 1997. "Using International and Japanese Regional Data to Determine when the Factor Abundance Theory of Trade Works." *American Economic Review* 87: 421–46.

Daxecker, Ursula E. 2004. "Perilous Polities? Regime Transition and Conflict 1950–2000." Paper presented at the Annual Meeting of the Midwest Political Science Association, Chicago, April 15–18.

Deardorff, Alan V. 1998. "Determinants of Bilateral Trade: Does Gravity Work in a Neoclassical World?" In *The Regionalization of the World Economy*, edited by J. A. Frankel. Chicago: University of Chicago Press.

DeBernardi, Jean. 1999. "Spiritual Warfare and Territorial Spirits: The Globalization and Localization of a 'Practical Theology'." *Religious Studies and Theology* 18 (2): 66–96.

De Soysa, Indra. 2000. "The Resource Curse: Are Civil Wars Driven by Rapacity or Paucity?" In *Greed and Grievance: Economic Agendas in Civil Wars*, edited by Mats Berdal and David M. Malone. Boulder, Colo.: Lynne Rienner, 113–35.

——— 2002. "Paradise Is a Bazaar? Greed, Creed, and Governance in Civil War, 1989–99." *Journal of Peace Research* 39 (4): 395–416.

Deutsch, Karl et. al. 1957. *Political Community and the North Atlantic Area.* Princeton, N.J.: Princeton University Press.

Diehl, Paul F. 1999a. "Territory and International Conflict: An Overview." In *A Road Map to War: Territorial Dimensions of International Conflict*, edited by Paul F. Diehl. Nashville, Tenn.: Vanderbilt University Press, viii–xx.

Diehl, Paul F., ed. 1999b. *A Road Map to War: Territorial Dimensions of International Conflict.* Nashville, Tenn.: Vanderbilt University Press.

Diehl, Paul F., and Gary Goertz. 1988. "No Trespassing: Territorial Changes and Militarized Conflict." *Journal of Conflict Resolution* 32: 103–22.

Dijkink, Gertjan, and H. Knippenberg. 2001. "The Territorial Factor: An Introduction." In *The Territorial Factor: Political Geography in a Globalizing World*, edited by Gertjan Dijkink and Hans Knippenberg. Amsterdam: Vossiuspers, 11–30.

Dion, Roger. 1947. *Les Frontières de la France.* Paris: Hachette.

Dittgen, Herbert. 2000. "The End of the Nation State? Borders in the Age of Globalization." In *Borderlands under Stress*, edited by Martin Pratt and Janet Allison-Brown. London: Kluwer Academic Publishers, 49–68.

Dodd, Stuart Carter. 1950. "The Interactance Hypothesis: A Gravity Model Fitting Physical Masses and Human Groups." *American Sociological Review* 15 (2): 245–56.

Dominguez, Jorge. 2001. "Territorial and Boundary Disputes in Latin America and the Caribbean." *Pensamiento Propio: Greater Caribbean Bilingual Journal of Social Sciences* 6 (14): 5–29.

Donnan, Hastings, and Thomas M. Wilson. 1999. *Borders: Frontiers of Identity, Nation and State.* New York: Berg.

Doyle, Michael. 1983a. "Kant, Liberal Legacies, and Foreign Affairs: Part 1." *Philosophy and Public Affairs* 12, 3 (summer): 205–35.

   1983b. "Kant, Liberal Legacies, and Foreign Affairs: Part 2." *Philosophy and Public Affairs* 12, 4 (Fall): 323–53.

Drury, Michael. 1981. "The Political Geography of Cyprus." In *Change and Development in the Middle East,* edited by John Clarke and Howard Bowen-Jones. London: Methuen, 289–304.

Duchacek, Ivo D. 1970. *Comparative Federalism: The Territorial Dimension of Politics.* New York: Reinhart and Winston.

Dudziak, Mary. 1988. "Desegregation as a Cold War Imperative." *Stanford Law Review* 41: 61–120.

Dumper, Michael. 1996. *The Politics of Jerusalem since 1967.* New York: Columbia University Press.

East, Maurice A., and Phillip M. Gregg. 1967. "Factors Influencing Co-operation and Conflict in the International System." *International Studies Quarterly* 11 (3): 244–69.

Easterly, William. 2001. *The Elusive Quest for Growth: Economists' Adventures and Misadventures in the Tropics.* Cambridge, Mass.: MIT Press.

Elazar, Daniel, ed. 1979. *Self Rule – Shared Rule: Federal Solutions to the Middle East Conflict.* Ramat Gan, Israel: Turtledove Press.

Elbadawi, Ibrahim, and Håvard Hegre. 2004. "Globalization, Economic Shocks, and Armed Conflict." Paper presented at the Conference on Territoriality, Globalization, and Conflict, San Diego, Calif., 16–18 January.

Elbadawi, Ibrahim, and Nicholas Sambanis. 2002. "How Much War Will We See? Explaining the Prevalence of Civil War." *Journal of Conflict Resolution* 46 (3): 307–34.

Ellingsen, Tanja. 2000. "Colorful Community or Ethnic Witches' Brew? Multiethnicity and Domestic Conflict during and after the Cold War." *Journal of Conflict Resolution* 44 (2): 228–49.

Engel, Charles, and John H. Rogers. 1996. "How Wide Is the Border?" *American Economic Review* 86 (5): 1112–25.

Englefield, Greg. 1992. *Yugoslavia, Croatia, Slovenia: Re-emerging Boundaries.* IBRU International Territory Briefing series No. 3. Durham, UK: International Boundaries Research Unit Press.

Escudé, Carlos. 1988. "Argentine Territorial Nationalism." *Journal of Latin American Studies* 20: 139–65.

   1992. "Education, Political Culture, and Foreign Policy: The Case of Argentina." Program in Latin American Studies Working Paper Series No. 4. Durham, N.C.: Duke–University of North Carolina Program in Latin American Studies.

Etherington, Norman. 1984. *Theories of Imperialism: War, Conquest, and Capital.* Totowa, N.J.: Barnes and Noble.

Evenett, Simon J., and Wolfgang Keller. 1998. "On Theories Explaining the Success of the Gravity Equation." In NBER Working Paper. No.6529. Cambridge, Mass.: National Bureau of Economic Research.

Faist, Thomas. 2000. "Transnationalization in International Migration: Implications for the Study of Citizenship and Culture." *Ethnic and Racial Studies* 23, 2 (March): 189–222.

Falah, Ghazi. 1994. "The Frontier of Political Criticism in Israeli Geographic Practice." *Area* 26 (1): 1–12.

　1996a. "Living Together Apart: Residential Segregation in Mixed Arab–Jewish Cities in Israel." *Urban Studies* 33: 823–57.

　1996b. "The 1948 Israeli–Palestinian War and its Aftermath: The Transformation and De-Signification of Palestine's Cultural Landscape." *Annals of the Association of American Geographers* 86 (2): 256–85.

　1997. "Re-envisioning Current Discourse: Alternative Territorial Configurations of Palestinian Statehood." *The Canadian Geographer* 41 (3): 307–30.

Falah, Ghazi, and David Newman. 1995. "The Spatial Manifestation of Threat: Israelis and Palestinians Seek a 'Good' Boundary." *Political Geography* 14: 689–706.

Fazal, Tanisha. 2002. "Born to Lose and Doomed to Survive: State Death and Survival in the International System." Ph.D. diss., Stanford University.

Fearon, James D. 1995. "Rationalist Explanations for War." *International Organization* 49, 3 (summer): 379–414.

　1998. "Commitment Problems and the Spread of Ethnic Conflict". In *The International Spread of Ethnic Conflict: Fear, Diffusion, and Escalation*, edited by David A. Lake and Donald Rothchild. Princeton, N.J.: Princeton University Press, 107–26.

　2004. "Why Do Some Civil Wars Last So Much Longer Than Others?" *Journal of Peace Research* 41, 3 (May): 275–301.

Fearon, James D., and David Laitin. 2003. "Ethnicity, Insurgency, and Civil War." *American Political Science Review* 97, 1 (February): 75–90.

Feld, Steven. 1996. "Waterfalls of Song: An Acoustemology of Place Resounding in Bosavi, Papua New Guinea." In *Senses of Place*, edited by S. Feld and K. H. Basso. Santa Fe, N.M.: School of American Research Press, 91–135.

Fettweis, Christopher J.. 2003. "Revising Mackinder and Angell: The Obsolescence of Great Power Geopolitics." *Comparative Strategy* 22 (2): 109–29.

Fischer, Stanley. 2003. "Globalization and Its Challenges." *American Economic Review* 93 (2): 1–30.

Fitzgerald, David. 2000. *Negotiating Extra-Territorial Citizenship: Mexican Migration and the Transnational Politics of Community.* Monograph Series No. 2. La Jolla, Calif.: Center for Comparative Immigration Studies.

Foner, Nancy. 2000. *From Ellis Island to JFK: New York's Two Great Waves of Migration.* New Haven, Conn.: Yale University Press.

Ford, Abiyi. 2003. "Ethiopian Diaspora and the Visual Arts: A Discussion." In Elizabeth Harney, *Ethiopian Passages: Contemporary Art from the Diaspora.* With contributions by Jeff Donaldson, Achamyeleh Debela, Kinsey Katchka, Abiyi Ford, and Floyd Coleman. London: Philip Wilson, 111–12.

Forsberg, Tuomas, ed. 1995. *Contested Territory: Border Disputes at the Edge of the Former Soviet Empire*. Aldershot: Edward Elgar.

Forsberg, Tuomas. 2002. "The Ground Without Foundation? Territory as a Social Construct." *Geopolitics* 8 (2): 7–24.

Fox, Annette Baker. 1959. *The Power of Small States: Diplomacy in World War II*. Chicago: University of Chicago Press.

Franck, Thomas. 1992. *Political Questions/Judicial Answers: Does the Rule of Law Apply to Foreign Affairs?* Princeton, N.J.: Princeton University Press.

Frankel, Jeffrey A., Ernesto Stein, and Shang-Jin Wei. 1997. *Regional Trading Blocs in the World Economic System*. Washington, D.C.: Institute for International Economics.

Frankel, Jeffrey A., and Shanjin Wei. 1993. "Continental Trading Blocs: Are They Natural or Supernatural?" NBER Working Paper No. 4588. Cambridge, Mass.: National Bureau of Economic Research.

Fraser, T. 1984. *Partition in Ireland, India, and Palestine: Theory and Practice*. London: Macmillan.

Friedman, David. 1977. "A Theory of the Size and Shape of Nations." *Journal of Political Economy* 85 (1): 59–77.

Friedman, Thomas. 1999. *The Lexus and the Olive Tree*. New York: Farrar, Straus, and Giroux.

Furlong, Kathryn, Nils Petter Gleditsch, and Håvard Hegre. 2005. "Geographic Opportunity and Neomalthusian Willingness: Boundaries, Shared Rivers, and Conflict." *International Interactions* 30 (4).

Galnoor, Itzhak. 1991. "Territorial Partition of Palestine: The 1937 Decision." *Political Geography Quarterly* 10 (4): 382–404.

Gartzke, Erik. 1999. "War Is in the Error Term." *International Organization* 53 (3): 567–87.

2001. "Democracy and the Preparation for War: Does Regime Type Affect States' Anticipation of Casualties?" *International Studies Quarterly* 45 (3): 467–84.

2004. "Rich Neighbors: War, Peace, and Economic Development." Unpublished ms., Columbia University.

Gartzke, Erik, and Kristian S. Gleditsch. Forthcoming. "Identity and Conflict: Ties that Bind and Differences that Divide." *European Journal of International Relations*.

Gartzke, Erik, and Quan Li. 2003a. "All's Well that Ends Well: A Reply to Oneal, Barbieri and Peters." *Journal of Peace Research* 40 (6): 727–32.

2003b. "How Globalization Can Reduce International Conflict." In *Globalization and Armed Conflict*, edited by Gerald Schneider, Katherine Barbieri, and Nils Petter Gleditsch. Lanham, Md.: Rowman and Littlefield, 123–40.

2003c. "War, Peace, and the Invisible Hand: Positive Political Externalities of Economic Globalization." *International Studies Quarterly* 47 (4): 561–86.

Gartzke, Erik, Quan Li, and Charles Boehmer. 2001. "Investing in the Peace: Economic Interdependence and International Conflict." *International Organization* 55 (2): 391–438.

Geary, Patrick J. 2002. *The Myth of Nations*. Princeton, N.J.: Princeton University Press.

Gellner, Ernst. 1983. *Nations and Nationalism*. Oxford: Blackwell.

Ghosn, Faten, and Glenn Palmer. 2003. "Codebook for the Militarized Inter-state Dispute Data, Version 3.0." http://cow2.la.psu.edu.

Gilbert, Emily, and Eric Helleiner. 1999. "Introduction: Nation-States and Money/Historical Contexts, Interdisciplinary Perspectives." In *Nation-States and Money: The Past, Present and Future of National Currencies*, edited by Emily Gilbert and Eric Helleiner. New York: Routledge, 1–21.

Gilbert, Paul. 1998. *The Philosophy of Nationalism*. Boulder, Colo.: Westview Press.

Gilpin, Robert. 1981. *War and Change in World Politics*. New York: Cambridge University Press.

Gissinger, Ranveig, and Nils Petter Gleditsch. 1999. "Globalization and Conflict: Welfare, Distribution, and Political Unrest." *Journal of World Systems Research* 5 (2): 327–65.

Gleditsch, Kristian Skrede. 2002a. "Expanded Trade and GDP Data." *Journal of Conflict Resolution* 46 (5): 712–24.

——— 2002b. *All International Politics is Local: The Diffusion of Conflict, Integration, and Democratization*. Ann Arbor: University of Michigan Press.

Gleditsch, Kristian S., and Michael D. Ward. 1999. "Interstate System Membership: A Revised List of the Independent States Since 1816." *International Interactions* 25: 393–413.

——— 2001. "Measuring Space: A Minimum-Distance Database and Applications to International Studies." *Journal of Peace Research* 38 (6): 739–58.

Gleditsch, Nils Petter. 1969. "The International Airline Network: A Test of the Zipf and Stouffer Hypotheses." *Papers, Peace Research Society (International)* 11: 123–53.

——— 1974. "Time Differences and International Interaction." *Cooperation and Conflict* 9 (2): 15–30.

——— 1995a. "Geography, Democracy, and Peace." *International Interactions* 21 (1): 297–323.

——— 1995b. "Thirty-Five Major Wars? A Brief Comment on Mueller." *Journal of Conflict Resolution* 39 (3): 584–87.

——— 1998. "Armed Conflict and the Environment: A Critique of the Literature." *Journal of Peace Research* 35 (3): 381–400.

Gleditsch, Nils Petter, and Håvard Hegre. 1997. "Peace and Democracy: Three Levels of Analysis." *Journal of Conflict Resolution* 41 (2): 283–310.

Gleditsch, Nils Petter, Peter Wallensteen, Mikael Eriksson, Margareta Sollenberg, and Håvard Strand. 2002. "Armed Conflict 1946–2001: A New Data Set." *Journal of Peace Research* 39 (5): 615–37.

Gochman, Charles S. 1990. "The Geography of Conflict: Militarized Interstate Disputes since 1816." Paper presented to the 31st Annual Convention of the International Studies Association, Washington, D.C., 10–14 April.

Gochman, Charles S., and Russell J. Leng. 1983. "Realpolitik and the Road to War." *International Studies Quarterly* 27 (1): 97–120.

Gochman, Charles S., and Zeev Maoz. 1984. "Militarized Interstate Disputes, 1816–1976: Procedure, Patterns, and Insights." *Journal of Conflict Resolution* 28 (4): 585–615.

Goertz, Gary, and Paul F. Diehl. 1992. *Territorial Changes and International Conflict*. London: Routledge.

Goldstein, Joshua S. 1988. *Long Cycles: Prosperity and War in the Modern Age*. New Haven, Conn.: Yale University Press.

Goldstein, Moris, and Michael Mussa. 1993. "The Integration of World Capital Markets." Paper presented at the conference Changing Capital Markets: Implications for Monetary Policy.

Gonen, Amiram. 1995. *Between City and Suburb: Urban Residential Patterns and Processes in Israel*. Aldershot: Avebury Press.

Gong, Gerrit. 1984. "China's Entry in International Society." In *The Expansion of International Society*, edited by Hedley Bull and Adam Watson. Oxford: Oxford University Press, 171–84.

Gottman, Jean. 1973. *The Significance of Territory*. Charlottesville: University of Virginia Press.

Gourevitch, Peter. 1978. "The Second Image Reversed: The International Sources of Domestic Politics." *International Organization* 32 (4): 881–911.

Gow, Greg. 2002. *The Oromo in Exile: From the Horn of Africa to the Suburbs of Australia*. Melbourne: Melbourne University Press.

Gowa, Joanne. 1999. *Ballots and Bullets: The Elusive Democratic Peace*. Princeton, N.J.: Princeton University Press.

Gray, Colin. 2004. "In Defense of the Heartland: Sir Halford Mackinder and His Critics a Hundred Years On." *Comparative Strategy* 23 (9): 9–25.

Green, Donald P., Soo Yeon Kim, and David H. Yoon. 2001. "Dirty Pool." *International Organization* 55 (2): 441–68.

Gregory, C. A. 1982. *Gifts and Commodities*. London: Academic Press.

Grieco, Joseph M. 1988. "Realist Theory and the Problem of International Cooperation: Analysis with an Amended Prisoner's Dilemma Model." *Journal of Politics* 50 (3): 600–24.

Griggs, Richard. 2000. "Designing Boundaries for a Continent: The Geopolitics of an African Renaissance." In *Borderlands under Stress*, edited by Martin Pratt and Janet Allison-Brown. London: Kluwer Academic Publishers, 227–50.

Guelke, Adrian. 1996. "The United States, Irish Americans, and the Northern Ireland Peace Process." *International Affairs* 72, 3 (July): 521–36.

Guldmann, Jean-Michel. 1999. "Competing Destinations and Intervening Opportunities: Interaction Models of Inter-city Telecommunication Flows." *Papers in Regional Science* 78 (2): 179–94.

Gupta, A. 1997. "Issues of South Asia: Geopolitics or Geoeconomics?" *International Studies* 34 (1): 15–24.

Gurr, Ted Robert. 1970. *Why Men Rebel*. Princeton, N.J.: Princeton University Press.

Gurr, Ted Robert, Keith Jaggers, and Will H. Moore. 1989. "Polity II: Political Structures and Regime Change, 1800–1986." Electronic resource. Boulder, Colo.: Center for Comparative Politics.

Hamilton, Carl, and L. Alan Winters. 1992. "Opening Up Trade with Eastern Europe." *Economic Policy* 14: 77–117.

Hancock, Kathleen J. 2001. "Surrendering Sovereignty: Hierarchy in the International System and the Former Soviet Union." Ph.D. diss., University of California, San Diego.

Hardin, Russell. 1995. *One for All: The Logic of Group Conflict*. Princeton, N.J.: Princeton University Press.

Hardy, Thomas. 1936. *The Dynasts: A Drama of the Napoleonic Wars, in Three Parts, Nineteen Acts, and One Hundred and Thirty Scenes.* London: Macmillan.

Harley, J. Brian. 1989. "Deconstructing the Map." *Cartographica* 26 (2): 1–20.

1990. "Cartography, Ethics, and Social Theory." *Cartographica* 27 (2): 1–23.

Harp, Stephen L. 1998. *Learning to be Loyal: Primary Schooling as Nation Building in Alsace and Lorraine.* DeKalb: Northern Illinois University Press.

Harris, William. 1978. "War and Settlement Change: The Golan Heights and the Jordan Rift Valley, 1967–1977." *Transactions of the Institute of British Geographers* 30 (3): 309–30.

Hasson, Shlomo, and Norman Gosenfeld. 1980. "Israeli Frontier Settlements: A Cross-Temporal Analysis." *Geoforum* 11: 315–34.

Havet, Julien. 1881. "La Frontière d'Empire dans l'Argonne; enquête faite par ordre de Rodolphe de Habsbourg? Verdun, en mai 1288." *Bibliothèque de l'école des chartes* 42: 383–428, 612.

Hechter, Michael. 2000. *Containing Nationalism.* New York: Oxford University Press.

Hegre, Håvard. 2000. "Development and the Liberal Peace: What Does it Take to Be a Trading State?" *Journal of Peace Research* 37 (1): 5–30.

Hegre, Håvard, Ranveig Gissinger, and Nils Petter Gleditsch. 2002. "Globalization and Internal Conflict." In *Globalization and Armed Conflict*, edited by Gerald Schneider, Katherine Barbieri, and Nils Petter Gleditsch. Lanham, Md.: Rowman and Littlefield, 251–75.

Hegre, Håvard, Tanja Ellingsen, Scott Gates, and Nils Petter Gleditsch. 2001. "Toward a Democratic Civil Peace? Democracy, Political Change, and Civil War, 1816–1992." *American Political Science Review* 95 (1): 33–48.

Heilbrunn, Jacob. 1998. "The Clash of Samuel Huntingtons." *The American Prospect* 39 (9): 22–28.

Held, Davids et al. 1999. *Global Transformationa: Politics, Economics, and Culture.* Stanford: Standford University Press.

Helleiner, Eric. 2003. *The Making of National Money: Territorial Currencies in Historical Perspective.* Ithaca, N.Y.: Cornell University Press.

Helliwell, John F. 1998. *How Much Do National Borders Matter?* Washington, D.C.: Brookings Institution.

Helpman, E. 1984. "Increasing Returns, Imperfect Markets, and Trade Theory." In *Handbook of International Trade*, edited by R. Jones and P. Kenen. Amsterdam: North Holland.

1987. "Imperfect Competition and International Trade: Evidence from Fourteen Industrial Countries." *Journal of Japanese and International Economics* 1: 62–81.

Henderson, Errol A. 1997. "Culture or Contiguity: Ethnic Conflict, the Similarity of States, and the Onset of War 1820–1989." *Journal of Conflict Resolution* 41 (5): 649–68.

Henderson, Errol A., and Richard Tucker. 2001. "Clear and Present Strangers: The Clash of Civilizations and International Conflict." *International Studies Quarterly* 45 (2): 317–38.

Hensel, Paul R. 1999. "Charting a Course to Conflict: Territorial Issues and Interstate Conflict, 1816–1992." In *A Road Map to War: Territorial*

Dimensions of International Conflict, edited by Paul F. Diehl. Nashville, Tenn.: Vanderbilt University Press. 115–46.

2000. "Territory: Theory and Evidence on Geography and Conflict." In *What Do We Know About War?*, edited by John A. Vasquez. Lanham, Md.: Rowman and Littlefield, 57–84.

2002. "The More Things Change. . . : Recognizing and Responding to Trends in Armed Conflict." *Conflict Management and Peace Science* 19 (1): 27–53.

Herb, Guntram H. 1999. "National Identity and Territory." In *Nested Identities: Nationalism, Territory, and Scale*, edited by Guntram H. Herb and David H. Kaplan. Lanham, Md.: Rowman and Littlefield, 9–30.

Herb, Guntram, and David Kaplan, eds. 1999. *Nested Identities: Nationalism, Territory, and Scale.* Lanham, Md.: Rowman and Littlefield.

Herbst, Jeffrey. 2000. *States and Power in Africa: Comparative Lessons in Authority and Control.* Princeton, N.J.: Princeton University Press.

Herz, John H. 1957. "Rise and Demise of the Territorial State." *World Politics* 9 (4): 473–93.

1968. "The Territorial State Revisited: Reflections on the Future of the Nation-State." *Polity* 1 (1): 11–34.

Hirsch, Eric. 2004. "Environment and Economy: Mutual Connections and Diverse Perspectives." *Anthropological Theory* 4 (4): 435–53.

Hirschman, Albert O. 1945. *National Power and the Structure of Foreign Trade.* Berkeley: University of California Press.

Hiscox, Michael J., and David A. Lake. 2000. "Democracy, Federalism, and the Size of States." Unpublished ms., Department of Political Science, University of California, San Diego.

Hobson, John A. 1938. *Imperialism.* Ann Arbor, Mich.: University of Michigan Press.

Holsti, Kalevi J. 1991. *Peace and War: Armed Conflicts and International Order 1648–1989.* New York: Cambridge University Press.

Homer-Dixon, Thomas F. 1991. "On the Threshold: Environmental Changes as Causes of Acute Conflict." *International Security* 16 (2): 76–116.

1994. "Environmental Scarcities and Violent Conflict, Evidence from Cases." *International Security* 19 (1): 5–40.

1999. *Environment, Scarcity, and Violence.* Princeton, N.J.: Princeton University Press.

Hooson, David, ed. 1994. *Geography and National Identity.* Oxford: Blackwell.

Horgan, John, and Max Taylor. 1999. "Playing the 'Green Card': Financing the Provisional IRA, Part I." *Terrorism and Political Violence* 11, 2 (summer): 1–38.

Horowitz, Donald L. 1985. *Ethnic Groups in Conflict.* Berkeley: University of California Press.

House, John. 1980. "The Frontier Zone: A Conceptual Problem for Policy Makers." *International Political Science Review* 1 : 456–77.

Hufbauer, Gary. 1991. "World Economic Integration: The Long View." *International Economic Insights* 2(3): 26–27.

Huntington, Samuel P. 1991. *The Third Wave: Democratization in the Late Twentieth Century.* Norman, Okla.: University of Oklahoma Press.

1993a. "If Not Civilizations, What?" *Foreign Affairs* 72 (4): 186–94.

1993b. "The Clash of Civilizations." *Foreign Affairs* 72 (3): 22–49.

1996. *The Clash of Civilizations and the Remaking of World Order.* New York: Simon and Schuster.

2000. "Try Again: A Reply to Russett, Oneal, and Cox." *Journal of Peace Research* 37 (5): 609–10.

Huth, Paul K. 1996. *Standing Your Ground: Territorial Disputes and International Conflict.* Ann Arbor: University of Michigan Press.

1999. "Enduring Rivalries and Territorial Disputes, 1950–1990." In *A Road Map to War: Territorial Dimensions of International Conflict,* edited by Paul F. Diehl. Nashville, Tenn.: Vanderbilt University Press, 37–72.

2000. "Territory: Why Are Territorial Disputes Between States a Central Cause of International Conflict?" In *What Do We Know About War?,* edited by John A. Vasquez. Lanham, Md.: Rowman and Littlefield, 85–110.

Huth, Paul K., and Todd L. Allee. 2003. *The Democratic Peace and Territorial Conflict in the Twentieth Century.* Cambridge: Cambridge University Press.

Inglehart, Ronald, and Pippa Norris. 2001. "The True Clash of Civilizations." *Foreign Policy* 135 (March): 62–70.

Inter-American Dialogue Task Force on Remittances. 2004. *All in the Family: Latin America's Most Important International Financial Flow.* Washington, D.C., January 2004.

Ireland, Gordon. 1938. *Boundaries, Possessions, and Conflicts in South America.* Cambridge, Mass.: Harvard University Press.

1941. *Boundaries, Possessions, and Conflicts in Central and North America and the Caribbean.* Cambridge, Mass.: Harvard University Press.

Irwin, Douglas, Michael Bordo, and Barry Eichengreen. 1999. *Is Globalization Today Really Different from Globalization a Hundred Years Ago?* Washington, D.C.: Brookings Institution.

Iwańska, Alicja. 1981. *Exiled Governments: Spanish and Polish.* Cambridge, Mass.: Schenkman.

Jackson, Robert H. 1990. *Quasi-States: Sovereignty, International Relations, and the Third World.* Cambridge: Cambridge University Press.

Jacob, M. C., ed. 1974. *Peace Projects of the Eighteenth Century.* New York: Garland.

Jaggers, Keith, and Ted R. Gurr. 1995. "Transitions to Democracy: Tracking Democracy's 'Third Wave' with the Polity III Data." *Journal of Peace Research* 32 (4): 469–82.

Jenkins, Philip. 2002. *The Next Christendom: The Coming of Global Christianity.* Oxford: Oxford University Press.

Jennings, R. Y. 1957. "Extraterritorial Jurisdiction and the United States' Anti-trust Laws." *British Yearbook of International Law* 33: 146–75.

Johnson, David, and David Post. 1995–96. "Law and Borders: The Rise of Cyberspace." *Stanford Law Review* 48: 1367–402.

Johnston, Ronald J. 1995. "Territoriality and the State." In *Geography, History and Social Sciences,* edited by Georges B. Benko and Ulf Strohmayer. Dordrecht: Kluwer Academic Publishers, 213–26.

Jones, Daniel, Stuart Bremer, and J. David Singer. 1996. "Militarized Interstate Disputes, 1816–1992: Rationale, Coding Rules, and Empirical Patterns." *Conflict Management and Peace Science* 15 (2): 163–213.

Joseph, J. S. 1996. "Cyprus at the Threshold of the European Union." *Mediterranean Quarterly* 7 (2): 112–22.

Juenger, Friedrich. 1983–84. "Judicial Jurisdiction in the U. S. and the EC: A Comparison." *Michigan Law Review* 82: 1205.

Kacowicz, Arie M. 1994. *Peaceful Territorial Change.* Columbia: University of South Carolina Press.

Kahler, Miles. 1984. *Decolonization in Britain and France.* Princeton, N.J.: Princeton University Press.

———. 2002. "The State of the State in World Politics." In *Political Science: The State of the Discipline,* edited by Ira Katznelson and Helen Milner. New York: W. W. Norton, 56–83

Kahler, Miles, and David A. Lake. 2003a. "Globalization and Governance." In *Governance in a Global Economy: Political Authority in Transition,* edited by Miles Kahler and David A. Lake. Princeton, N.J.: Princeton University Press, 1–30.

———. 2003b. "Globalization and Changing Patterns of Political Authority." In *Governance in a Global Economy: Political Authority in Transition,* edited by Miles Kahler and David A. Lake. Princeton, N.J.: Princeton University Press, 412–38.

Kahn, Miriam. 1996. "Your Place and Mine: Sharing Emotional Landscapes in Wamira, Papua New Guinea." In *Senses of Place,* edited by S. Feld and K. H. Basso. Santa Fe, N.M.: School of American Research Press, 167–96.

Kaldor, Mary. 1998. "Reconceptualizing Organized Violence." In *Re-imagining Political Community,* edited by Daniele Archibugi, David Held, and Martin Köhler. Stanford, Calif.: Stanford University Press, 91–110.

Kant, Immanuel. 1957. *Perpetual Peace.* New York: Liberal Arts Press.

Kantorowicz, Ernst Hartwig. 1997. *The King's Two Bodies: A Study in Mediaeval Political Theology.* Princeton, N.J.: Princeton University Press.

Kaplan, D., and J. Häkli, eds. 2002. *Boundaries and Place: European Borderlands in Geographical Context.* Lanham, Md.: Rowman and Littlefield.

Kaplan, Robert D. 1994. "The Coming Anarchy: How Scarcity, Crime, Overpopulation, Tribalism, and Disease are Rapidly Destroying the Social Fabric of our Planet." *Atlantic Monthly* 273 (2): 44–76.

———. 1997. *The Ends of the Earth: From Togo to Turkmenistan, from Iran to Cambodia: A Journey to the Frontiers of Anarchy.* New York: Random House.

———. 2000. *The Coming Anarchy: Shattering the Dreams of the Post–Cold War World.* New York: Random House.

Kapstein, Ethan B. 1994. *Governing the Global Economy: International Finance and the State.* Cambridge, Mass.: Harvard University Press.

Katznelson, Ira. 2002. "Rewriting the Epic of America." In *Shaped by War and Trade: International Influences on America Political Development,* edited by Ira Katznelson and Martin Shefter. Princeton, N.J.: Princeton University Press, 1–23.

Kautsky, Karl. 1914. "Imperialism and the War." *International Socialist Review* 15 (5): 282–86.

Kay, Sean. 2004. "Globalization, Power, and Security." *Security Dialogue* 35 (1): 9–25.

Keene, Derek. 1996. "Landlords, and Property Market and Urban Development in Medieval England." In *Power, Profit, and Urban Land: Landownership in Medieval and Early Modern Northern European Towns*, edited by Finn-Einar Eliassen and Geir Atle Ersland. Brookfield, Vt.: Ashgate, 93–119.

Kellerman, Aharon. 1993. *Society and Settlement: Jewish Land of Israel in the Twentieth Century.* Albany, N.Y.: SUNY Press.

———. 1995. "Comment on Falah." *Area* 27 (1): 76–77.

Kennan, George. 1962. *Russia and the West under Lenin and Stalin.* Boston, Mass.: Little, Brown.

Kennedy, Paul M. 1987. *The Rise and Fall of the Great Powers: Economic Change and Military Conflict from 1500 to 2000.* New York: Random House.

Kennedy, Paul, and Mathew Connelly. 1994. "Must It Be the Rest Against the West?" *Atlantic Monthly* 274 (6): 61–84.

Keohane, Robert O. 1984. *After Hegemony: Cooperation and Discord in the World Political Economy.* Princeton, N.J.: Princeton University Press.

Keohane, Robert O., and Joseph S. Nye. 1989. *Power and Interdependence.* New York: HarperCollins.

———. 2000. "Introduction." In *Governance in a Globalizing World*, edited by Joseph S. Nye and John D. Donahue. Washington, D.C.: Brookings Institution, 1–41.

Kern, Fritz. 1910. *Die Anfänge der französischen Ausdehnungspolitik bis zum Jahr 1308.* Tübingen: J. C. B. Mohr.

Kern, Fritz, ed. 1911. *Acta Imperii Angliae et Franciae ab a. 1267 ad a. 1313.* Tübingen: J. C. B. Mohr.

Kimmerling, Baruch. 1983. *Zionism and Territory: The Socio-Territorial Dimension of Zionist Politics.* Berkeley, Calif.: University of California Press.

Kindleberger, Charles P. 1969. *American Business Abroad: Six Lectures on Direct Investment.* New Haven, Conn.: Yale University Press.

King, Gary. 1996. "Why Context Should Not Count." *Political Geography* 15 (2): 159–64.

Kirkpatrick, Jeane F., et al. 1993. "The Modernizing Imperative: Tradition and Change." *Foreign Affairs* 72: 22–26.

Klemencic, Mladen. 2000. "The Boundaries, Internal Order, and Identities of Bosnia and Herzegovina." *Boundary and Security Bulletin* 8 (4): 63–71.

———. 2001. "Threats to Macedonia's Stability and Borders." *Boundary and Security Bulletin* 9 (1): 73–78.

Klieman, Aaron. 1980. "The Resolution of Conflicts Through Territorial Partition: The Palestine Experience." *Comparative Studies in Society and History* 42: 281–300.

Kliot, Nurit. 1986. "Lebanon: A Geography of Hostages." *Political Geography Quarterly* 5 (3): 199–220.

———. 2002. "Transborder Peace Parks: The Political Geography of Cooperation (and Conflict) in Borderlands." In *The Razor's Edge: International Boundaries and Political Geography*, edited by Clive Schofield et al. London: Kluwer Academic Publishers, 407–37.

Kliot, Nurit, and Yoel Mansfield. 1997. "The Political Landscape of Partition: The Case of Cyprus." *Political Geography* 16 (6): 495–521.

Kliot, Nurit, and Stanley Waterman. 1990. "The Political Impact on Writing the Geography of Palestine/Israel." *Progress in Human Geography* 14 (2): 237–60.

Knight, David B. 1994. "People Together, Yet Apart: Rethinking Territory, Sovereignty, and Identities." In *Reordering the World: Geopolitical Perspectives on the Twenty-First Century*, edited by George J. Demko and William B. Wood. Boulder, Colo.: Westview Press, 71–86.

———. 1999a. "Bounding Whose Territory? Potential Conflict between a State and a Province Desiring Statehood." *Geopolitics* 4 (2): 209–38.

———. 1999b. "Afterword: Nested Identities: Nationalism, Territory, and Scale." In *Nested Identities: Nationalism, Territory, and Scale*, edited by Guntram H. Herb and David H. Kaplan. Lanham, Md.: Rowman and Littlefield, 317–29.

Knox, Paul. 1995. *Urban Social Geography: An Introduction*. Harlow, UK: Longman.

Kobrin, Stephen J. 1997. "Beyond Symmetry: State Sovereignty in a Networked Global Economy." In *Governments, Globalization, and International Business*, edited by J. Dunning. Oxford: Oxford University Press.

Kocs, S. 1995. "Territorial Disputes and International War, 1943–1987." *Journal of Politics* 57 (1): 59–175.

Kolossov, Vladimir. 1998. "The Political Geography of European Minorities: Past and Future." *Political Geography* 17 (5): 517–34.

Kolossov, Vladimir, and John O'Loughlin. 1998. "New Borders for New World Orders: Territorialities at the Fin de Siecle." *GeoJournal* 44 (3): 259–73.

Koo, Won W., and David Karemera. 1991. "Determinants of World Wheat Trade Flows and Policy Analysis." *Canadian Journal of Agricultural Economics* 39 (3): 439–55.

Koslowski, Rey. 2001. "Demographic Boundary Maintenance in World Politics: Of International Norms on Dual Nationality." In *Identities, Borders, Orders: Rethinking International Relations Theory*, edited by Mathias Albert, David Jacobson, and Yosef Lapid. Minneapolis: University of Minnesota Press, 203–23.

Kosonen, Katariina. 1999. "Maps, Newspapers, and Nationalism: The Finnish Historical Experience." *GeoJournal* 48: 91–100.

Kraft, C. H. 2002. "Spiritual Warfare: A Neocharismatic Perspective." In *The New International Dictionary of Pentecostal and Charismatic Movements*, edited by S. M. Burgess and E. M. van der Maas. Grand Rapids, Mich.: Zondervan, 1091–96.

Kramer, Larry. 1991. "Vestiges of Beale: Extraterritorial Application of American Law." *Supreme Court Review* (1991): 179–224.

Krasner, Stephen D. 1999. *Sovereignty: Organized Hypocrisy*. Princeton, N.J.: Princeton University Press.

Kratochwil, Friedrich. 1986. "Of Systems, Boundaries, and Territoriality: An Inquiry into the Formation of the State System." *World Politics* 39, 1 (October): 27–52.

Kreps, David M. 1990. "Corporate Culture and Economic Theory." In *Perspectives on Positive Political Economy*, edited by James E. Alt and Kenneth A. Shepsle. New York: Cambridge University Press, 90–143.

Kugler, Jacek, and Mariana Arbetman. 1997. *Political Capacity and Economic Behavior*. Boulder, Colo.: Westview Press.

Kugler, Jacek, and Douglas Lemke. 1996. *Parity and War: Evaluations and Extensions of "The War Ledger."* Ann Arbor, Mich.: University of Michigan Press.

Kugler, Jacek, and A. F. K. Organski. 1989. "The Power Transition: A Retrospective and Prospective Evaluation." In *The Handbook of War Studies*, edited by Manus Midlarsky. Boston: Unwin Hyman, 171–94.

Kugler, Richard L., and Ellen L. Frost, eds. 2001. *The Global Century: Globalization and National Security.* Washington, D.C.: National Defense University Press.

Kuznets, Simon. 1966. *Modern Economic Growth.* New Haven, Conn.: Yale University Press.

1973. "Modern Economic Growth: Findings and Reflections." *American Economic Review* 63 (3): 247–58.

Lacina, Bethany and Nils Petter Gleditsch. 2005. "Monitoring Trends in Global Combat? A New Dataset of Battle Deaths." *European Journal of Population* 21 (2–3): 145–66.

Lacina, Bethany, Bruce Russett, and Nils Petter Gleditsch. 2005. "The Declining Risk of Death in Battle." Paper prepared for the 46th Annual Convention of the International Studies Association, Honolulu, HI, March 2–5.

Lake, David A., and Angela O'Mahony. 2004. "The Incredible Shrinking State: Explaining Change in the Territorial Size of Countries." *Journal of Conflict Resolution* 48, 5 (October): 699–722.

Leamer, Edward E. 1974. "The Commodity Composition of International Trade in Manufactures: An Empirical Analysis." *Oxford Economic Papers* 26: 350–74.

Leamer, Edward E., and James Levinsohn. 1995. "International Trade Theory: The Evidence." In *Handbook of International Economics*, edited by G. M. Grossman and K. Rogoff. Elsevier: North Holland.

Lemke, Douglas. 2002. *Regions of War and Peace.* Cambridge: Cambridge University Press.

2003. "Development and War." *International Studies Review* 5 (4): 55–63.

Lemon, Anthony. 2002. "South Africa's Internal Boundaries: The Spatial Engineering of Land and Power in the Twentieth Century." In *The Razor's Edge: International Boundaries and Political Geography*, edited by Clive Schofield et al. London: Kluwer Academic Publishers, 303–22.

Lenin, V. I. 1939. *Imperialism: The Highest Stage of Capitalism.* New York: International Publishers.

1965. *Imperialism, the Highest Stage of Capitalism.* Beijing, PRC: Foreign Languages Press. Reprint of the text as given in V. I. Lenin, *Selected Works*, Moscow, 1952.

1978. *The Proletarian Revolution and the Renegade Kautsky.* 7th edn. Moscow: Progress.

Levi, Margaret. 1997. *Consent, Dissent, and Patriotism.* Cambridge: Cambridge University Press.

Levy, Jack S. 1983. *War in the Modern Great Power System, 1495–1975.* Lexington: University of Kentucky Press.

Lewis, David K. 1969. *Convention: A Philosophical Study.* Cambridge, Mass.: Harvard University Press.

Liebknecht, Karl. 1969. *Militarism and Anti-Militarism: With Special Regard to the International Young Socialist Movement.* New York: Howard Fertig.

Lilley, Keith D. 2002. *Urban Life in the Middle Ages, 1000–1450.* New York: Palgrave Macmillan.

Linge, G. J. R. 1995. "The Kuriles: The Geopolitical Spanner in the Geoeconomic Works." *Australian Geographical Studies* 33 (1): 116–32.

Linnemann, Hans. 1966. *An Econometric Study of International Trade Flows.* Amsterdam: North-Holland.

Lipson, Charles. 1991. "Why Are Some International Agreements Informal?" *International Organization* 45 (4): 495–538.

Locke, John. 1988. *Two Treatises of Government: Second Treatise.* Student edn. Edited by Peter Laslett. New York: Cambridge University Press.

Long, David. 1996. *Towards a New Internationalism: The International Theory of J. A. Hobson.* Cambridge: Cambridge University Press.

Longnon, Auguste. 1922. *La Formation de l'unité française. Leçons professées au Collège de France en 1889–1890.* Paris: Auguste Picard.

Lorenz, Konrad. 1966. *On Aggression.* New York: Harcourt, Brace, and World.

Low, D. A. 1991. *Eclipse of Empire.* Cambridge: Cambridge University Press.

Luard, Evan. 1986. *War in International Society: A Study in International Sociology.* London: I. B. Tauris.

1988. *Conflict and Peace in the Modern International System: A Study of the Principles of International Order.* Houndmills, UK: Macmillan.

Lugge, Margret. 1960. *"Gallia" und "Francia" im Mittelalter.* Bonn: Ludwig Röhrsched Verlag.

Luke, Timothy W. 1991. "The Discipline of Security Studies and the Codes of Containment: Learning from Kuwait." *Alternatives* 16 (3): 315–44.

Lustick, Ian S. 1993. *Unsettled States, Disputed Lands: Britain and Ireland, France and Algeria, Israel and the West Bank–Gaza.* Ithaca, N.Y.: Cornell University Press.

Luxemburg, Rosa. 1971. *The Mass Strike, The Political Party and the Trade Unions, and The Junius Pamphlet.* New York: Harper and Row.

Lyons, Terrence. 1996. "Closing the Transition: The May 1995 Elections in Ethiopia." *Journal of Modern African Studies* 34, 1 (March): 121–42.

Lyons, Terrence, Christopher Mitchell, Tamra Pearson d'Estree, and Lulsegged Abebe. 2004. *The Ethiopian Extended Dialogue: An Analytical Report, 2000–2003.* Fairfax, Va.: Institute for Conflict Analysis and Resolution.

Mackinder, Halford John. 1904. "The Geographical Pivot of History." *The Geographical Journal* 23 (4): 421–44.

1962. *Democratic Ideals and Reality.* Westport, Conn.: Greenwood.

Mahan, A. T. 1915. *The Interest of America in International Conditions.* Boston: Little, Brown.

1987 [1890]. *The Influence of Sea Power on History, 1660–1783.* 5th edn. New York: Dover.

Maier, Charles S. 2000. "Consigning the Twentieth Century to History: Alternative Narratives for the Modern Era." *American Historical Review* 105 (3): 807–31. Available at http://www.historycooperative.org/journals/ahr/105.3/ah000807.html.

Malthus, T. R. 1958. *An Essay on Population.* London: Dent.

Mandell, Robert. 1980. "Roots of Modern Interstate Border Disputes." *Journal of Conflict Resolution* 24: 427–54.

Maney, Gregory M. 2000. "Transnational Mobilization and Civil Rights in Northern Ireland." *Social Problems* 47 (2): 153–79.

Maoz, Zeev. 2001. "Dyadic MID Data Set, Version 1.1 Codebook." Electronic resource. School of Government and Policy, Department of Political Science, Tel-Aviv University. http://spirit.tau.ac.il/poli/faculty/maoz/dyadmid. html.

Maoz, Zeev, and Bruce Russett. 1992. "Alliances, Contiguity, Distance, Wealth, and Political Stability: Is the Lack of Conflict among Democracies a Statistical Artifact?" *International Interactions* 17 (3): 245–68.

Marcusen, J., and R. Wigle. 1990. "Explaining the Volume of North–South Trade." *Economic Journal* 100: 1206–15.

Marshall, Monty G., and Keith Jaggers. 2000. *Polity IV.* Available at http://www. cidcm.umd.edu/inscr/polity/

Martin, David. 2002. *Pentecostalism: The World Their Parish.* Oxford: Blackwell.

Martinez, Oskar. 1994. The Dynamics of Border Interaction: New Approaches to Border Analysis." In *Global Boundaries*, edited by Clive Schofield. London: Routledge, 1–15.

Mason, T. David. 2003. "Globalization, Democratization, and the Prospects for Civil War in the New Millennium." *International Studies Review* 5 (4): 19–35.

Masson, Paul. 2001. "Globalization: Facts and Figures." IMF Policy Discussion Paper 4. Washington, D.C.: International Monetary Fund.

Matthes, Norbert. 1994. "Allocation of Mobile Communication Flows: From Microeconomic Demand Theory to a Gravity Model." *Annals of Regional Science* 28 (4): 395–409.

Maurseth, Per Botolf. 2003. "Geography and Growth: Some Empirical Evidence." *Nordic Journal of Political Economy* 29 (1): 25–46.

Mauss, Marcel. 1990 [1925]. *The Gift: The Form and Reason for Exchange in Archaic Societies.* Translated by W. D. Halls. London: Routledge.

May, Ernest. 1991[1961]. *Imperial Democracy: The Emergence of America as a Great Power.* 2nd edn. New York: Harcourt Brace.

Maynes, Charles William. 1995. "The New Pessimism." *Foreign Policy* 100: 33–49.

McCallum, John. 1995. "National Borders Matter: Canada–U.S. Regional Trade Patterns." *American Economic Review* 85 (3): 615–23.

McGuire, Martin C., and Mancur Olson. 1996. "The Economics of Autocracy and Majority Rule: The Invisible Hand and the Use of Force." *Journal of Economic Literature* 34 (1): 72–96.

Mearsheimer, John J. 1983. *Conventional Deterrence.* Ithaca, N.Y.: Cornell University Press.

    1994/95. "The False Promise of International Institutions." *International Security* 19 (3): 5–26.

    2001. *The Tragedy of Great Power Politics.* New York: W. W. Norton.

Meyer, P. F. 1998. "Russo-Japanese Relations: Opportunity for Rapprochement?" *Demokratizatsiya* 6 (2): 363–79.

Michaud, Joseph François. 1973 [1852]. *History of the Crusades*, vol III. Translated by W. Robson. New York: AMS Press.

Michaels, Ralf. 2004. "Territorial Jurisdiction after Territoriality." In *Globalisation and Jurisdiction*, edited by P. J. Slot and M. Bulterman. New York: Kluwer.

Milenkoski, Mile, and Jove Talevski. 2001. "The Borders of the Republic of Macedonia." *Boundary and Security Bulletin* 9 (1): 79–85.

Mill, John Stuart. 1864. *Principles of Political Economy*. New York: Appleton.

Modelski, George A. 1987. *Long Cycles in World Politics*. Seattle: University of Washington Press.

Modelski, George, and William R. Thompson. 1988. *Seapower in Global Politics, 1494–1993*. Seattle: University of Washington Press.

Mohamoud, A. A. 2005. "Diaspora: Untapped Potential for Peacebuilding in the Homelands." In *People Building Peace II: Successful Stories of Civil Society*, edited by Paul van Tongeren, Malin Brenk, Marte Hellema, and Juliette Verhoeven. Boulder, Colo.: Lynne Rienner.

Monmonier, Mark. 1995. *Drawing the Line: Tales of Maps and Cartocontroversy*. New York: Henry Holt.

Montague, Dena. 2002. "Stolen Goods: Coltan and Conflict in the Democratic Republic of Congo." *SAIS Review* 22 (1): 103–18.

Montesquieu, Baron de. 1989 [1748]. *Spirit of the Laws*. Cambridge: Cambridge University Press.

Mooradian, Moorad. 2004. "Reconciliation: A Case Study of the Turkish Armenian Reconciliation Commission." Institute for Conflict Analysis and Resolution Working Paper. Institute for Conflict Analysis and Resolution, Fairfax, Va.

Morgenthau, Hans J. 1948. *Politics among Nations: The Struggle for Power and Peace*. New York: Knopf.

1985. *Politics among Nations: The Struggle for Power and Peace*. 6th edn. New York: Alfred Knopf.

Morley, David, and Kevin Robins. 1993. "No Place like Heimat: Images of Home(land) in European Culture." In *Space and Place: Theories of Identity and Location*, edited by Erica Carter, James Donald, and Judith Squires. London: Lawrence and Wishart, 3–31.

Morrow, James D. 1999. "How Could Trade Affect Conflict?" *Journal of Peace Research* 36, 4 (July): 481–89.

Morse, Edward. 1976. *Modernization and the Transformation of International Relations*. New York: Basic Books.

Most, Benjamin A., and Harvey Starr. 1980. "Diffusion, Reinforcement, Geopolitics, and the Spread of War." *American Political Science Review* 74 (4): 932–46.

1989. *Inquiry, Logic, and International Politics*. Columbia: University of South Carolina Press.

1990. "Opportunity, Willingness, and the Diffusion of War." *American Political Science Review* 84 (1): 47–67.

Motyl, Alexander. 2001. "Reifying Boundaries – Fetishizing the Nation: Soviet Legacies and Elite Legitimacy in Post-Soviet States." In *Right-Sizing the State: The Politics of Moving Borders*, edited by B. O'Leary, I. Lustick, and T. Callaghy. Oxford: Oxford University Press, 201–21.

Mueller, John. 1989. *Retreat from Doomsday: The Obsolescence of Major War*. New York: Basic Books.

1995. "The Catastrophe Quota: Trouble after the Cold War." *Journal of Conflict Resolution* 38 (3): 355–75.

Murdoch, James C., and Todd Sandler. 2002. "Economic Growth, Civil Wars, and Spatial Spillovers." *Journal of Conflict Resolution* 46 (1): 91–110.

2004. "Civil Wars and Economic Growth: Spatial Dispersion." *American Journal of Political Science* 48 (1): 138–51.

Murphy, Alexander B. 1989. "Territorial Policies in Multiethnic States." *Geographical Review* 79: 410–21.

1990. "Historical Justifications for Territorial Claims." *Annals of the Association of American Geographers* 80 (4): 531–48.

1996. "The Sovereign State System as a Political-Territorial Ideal: Historical and Contemporary Considerations." In *State Sovereignty as Social Construct*, edited by T. Biersteker and C. Weber. Cambridge: Cambridge University Press, 81–120.

1999. "International Law and the Sovereign State System: Challenges to the Status Quo." In *Reordering the World: Geopolitical Perspectives on the Twenty-first Century*, edited by G. J. Demko and W. B. Woods. Boulder, Colo.: Westview Press.

2001. "Political Geography." In *International Encyclopedia of the Social and Behavioral Sciences*, edited by N. D. Smelser and P. B. Baltes. Amsterdam: Pergamon.

2002. "National Claims to Territory in the Modern State System: Geographical Considerations." *Geopolitics* 7 (2): 193–214.

Nadelmann, Ethan. 1993. *Cops across Borders: The Internationalization of U.S. Criminal Law Enforcement*. University Park: Pennsylvania State Press.

Naficy, Hamid. 1991. "The Poetics and Practice of Iranian Nostalgia in Exile." *Diaspora* 1, 3 (winter): 285–302.

Neuman, Gerald. 1996a. "Anomalous Zones." *Stanford Law Review* 48: 1197–234.

1996b. *Strangers to the Constitution*. Princeton, N.J.: Princeton University Press.

Newman, David. 1989. "The Role of Civilian and Military Presence as Strategies of Territorial Control: The Arab–Israel Conflict." *Political Geography Quarterly* 8 (3): 215–27.

1996a. "The Territorial Politics of Exurbanization: Reflections on Thirty Years of Jewish Settlement in the West Bank." *Israel Affairs* 3 (1): 61–85.

1996b. "Writing Together Separately: Critical Discourse and the Problems of Cross-Ethnic Coauthorship." *Area* 28 (1): 1–12.

1998a. "Metaphysical and Concrete Landscapes: The Geopiety of Homeland Socialization in the 'Land of Israel'." In *Land and Community: Geography in Jewish Studies*, edited by Harold Brodsky. Bethesda: University Press of Maryland, 153–84.

1998b. "Creating the Fences of Territorial Separation: The Discourse of Israeli–Palestinian Conflict Resolution." *Geopolitics and International Boundaries* 2 (2): 1–35.

1999. "Real Spaces, Symbolic Spaces: Interrelated Notions of Territory in the Arab–Israeli Conflict." In *A Road Map to War*, edited by Paul Diehl. Nashville, Tenn.: Vanderbilt University Press, 3–34.

2002a. "From 'Moribund Backwater' to 'Thriving into the Next Century': The Changing Research Agenda of Political Geography." In *The Razor's Edge: International Boundaries and Political Geography*, edited by Clive Schofield et al. London: Kluwer Academic Publishers, 3–24.

2002b. "Boundaries." In *A Companion to Political Geography*, edited by John Agnew, Katharyne Mitchell, and Gerard Toal. Oxford: Blackwell, 123–37.

2002c. "The Geopolitics of Peacemaking in Israel–Palestine." *Political Geography* 21 (5): 629–46.

2003. "On Borders and Power: A Theoretical Framework." *Journal of Borderland Studies* 18 (1): 13–24.

2004. "Conflict at the Interface: The Impact of Boundaries and Borders on Contemporary Ethno-National Conflict." In *The Geography of War and Peace*, edited by Colin Flint. London: Oxford University Press, 321–44.

Newman, David, and Anssi Paasi. 1998. "Fences and Neighbors in the Post-Modern World: Boundary Narratives in Political Geography." *Progress in Human Geography* 22 (2): 186–207.

O'Brien, Richard. 1992. *Global Financial Integration: The End of Geography*. London: Pinter Publishers.

O'Grady, Joseph. 1996. "An Irish Policy Born in the U.S.A.: Clinton's Break with the Past." *Foreign Affairs* 75, 3 (May–June): 2–7.

O'Loughlin, John. 2000. "Geography as Space and Geography as Place: The Divide between Political Science and Political Geography Continues." *Geopolitics* 5 (3): 126–37.

2004. "Democratic Values in a Globalizing World: A Multilevel Analysis of Geographic Contexts." *Geojournal* 60 (1): 3–17.

O'Loughlin, John, Michael D. Ward, Corey L. Lofdahl, Jordin S. Cohen, David S. Brown, David Reilly, Kristian S. Gleditsch, and Michael Shin. 1998. "The Diffusion of Democracy, 1946–1994." *Annals of the Association of American Geographers* 88 (4): 545–74.

O'Rourke, Kevin H., and Jeffrey G. Williamson. 2000. *Globalization and History: The Evolution of a Nineteenth-Century Atlantic Economy*. Cambridge, Mass.: MIT Press.

Obstfeld, Maurice, and Kenneth Rogoff. 2001. "The Six Major Puzzles in International Macroeconomics. Is There a Common Cause?" NBER Working Paper 7777. Washington, D.C:. National Bureau of Economic Research.

Oguledo, Victor Iwuagwu, and Craig R. MacPhee. 1996. "Gravity Models: A Reformulation and an Application to Discriminatory Trade Arrangements." *Applied Economics* 24: 107–20.

Ohmae, Ken'ichi. 1990. *The Borderless World: Power and Strategy in the Interlinked Economy*. New York: Harper Business.

1995. *The End of the Nation State: The Rise of Regional Economies*. New York: Free Press.

Olson, Mancur. 1993. "Dictatorship, Democracy, and Development." *American Political Science Review* 87 (3): 567–76.

2000. *Power and Prosperity: Outgrowing Communist and Capitalist Dictatorships*. New York: Basic Books.

Oneal, John R., and Bruce Russett. 1999a. "Assessing the Liberal Peace with Alternative Specifications: Trade Still Reduces Conflict." *Journal of Peace Research* 36 (4): 423–42.

1999b. "The Kantian Peace: The Pacific Benefits of Democracy, Interdependence, and International Organizations, 1885–1992." *World Politics* 52 (1): 1–37.

Oommen, T. K. 1995. "Contested Boundaries and Emerging Pluralism." *International Sociology* 10: 251–68.

Oren, Ido, and Jude Hays. 1997. "Democracies May Rarely Fight One Another, but Developed Socialist States Rarely Fight at All." *Alternatives: Social Transformation and Humane Governance* 22 (4): 493–521.

Organski, A. F. K. 1958. *World Politics.* New York: Knopf.

Organski, A. F. K., and Jacek Kugler. 1980. *The War Ledger.* Chicago: University of Chicago Press.

Orridge, Andrew W. 1982. "Separatist and Autonomist Nationalisms: The Structure of Regional Loyalties in the Modern State." In *National Separatism*, edited by Colin H. Williams. Cardiff: University of Wales Press, 43–74.

Osiander, Andreas. 2001. "Sovereignty, International Relations, and the Westphalian Myth." *International Organization* 55, 2 (spring): 251–88.

Ostrom, Elinor. 2000. "Collective Action and the Evolution of Social Norms." *Journal of Economic Perspectives* 14 (1): 137–58.

Paasi, Anssi. 1995. "Constructing territories, boundaries and regional identities." In *Contested Territory: Border Disputes at the Edge of the Former Soviet Empire*, edited by Tuomas Forsberg. Aldershot, UK: Edward Elgar, 42–61.

1996. *Territories, Boundaries, and Consciousness: The Changing Geographies of the Finnish–Russian Border.* New York: John Wiley and Sons.

1998. "Boundaries as Social Processes: Territoriality in the World of Flows." *Geopolitics* 3 (1): 69–88.

1999. "Boundaries as Social Processes: Territoriality in the World of Flows." In *Boundaries, Territoriality, and Postmodernity*, edited by David Newman. London: Frank Cass, 69–88.

2002. "Territory." In *A Companion to Political Geography*, edited by John Agnew, Katharyne Mitchell, and Gerard Toal. Oxford: Blackwell, 109–22.

Pahl, Ray. 1969. "Urban Social Theory and Research." *Environment and Planning A*: 143–53.

Papastergiadis, Nikos. 2000. *The Turbulence of Migration: Globalization, Deterritorialization, and Hybridity.* Cambridge: Polity Press.

Papayoanou, Paul A. 1996. "Interdependence, Institutions, and the Balance of Power: Britain, Germany, and World War I." *International Security* 20 (4): 42–76.

1999. *Power Ties: Economic Interdependence, Balancing, and War.* Ann Arbor: University of Michigan Press.

Papayoanou, Paul, and Scott L. Kastner. 1999. "Sleeping with the (Potential) Enemy: Assessing the U. S. Policy of Engagement with China." *Security Studies* 9 (1/2): 157–87.

Peceny, Mark, Caroline C. Beer, and Shannon Sanchez-Terry. 2002. "Dictatorial Peace?" *American Political Science Review* 96 (1): 15–26.

Peckham, Robert Shannan. 2000. "Map Mania: Nationalism and the Politics of Place in Greece, 1870–1922." *Political Geography* 19: 77–95.

Pegg, Scott. 2003. "Globalization and Natural-Resource Conflicts." *Naval War College Review* 56 (4): 82–96.

Peninou, Jean-Louis. 1998. "The Ethiopian-Eritrean Border Conflict." *Boundary and Security Bulletin* 6 (2): 46–50.

Petersen, Roger D. 2001. *Resistance and Rebellion: Lessons from Eastern Europe.* New York: Cambridge University Press.

Polachek, Solomon W. 2002. "Trade-Based Interactions: An Interdisciplinary Perspective." *Conflict Management and Peace Science* 19 (2): 1–21.

Polachek, Solomon W., John Robst, and Yuan-Ching Chang. 1998. "Geographic Proximity and Interdependence: The Relationship between Distance, Trade and International Interactions." Working Paper 9805. Binghamton, N.Y.: Department of Economics, Binghamton University.

Polanyi, Karl. 1957. *The Great Transformation.* New York: Octagon.

Polak, Jacques J. 1996. "Is APEC a Natural Trading Bloc? A Critique of the 'Gravity Model' of International Trade." *World Economy* 19 (5): 533–43.

Polat, Necati. 2002. *Boundary Issues in Central Asia.* Ardsley, N.Y.: Transnational Publishers.

Pollins, Brian M. 1989. "Conflict, Cooperation, and Commerce: The Effect of International Political Interactions on Bilateral Trade Flows." *American Journal of Political Science* 33 (3): 737–61.

Portes, Alejandro. 1999. "Toward a New World Order: The Origins and Effects of Transnational Activities." *Ethnic and Racial Studies* 22 (2): 463–77.

Portugali, Juval. 1991. "Jewish Settlements in the Occupied Territories: Israeli Settlement Structure and the Palestinians." *Political Geography Quarterly* 10 (1): 26–53.

Pounds, Norman J. G. 1951. "The Origin of the Idea of Natural Frontiers in France." *Annals of the Association of American Geographers* 41 (2): 146–57.

Povrzanovic-Frykman, Maja. 2001. "Challenges of Belonging in Diaspora and Exile." In *Beyond Integration: Challenges of Belonging in Diaspora and Exile,* edited by Maja Povrzanovic-Frykman. Lund: Nordic Academic Press, 11–40.

Powell, Robert. 1999. *In the Shadow of Power: States and Strategies in International Politics.* Princeton, N.J.: Princeton University Press.

Poyhonen, Pentti. 1963. "A Tentative Model for the Volume of Trade between Countries." *Weltwirtschaftliches Archiv* 90: 93–99.

Prescott, J. R. V. 1987. *Political Frontiers and Boundaries.* London: Unwin Hyman.

Pringle, Dennis. 1997. "Globalization, Reterritorialization and National Identity." *Geopolitics* 3 (3): 1–13.

Quester, George H. 1977. *Offense and Defense in the International System.* New York: John Wiley and Sons.

Ratner, Steven R. 1996. "Drawing a Better Line: *Uti possidetis* and the Borders of New States." *American Journal of International Law* 90 (4): 590–624.

Raustiala, Kal. 1999. "Law, Liberalization, and International Narcotics Trafficking." *NYU Journal of International Law and Politics* 32 (1): 89–145.

2002. "The Architecture of International Cooperation." *Virginia Journal of International Law.* 43: 1–92.

Ray, James Lee. 1998. "Does Democracy Cause Peace?" *Annual Review of Political Science* 13 (1): 27–46.

Rector, Chad. 2003. "Federations and International Politics." Ph.D. diss., University of California, San Diego.

Reichmann, Shalom. 1986. "Policy Reduces the World to Essentials: A Reflection on the Jewish Settlement Process in the West Bank since 1967." In *Planning in Turbulence,* edited by David Morley and Aryeh Shachar. Jerusalem: Magness Press.

Reimitz, Helmut. 2000. "Grenzen und Grenzüberschreitungen im Karolingischen Mitteleuropa." In *Grenze und Differenz im frühen Mittelalter,* edited by Walter Pohl and Helmut Reimitz. Wien: Verlag der Oesterreichischen Akademie der Wissenschaften, 105–66.

Reynolds, Susan. 1997. *Kingdoms and Communities in Western Europe, 900–1300.* Oxford: Clarendon Press.

Richardson, Lewis F. 1960. *Statistics of Deadly Quarrels.* Pittsburgh, Pa.: Quadrangle/Boxwood.

Robbins, Joel. 1995. "Dispossessing the Spirits: Christian Transformations of Desire and Ecology among the Urapmin of Papua New Guinea." *Ethnology* 34 (3): 211–24.

1998. "On Reading 'World News': Apocalyptic Narrative, Negative Nationalism, and Transnational Christianity in a Papua New Guinea Society." *Social Analysis* 42 (2): 103–30.

1999. "'This Is Our Money:' Modernism, Regionalism, and Dual Currencies in Urapmin." In *Money and Modernity: State and Local Currencies in Contemporary Melanesia,* edited by J. Robbins and D. Akin. Pittsburgh, Pa.: University of Pittsburgh Press, 82–102.

2003. "Properties of Nature, Properties of Culture: Possession, Recognition, and the Substance of Politics in a Papua New Guinea Society." *Journal of the Finnish Anthropological Society (Suomen Antropologi)* 28 (1): 9–28.

2004a. *Becoming Sinners: Christianity and Moral Torment in a Papua New Guinea Society.* Berkeley: University of California Press.

2004b. "The Globalization of Pentecostal and Charismatic Christianity." *Annual Review of Anthropology* 33: 117–43.

Robertson, Roland. 1992. *Globalization: Social Theory and Global Culture.* London: Sage.

Rodrik, Dani. 1997. *Has Globalization Gone Too Far?* Washington, D.C.: Institute for International Economics.

1999. *The New Global Economy and Developing Countries: Making Openness Work.* Washington, D.C.: Overseas Development Council.

Romann, Michael, and Alex Weingrod. 1991. *Living Together Separately: Jews and Arabs in Contemporary Jerusalem.* Princeton, N.J.: Princeton University Press.

Rose, Andrew. 1999. "One Money, One Market: Estimating the Effect of Common Currencies on Trade." NBER Working Paper No. 7432. Cambridge, Mass.: National Bureau of Economic Research.

Rosecrance, Richard N. 1985. *The Rise of the Trading State: Commerce and Conquest in the Modern World*. New York: Basic Books.

1996. "The Rise of the Virtual State." *Foreign Affairs* 75 (4): 45–61.

Rostow, W. W. 1998. "The Five Stages of Economic Growth." In *Development and Under-Development: The Political Economy of Global Inequality*, edited by Mitchell Seligson and John Passe-Smith. Boulder, Colo.: Lynne Rienner, 9–16.

Rowe, David M. 1999. "World Economic Expansion and National Security in Pre-World War I Europe." *International Organization* 53 (2): 195–231.

Ruggie, John Gerard. 1993. "Territoriality and Beyond: Problematizing Modernity in International Relations." *International Organization* 47, 1 (winter): 139–74.

Rumley, Dennis, and Julian Minghi, eds. 1991. *The Geography of Border Landscapes*. New York: Routledge.

Rummel, Rudolph J. 1967. "Some Attributes and Behavioral Patterns of Nations." *Journal of Peace Research* 4 (2): 196–206.

Runciman, Steven. 1954. *A History of the Crusades*. 3 vols. Vol. III, *The Kingdom of Acre and the Latter Crusades*. New York: Cambridge University Press.

Russett, Bruce M. 1967. *International Regions and the International System: A Study in Political Ecology*. Chicago: Rand McNally.

Russett, Bruce M., and John Oneal. 2001. *Triangulating Peace: Democracy, Interdependence, and International Organizations*. New York: W. W. Norton.

Russett, Bruce M., John R. Oneal, and Michaelene Cox. 2000. "Clash of Civilizations, or Realism and Liberalism Deja Vu?: Some Evidence." *Journal of Peace Research* 37 (5): 583–608.

Rutherglen, George. 2001. "International Shoe and the Legacy of Legal Realism." *Supreme Court Review* (2001): 347.

Sachs, Jeffrey D., and Andrew Warner, 1995. "Economic Reform and the Process of Global Integration." *Brookings Papers on Economic Activity* 1.

Sack, Robert David. 1986. *Human Territoriality: Its Theory and History*. Cambridge: Cambridge University Press.

Safran, William. 1991. "Diasporas in Modern Societies: Myths of Homeland and Return." *Diaspora* 1 (1): 89–99.

Sagan, Scott D., and Kenneth N. Waltz. 1995. *The Spread of Nuclear Weapons: A Debate*. New York: Norton.

Sahlins, Marshall. 1992. "The Economics of Develop-Man in the Pacific." *Res* 21: 13–25.

2001. "Reports of the Deaths of Cultures Have Been Exaggerated." In *What Happens to History: The Renewal of Ethics in Contemporary Thought*, edited by H. Marchitello. New York: Routledge, 189–213.

Sahlins, Peter. 1989. *Boundaries: The Making of France and Spain in the Pyrenees*. Berkeley: University of California Press.

1990. "Natural Frontiers Revisited: France's Boundaries since the Seventeenth Century." *American Historical Review* 95 (5): 1423–51.

1991. *Boundaries: The Making of France and Spain in the Pyrenees*. 1st paperback edn. Berkeley: University of California Press.

Said, Edward W. 2001. "The Clash of Ignorance." *The Nation* 273 (12): 11–13.

Saltman, Michael. 2002. "From Cattle Herding to Cultivation – From Territoriality to Land." In *Land and Territoriality*, edited by Michael Saltman. New York: Berg, 159–73.

Salvadori, Massimo. 1979. *Karl Kautsky and the Socialist Revolution, 1880–1938*. London: NLB.

Samaddar, Ranabir, Rada Ivekovic, Sanjay Chaturvedi, and Stefano Bianchini. 2004. *Partitions: Reshaping States and Minds*. London: Frank Cass.

Sarkees, Meredith Reid, Frank Whelon Wayman, and J. David Singer. 2003. "Inter-State, Intra-State, and Extra-State Wars: A Comprehensive Look at Their Distribution over Time, 1816–1997." *International Studies Quarterly* 47 (1): 49–70.

Sassen, Saskia. 2000. "Territory and Territoriality in the Global Economy." *International Sociology* 15.

Saunders, Harold H. 1999. *A Public Peace Process: Sustained Dialogue to Transform Racial and Ethnic Conflicts*. New York: St. Martin's Press.

Sayrs, Lois W. 1993. "The Long Cycle in International Relations: A Markov Specification." *International Studies Quarterly* 37 (2): 215–37.

Schelling, Thomas C. 1960. *The Strategy of Conflict*. Cambridge, Mass.: Harvard University Press.

1966. *Arms and Influence*. New Haven, Conn.: Yale University Press.

1978. *Micromotives and Macrobehavior*. New York: W. W. Norton.

1980. *The Strategy of Conflict*. Rev. edn. Cambridge, Mass.: Harvard University Press.

Schieffelin, Edward L. 1976. *The Sorrow of the Lonely and the Burning of the Dancers*. New York: St. Martin's Press.

Schneider, Gerald, Katherine Barbieri, and Nils Petter Gleditsch. 2003a. "Does Globalization Contribute to Peace? A Critical Survey of the Literature." In *Globalization and Armed Conflict*, edited by Gerald Schneider, Katherine Barbieri, and Nils Petter Gleditsch. Lanham, Md: Rowman and Littlefield, 3–29.

Schneider, Gerald, Katherine Barbieri, and Nils Petter Gleditsch, eds. 2003b. *Globalization and Armed Conflict*. Lanham, Md.: Rowman and Littlefield.

Schofield, R. 1997. "The Last Missing Fence in the Desert: The Saudi-Yemeni Boundary." *Geopolitics and International Boundaries* 1 (3): 247–99.

Schultz, H.-D. 1991. "Deutschlands 'natürliche Grenzen.'" In *Deutschlands Grenzen in der Geschichte*, 1st edn, edited by A. Demandt. München: A. Demandt, 33–88.

Scully, Eileen. 2001. *Bargaining with the State from Afar*. New York: Columbia University Press.

Seligson, Mitchell A., and John T. Passe-Smith, eds. 1998. *Development and Underdevelopment: The Political Economy of Global Inequality*. Boulder, Colo.: Lynne Rienner.

Senese, Paul D. 1996. "Geographical Proximity and Issue Salience: Their Effect on the Escalation of Militarized Interstate Conflict." *Conflict Management and Peace Science* 15: 133–61.

Serbin, Andres. 2001. "Relations between Venezuela and Guyana and the Dispute over the Essequibo Territory: One Step forward, Two Back?" *Pensamiento Propio: Greater Caribbean Bilingual Journal of Social Sciences* 14: 135–58.

Shain, Yossi. 2002. "The Role of Diasporas in Conflict Perpetuation or Resolution." *SAIS Review* 22, 2 (summer–fall): 115–44.

Shain, Yossi, and Aharon Barth. 2003. "Diasporas and International Relations Theory." *International Organization* 57, 3 (summer): 449–79.

Shapiro, Michael, and H. Alker, eds. 1996. *Challenging Boundaries: Global Flows, Territorial Identities.* Minneapolis: University of Minnesota Press.

Sheckler, Annette C. 1998. "Evidence of Things Unseen: Secrets Revealed at the Voice of America." *Horn of Africa* 16, 1/4 (December): 31–50.

Sheffer, Gabriel. 2003. *Diaspora Politics: At Home Abroad.* Cambridge: Cambridge University Press.

Sibley, David. 1995. *Geographies of Exclusion: Society and Difference in the West.* London: Routledge.

Simmons, Beth A. 1999. *Territorial Disputes and Their Resolution: The Case of Ecuador and Peru.* Washington, D.C.: United States Institute of Peace.

2002. "Capacity, Commitment, and Compliance: International Institutions and Territorial Disputes." *Journal of Conflict Resolution* 46, 6 (December): 829–56.

2005. "Forward Looking Dispute Resolution: Ecuador, Peru, and the Border Issue." In *Peace v. Justice*, edited by I. W. Zartman and G. O. Faure. Lanham, Md.: Rowman and Littlefield, 283–308.

Simmons, Beth A., and Lisa Martin. 2002. "International Organizations and Institutions." In *Handbook of International Relations*, edited by W. Carlsnaes, T. Risse, and B. A. Simmons. London: Sage Publications, 192–211.

Singer, J. David, and Melvin Small. 1966. "Formal Alliances, 1815–1939: A Quantitative Description." *Journal of Peace Research* 3 (1): 1–32.

1994. "Correlates of War Project: International and Civil War Data, 1816–1992." Electronic resources. Ann Arbor, Mich.: Inter-University Consortium for Political and Social Research.

Singer, J. David, Stuart Bremer, and John Stuckey. 1972. "Capability Distribution, Uncertainty, and Major Power War, 1820–1965." In *Peace, War, and Numbers*, edited by Bruce Russett. Beverly Hills, Calif.: Sage, 19–48.

Siverson, Randolph M., and Harvey Starr. 1990. "Opportunity, Willingness, and the Diffusion of War." *American Political Science Review* 84 (1): 47–67.

Slantchev, Branislav. 2003. "The Power to Hurt: Costly Conflict with Completely Informed States." *American Political Science Review* 47 (1): 123–35.

Slaughter, Anne-Marie. 2004. *A New World Order.* Princeton, N.J.: Princeton University Press.

Small, Melvin, and J. David Singer. 1982. *Resort to Arms.* Beverly Hills, Calif.: Sage.

1990. "Formal Alliances, 1816–1965: An Extension of the Basic Data." In *Measuring the Correlates of War*, edited by J. David Singer and Paul F. Diehl. Ann Arbor: University of Michigan Press, 159–90.

Smith, Anthony D. 1992. "Ethnic Identity and Territorial Nationalism in Comparative Perspective." In *Thinking Theoretically about Soviet Nationalities: History and Comparison in the Study of the USSR*, edited by Alexander J. Motyl. New York: Columbia University Press, 45–66.

Smith, Jonathan Z. 1978. *Map is Not Territory: Studies in the History of Religions.* Chicago: University of Chicago Press.

1987. *To Take Place: Toward Theory in Ritual.* Chicago: University of Chicago Press.

Sobel, Andrew. 1994. *Domestic Choices, International Markets: Dismantling National Barriers and Liberalizing Securities Markets*. Ann Arbor: University of Michigan Press.

Soja, Edward. 1971. "The Political Organization of Space." Commission on College Geography Resource Paper No. 8. Washington, D.C.: Association of American Geographers.

Sørli, Mirjam E., Nils Petter Gleditsch, and Håvard Strand. 2005. "Why Is There So Much Conflict in the Middle East?" *Journal of Conflict Resolution* 49 (1): 141–65.

Spears, Russell, Bertjan Doosje, and Naomi Ellemers. 1997. "Self-Stereotyping in the Face of Threats to Group Status and Distinctiveness: The Role of Group Identification." *Personality and Social Psychology Bulletin* 23 (5): 538–53.

Spiro, Peter. 2002. "Globalization and the (Foreign Affairs) Constitution." *Ohio State Law Journal* 63: 649–730.

Spruyt, Hendrik. 1994. *The Sovereign State and Its Competitors*. Princeton, N.J.: Princeton University Press.

Spykman, Nicholas J. 1942. *America's Strategy in World Politics: The United States and the Balance of Power*. New York: Harcourt, Brace, and Co.

Squatriti, Paolo. 2002. "Digging Ditches in Early Medieval Europe." *The Past and the Present* 176 (1): 11–65.

Stiglitz, Joseph E. 2002. *Globalization and Its Discontents*. New York: W. W. Norton.

Stinnett, Douglas M., Jaroslav Tir, Philip Schafer, Paul F. Diehl, and Charles Gochman. 2002. "The Correlates of War Project Direct Contiguity Data, Version 3." *Conflict Management and Peace Science* 19 (2): 58–66.

Stopford, John, and Susan Strange. 1991. *Rival States, Rival Firms: Competition for World Market Shares*. Cambridge: Cambridge University Press.

Stouffer, Samuel. 1940. "Intervening Opportunities: A Theory Relating Mobility to Distance." *American Sociological Review* 5 (4): 845–67.

Strange, Susan. 1996. *The Retreat of the State: The Diffusion of Power in the World Economy*. Cambridge: Cambridge University Press.

———. 1998. *Mad Money: When Markets Outgrow Governments*. Ann Arbor: University of Michigan Press.

Strathern, Marilyn. 1988. *The Gender of the Gift: Problems with Women and Problems with Society in Melanesia*. Berkeley: University of California Press.

Strayer, Joseph R. 1970. *On the Medieval Origins of the Modern State*. Princeton, N.J.: Princeton University Press.

———. 1971. *Medieval Statecraft and the Perspectives of History*. Princeton, N.J.: Princeton University Press.

———. 1980. *The Reign of Philip the Fair*. Princeton, N.J.: Princeton University Press.

Stump, Roger W. 2000. *Boundaries of Faith: Geographical Perspectives on Religious Fundamentalism*. Lanham, Md.: Rowman and Littlefield.

Sukhwal, B. L. 1971. *India: A Political Geography*. Bombay: Allied Publishers.

Summary, Rebecca M. 1989. "A Political-Economic Model of U.S. Bilateral Trade." *Review of Economics and Statistics* 71 (1): 179–82.

Svalastoga, Kaare. 1956. "Homicide and Social Contacts in Denmark." *American Sociological Review* 52 (1): 37–41.

"Symposium: Globalization and Governance: The Prospects for Democracy." 2003. *Indiana Journal of Global Legal Studies* (special issue), 10 (1).

Tangredi, Sam J., ed. 2002. *Globalization and Maritime Power*. Washington, D.C.: National Defense University Press.

Taylor, Peter J. 1994. "The State as a Container: Territoriality in the Modern World System." *Progress in Human Geography* 18: 151–62.

1995. "Beyond Containers: Internationality, Interstateness, Interterritoriality." *Progress in Human Geography* 19: 1–15.

1996. "Territorial Absolutism and Its Evasions." *Geography Research Forum* 16: 1–12.

Theophylactou, D. A. 1995. "A 'German Solution' for Cyprus's Reunification or United Nations 'Enforcement' of Peace?" *Mediterranean Quarterly* 6 (3): 39–51.

Thompson, William R. 1982. "Phases of the Business Cycle and the Outbreak of War." *International Studies Quarterly* 26: 301–11.

1988. *On Global War: Historical-Structural Approaches to World Politics*. Columbia: University of South Carolina Press.

Tilly, Charles. 1990. *Coercion, Capital, and European States, AD 990–1990*. Cambridge, Mass.: Blackwell.

Timothy, D. J. 1995. "Political Boundaries and Tourism: Borders as Tourist Attractions." *Tourism Management* 16 (7): 525–32.

Tinbergen, Jan. 1962. *Shaping the World Economy: Suggestions for an International Economic Policy*. New York: Twentieth Century Fund.

Tir, Jaroslav, and Paul Diehl. 1998. "Demographic Pressure and Interstate Conflict: Linking Population Growth and Density to Militarized Disputes and Wars, 1930–89." *Journal of Peace Research* 35 (3): 319–39.

Tir, Jaroslav, Philip Schafer, Paul Diehl, and Gary Goertz. 1998. "Territorial Changes, 1816–1996: Procedures and Data." *Conflict Management and Peace Science* 16 (1): 89–97.

Toft, Monica Duffy. 2001. "Indivisible Territory and Ethnic War." Working Paper 01–08. Weatherhead Center for International Affairs, Harvard University, Cambridge, Mass.

2003. *The Geography of Ethnic Violence: Identity, Interests, and the Indivisibility of Territory*. Princeton, N.J.: Princeton University Press.

Tölölyan, Khacig. 2000. "Elites and Institutions in the Armenian Transnation." *Diaspora* 9 (1): 107–35.

Torpey, John. 1998. "Coming and Going: On the State Monopolization of the Legitimate 'Means of Movement'." *Sociological Theory* 16 (3): 239–59.

2000. *The Invention of the Passport: Surveillance, Citizenship, and the State*. Cambridge: Cambridge University Press.

Toset, Hans Petter Wollebæk, Nils Petter Gleditsch, and Håvard Hegre. 2000. "Shared Rivers and Interstate Conflict." *Political Geography* 19 (8): 971–96.

Toynbee, Arnold. 1961. *A Study of History*. Oxford: Oxford University Press.

Trochim, William M. K. 2001. *The Research Methods Knowledge Base*. 2nd edn. Cincinnati, Ohio: Atomic Dog Publishing.

Tuan, Yi-Fu. 1976. "Geopiety: A Theme in Man's Attachment to Nature and Place." In *Geographies of the Mind*, edited by David Lowenthal and M. Bowden. New York: Oxford University Press, 11–39.

Tucker, Richard. 1999. "BTSCS: A Binary Time-Series–Cross-Section Data Analysis Utility, Version 4.0.4." Computer program. Vanderbilt University.

Tures, John. 2000. "The Onset and Escalation of Regime Claims in the Western Hemisphere, 1816–1992." Ph.D. diss., Florida State University.

US Bureau of Statistics. 2000 Census. Available at http://factfinder.census.gov.

US State Department. 2004. "International Boundary Study." Available at http://www.law.fsu.edu/library/collection/LimitsinSeas/numericalibs.php.

van Creveld, Martin. 1999. *The Rise and Decline of the State*. Cambridge: Cambridge University Press.

Van Houtum, H. 2002. "Borders, Strangers, Doors, and Bridges." *Space and Polity* 6 (2): 141–46.

Van Houtum, H., and T. Van Naerssen. 2002. "Bordering, Ordering, and Othering." *Tijdschrift voor Economische en Sociale Geografie* 93 (2): 125–36.

van Schendel, Willem. 2003. "Stateless in South Asia: The Making of the India–Bangladesh Enclaves." In *Routing Borders between Territories: Discourses and Practices*, edited by Eiki Berg and Henk van Houtum. Burlington, Vt.: Ashgate, 237–74.

Vasquez, John A. 1983. "The Tangibility of Issues and Global Conflict: A Test of Rosenau's Issue Area Typology." *Journal of Peace Research* 20: 179–92.

    1993. *The War Puzzle*. Cambridge: Cambridge University Press.

    1995. "Why Do Neighbours Fight? Proximity, Interaction, or Territoriality." *Journal of Peace Research* 3 (2): 277–93.

    2004. "The Probability of War, 1816–1992." *International Studies Quarterly* 48, 1 (March): 1–27.

Vasquez, John A., ed. 2000. *What Do We Know about War?* New York: Rowman and Littlefield.

Vasquez, John A., and Marie T. Henehan. 2001. "Territorial Disputes and the Probability of War, 1816–1992." *Journal of Peace Research* 38 (2): 123–38.

    2004. "Globalization, Territoriality, and Interstate War." Paper presented to the Conference on Globalization, Territoriality, and Conflict, IICAS, UCSD, 16–18 January.

Vernon, Raymond. 1971. *Sovereignty at Bay: The Multinational Spread of U.S. Enterprises*. New York: Basic Books.

Vigarello, Georges. 1997. "The Tour de France." In *Realms of Memory: Rethinking the French Past*, edited by Pierre Nora, translated by Arthur Goldhammer. 3 vols. Vol. II: *Traditions*. New York: Columbia University Press, 468–500.

Viner, Jacob. 1937. *Studies in the Theory of International Trade*. New York: Harper and Brothers.

Volkan, Vamik. 1997. *Bloodlines: From Ethnic Pride to Ethnic Terrorism*. New York: Farrar, Straus, Giroux.

Wade, Robert. 1996. "Globalization and Its Limits: Reports of the Death of the National Economy Are Greatly Exaggerated." In *National Diversity and Global Capitalism*, edited by Suzanne Berger and Ronald Dore. Ithaca, N.Y.: Cornell University Press.

Wagner, R. Harrison. 2004. "War and the State: An Introduction to the Study of International Politics." Unpublished MS, University of Texas at Austin.

Wahlbeck, Östen. 1999. *Kurdish Diasporas: A Comparative Study of Kurdish Refugee Communities*. Basingstoke, UK: Macmillan.

Wallensteen, Peter. 1984. "Universalism Versus Particularism: On the Limits of Major Power Order." *Journal of Peace Research* 21 (3): 243–57.

Wallensteen, Peter, Birger Heldt, Mary B. Anderson, Stephen John Stedman, and Leonard Wantchekon. 2001. "Conflict Prevention through Development Co-Operation." Research Report No. 59. Uppsala, Sweden: Department of Peace and Conflict Research, Uppsala University.

Walt, Stephen M. 1997. "Building Up the New Bogeyman." *Foreign Policy* 106: 176–89.

Walter, Barbara. 2003. "Explaining the Intractability of Territorial Conflict." *International Studies Review* 5 (4): 137–53.

2006. "War as a Reputation Problem: Explaining Government Responses to Self-Determination Movements." *American Journal of Political Science* 50, 1 (January).

Waltz, Kenneth N. 1959. *Man, the State, and War: A Theoretical Analysis*. New York: Columbia University Press.

1979. *Theory of International Politics*. New York: McGraw-Hill.

1999. "Globalization and Governance." *PS: Political Science and Politics* 32 (4): 693–700.

2000. "Globalization and American Power." *National Interest* 59: 46–56.

Ward, Michael D., and Kristian S. Gleditsch. 2002. "Location, Location, Location: An MCMC Approach to Modeling the Spatial Context of War and Peace." *Political Analysis* 10 (3): 244–60.

Wasserstein, Bernard. 2001. *Divided Jerusalem: The Struggle for the Holy City*. London: Profile Books.

Waterman, Stanley. 1987. "Partitioned States." *Political Geography Quarterly* 6 (2): 151–70.

1996. "Partition Secession and Peace in Our Time." *GeoJournal* 39: 345–52.

2002. "States of Segregation." In *The Razor's Edge: International Boundaries and Political Geography*, edited by Clive Schofield et al. London: Kluwer Academic Publishers, 57–76.

Weber, Eugen. 1976. *Peasants into Frenchmen: The Modernization of Rural France 1870–1914*. Stanford, Calif.: Stanford University Press.

1984–86. "L'Hexagone." In *Les Lieux de mémoire*, edited by Pierre Nora. Vol. II, *La Nation*. Paris: Gallimard.

Weede, Erich. 2003. "Globalization: Creative Destruction and the Prospect of a Capitalist Peace." In *Globalization and Armed Conflict*, edited by Gerald Schneider, Katherine Barbieri, and Nils Petter Gleditsch. Lanham, Md: Rowman and Littlefield, 311–23.

Weiner, James F. 1991. *The Empty Place: Poetry, Space, and Being among the Foi of Papua New Guinea*. Bloomington: Indiana University Press.

Weingast, Barry R. 1997. "The Political Foundations of Democracy and the Rule of Law." *American Political Science Review* 91 (2): 245–63.

Weissberg, Günter. 1963. "Maps as Evidence in International Boundary Disputes: A Reappraisal." *American Journal of International Law* 57: 781–803.

Wells, Peter S. 2002. *The Battle that Stopped Rome: Emperor Augustus, Arminius, and the Slaughter of the Legions in the Teutoburg Forest.* New York: W. W. Norton.

Wendt, Alexander. 1999. *Social Theory of International Politics.* Cambridge: Cambridge University Press.

Werbner, Pnina. 2002. "The Place Which is Diaspora: Citizenship, Religion, and Gender in the Making of Chaordic Transnationalism." *Journal of Ethnic and Migration Studies* 28, 1 (January): 119–34.

Wheaton, Henry. 1936[1866]. *Elements of International Law,* text of the 1866 edition, edited with notes by George Grafton Wilson. Carnegic Endowment, Classics of International Law series. Oxford: Clarendon Press.

White, George C. 2000. *Nationalism and Territory: Constructing Group Identity in Southeastern Europe.* New York: Rowman and Littlefield.

Wohlstetter, Albert. 1968. "Illusions of Distance." *Foreign Affairs* 6 (2): 242–55.

Wolfe, Roy I. 1963. *Transportation and Politics.* Princeton, N.J.: Van Nostrand.

Wood, Charles T. 1967. "*Regnum Francie*: A Problem in Capetian Administrative Usage." *Traditio* 23: 117–47.

Wood, Denis. 1992. *The Power of Maps.* New York: The Guilford Press.

Woods, Frederick Adams, and Alexander Baltzly. 1915. *Is War Diminishing?* Boston: Houghton Mifflin.

Woods, Ngaire. 2000. "The Political Economy of Globalization." In *The Political Economy of Globalization,* edited by Ngaire Woods. Basingstoke: Palgrave.

World Bank. 2001. *World Development Indicators* CD-ROM. Washington, D.C.: World Bank. http://devdata.worldbank.org.ezp2.hardvard.edu/dataonline/.

Wright, J. 1947. "Terrae Incognitae: The Place of Imagination in Geography." *Annals of the Association of American Geographers* 37: 1–5.

Wright, Quincy. 1942. *A Study of War.* Chicago: University of Chicago Press.

Yarbrough, Beth V., and Robert M. Yarbrough. 1994. "International Contracting and Territorial Control: The Boundary Question." *Journal of Institutional and Theoretical Economics* 150 (1): 239–64.

Yates, Nigel, and James M. Gibson. 1994. *Traffic and Politics: The Construction and Management of the Rochester Bridge, A.D. 43–1993.* Rochester, N.Y.: Boydell.

Yiftachel, Oren. 1997. "Israeli Society and Jewish-Palestinian Reconciliation: Ethnocracy and Its Territorial Contradictions." *Middle East Journal* 51: 505–19.

    2001a. "'Right Sizing' or 'Right Shaping'? Politics, Ethnicity and Territory in Plural States." In *Right-Sizing the State: The Politics of Moving Borders,* edited by B. O'Leary, I. Lustick, and T. Callaghy. Oxford: Oxford University Press, 358–87.

    2001b. "The Homeland and Nationalism." In *Encyclopedia of Nationalism,* vol. I, edited by Alexander J. Motyl. New York: Academic Press, 359–83.

Yiftachel, Oren, and Haim Yacobi. 2003. "Urban Ethnocracy: Ethnicization and the Production of Space in an Israeli 'Mixed City.'" *Society and Space* 21 (6): 673–93.

Zacher, Mark W. 2001. "The Territorial Integrity Norm: International Boundaries and the Use of Force." *International Organization* 55, 2 (spring): 215–50.

Zeller, Gaston. 1933. "La Monarchie d'ancien régime et les frontières naturelles." *Revue d'histoire moderne* 8 (20): 305–33.

Zipf, George K. 1949. *Human Behavior and the Principle of Least Effort*. Cambridge, Mass.: Addison–Wesley.

Zuk, Gary. 1985. "National Growth and International Conflict: A Reevaluation of Choucri and North's Thesis." *Journal of Politics* 47 (1): 269–81.

Zunzer, Wolfram. 2004. "Diaspora Communities and Civil Conflict Transformation." Occasional Paper 26. Berlin: Berghof Research Center for Constructive Conflict Management.

Index

Adams, Gerry 126–27
Afghanistan 198, 212
Africa 104, 191, 192–93, 199
Albania 106
Albanian diaspora 125
aliens 18
  detention of 220, 221, 231, 233
  rights of 225, 234, 245, 246
  security threats by 233, 244–45
alliances 171
American Banana 226, 228, 240
Americans for a New Irish
  Agenda (ANIA) 126–27
Andean Pact 264
Anomalous zones 224
antitrust regulation 226, 230, 238
Argentina 40, 257, 266, 269, 272, 276,
  279, 295
Armenia 119–20
Armenian diaspora 114, 118, 119, 120
Asian financial crisis 20
attachment, territorial *see* territorial
  attachment
Australia 136, 201
autarkic economies 169, 177, 178
autocracies 139

Balkans 85, 90, 93, 100, 104, 106, 109
bargaining 4, 10, 26, 90, 163, 168
bargaining range 140, 141
behavior, territorial 86, 91, 95–101
Belfast 94, 95
Belize 269, 277
bilateral trade 18, 159, 255, 257, 259
Bill of Rights 220, 230, 242
bitter pill arguments 167
Bolivia 257, 276
border delimitation 5, 15, 17
border effects 255, 259–61
bordering process 92, 101, 103,
  107, 108
border regime 18

borders
  cultural 103
  functions of 1, 101, 102–03
  as institutions 18, 101–02, 251, 253–59
  neighborhood 91–94
  perceived 88
  permeability of 88, 107–08
  in resilient territoriality 87
  settled 3, 252, 259, 276–77
  study of 1, 101–02
Bosnia-Herzegovina border 54
boundaries
  described 3
  focal principles and 51–55
  international 252, 253–59
  permeability of 101
  superimposition of 104
boundary regime 14
Bowman v. US 229
Brazil 257
brinkmanship 169
British Guiana 8
Bulgaria 54
Burgundy 50
Bush administration 234, 244–45

Camp David summit 100
Canada 38, 136, 239, 255
capital 157, 161, 162, 164–65
capitalism 137, 167
capital markets 162
CARICOM 277
cartographic principle 38–40
cartography 27, 32, 38
Central America 114, 136, 277
Central American Common
  Market 264, 277
chain-store paradox 28
Chile 257, 266, 269, 272, 276, 279, 295
China 38, 164, 224
Christianity 46, 47, 48, 74
civil rights 230, 243

Macedonia 54–55, 125
Madsen v. *Kinsella* 230
major powers 171, 174
managerialism 92–93
Marxism 159–60, 162, 167
Mercosur 258, 264, 272
Mexico 232
Middle East conflicts 85–107, 191
migrants 4, 9, 62, 112–13
migration 6, 17, 62, 112–14
militarized interstate disputes
    (MIDs) 170, 199
  see also interstate conflict; war
military courts 224, 230–31
military technology 13, 197–98
Milosevic, Slobodan 291
Miranda warnings 234
missile warfare 190, 197
mobility 5, 157, 161, 162, 164
Mongols 5
multilateralism 238, 248
multinationals 237

NAFTA 260
nationalism 27, 28, 35, 42, 43, 97, 263,
    264, 278
nation-state 1–2, 15, 87, 192
NATO 106, 241
natural frontiers principle 32, 33, 36–38
neighborhoods 91–94, 206–08
New Irish Agenda *see* Americans for a New
    Irish Agenda (ANIA)
New Zealand 199, 201
Nicaragua 269, 272, 277, 279
Nijmegen, Treaty of 37, 55
non-equivalent dependent variables
    research design (NEDV) 149
North America 146
Northern Ireland 104, 119, 124,
    126–27, 290
North–South Korea conflict 104
nuclear warfare 190

occupation 157, 162
  bitter pill arguments of 167
  reduced benefits of 164–66
  repatriation of assets in 164
  US 224, 231–32, 243
O'Dowd, Niall 126, 127
OECD 241
opportunity 187
opportunity cost 252, 277
ordering 88, 92, 101, 103
Oromo diaspora 114, 121, 122–23,
    124–25
Oromo Liberation Front (OLF) 120, 121

Pakistan 104
Palestine 97, 98, 100, 109
Palestinian diaspora 114
Panama 226
Papua New Guinea (PNG) 63, 153, 289
partition 104
peacekeeping forces 106
Peking, Treaty of 38
Pentecostalism 8, 63, 66, 74, 75–76,
    82–83, 289
Peru 257, 258–59, 266, 269, 272,
    276–77, 278
Philip the Fair 28, 37, 45–51
Philippines 223, 227
Poland 190
political geography 85, 86
political power 85, 90, 190
Polity project –[–7.182–]
preference heterogeneity 139
prior historical formation principle 32,
    42–44, 51–55, 95
production networks 165, 237
property rights 165, 257
proximity 210, 211
Puerto Rico 220, 224, 227, 228
Pyrenees border 5
Pyrenees, Treaty of the 15, 44

quasi-states 14

Rasul v. *Bush* 245
rationalist war theory 25–26, 140, 146
realist theory 159–60, 253–55,
    256, 258
regime claims 263, 272
regimes 3, 4–5, 14, 15, 16, 138
regime types 133, 134, 143,
    263–64, 272
Reid v. *Covert* 228, 230–31, 232, 234,
    242–44
religion 19, 66, 74, 82, 94, 97–98,
    289–90
remittance economy 112–13
resources
  competition for 94
  control of 104, 162, 165
  distribution of 94, 194, 291
  national power and 253
  shared 190
  tradable 14, 156
reterritorialization 8, 87, 88
Romanian nationalism 43
Rome 179
Ross, John 225–26, 231
Russia 135, 257
Ryswyck, Treaty of 37, 55